D0205503

The United States
and the
Caribbean Republics
1921-1933

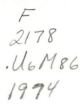

The United States and the Caribbean Republics

1921-1933

Dana G. Munro

PRINCETON UNIVERSITY PRESS

Library of Congress Cataloging in Publication Data will
be found on the last printed page of this book

This book has been composed in Linotype Caledonia

Printed in the United States of America
by Princeton University Press, Princeton, New Jersey

To My Wife

CONTENTS

PREFACE

In this account of the American government's policy in the Caribbean between 1921 and 1925, I have tried to describe and explain what happened rather than to defend what the State Department did. I believe that the people who were responsible for the American government's actions were trying to do what was best for the United States and for the people of the Caribbean states, but some of these actions were undoubtedly unfortunate. It has often been pointed out that statesmen dealing with problems of foreign policy are usually confronted, not by a choice between a good and a bad course of action, but by a choice among courses of action all of which are bad. This is especially true of the sort of problems which the Caribbean states presented in the 1920's, and which some of them still present.

I cannot pretend to be wholly objective in my treatment of these matters because I was involved, in one capacity or another, in a great many of the situations that are described. On the strength of two years of travel and study in Central America as a graduate student between 1914 and 1916, I was employed as regional economist for Mexico and Central America in the State Department in 1919-1920 and then entered the Foreign Service. I continued to work chiefly on Caribbean problems as a member of the Latin American division in the department from 1921-1925, as secretary of legation in Panama, 1925-1927, as secretary in Nicaragua, 1927-1929, and as chief of the Latin American division, 1929-1930. I was American minister in Haiti from 1930 to 1932. I consequently knew most of the people who are mentioned in the pages that follow and took part in discussions and negotiations with them.

I have of course checked my own recollection against the State Department's records. References to unpublished material in the files are cited where this seems appropriate, but to avoid the accumulation of footnotes I have not generally cited references to correspondence which is available in *Foreign Relations*. The study is based mainly on material from the State Department's record, because it deals primarily with the development of the State Department's policy. I have not made exhaustive use of much other material which would have to be used in a more comprehensive study of our relations with the Caribbean republics, and I have not attempted to discuss some phases of these relations, like the mediation in boundary disputes, which have little bearing on the main theme of the book. I have not tried to deal with Panama, because Panama is a very special case and an account of the complicated problems that have arisen in connection with the canal would require virtually another book.

The courtesy and competence of the staff of the National Archives make doing research there a pleasure, and I am especially grateful to Mrs. Patricia Dowling, whose familiarity with the material under her charge was very helpful. I am also grateful to Miss Judith Schiff of the Yale University Library for her assistance in connection with my examination of the Stimson diary.

The United States
and the
Caribbean Republics
1921-1933

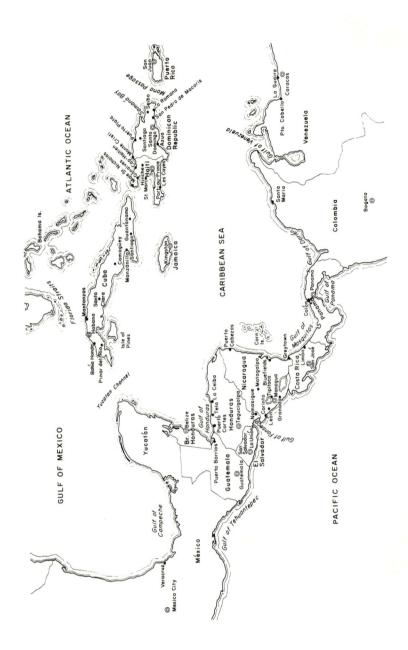

Chapter One

INTRODUCTION

President Harding and Secretary of State Hughes faced several troublesome problems in the Caribbean when they took office in March 1921. The most urgent was in Cuba, where General Crowder, as personal representative of the president of the United States, was trying to cope with a political and economic crisis which threatened to compel the American government to intervene under the Platt amendment. In the Dominican Republic, things were obviously going badly under a military government headed by an American admiral. In Haiti, also occupied by American forces, the treaty of 1915, which gave American officials control of most of the government's important functions, was not working well. There had been much friction with the Haitian officials, and American marines had had to suppress a peasant revolt, with a shocking amount of bloodshed. In Nicaragua, where American intervention had put down a revolution in 1912, the continued presence of a small legation guard of American marines had enabled one party to control elections and remain in power since that time. The American government had not dared to withdraw the guard because its departure would probably have precipitated a civil war, but the situation was obviously one which could not continue.

Most of these problems had developed from efforts to discourage revolutions and promote economic progress in the Caribbean states. After it acquired Puerto Rico and assumed responsibility for the future of Cuba, and more particularly after it decided to build the Panama Canal, the American government began to take more interest in a region which had suddenly taken on a new strategic importance. It was especially concerned about the internal disorder which made it impossible for some of the Central American and West Indian states to protect foreigners or pay their foreign debts. In the first years of the century, European governments seemed increasingly disposed to attempt to take control of countries where such conditions invited intervention, and the United States did not want to see any potentially hostile

3

power get a foothold in a region that lay between its own territory and the canal.

In 1903 the United States made treaties with Cuba and Panama in which it guaranteed the independence of the two states and reserved the right to intervene if necessary to maintain orderly government. Soon afterward President Theodore Roosevelt enunciated his corollary to the Monroe Doctrine: that the United States, if it wished to prevent foreign interference in the Caribbean, must help the Caribbean states to correct the conditions that threatened to bring on foreign intervention. Acting on this idea, he set up a customs receivership in the Dominican Republic in 1905 and used his good offices to persuade the Central American republics to adopt the 1907 treaties, which were intended to prevent international and internal wars in that area.

Roosevelt acted in these cases because serious crises seemed to justify diplomatic intervention. His successors attempted to forestall such crises by insisting on reforms that would make them less likely to arise. The Taft administration attempted to set up customs receiverships in Honduras and Nicaragua, but its plans were defeated by opposition in the United States Senate. It was more successful in a vigorous diplomatic intervention to stop a civil war in the Dominican Republic in 1912 and in its armed intervention to stop one in Nicaragua in the same year. The Wilson administration went still farther. President Wilson thought that the United States had a duty to promote democratic government among its neighbors, by compulsion if necessary. To discourage the use of force to settle political disputes, he opposed revolutions against constituted governments. When conditions in Haiti and the Dominican Republic seemed to become intolerable and his offers of help were rejected, he sent military forces to occupy each country.

During the presidential campaign of 1920, Senator Harding criticized these actions, and some observers thought that his election would mean a change in American policy. As usually happens when a new administration takes office, however, no sudden change occurred. General Crowder was making good progress in his efforts to avert a political and economic collapse in Cuba, and it was clearly advisable to let him continue. The State Department had already started to do something about the problems in the other countries. It had persuaded President Wilson in December 1920 to take the first steps toward the withdrawal of the military government at Santo Domingo, and it was trying to bring about a better coordination of the treaty services in Haiti. It had made the Nicaraguan government promise to employ an expert to draft an electoral law as a first step toward the creation of a situation which would allow the American marines to be safely withdrawn.

There was nothing to suggest any sharp break with past policy in the new administration's appointments to the higher positions in the State Department. Henry Fletcher, who became undersecretary, was a career diplomat who had been ambassador to Chile and to Mexico and had worked on Latin American problems in the Department under Wilson. The assistant secretary, Fred Dearing, and the third assistant secretary, Robert Woods Bliss, were also veterans of the career service. Alvee A. Adee, who had been second assistant secretary of state since 1886, continued in his position, as did Sumner Welles, the chief of the Latin American division.

Secretary Hughes' basic ideas about Caribbean policy were not very different from his predecessors'. After he took office, he became much interested in inter-American relations and discussed them in a series of addresses which he wrote himself in longhand and often tried out on his subordinates before delivery. He thought that considerations of national security, and especially the need to defend the approaches to the Panama canal, required the United States to take a special interest in the West Indies and Central America. The Monroe Doctrine, as he saw it, had lost none of its importance from the fact that there seemed for the moment to be no danger of non-American intervention in the hemisphere, for "the future holds infinite possibilities and the Doctrine remains as an essential policy to be applied whenever any exigency may arise requiring its application."[1] On the other hand, he insisted that "the declaration of our purpose to oppose what is inimical to our safety does not imply an attempt to establish a protectorate."[2] He thought that the United States should not forego its right to intervention if its security were endangered or if a breakdown of local government imperiled the lives and property of its citizens, but he knew that any intervention was re-

---

[1] *The Centenary of the Monroe Doctrine*, address delivered at Philadelphia, Nov. 30, 1923.

[2] *Observations on the Monroe Doctrine*, address delivered before the American Bar Association at Minneapolis, Aug. 30, 1923.

sented by the other American countries and thought that it should be avoided wherever possible.

Hughes had more control over the foreign policy of the United States than most of his predecessors had had. In the first months of the new administration he had some difficulty with colleagues who tried to interfere in matters affecting relations with other countries,[3] but he was soon able to obtain recognition of the State Department's predominant interest in the field. He consulted the president on important questions of policy, but his recommendations were almost always approved. In the State Department itself he exercised a close control over what went on. The astonishing rapidity with which he could read and understand long documents dealing with complicated questions enabled him to cope with a great volume of work. He made the State Department a more efficient organization than it had been because he demanded a high standard of performance and had no patience with carelessness or complacency.

Even Hughes, however, could not follow closely the multifarious problems with which the department had to deal. Deciding what to do about a political problem in a Central American country, for example, often required a knowledge of the background and of the personalities involved, and a consideration of the implications of any step that might be taken, for which only a person who dealt with the problems of one relatively small region could possibly have time. In dealing with matters of this sort, the secretary had to rely on the advice of his staff.

The organization of the department was less complex in 1921 than it became later. Under the secretary and the undersecretary, only one assistant secretary, *the* assistant secretary, dealt chiefly with questions of policy. The second assistant secretary, the venerable Alvee A. Adee, had once been a power in the department, but was now very deaf and unable to speak intelligibly. He no longer wrote the witty policy memoranda which had once instructed and delighted his colleagues, but nearly all outgoing instructions and letters still had to pass through his office before being presented to other officials for signature. His two very efficient secretaries, Miss Margaret Hanna and Mrs. Ruth Shipley, exercised an autocratic authority in matters relating to the form and style of the department's correspondence and compelled several generations of young officers to learn to write State

[3] Mr. Hughes told me this, in very general terms.

Department English. Not infrequently they influenced decisions on policy, especially where precedents were involved. The third assistant secretary dealt chiefly with administrative problems in the diplomatic service. In 1924 all of the assistant secretaries were made equal in rank, and a fourth assistant secretaryship was created for Wilbur J. Carr, the director of the consular service.

Most incoming correspondence went first to the geographical divisions. These handled economic as well as political matters, for the staff of the economic intelligence section of the trade adviser's office, which was beginning to take over economic policy at the end of the Wilson administration, was broken up and distributed among the geographical divisions in 1921. The trade adviser, later called the economic adviser, continued to be consulted on financial problems and to deal with economic matters which involved more than one part of the world. The office had much influence, as did that of the solicitor, with his large staff of lawyers, who handled claims and passed on the legal aspects of policy questions. Usually, however, it was the geographical divisions which formulated policy and drafted instructions. Questions of interest to more than one division were discussed informally by the officers concerned and there were few committees. There was also much informal contact with other departments of the government. The relatively small number of persons involved made the transaction of business easier than it is today.

Relations with all of the Latin American republics, except Mexico, which was the province of a separate division, were handled by the division of Latin American affairs, of which I was a member from 1921 to 1925 and again in 1929-1930. This had a chief and from six to eight other officers, most of them in charge of groups of countries. Except for one or two permanent "drafting officers," the staff were members of the diplomatic or consular services, detailed to Washington for periods of not more than four years. The chief of the division usually saw the secretary, or talked with him over the intercom, several times each week. In 1921, though the volume of correspondence was rapidly increasing, he was expected to see every dispatch and letter that came to the division and to satisfy himself of the accuracy and advisability of every instruction and letter that went out. Particularly in dealing with Caribbean problems, which were usually the most important ones that it handled, the division had to follow troubled political

7

situations from day to day. It drafted instructions or memoranda for the secretary's consideration and in most cases made the decision as to what the American government should do, within the outlines of general policy which the secretary laid down.

Though the department, even under Hughes, was not free from the overcautiousness and adherence to precedent and the propensity for double-talk which seems characteristic of foreign offices, and though the general level of competence in the career diplomatic service was perhaps not so high as it is today, the staff was for the most part capable and conscientious. Loyalty and integrity were taken for granted. Leaks of information to the press were very rare. Occasionally a higher official told the newspapers something which those closer to the problem would have preferred to keep from them, but we should all have been amazed and shocked if one of our colleagues had revealed information in an effort to sabotage the department's policies. I can remember only one or two cases where this occurred in connection with Latin American problems in the twelve years that I was in the foreign service.

The American government's representation abroad, and especially in the Caribbean, left more to be desired. Ministers and ambassadors were usually appointed as a reward for services to the party in power, and the posts in the Caribbean too often went to totally unqualified people. Hughes, when he first took office, seems to have made little effort to change this situation. There was no immediate occasion for the appointment of new chiefs of mission in Cuba, where General Crowder was acting as the president's personal representative, or in Haiti and the Dominican Republic, where the military occupations created special problems; but in Central America political appointments were made in all five countries. One or two turned out well, but two of the ministers were removed for manifest incompetence, after they had been dealing with critical situations for more than two years.

It was especially bad to have a stupid or foolish American minister in a Caribbean state, because the State Department rarely provided the legations in the smaller Latin American capitals with competent staffs. For a time in 1922, when the embassy at Brussels had a counselor and three diplomatic secretaries, there was only one diplomatic secretary in all of Central America, though each of the five missions there had vastly more work to do.[4] At most, a minister in Central America usually had one young inexperienced diplomatic secretary, and, with luck, one clerk. Those who handled diplomatic assignments considered the missions in Europe more important, and the wealthy and often spoiled young career diplomats were reluctant to go to posts where social life and living conditions were unattractive. As time went on, the general improvement in the Foreign Service, brought about chiefly by the Rogers Act of 1924, and the fact that many of the ablest officers in the service became interested in Latin America, ameliorated the situation.

The basic ideas of the officers who staffed the Latin American division, like those of the secretary himself, were not very different from the ideas which had shaped the Caribbean policy of the American government from the time when Elihu Root was secretary of state. We thought that the United States must try to promote orderly government in the Caribbean because disorder would invite interference by other powers. After the world war there was no immediate danger that any foreign power might challenge our position in the Caribbean, but we still felt that any extension of foreign influence would be unacceptable in a region so important to our own security. We certainly had no desire to see the United States take control permanently of any of the Caribbean states, but we saw nothing wrong in exercising a measure of control to stop disorder and bring about needed reforms.

We also saw nothing wrong in sending a warship from time to time to prevent injury to Americans and other foreigners when a breakdown of law and order endangered their lives. In 1921 most governments considered that they had a right and a duty to protect their citizens if local authorities were unable to do so. Our protection was also extended to other foreigners. Other governments expected this because we had asserted that we had a predominant interest in the Caribbean and had made it clear that we did not want anyone else to intervene there. The vessels of the Special Service Squadron, a group of small cruisers operating out of the Canal Zone, were frequently sent to Central American ports where disturbances had occurred or seemed likely. If con-

[4] Francis White to Herbert Stabler, May 15, 1926, Francis White papers, National Archives, Box 35. White thought that the Brussels embassy had less work in a year than a Central American legation had in a week.

ditions were sufficiently serious, an armed force was landed and a neutral zone set up in which no fighting was allowed. This arrangement usually served to protect the most important foreign properties in the area. The arrival of a warship also gave notice to troublemakers that the United States opposed their activities, and this was frequently the real purpose of the visit. As the policy of non-interference developed, the State Department became more reluctant to send warships except in cases where American lives were clearly in imminent danger. It was not easy, however, to decide not to send a warship when American citizens in a banana port were terrified and begging for protection.

We thought that the first requisite for progress in the Caribbean was the development of orderly republican government. Revolutions in the 1920's were apt to be more disastrous than the military revolts by which governments are changed today. Frequently they were civil wars, fought by untrained and undisciplined forces equipped with antiquated firearms and machetes, but nonetheless bloody and destructive. The contending armies lived off the country, killing livestock and stealing crops, with little consideration for civilians. A country which was exposed to periodic convulsions of this sort had little chance for progress. It seemed clear that stable government could not be attained until elections took the place of revolutions as the way of changing administrations, and whenever possible we used our influence to bring about better elections. We realized, however, that there were great obstacles to the holding of free elections in many of the Caribbean countries, and we were inclined to support constituted governments against any attempt to overthrow them by force, in the belief that only the maintenance of peace would permit the sort of progress that was necessary for the development of democratic institutions. For the same reason we endeavored, with little success, to persuade the Central American states to replace their graft-ridden, undisciplined armies with police forces trained by foreign instructors. We appreciated the inconsistency of advocating democratic practices and at the same time giving moral support to governments like those of Guatemala and El Salvador, which were not democratic, but it was apparent that these were the only sort of governments that some of the Central American states were likely to have in the foreseeable future. Fortunately there were no particularly objectionable dictatorships in the Caribbean in the early 1920's.

We were interested in economic development in the Caribbean because the poorer countries were not likely to have better governments so long as the masses of the people lived in ignorance and poverty in communities which were cut off from the outside world by lack of roads and railroads. In the 1920's there was no possibility of obtaining funds for foreign aid from the United States Treasury, but we hoped that the maintenance of peace might encourage the establishment of new productive enterprises by foreign capital. In practice, however, we probably did as much to discourage as to encourage foreign investment, because we repeatedly refused to support or consent to the kind of concessions that American promoters thought they needed in countries where the possibility of political upheavals made the risk great. We had to discourage anything that looked like exploitation in countries where we exercised political influence.

One obvious way to improve both economic and political conditions was to improve the governments' financial administration, which was often so inefficient and corrupt that there was no money for salaries and pressing bills, to say nothing of building roads or schools. The smaller Caribbean states depended for their income almost wholly on the duties which they collected on imports and exports. Between 1905 and 1915, the American government had succeeded in having the customs collection in the Dominican Republic and Nicaragua and Haiti put under the control of officials appointed by it or with its approval, and we thought that the results, on the whole, had been good. We were consequently disposed to encourage new loans which would bring about similar arrangements. Nationalist sentiment in the Caribbean states and an increasing reluctance in Washington to assume new responsibilities in connection with their affairs ruled out the possibility of setting up any more collectorships headed by appointees of the American government; but the State Department was willing to cooperate in seeing that suitable persons were chosen as collectors, if the borrowing government wanted help. Consequently, we sometimes became involved in loan negotiations and assumed some responsibility for the result. In 1922 the State Department asked American bankers to inform it about all foreign loans which they were about to make, so that it might consider the bearing of the loans on American foreign policy.[5] Ordinarily we did not comment on the soundness of the

[5] The press release was published in *Foreign Relations, 1922*, Vol. I, p. 557.

transaction from a financial point of view, but where a loan to a Caribbean state was involved we felt that we had to see that the terms were fair and that the loan was a sound proposition for the borrowing government.

The State Department had always thought that its efforts to promote peace and economic progress in the Caribbean would be welcomed by intelligent and peace-loving people in the countries concerned. This assumption was less naïve, in the first decades of the century, than it would seem today. Many property owners and professional men, and many small farmers, were sick of civil wars and misgovernment and economic stagnation, and thought that American help offered the only hope for improvement. Diplomats in the field and officers in the State Department naturally had more contact with people who held these views, and with political leaders who wanted American support for more selfish reasons, than with unfriendly persons. President Wilson and his advisers had been honest in their belief that their efforts to enforce peace and better government were opposed chiefly by selfish and corrupt professional politicians. They were not wholly correct, because there were many people in the Caribbean states who were jealous of their national independence, and many others who might have welcomed American help but were alienated by the clumsy way in which it was sometimes imposed on them.

By 1921, it was clear that our interventions had aroused much resentment in the Caribbean region and that this resentment was being reflected in a growing feeling of hostility in South America. Few South Americans had any real sympathy for the Haitians and Dominicans, but many of them disliked and distrusted the United States and were responsive to propaganda portraying it as a greedy and imperialistic power. After the world war they began to receive more information about what the United States had been doing. The nationalists in the Dominican Republic sent emissaries who described the oppressive conduct of the American military government, and the activities of the anti-imperialist organizations in the United States were reported by the American press services. These services found it profitable to offer their Latin American customers reports of speeches and articles by critics of American policy, even though they had little news value in the United States. Exaggerated and violent attacks were of course more salable than more moderate discussions. The dis-

12

semination of anti-American propaganda was encouraged by European interests which were trying desperately to recover the preeminent position in the South American market which they had lost during the war. It became evident that our efforts to help the Caribbean states had done us a great deal of harm in other parts of the hemisphere.

At the same time there was a growing anti-imperialist sentiment in the United States. This caused the State Department less concern than the hostility in South America, but domestic criticism probably actually had more effect on American policy. There had been opposition to intervention in the Caribbean during the Taft administration, but there had been less criticism of Wilson's actions because the war in Europe distracted attention from them. The press, at least in the larger cities, reported the landing of marines in Haiti in 1915 and the establishment of the military government in the Dominican Republic in 1916, but there was little informed discussion of the background of these events and little coverage of what followed. There are almost no references to Haiti in the *New York Times Index* between October 1917 and July 1919. Until late in 1919 the American naval commanders were able to prevent the foreign press from receiving any but the scantiest reports of the insurrections which the marines had to suppress in Haiti and the Dominican Republic, a performance which would hardly have been possible if the press had been interested in the situation. The Nicaraguan liberals received equally little attention when they complained that American marines were keeping an unpopular government in power there.

By 1920 this situation was changing. After the world war, when political leaders in Haiti and the Dominican Republic began to organize protest movements against the American occupation, their efforts attracted attention in the United States as well as in South America. In July 1920 the *Nation* of New York began to publish a series of articles accusing the American authorities in the two countries of ineptitude and oppressive conduct and describing atrocities alleged to have been perpetrated by American marines. It was perhaps these articles that encouraged Harding to make Caribbean policy a minor issue in the electoral campaign by criticizing Wilson for making war on Haiti and the Dominican Republic without a declaration by Congress. In the same month, the military government at Santo Domingo helped to make the charges against it more credible by arresting the poet Fabio Fiallo and several other persons for criticizing the occupation in speeches and newspaper articles. In October, the Navy Department itself created a sensation, when it published a letter in which Major General Barnett, the commandant of the marine corps, wrote Secretary Daniels that he had found evidence that practically indiscriminate killing of natives had gone on for some time during the *caco* revolt in Haiti, and that he had ordered an investigation. The General later said that this statement had been misinterpreted, and that he was referring to the killing of only two Haitians. An inquiry, headed by Admiral Mayo, found no evidence that any considerable number of atrocities had been committed by the marines, but this did not satisfy critics who thought that American forces should not have been fighting in Haiti at all.

Throughout the next twelve years there was much criticism of the American government's policy in the Caribbean by magazines like the *Nation* and the *New Republic* and by a small group of anti-imperialists in the United States Senate, of whom Senator King of Utah was the most vocal. Many liberal-minded people thought that it was wrong to interfere in the internal affairs of small states and were shocked at the idea of American marines killing people who resisted interference. In academic circles a generation trained to look for economic motives in all governmental action explained the policy of the United States as primarily an effort to promote American trade and get profits for American bankers. Like many crusaders, some of the more ardent anti-imperialists tended to accept uncritically any evidence that seemed to support their case. Others were sound scholars who produced some of the best studies of Caribbean relations that were written during the 1920's. The people who worked on Latin American problems in the State Department thought that much of the anti-imperialist propaganda was untruthful or exaggerated. They resented especially the totally unfair allegation that the purpose of their policy was to subjugate small neighboring countries for the benefit of American business. They could not but realize however that many people who did not believe everything that the anti-imperialists said felt that there was something wrong with a policy which could lead to armed intervention in other countries, and they knew also that intervention in the Caribbean had a bad effect on hemisphere relations. At the same time some of them were increasingly coming to doubt whether diplomatic pressure, backed up on occasion by the threat of force, was the best way to bring about stable government in small disorderly countries. They still felt that what happened in the Caribbean was vitally important to the security of the United States, but from 1923 on there was a definite trend toward a policy of less interference in the internal political affairs of the Central American and West Indian republics.

The major decisions which marked this change in policy were made by presidents and secretaries of state, but it was the officers who dealt with Caribbean affairs in the State Department from day to day who carried them out. The man chiefly responsible for the form which the new policy took was Francis White, who was chief of the Latin American division from June 1922 to June 1926 and assistant secretary in charge of Latin American affairs from the spring of 1927 until 1933. White, a career diplomat, was an indefatigable worker who usually had well-thought-out views about what should be done and supported them tenaciously and effectively. He tended to be conservative in his approach to questions of policy, and he did not advocate abandoning the authority and responsibility which the United States was exercising under treaties with countries like Haiti and the Dominican Republic. In his first years as chief of the Latin American division he was perhaps more inclined than Secretary Hughes to take a strong line in efforts to discourage revolutions and insist on constitutional procedures in the Caribbean states, but as time went on he became more and more convinced that the American government should so far as possible avoid interference in purely internal political affairs, even in countries where it had special responsibilities. In this attitude he was generally supported by Secretary Kellogg, and it is perhaps unfortunate that White was away from Washington during most of the period in 1926-1927 when the American government was becoming involved in the second intervention in Nicaragua. The policy of non-interference took a more definite form under President Hoover, who was averse to any form of intervention in the Caribbean. By 1933, at least some of the distrust which earlier policies had aroused in other American countries seemed to be diminishing.

Chapter Two

GENERAL CROWDER'S MISSION
TO CUBA

One of the first problems that confronted Secretary Hughes in March 1921 was the political and financial crisis in Cuba, where Major General Enoch H. Crowder was attempting to prevent a civil war and to help the Cubans to deal with a desperate economic situation. Crowder had gone to Habana as the personal representative of President Wilson in the first days of January, and President-elect Harding had told the State Department in February that he wished his special mission to continue after the new administration took office.

The American government had felt a special responsibility for Cuba since it made the island independent after the Spanish-American war. The Platt amendment, embodied in the Cuban constitution and in the permanent treaty of 1903, gave the United States the right to intervene to preserve the country's independence and to maintain a government "adequate for the protection of life, property, and individual liberty"; and the reciprocity treaty of 1902 gave Cuba a favored position in the American market which helped to make her one of the world's greatest sugar producers. Much American and other foreign capital was invested there, and the country became the richest of the Caribbean states. The quality of the government, however, left much to be desired. Violence and crime played a large part in political contests and there was an extraordinary amount of corruption. The first presidential election after independence caused a civil war which forced the United States to intervene and to take over the government of the island in 1906. In 1909 a freely elected Cuban president was installed and the American forces were withdrawn, but during the next four years the State Department constantly interfered to discourage what it considered improvident or corrupt actions. There was less interference after new administrations came into office in both countries in 1913, but a disputed election in 1916 caused another revolt. The United

16

States contributed to the rebels' defeat by announcing publicly that it would support the constituted government, but as the presidential election of 1920 approached the American government insisted that President Menocal invite General Crowder to come to Cuba to draft an electoral law which might prevent the abuses that had caused the revolts of 1906 and 1917.

The law which Crowder drafted was approved by the Cuban congress, but Menocal turned down the American government's offer to supervise the election. The American legation at Habana sent a representative to each province to "observe" the voting, which took place on November 1, 1920, but their presence had little effect. Much violence and intimidation occurred and there were many charges of fraud. The result, on the face of the returns, was a victory for Alfredo Zayas, the leader of a faction of the liberal party, who had been supported by Menocal and his fellow conservatives because there seemed to be no other way to defeat General José Miguel Gómez, the candidate of the majority of the liberal party.

The liberals were not disposed to accept the result without a fight. They had gone to the polls only because the American government insisted that they should and led them to think that it would endeavor to assure fair play. They proposed to send a mission to Washington to demand the annulment of the election, but the State Department insisted that they pursue the remedies provided by the electoral law. The liberals presented a great number of complaints in the form that the law required, but it was soon evident that red tape and procrastination in the electoral boards and the courts would make it hard for them to get fair treatment. There was much talk of a revolt, and the situation was made worse by an economic crisis. Cuba was particularly hard hit by the post-war depression. The price of sugar, which had reached unprecedented heights when sugar was released from war-time controls, suddenly collapsed in the autumn of 1920. The local banks, which had financed an orgy of speculation and extravagance during what was called "the dance of the millions," were severely affected, and President Menocal proclaimed a moratorium in an effort to save them. This paralyzed business and threw thousands of people out of work.

The American government sent Crowder to Habana again in an effort to help the Cubans to deal with the situation. Crowder was well known in Cuba and had many friends there. He had

17

been chairman of a Cuban-American commission which drafted new laws for the republic during the intervention of 1906-1909 and had continued to take a special interest in Cuba's problems. As the author of the law under which the recent election was held, he was peculiarly fitted to deal with the political crisis. He went to Cuba with greater prestige after his distinguished service as provost marshal general during the world war.

Boaz Long, the American minister, stayed at his post for the time being, but Crowder became the principal spokesman for the United States in dealing with the election and in giving advice on economic matters. As he very explicitly told the Cubans, the purpose of his mission was to prevent the development of a situation where the United States would be compelled to take more drastic action. It might be difficult to avoid actual intervention if the electoral dispute led to civil war, or if it dragged on, as it threatened to, beyond the time when a new government should take office under the constitution. The solution of the electoral dispute, as he saw it, was simply to insist on the application of the electoral law, which permitted aggrieved parties to demand that the electoral boards order new elections in districts where it could be shown that the first vote had been vitiated by intimidation or fraud. If the boards failed to act, the complainants could appeal to the courts. He insisted that the liberals pursue their remedies and that the electoral boards and the courts act more promptly on cases before them.

Under Crowder's energetic prodding, the electoral machinery began to function. The electoral boards and the courts found it hard to reject or ignore complaints which were supported by evidence, and by the beginning of March, new elections had been ordered in enough districts to give the liberals at least an outside chance to win. Crowder thought that the decisions of the electoral boards and the courts had on the whole been correct and that the central electoral board and President Menocal had taken all reasonable measures to assure fairness in the approaching partial elections.[1] The liberals, however, were not satisfied. They had failed to persuade the courts to order new elections in many districts where they claimed there had been fraud or intimidation in November, and they insisted that the new elections would

[1] Crowder to Hughes, March 7, 1921, State Department decimal file, National Archives, 837.00/2017. Except where otherwise indicated, all numerical references are to these files.

18

not be fair unless they were controlled by the United States, a proposal which Crowder refused to consider.

In the meantime, the Cuban government, with Crowder's help, had taken measures which somewhat improved the economic situation. The so-called Torriente laws provided for the gradual lifting of the moratorium and the orderly liquidation of any banks that proved to be insolvent, and a sugar finance commission was set up to take over the sale and shipment of the 1920-21 sugar crop. These measures had been proposed by the Cubans, and the United States government, which had other ideas, had acquiesced in them rather reluctantly on Crowder's recommendation after the general had helped to redraft the proposed legislation. The State Department and American sugar refiners objected especially to the sugar finance commission, which seemed likely to increase prices paid by consumers in the United States.

Crowder still feared that the electoral process might break down and he also looked forward with misgivings to what might happen if either Zayas or Gómez became president. He did not think that either man could bring about the reforms which Cuba desperately needed, and in February he suggested privately to officials in the State Department that both candidates might be persuaded to withdraw in favor of a third man who could then be made president by the electoral college. He evidently thought that the conservatives would be glad to abandon Zayas, and the liberals had already indicated that they would accept a compromise.[2] Crowder discussed this idea informally with President Menocal and a few other prominent Cubans and found them receptive to it. In the latter part of February, Sumner Welles, the chief of the Latin American division in the State Department, went to Habana to explore it. He and Crowder and Boaz Long drew up a list of preferred candidates, headed at Welles' suggestion by the name of Carlos Manuel de Céspedes, the Cuban minister at Washington. Apparently Crowder was to work to have the plan adopted, if the electoral process broke down, but the State Department was not to be involved. Welles seems to have acted on his own initiative, presumably with the acquiescence of higher officials in the outgoing administration, but after his return to Washington he explained the plan to Henry Fletcher, who was to become undersecretary of state a few days later, and

[2] For the liberals' attitude, see Long's dispatch of Feb. 18, 1921, 837.00/2008.

got Fletcher's tentative approval.[3] On March 12 Crowder cabled that he thought it possible, though not probable, that liberal opposition and defections among his own followers might lead Zayas to withdraw his candidacy even after the electoral process was completed. In this case, unless otherwise instructed, he would carry out the procedure discussed with Welles. The State Department approved.[4]

The new partial elections were to take place on March 15, except in the province of Santiago, where they were set for March 26. Crowder exerted much pressure on Menocal to assure fair play, and persuaded the political parties to set up a conciliation committee which at the end of February reached an apparently satisfactory agreement about the conduct of the elections. Nevertheless the liberals decided on March 10 not to go to the polls, citing several recent minor disturbances as evidence that it would be dangerous to do so. Crowder thought their action unjustified. He had just made a tour of the districts where the sharpest contests were likely, and he was satisfied that the measures which he had persuaded the government to take and the presence of a large number of inspectors would prevent organized intimidation or violence. There was reason to suspect that the liberals themselves had staged the recent incidents as a pretext for their withdrawal.[5] Crowder rejected the liberals' proposal that new general elections be held in November under a provisional president to be chosen by Congress. Since there was no possibility that the partial elections in Santiago would overcome the majority which Zayas already had in that province, the elections of March 15, in which few liberals voted, virtually ended the contest. Crowder thought that the Cuban people had been compelled "to respect the results obtained under the law which they themselves had duly enacted, as construed by their own courts."

It seemed likely that the liberals might still prevent the Congress from proclaiming Zayas president-elect because the consti-

[3] There are only vague references to this plan in the official record, but a copy of Welles' memorandum of March 1, 1921, describing his visit, and letters to and from Crowder discussing it, are in the Latin American division file, now in the National Archives.

[4] Crowder to Hughes, March 12, and Hughes to Crowder, March 14, 1921, 837.00/2026.

[5] Crowder to Hughes, March 12, 1921, 837.00/2026.

tution required that two-thirds of the members must be present for the opening of a new legislative term. Crowder seems to have regarded this possibility with equanimity. A deadlock would offer an opportunity to carry out the plan which he had discussed with Welles. He even got Menocal and the central electoral board to promise that they would consult him before setting the date for the meeting of the presidential electors, so as to gain time for the choice of a compromise candidate if the liberals prevented a quorum in Congress. When the party leaders began to discuss terms on which the liberals might agree to permit the Congress to meet, he did nothing to encourage the negotiations.

The State Department seems to have been less interested in the idea of selecting a compromise candidate. When Gómez went to Washington to lay his case before the department, Secretary Hughes told him courteously but firmly on April 15 that the United States considered that Zayas had been properly elected and would view with regret and apprehension any further effort to prevent him from taking office. Gómez said that he would accept the American government's decision. When he returned to Habana he urged his party to resign itself to defeat rather than risk American intervention. On April 17 the legation at Habana issued a long public statement reviewing the history of the election and urging the cessation of any effort to obstruct final action by Congress. The liberals gave up, and Zayas was proclaimed president-elect on April 29.

The election showed how difficult it is to impose democracy by pressure from outside. It was by no means clear that the outcome represented the wishes of a majority of the Cuban voters. Crowder thought that Menocal had done less than he should have to prevent abuses.[6] Even if the president had wished to hold a free election, it would have been difficult to do so. Too many of the military and civil officials in the provinces would have found it impossible to imagine that they must really refrain from the fraud and intimidation which were a normal part of the electoral procedure. They had too much at stake in the victory of their own party. Under the electoral law, the liberals could complain to the electoral boards and the courts, but there were undoubtedly many cases where it was difficult to prove that fear of mistreatment had kept voters away from the polls or that bribery or

[6] See Crowder's final report on the election, April 7, 1921, 837.00/2082.

coercion had influenced the decisions of local electoral boards. In the situation that confronted him, however, Secretary Hughes could hardly have acted otherwise than he did. The alternatives were to hold aloof and risk a civil war in Cuba, or to compel the holding of a new election, presumably under complete American control. Ten years later, the American government might conceivably have adopted a hands-off policy and let the Cubans fight it out. In 1921, especially in view of the extent to which the United States was already involved in the situation, a secretary of state who had only been in office a few days could hardly be expected to adopt a course so inconsistent with the American government's traditional policy. It would have been still harder to justify insisting on a new general election after the Cuban courts had ordered new partial elections in the districts where there was proof that there had been violence or fraud in November, and after the liberals had refused to participate in them.

In dealing with the electoral dispute, the new administration could do little but continue the policy to which its predecessor had committed it. After the dispute was resolved, it had to determine what its own policy would be. Presumably on the advice of Sumner Welles, Secretary Hughes was persuaded that the Cubans would continue to need the sort of help that Crowder could give them and that the United States, in view of its historic relationship to Cuba, had a duty to extend it. The immediate danger of a civil war had passed, but there was still danger of an economic collapse which might have disastrous political consequences. The price of sugar was low and the sugar finance commission had had little success in disposing of the great stocks that glutted the market. Though the Torriente laws had ended the moratorium, the Cuban banks were in such bad shape that practically all of them went into liquidation between April and June 1921. The failure of the Banco Nacional, early in April, was especially serious because several million dollars of government funds were on deposit there. This aggravated an already bad situation in the national treasury, and the government's inability to pay bills and current salaries made general economic conditions worse.

Crowder was reluctant to continue. He was about to retire from the army and had already made arrangements for what promised to be a lucrative legal practice in the United States. President Harding had offered to make him minister to Cuba, but to accept this position he would have to give up his pay as a retired army officer. He also realized, and pointed out to the State Department, that an indefinite prolongation of his mission would cause resentment in Cuba. Nevertheless Hughes asked him on May 6 to stay at Habana until after Zayas' inauguration, to give advice and assistance to the new government.[7] Minister Long's resignation was accepted and Crowder was instructed to move into the legation. As it turned out the general continued to represent the United States at Habana until 1927, as personal representative of the president of the United States until 1923 and thereafter as American ambassador.

Crowder's mission was later criticized in the United States as an effort to exercise imperialistic control over Cuba. It is true that his activities during the first years of Zayas' administration involved a great deal of interference in Cuba's internal affairs. His purpose, however, was not to establish permanent American control but to correct conditions which would expose the republic to foreign interference or eventual armed intervention. He was genuinely interested in the effort to develop stable republican government in Cuba and he thought that this effort could not succeed unless the political evils and the gross corruption which had brought the country to the verge of disaster were eliminated. He thought that the United States had a duty, under the Platt amendment, to insist on reforms and to resort to compulsion if its advice were disregarded.

Even before Zayas was officially proclaimed as president-elect, Crowder had asked the State Department's permission to begin the discussion of measures to improve the electoral system and to reduce corruption and inefficiency in the government. Without such reforms, he thought that American intervention would sooner or later be unavoidable. The department approved,[8] and when Crowder reported that Zayas seemed likely to make some undesirable appointments to his cabinet he was told to impress on the president-elect the American government's "earnest desire" that "there may be no repetition in the future" of the electoral failure which had provoked such a serious crisis in the national life of the republic. He was to tell Zayas that "the Government of the United States believes that there is implicit

[7] Hughes to Crowder, May 6, 1921, 837.00/2097.

[8] Crowder to Hughes, March 23, and Hughes to Crowder, March 28, 1921, 837.00/2048, 2049.

23

in the treaty of 1903 the obligation on the part of the Republic of Cuba to maintain an honest and efficient government in return for the obligations assumed by the United States." This instruction seemed to indicate that the new administration subscribed to an interpretation of the Platt amendment which would permit more interference in Cuba's internal affairs than the Wilson administration had practiced. Crowder immediately laid before the president-elect a broad program of reform designed to do away with some of the bad political and financial practices which had characterized the Cuban government since the withdrawal of the American occupation in 1909.

Zayas, as was later evident, had no interest in reforms, but he was not in a position to resist Crowder's forcefully presented recommendations. The president-elect knew that he would have to have American help in dealing with the economic and political problems that confronted him. The general economic situation was still bad and the government's financial condition was worse. His political situation was precarious, for he had no real friends among the conservatives who had supported his election and the liberals were angry about their defeat. Furthermore, he knew that many of his influential fellow-citizens would support Crowder's program. Some Cubans, including many politicians, resented the general's interference, but many others considered him one of the republic's best friends. Under the circumstances, it was expedient to profess a willingness to follow Crowder's advice.

Zayas consequently accepted the State Department's interpretation of the Platt amendment and agreed to go forward with the reforms which Crowder considered indispensable: the reduction of government expenditures, the elimination of *botellas*, positions in which favored politicians drew salaries but did no work, and a general reform of the national lottery, which was one of the principal sources of corruption. He eliminated from his list of candidates for cabinet appointments several persons whom the general disapproved, and he accepted the general's help in drafting his inaugural message, in which he set forth his program. A few days before his inauguration, in answer to newspaper criticism of Crowder's continued presence, Zayas publicly stated that he would be glad to have the general stay in Cuba and would not hesitate to "utilize his valuable and distinguished services."

24

When Zayas took office on May 20, Crowder was cautiously optimistic. He thought that the passage of the presidency "from the soldier class of statesmen to the lawyer class" was perhaps a change for the better, and he wrote that Zayas was as good a lawyer in Cuba as Root was in New York. He spoke highly of the new president's intelligence and his understanding of the government's problems. Crowder feared however that Zayas' many political obligations would make it hard to adhere to a policy of economy, and he was not sure that Zayas would actually go through with the program in which he professed to want American help. He knew that Zayas had been less than enthusiastic about making his recent statement to the press.[9]

Crowder's misgivings were confirmed during the first month of Zayas' administration. The government's most urgent problem was the alarming state of its finances. During the post-war boom, revenues had reached the highest point in history, but extravagance and graft had pushed expenditures to a still higher figure. Future revenues had been recklessly obligated in contracts for public works and other purposes, and after the government's income suddenly fell off at the end of 1920 a large floating debt accumulated. Menocal did little to correct the situation, and when Zayas took office, the government was still unable to pay current bills and many employees were not receiving their salaries. There was still an excessive number of persons on the payroll. Early in July 1921, Zayas signed decrees ordering the abolition of *botellas,* or sinecures, and suspending the salary bonuses which had been promised the government employees by Menocal, but it soon became clear that he would not make the sort of economies which Crowder thought necessary. He made little effort actually to get rid of *botellas* or to correct other administrative abuses. Crowder could obtain little information about what the government was doing. By August he felt that his effort to obtain reforms "by advice firmly and insistently given" had accomplished little, and that it might be necessary in the future "to speak to the Zayas administration upon important matters more or less in terms of an ultimatum."[10]

Zayas became more amenable, however, when he realized that he could not emerge from his financial difficulties without a foreign loan. In the first months of his administration he had appar-

[9] Crowder to Hughes, personal, May 21, 1921, 837.00/2210.
[10] Crowder to Hughes, Aug. 22, 1921, 837.00/2158.

25

ently hoped to avoid borrowing because he knew that the lenders would insist on financial reforms. By September 1921 it was clear both to him and to Crowder and the State Department that he must have financial help. He could not get a loan without the American government's approval. Article II of the Platt amendment, which provided that the Cuban government

> shall not assume or contract any public debt, to pay the interest upon which, and to make reasonable sinking-fund provision for the ultimate discharge of which, the ordinary revenues of the island after defraying the current expenses of Government shall be inadequate.

had always been interpreted as requiring the consent of the United States for any Cuban loan; and even if it had not been so interpreted no banker would be likely to make a loan without the State Department's approval. J. P. Morgan and Company, who had floated earlier Cuban loans, told the State Department soon after Zayas' inauguration that they would consider a loan of up to $50,000,000 if the American government gave its consent, provided that the Cuban government reduced its expenditures and found new sources of revenue to make better provision for the service of the bonds. Crowder, too, insisted that the government reduce its expenditures before it tried to borrow. He could not very well insist on specific reductions without a detailed inspection of the government services, which he thought it inadvisable to undertake, but he urged that the total budget be kept down to $55,000,000. Zayas maintained that he must have $65,000,000.

While this matter was being discussed, the situation grew worse. The government had failed to keep up service on its internal bonds and it seemed likely that it would have to default on the service of its existing foreign debt. Zayas consequently asked the bankers for an emergency short-term advance of $5,000,000, and at the end of September Dwight Morrow and Norman Davis of the Morgan firm went to Habana to discuss the matter. The bankers said they would consider a short-term loan only if it were the first step toward constructive financial reform. They offered to lend Cuba $5,000,000 for one year, to be repaid from a $50,000,000 loan to be made later, on condition that the budget be reduced and that the customs and internal revenue laws be revised to provide an annual surplus of $10,000,000. Under pressure from Crowder, Zayas accepted the proposal and promised to reduce the current budget and to propose a budget of $55,000,000, plus $5,000,000 for contingencies, for the fiscal year 1922-1923. He also agreed to the appointment of an advisory commission on tariffs and taxes to study ways of increasing the govenment's revenues, and in November he appointed John S. Hord, an American tax expert, as its chairman.

Before the loan contract was signed, however, Zayas apparently changed his mind. The provisional budget which he submitted to Congress for 1922-1923 totaled $64,422,664.68. He asked the Congress to delay action on it because he planned to propose reductions, but he was evasive when Crowder questioned him. Other bankers who were interested in the proposed larger loan had evidently encouraged him to think that he might obtain help without submitting to the conditions on which Morgan and Crowder were insisting. He was also perhaps influenced by persistent reports that the State Department was about to terminate Crowder's mission. His attitude made the State Department fear that the whole effort to rehabilitate Cuba's finances was breaking down,[11] and on December 20 it asked Crowder to come to Washington for a conference. Before leaving Habana he was to demand a definite statement about the reduction of the budget and to say that the United States regarded the situation with the "utmost concern." He was also to tell Zayas that he would return to Cuba and would remain until the financial situation was satisfactorily solved. The State Department's attitude and his own urgent need for money convinced Zayas that he had to yield. He issued a decree cutting expenditures for the current fiscal year to about $63,000,000, and on January 14, 1922 the American government gave its consent for the short-term loan. J. P. Morgan and Company bought the Cuban government's note for $5,000,000 at a discount of ½% and a 6% interest rate.

Meanwhile, in January 1922, the American government removed a potential source of friction by withdrawing to Guantánamo a small force of marines which had been stationed in Camaguey province since 1917. The marines had been sent to eastern Cuba during the world war to help maintain order and prevent interference with sugar production, and the Americans in the province would have been glad to have them stay. Crow-

[11] Latin American division memorandum of Dec. 17, 1921, 837.51/713.

der at first thought it would be wise to keep them there for the time being, but by December, when the Cuban government asked that they leave, he saw no adequate reason to object.

Crowder discussed the Cuban problem with the State Department while he was in Washington in January and returned to Habana with instructions to insist on a broad program of reform. He was authorized to present a note saying that the Cuban government's default on its internal bonds and its failure to meet other obligations was a violation of the Platt amendment which justified the United States in making recommendations for reform in fiscal policy. The United States would consequently expect the government to give Crowder free access to all sources of information and to permit him to make all necessary inspections, so that the American government would have the information necessary for action on any proposed loan or for the determination of measures to protect those who had already lent money to Cuba. When Zayas received the note he drafted a reply politely questioning the American interpretation of the Platt amendment, but Crowder apparently persuaded him not to deliver it. Zayas was in no position to refuse American help. The $5,000,000 loan had averted default on the foreign debt, but many of the government employees and other creditors, including the holders of the internal bonds, were still going unpaid.

The proposed $50,000,000 loan would clearly be needed, but Crowder thought that the United States would not be justified in consenting to it until the government had balanced its budget and had carried out basic reforms which would eliminate some of the corruption and extravagance which had helped to bring on the situation in which the government found itself. Beginning in March 1922, he gave Zayas a series of memoranda discussing fiscal and administrative problems and describing many of the worst abuses which needed correction. These papers represented a great amount of research and supported proposals for reform with arguments which no Cuban official could easily refute. Zayas seemed to receive them in a friendly spirit, but he showed little disposition to act on them, and by the end of March Crowder was again suggesting to the State Department that the time was approaching when he should resort to an ultimatum in demanding reforms. He thought that Cuban public opinion would support him in doing so.[12]

[12] Crowder to Hughes, March 31, 1922, 837.51/748.

The general apparently thought after his visit to Washington in January that the State Department agreed with his view that the United States would ultimately have to intervene in Cuba if economic or political conditions grew intolerably bad, and that he would therefore be justified in exerting vigorous diplomatic pressure, with the threat of intervention in the background, to compel the adoption of reforms. He had discussed the situation with Fletcher and Welles, but it is probable that he had not discussed it so fully with Hughes, who had been occupied with the Washington naval conference and had left Latin American affairs in the hands of the undersecretary and the Latin American division. Hughes had approved the instruction asserting the rights of the United States under the Platt amendment, but this had contained no threat to intervene. Early in April 1922, when Crowder asked the Department to approve the presentation of two memoranda dealing with the budget and the elimination of *botellas*, couched in language that conveyed a rather definite threat of intervention, Hughes told his subordinates emphatically that intervention was out of the question.[13] Crowder was told to say merely that the United States regarded the problems dealt with in the memoranda, "with the gravest concern." A month later, when he submitted memoranda on "Graft, Corruption, and Immorality in the Public Administration" and on the lottery, he was asked to make verbal changes to eliminate preemptory demands or the appearance of a threat. He was authorized to say that the continuance of abuses in the lottery would be "a most serious obstacle to any rehabilitation of Cuba's finances," but he was to emphasize Zayas' promises of reforms and the urgent need for all available revenue rather than any obligations growing out of the Platt amendment.

For the time being the State Department's more cautious attitude did not have much effect on the course of events. The department was still prepared to support Crowder vigorously, and at the end of May, when he reported that he was about to press Zayas for action on the reform program, and that he would need effective help from Washington, Hughes asked the Cuban minister to tell Zayas that the United States fully supported the general in the recommendations which he would make. It was hard

[13] He said emphatically to me on one occasion that there would be no intervention, "because public opinion would not stand for it." I dealt with Cuban affairs during this period only at times when Welles was absent.

for Zayas to resist the demands which Crowder presented. His political situation was growing weaker, for his conservative allies were beginning to desert him and the liberals were still hostile. Crowder's memoranda had not been published, but it was known that he was urging a sounder fiscal policy and the elimination of graft, and most of the Cuban newspapers supported him.[14] Everyone appreciated the need for continued American help in dealing with the financial situation.

Crowder began by insisting that the president replace several members of his cabinet with men of greater ability and integrity. Zayas at first resisted, but after several conferences, in which Crowder refused to accept anyone in whom he did not have confidence, new secretaries were chosen to head the Treasury and Interior and Public Works Departments. Though the general later insisted that he had not suggested a single name, it is clear that he was able in some way to bring about the appointment of men in whom he had confidence and whom Zayas, in some cases, was rather unwilling to accept. Crowder's friend Colonel Manuel Despaigne became secretary of the treasury and Demetrio Castillo, who had been the general's personal aide, became secretary of public works. Crowder at first objected to the appointment of Ricardo Lancis to the key post of secretary of government, but he withdrew his opposition after Lancis showed an independent spirit by refusing to accept Zayas' nephew as subsecretary in the department.[15] The whole affair must have been painful and humiliating to Zayas, but the "honest cabinet," as it was called in Cuba, was well received by the press and by public opinion.

The next step was to reform the national lottery, which put millions of dollars each month into the pockets of favored politicians. The legal price of a lottery ticket was $20, but the tickets could usually be sold to the public for at least $30. The difference went not to the national treasury but to dealers, and especially to the "collectors," who had the privilege of buying tickets from the government at the legal price less three percent. This privilege was valuable, because each *colecturía* gave its holder fourteen tickets for each drawing and there were at least three drawings every month. It involved no work or responsibility because other dealers took over and distributed the tickets. Most of the

[14] Crowder to Hughes, June 12, 1922, *Foreign Relations, 1922*, Vol. I, p. 1032.
[15] Crowder to Hughes, June 19, 1922, 837.002/53.

2,000 *colecturías* were distributed among congressmen and newspaper editors and other persons whose support the government wished to buy, and their efficacy as a means of corruption was the greater because they could be withdrawn at any time. One large block of tickets was usually sold directly to wholesalers for the benefit of the director general of the lottery and the president of the republic, giving them a profit which Crowder estimated as $200,000 to $250,000 each month. Alfredo Zayas Jr., the president's son, was director general.

Crowder thought that graft could be stopped in the lottery and the government's revenue from it increased if the tickets were sold to the dealers at the price which the public paid less a reasonable discount. His proposal would deprive many of the government's friends of a substantial part of their income, and was certain to be violently opposed by members of Congress and many newspapermen. Zayas signed the decree which Crowder drafted for him only under "extreme pressure" from the general and from members of the new cabinet, and when he did so he asked Crowder whether the United States would support him against a possible attempt at impeachment by Congress. Crowder replied that he would recommend action by the American government only if Zayas aggressively supported the reform program and supported his new cabinet in its campaign against graft and other abuses.[16]

With the reform of the lottery apparently accomplished, Crowder resumed his efforts to help the government with its financial problems. He was convinced that the government needed a large foreign loan because its inability to pay its debts was retarding the country's recovery from the post-war depression, but he thought that other reforms should be made before the United States should consent to the loan. He urged the temporary suspension of parts of the civil service law to make possible a reorganization of some government services; the passage of legislation to permit the removal of dishonest judges; the establishment of a stricter system of accounting; and the appointment of a commission to determine the amount of the internal debt. During the summer of 1922, he and the new cabinet pressed Zayas and the leaders in Congress for action on this program and for the enactment of a law authorizing a foreign loan and creating new taxes

[16] Crowder to Hughes, June 30, 1922, 837.513/54. A part of this telegram is printed in *Foreign Relations, 1922*, Vol. I, p. 1035.

for its service. Earlier in the year Hord, the American tax expert, had given Zayas' drafts of legislation providing for several new taxes.

Zayas and the congressional leaders realized that the government must have a loan, but they showed no enthusiasm for the rest of the program. The congressional leaders had even less interest in reform than the president had, and many of them were angry about the loss of their *colecturías*. When they failed to act on the honest cabinet's proposals, Crowder sought help from the State Department and Hughes issued a public statement, describing the reform program and expressing the hope that its adoption would restore tranquillity and confidence and improve business conditions in Cuba.[17] A few days later Crowder told one of the congressional leaders that he would give Congress ten days more to act, before reporting to the State Department and if necessary going to Washington for conference. When press reports from Habana described this threat as an "ultimatum," Undersecretary Phillips, who was in charge while Hughes was visiting Brazil, denied that there had been an ultimatum and said that the American government was not considering intervention in Cuba. This encouraged the opposition in the Cuban Congress, and the State Department had to issue another statement emphasizing the imperative need to adopt the reform program, and saying that Crowder had the American government's complete confidence and support.

Crowder's firmness and persistence finally overcame the Cubans' resistance and early in October the Congress completed action on the measures which he had been urging. The only remaining obstacle to an agreement between the two governments on the loan was an amnesty bill pending in Congress which would have freed several persons recently indicted in connection with scandals in the lottery. The Cuban Congress' propensity for granting amnesty periodically to great numbers of criminals had always been a source of concern to the State Department and the proposal under consideration seemed particularly ill-timed. Zayas, however, assured the general that the bill would not become law.

On October 18 the Cuban chargé d'affaires at Washington formally asked if the American government had any objection to the

---

[17] Press release of Aug. 23, *Foreign Relations, 1922*, Vol. I, p. 1036.

negotiation of a loan of $50,000,000. The State Department was about to reply when Zayas, without asking the approval of Congress, issued an executive decree appropriating $182,000 for expenses of the national palace. This was a flagrant violation of promises to Crowder to refrain from illegally appropriating money in this way. At the same time it became known that Zayas was about to reappoint his son as director of the lottery, despite the fact that Zayas Jr. was under indictment for malfeasance during his previous tenure of office. It was difficult to approve the loan in the face of such glaring evidence of the president's lack of interest in the reform program, but the State Department gave its consent on November 4 after Crowder and Despaigne persuaded the president to ask Congress for the funds for the palace and to appoint his son to another position. Undersecretary Phillips asked the Cuban chargé to tell his government that the consent was being given because of the assurances which Zayas had given Crowder about reform. Phillips said that the American government was especially interested in two matters which were still pending: the proposed amnesty bill and the preservation of the cabinet substantially as it was. The secretary of state, he said, strongly endorsed the position which Crowder had taken on both matters.[18]

Action on the loan was delayed for a time because Zayas was ill, but in the latter part of December the Cuban government invited bankers to bid for the proposed bond issue. J. P. Morgan and Company had waived any claim to a preferential right to the business, but their offer of 96.77 for 5½% thirty-year bonds was higher than those of Speyer and Company and Lee Higginson and Company who also submitted bids. Contrary to earlier expectations, the bankers made no demand for any outside control of Cuba's financial administration, perhaps because they counted on the State Department's continued support of the reform program. The Cuban government accepted the Morgan bid on January 13, 1923.

The loan was an example of the brighter side of dollar diplomacy. The plan for it had been carefully worked out by Crowder and by Dwight Morrow, the Morgan partner who handled the matter, as a part of the broader effort to pull Cuba out of the political and financial crisis. The terms were remarkably

[18] Phillips' memorandum of Nov. 4, 1922, 837.51/929.

favorable to the Cuban government and distinctly better, because of Cuba's relationship to the United States, than those on which most Latin American governments could borrow. The proceeds were used chiefly to pay debts, including back salaries and pensions. A smaller amount was available for public works. The loan stimulated the economic recovery and the improvement in the government's financial situation which were already beginning to become evident in the last months of 1922.

In January 1923, the United States Congress, by an amendment to a deficiency appropriation act, made it possible for General Crowder to receive salary as ambassador to Cuba without giving up his military retirement pay. He was appointed ambassador on February 10. The termination of his special mission put relations on a somewhat more normal basis and perhaps made his presence more acceptable to the more senstive Cuban nationalists, but otherwise made little practical difference. It was a coincidence that the general's change in status occurred just a few months before the breakdown of his reform program.

Up to this point Crowder's mission had been remarkably successful. Civil war had been averted and economic conditions were improving. Under the new cabinet the public administration was becoming more efficient. Many useless employees had been discharged. The worst aspects of the lottery had been corrected, and improvident or corrupt public works contracts granted by the Menocal administration and involving some $49,000,000, were being canceled. Legitimate debts were being examined by a commission and paid with funds from the foreign loan. The new 1% sales tax, proposed by Hord, was producing less than it should because it was inefficiently administered, but there was every prospect that the treasury would have a substantial surplus at the end of the fiscal year.

Crowder and the State Department and the bankers had gone ahead with the loan on the assumption that what Crowder called the "moralization" program would continue. They knew that Zayas had little interest in the program, but they thought that the American government could exert enough influence to prevent its abandonment. Much would depend, of course, on the continuance in office of the honest cabinet. Secretary Hughes had not thought it advisable to require Zayas to commit himself definitely on this point as a condition of the loan, but Zayas had assured Crowder before the State Department gave its consent in November that no changes were contemplated. In January, before the loan contract was signed, the bankers wrote Crowder that they had bid for the bonds because they understood the United States had approved the loan on the understanding that a good cabinet would be retained, and expressed concern about press reports in Cuba that the cabinet might be changed. Crowder discussed the matter with Zayas and with some difficulty obtained an oral promise that the cabinet would remain for the time being and that any changes that might eventually be made would not affect the moralization program.[19]

It soon became clear that Zayas did not intend to go ahead with the reform program unless he had to. He had yielded to Crowder's demands, often unwillingly and after much resistance, because he needed the loan. With the money in hand, he could hardly be expected to continue indefinitely to retain ministers who were closer to the American ambassador than to himself. The reform program made it hard for him to build up his political following and threatened to prevent him and his friends from profiting by their official positions as Cuban politicians expected to profit.

On March 13, 1923, the president published a decree providing for the purchase of the so-called Santa Clara convent property for use for government offices. This was another violation of his promise not to appropriate money by decree and it was clear that the transaction involved a large amount of graft. Crowder protested and pointed out that the purchase price of $2,350,000 was excessive for a property which had been sold for $1,000,000 in April 1920, when real estate prices were high. Zayas agreed not to conclude the purchase until he had obtained the approval of Congress, but he expressed resentment against the secretary of finance and the secretary of public health, who publicly criticized his action. It soon became evident that he was attempting to obtain the support of public opinion in an effort to throw off Crowder's tutelage.[20] By the end of March the Cuban press was publishing stories about an impending cabinet crisis and speculating whether public opinion would support the president in a

[19] Crowder to Hughes, Feb. 3, 1923, 837.51/931. A part of this dispatch was published in *Foreign Relations, 1923*, Vol. I, p. 838.

[20] The correspondence about the Santa Clara convent property is in file 837.157. The Cuban Congress approved the purchase of the property in 1924.

conflict with ministers imposed on him by the United States government.

Crowder sent Zayas a note denying that he had imposed the cabinet on the president but saying that the United States assumed, in view of Zayas' assurances, that there would be no cabinet changes without an exchange of views between the two governments. At Washington, Undersecretary Phillips warned the Cuban chargé that the United States would take a serious view of any steps that might endanger the moralization program. On April 3 the State Department told Crowder to say that because of its participation in the establishment of the Cuban Republic and its treaty relations, it had been giving the Cuban government advice as a special friend. It would regret actions not in conformity with its advice but it would not stop giving advice. Crowder was to urge Zayas to proceed loyally with the moralization program and the United States would carefully observe any failure to do so. If there were changes in the cabinet Crowder was to ask Zayas to dissipate any doubt as to their effect on the program. On the next day, however, apparently fearing that Crowder might take too vigorous a position, Hughes cautioned the ambassador not to deliver any ultimatum or to intimate intervention. The department, he said, did not wish to be put in a position where it had to make good a threat. Intervention could come only as a result of a complete breakdown of government which would clearly leave no other alternative; the United States could not contemplate intervention to eliminate graft.

In the meantime, on April 3, Zayas asked for the resignations of all the cabinet, and on the fourth, in reply to Crowder's first note, he denied that he had made any commitment to retain the cabinet permanently. He assured the ambassador that he would continue the moralization program, but he would try to find new ministers who did not think themselves "elements of greater authority than the president." He offered to discuss the matter with Crowder before taking any definite action. At the same time Zayas instructed the Cuban chargé at Washington to tell the State Department that he had never agreed to keep this cabinet permanently but that any changes that he might make would not weaken the moralization program.[21]

Crowder discussed the cabinet crisis and the moralization pro-

---

[21] The correspondence about the cabinet change is in decimal file 837.002, enclosures 59ff.

gram with Zayas in three days of conferences totalling nine and a half hours. The president argued that he had been compelled to remove some of his ministers when they openly criticized the Santa Clara convent decree and he insisted that the responsibility for choosing new ones rested wholly on himself. He finally gave Crowder the names of prospective appointees, unofficially, but he paid little attention to the ambassador's comments on them. He wished, he wrote Crowder, to avoid having any secretary consider himself "the guide and mentor of the president." On the other hand, in a proclamation issued on April 20, in which he referred to his constitutional right to appoint his own cabinet, he spoke warmly of the United States and the advice which Cuba had received from the American government and expressed personal friendship for Crowder.

Crowder was not at first convinced that the removal of the honest cabinet meant the end of his effort for reform. He thought that most of the new ministers were men of little standing or ability, but all of them promised to cooperate in the moralization program. The ambassador thought that neither they nor Zayas were under any illusions about the embassy's continued determination to press the program and it would be more difficult for Zayas to abandon it now that the whole country knew about it and about Zayas' commitment to it. The ambassador assured the State Department that the new situation would not make his own position more difficult than it had been. In a personal letter to Francis White, he seemed less sanguine. He thought that he would not press aggressively for further reforms for a few weeks until the political situation was somewhat clearer.[22] During the next two months Crowder continued to gather information about the evils in Cuba's political life. In July he sent the State Department three additional memoranda: one about graft in the provincial and municipal governments, another discussing electoral practices, and a third describing the irresponsible and venal conduct of the Cuban Congress during the past quarter century. He hoped that these would give the department a basis for a restatement of its policy, which he thought "urgently necessary."[23]

[22] Crowder to Hughes, April 23, 1923, 837.002/85; Crowder to White, April 26, 1923, 837.00/2610.

[23] The memorandum on corruption in the local governments was sent with Crowder's dispatch of July 12, 1923, 837.00/2318, and those on electoral reform and on Congress were sent on July 17, 837.00/2319 and 837.032/68.

Zayas, however, had clearly decided to run the government in his own way. On July 11 Crowder reported that the Cuban Congress had very secretly passed a bill increasing the number of lottery *colecturías* from 961 to 2000 and removing restrictions on the sale price of the tickets. The president vetoed the measure, under pressure from the ambassador and the State Department, but both houses passed it again by overwhelming majorities, with a resolution saying that they did so because of rumors that the United States had urged Zayas' veto, and denying that the Platt amendment justified the American government in interfering in Cuba's internal affairs.[24] The new law, which restored some of the worst abuses in the lottery, had apparently been drafted in the national palace and undoubtedly had Zayas' support. Crowder thought that the Cubans were deliberately testing the willingness of the United States to insist on reform. Unless the American government took some vigorous action, he feared that the Congress would proceed to pass an amnesty bill and other measures from which the members could benefit financially.[25]

The State Department was indignant but it was not prepared to go farther than it had already gone. It seemed clear that there was little hope of saving the reform program unless the American government applied strong pressure, backed by at least an implied threat of intervention. The department had repeatedly told Crowder that the United States would not intervene in Cuba simply to eliminate governmental corruption. When Crowder was called to Washington for conference and then given a long overdue vacation which kept him away from Habana from August 2 until December 14, 1923, it was evident that the American government did not intend to respond to the challenge posed by the lottery bill. The State Department, in statements to the press and to Cuban officials, continued to emphasize its interest in the elimination of corruption in Cuba, and in November the secretary spoke very frankly to the new Cuban ambassador about Zayas' violation of the promises which he had made when he obtained the $50,000,000 loan; but statements of this sort were not likely to dissuade the president from actions which would improve his political situation or put money in his pocket. He perceived that the American government was unwilling to resort to coercion, and with the loan in hand he no longer needed its help.

[24] Crowder to Hughes, July 24, 1923, 837.513/63.
[25] Crowder to Hughes, July 26, 1923, 837.032/71.

38

It was safe, and politically profitable, to defy the United States and assert his independence.

Zayas' appeal to Cuban nationalism, however, was only partly successful. Outside of political circles there were many people who regretted his break with the American government and were apprehensive about its possible consequences. Crowder could not have accomplished what he did if he had not had the support of influential Cubans who deplored the corruption which permeated the government and were glad to have help from the United States in correcting it. Few except the politicians and newspaper men who hoped to obtain *colecturías* wanted to see the abuses in the lottery return. Even among politicians who had no interest in reform there were many who opposed Zayas because they feared he would use his control of the government machinery to bring about his reelection. The president still had few real friends outside of his own small "popular party."

In the summer of 1923 some of the president's enemies organized the "Veterans and Patriots Movement" under the leadership of Carlos García Vélez, the Cuban minister in London. This soon had strong support throughout the island. The veterans tried to achieve their ends by demonstrations and moral pressure, but it seemed clear that they might resort to revolution if their demands were not met. Since Colonel Despaigne, who had been secretary of the treasury in the honest cabinet, was one of the chief leaders and since one of its avowed purposes was to support Crowder's program, many Cubans assumed that the movement had at least the moral support of the United States. The American government, however, did nothing to encourage it. It was glad to see Cuban support of the moralization program, but there was reason to suspect that the leaders of the movement were more interested in blocking Zayas' reelection than in moralization. The State Department expressed disapproval when it learned that the military attaché at Habana and Captain Rock, Crowder's personal aide, were keeping in close touch with the veterans' movement.

One of the targets of the veterans' propaganda was the so-called Tarafa bill, which was before the Cuban Congress when Crowder left Habana for Washington in August 1923. This would have authorized the merger of the Northern Railways of Cuba and the Cuba Railroad Company on terms which would give them a virtual monopoly of rail transport in eastern Cuba and

would have forced the closing of the private ports through which many of the large sugar producers shipped their crop. Colonel José M. Tarafa, its sponsor, was the president and chief stockholder of the Northern Railways and a large stockholder in the Cuba Railroad Company. Tarafa claimed that the measure was needed to protect the business of the two companies and to put the sugar producers who did not have private ports in a better competitive position. He also asserted that it would put an end to abuses in the customhouses which many of the big companies had been permitted to set up at their own expense in their ports. As was often the case with measures which were likely to arouse criticism, there was an effort to keep the project secret while Congress was considering it, but in July some of the larger American sugar companies got wind of it and asked the State Department's help. Crowder had apparently known little about the bill, but he obtained a copy from Colonel Tarafa before he left, and the State Department instructed the chargé to ask Zayas to see that no final action was taken until the interested parties had an opportunity to present their views. The House of Representatives had already passed the bill, but the Senate suspended action while Colonel Tarafa went to the United States to discuss the matter with the State Department and the sugar companies.

By this time not only the American sugar and mining companies which had private ports but also powerful Cuban organizations like the Association of Sugarmill Owners and Planters were opposing the Tarafa bill and the veterans' movement was making it a central issue in its campaign. The State Department approached the matter rather cautiously. There were plausible arguments for the consolidation of the railroads and the abolition of private ports and customhouses. In most cases it was not clear that the American companies had any contractual right to use the private ports, though they had been encouraged or permitted by the Cuban government to make heavy investments which would lose their value if the ports were closed. When Colonel Tarafa called at the State Department on August 21 and said that he would be willing to accept amendments which would make the bill less objectionable to the American sugar producers, he was encouraged to talk the matter over with the interested groups in New York. Conferences there and later in Habana finally produced a compromise which permitted the American companies to use their ports, under some restrictions; and the bill was

40

signed by Zayas on October 9, 1923. It was alleged that Zayas and the members of Congress received a total of $1,600,000 from the sponsors of the measure.[26]

The compromise did not make the bill more acceptable to some of the Cuban interests which it affected, and there was resentment because the matter had been settled in New York rather than in Habana. The veterans continued to criticize it and continued to attack the government on other grounds. There was still talk of revolution, and in October the government charged several of the veterans' leaders with sedition and prohibited public meetings. By this time, however, dissensions among the leaders and lack of funds were weakening the movement, and it collapsed when the government easily suppressed a small uprising near Cienfuegos in April 1924. The American government showed its disapproval of the revolt by imposing an embargo on the shipment of arms to Cuba.

After Crowder's return to Habana in December 1923, he made little effort to revive his reform program. In May 1924, when Zayas signed the amnesty bill which the American government had been opposing since 1921, the ambassador protested, without result, but the State Department took no action. Any lingering doubts about the Cuban president's attitude disappeared when he reappointed his son as director of the lottery in September. A Cuban court had recently acquitted Zayas, Jr. of the charge that he had embezzled funds during his previous tenure of the office, but there were few who thought his reputation had been cleared.

The State Department's changed attitude toward Cuban problems became more evident as the presidential election of November 1924 approached. Between 1921 and 1923 it had agreed with Crowder on the need for reforms which would help to prevent another dangerous electoral dispute. In 1924 it showed little inclination to interfere in the way the election was conducted. Zayas' hope for reelection vanished when the conservatives, who had supported him in 1920, chose ex-President Menocal as their candidate, and in August 1924, he threw his support to Gerardo Machado, the liberal nominee. Crowder watched the work of the electoral boards, and from time to time urged the Cuban government to take steps which the electoral law required or to remedy improprieties like the excessive padding of registration lists, but

[26] The correspondence about the Tarafa bill is in file 637.0023.

his advice was often disregarded. As the time for the election approached he recommended that the United States appoint an unofficial adviser to the central electoral board, in the hope of reducing fraud and violence. The State Department, however, was unwilling to act in the absence of any request from the Cuban government.[27] Later, when Menocal asked that American observers be sent to a few municipalities in Santa Clara Province, the department seemed willing to do so but dropped the idea when Zayas objected.[28]

The State Department's reluctance to interfere did not arise from any desire to see Machado win. In a dispatch written in October, Crowder suggested that the United States might be asked to give the Cuban government its moral support if the conservatives should start a revolution, and urged that the State Department bear in mind Zayas' abandonment of the moralization program and the fact that Machado was expected to continue Zayas' policies. Hughes assured him that the department had not changed its attitude toward the reform program.[29] Later, the ambassador reported a rumor that the administration press was fabricating a statement, like the one issued by the State Department in 1917, to be published immediately before the election, warning the conservatives against any resort to violence. This would have given the impression that the United States would support Zayas in forcing the election of Machado, and to forestall such a maneuver Crowder suggested that the department tell the American press that it expected orderly elections and would not recognize any Cuban government which was elected by intimidation or fraud. The department did not wish to tie its hands by so definite a statement, but on October 29 Undersecretary Grew told the press that the United States earnestly hoped for free and orderly elections and that there would be no occasion to issue a statement like that of 1917 because conditions were entirely different.[30]

There was in fact no occasion for the American government to interfere. There was no time when either party seemed likely to

[27] Hughes to Crowder, Oct. 8, 1924, 837.00/2555.

[28] See White's memorandum of October 29, 1924, 837.00/2575.

[29] Crowder to Hughes, Oct. 4, 1924, and Hughes to Crowder Oct. 8, 837.00/2555.

[30] Crowder to Hughes, Oct. 22, 1924, and Grew to Crowder, Oct. 25 and Oct. 29, 837.00/2563.

withdraw from the contest and resort to revolution. When Machado defeated Menocal with 200,000 votes to less than 136,000, the conservatives charged that there had been intimidation and corruption, but Menocal discouraged talk of revolt and at Crowder's suggestion sent a letter of congratulation to Machado. The new president, during his first years in office, did better than Crowder expected. He was an able administrator and he made a real effort to reduce graft and inefficiency. Before his inauguration he asked Crowder to feel free to give him personal advice on internal problems as well as on matters affecting relations with the United States. Crowder, who stayed at Habana until his retirement from the public service in May 1927, did not attempt to revive his reform program.

Chapter Three

GETTING OUT OF SANTO DOMINGO

Another problem that required immediate attention when the Harding administration took office was the status of the military government at Santo Domingo. The United States had had a special relationship with the Dominican Republic since 1905, when it took over the collection of the customs revenues at a time when several European governments were pressing for the payment of debts due their nationals. It helped to work out a plan for the adjustment of the debts, and a treaty signed in 1907 provided that the American collectorship should continue until the retirement of the bonds issued under the plan. For a time after 1907 there was less of the disorder which had frequently invited foreign intervention during the nineteenth century. After 1911, however, a new series of civil wars brought the country to the verge of bankruptcy, and in 1915 the Wilson administration demanded that the Dominicans accept a more complete control of their finances and agree to the organization of an American-trained constabulary which could maintain order. The Dominicans rejected these proposals, and in November 1916 Wilson ordered the military occupation of the Republic. An American admiral became military governor.

The military government maintained peace, except in a few remote districts, and for a time high war-time prices for Dominican products made the country unusually prosperous. The American officials devoted much attention to education and public works. The number of children in school increased from 12,000 to more than 100,000, and automobiles began to replace saddle horses and small boats as the means of travel between the principal towns. Unfortunately these programs had to be suspended when sugar prices collapsed at the end of 1920, and the military government found itself in a position almost as bad as that with which General Crowder was dealing in Cuba. The resulting discontent was made worse by the tactlessness and ineptitude of some of the American officials, who repressed all criticism and imposed a stupid press censorship.

When the military government was set up, the Wilson administration apparently intended that it should continue for a year or two, to restore order and carry out the financial and military reforms on which the United States had been insisting. It was not long, however, before the naval officers who took over the government began to feel that a much longer period of American rule would be needed. The State Department apparently accepted this view. It paid little attention to what went on in the country during the world war, but in 1919 it began to be concerned about the painful impression which the military government's policies were causing in other Latin American countries. In November 1920 Secretary Colby obtained President Wilson's approval of a plan for the gradual withdrawal of the occupation. As a first step, the military governor was to appoint a commission of Dominicans, with a North American adviser, to draw up constitutional amendments and other laws designed to prevent a return of the conditions which had existed before 1916. The military governor, under instructions from the president, issued a proclamation on December 23 saying that the United States believed that the time had arrived when it might "inaugurate the simple processes of its rapid withdrawal" from the republic, and that a commission of Dominicans would be appointed to formulate needed constitutional amendments and laws.

The proclamation did not indicate what sort of laws the commission would be asked to draft, or what conditions would be imposed, but it was not hard to guess that the United States would insist on the same reforms which it had demanded in 1915-1916. This would be unacceptable to most Dominicans. The political leaders, who had been encouraged by some of Harding's statements during the electoral campaign, wanted an immediate unconditional withdrawal of the occupation. It was only with great difficulty that the military governor and the American minister, who had remained at his post during the occupation, persuaded seven eminent Dominicans to serve on the commission, which was finally organized only about two weeks before the change of administration in Washington. Further steps toward the execution of the plan for withdrawal had to wait until the new secretary of state had an opportunity to consider it.

On April 6, 1921 Sumner Welles presented to Secretary Hughes a detailed plan which was essentially the one which the Wilson administration had approved. The constitutional amendments and laws drawn up by the Dominican commission under the guidance of its American technical adviser would be adopted by an elected Congress and a constitutional convention, and thereafter the Dominicans would elect a president to whom the military governor would turn over the executive power. The two governments would then negotiate a treaty which would ratify all acts of the American occupation and assure the stability of the new government. The general receiver of customs would be given control over the collection of all revenues and also over the government's expenditures; and the training of the constabulary which the military government had organized would be completed under American officers. The United States would be authorized to intervene at any time to maintain a stable government. American officials would control the Dominican government's finances until the treaty was ratified and American forces would maintain order until the constabulary was ready to take over. Welles told the secretary that educated Dominicans wanted a gradual withdrawal of the military government but wished the United States to retain control of the financial administration and the constabulary.[1]

Welles' plan would have set up a relationship very similar to that between the United States and Haiti. Hughes was evidently unwilling to go so far. The plan that he approved, and that was set forth in a proclamation which the military governor issued on June 14, 1921, did not provide for any right to intervene or any American control of the Dominican government's expenditures. It did provide that the acts of the occupation would be ratified, that an American military mission would complete the training of the constabulary, and that the general receiver of customs would have authority to collect a portion of the internal revenues if this should be necessary to assure the service of the Republic's debts. A Dominican Congress, to be elected as soon as possible, would ratify a convention of evacuation containing these provisions, and a Dominican president would then be chosen. Since there was no requirement for the prior adoption of any program of basic reforms, it was hoped that the process of withdrawal would be completed within about eight months.

The new plan seemed reasonable. The ratification of the acts of the military government was necessary for the protection of

[1] Welles to Hughes, April 6, 1921, 839.00/2480.

the Dominicans and foreigners who had acquired rights under laws and contracts, and it was obviously desirable to complete the training of the new constabulary which as yet had few Dominican officers. The extension of the general receiver's authority would not seriously curtail the new Dominican government's control over its finances, especially as it would not take effect unless there was danger of a default on the public debt. Welles thought the Dominicans would accept the plan. He had discussed it in advance with Dr. Francisco Henríquez y Carbajal, who had been provisional president before the military government was set up and was the leader of one of the more nationalistic political groups, and he understood that Henríquez approved all of the articles of the proposed convention of evacuation.[2] Nevertheless the proclamation was received with what the American minister described as "a hot blast of protest from the press." The provisions of the proposed convention of evacuation were attacked as an effort to continue American control over the country. Henríquez y Carbajal demanded that he be simply reinstated in the presidency, though his term had expired. The other leaders wanted a presidential election, but not under the conditions set forth in the proclamation. Most of the members of the commission appointed in February joined in denouncing the American government's proposals.

All of the political leaders insisted they would not take part in elections run by the military government. The State Department apparently did not realize how much they detested and distrusted the higher officials of the occupation. Relations between Americans and Dominicans had become much worse during the previous two years. Rear Admiral Snowden, the military governor, had little contact with the Dominican leaders, and he had aroused animosity by public statements reflecting on their ability to manage their own affairs. The principal American officials at Santo Domingo made no secret of their opposition to any early withdrawal of the occupation, and their attitude caused many Dominicans to doubt the American government's good faith. The military government had been compelled under pressure from the State Department to relax some of its restrictions on freedom of speech and of the press, but the Dominicans still felt that they were living under an oppressive alien regime.

[2] Welles to Hughes, July 20, 1921, 839.00/2432.

The State Department attempted to meet some of the Dominicans' objections to the plan in a statement which Rear Admiral Samuel S. Robison, who had replaced Snowden, was instructed to issue on July 6. It said that the Dominican Congress would be asked to agree upon the names of the Dominicans who would negotiate the convention of evacuation and that the ratification of the acts of the occupation would not prevent their being repealed later in cases where the security of outstanding obligations was not involved. It pointed out that the collector general would take control of part of the internal revenues only if this were necessary to meet the debt service. During the next few days the Admiral and William W. Russell, the American minister, talked with the Dominican political leaders in an effort to persuade them to take part in the congressional election, which had been set for August 13. At first the Dominicans seemed ready to try to find a basis for cooperation. They insisted, however, that they could not accept the terms of the proclamation of June 14.

Neither Robison nor Russell made any very earnest effort to find out what changes would make the plan of withdrawal more acceptable. Robison, who had been appointed in the hope that a change in the governor's office would improve relations with the Dominicans, was a capable naval officer, but he made no claim to competence as a diplomat, and he had no enthusiasm for a proposal which he considered premature and unwise. Russell apparently took little part in the discussions. What influence he had once had in Santo Domingo was impaired by the recollection of his connection with the events leading up to the American occupation and by his association with the military government since 1916. After two conferences with a group of Dominican leaders, the military governor thought the Dominicans had been persuaded to accept most of the terms of the proclamation and that the principal remaining difficulty was with respect to the powers and the duration of the proposed military mission. A third conference was arranged, with the understanding that the election might be postponed to give the political parties time to organize. On July 17, however, the Dominican leaders told Robison that they would attend no further meetings until his proclamation of June 14 had been withdrawn. The admiral and the minister attributed this sudden change of attitude partly to a violent campaign which the nationalists had been carrying on in the local press, and partly to the receipt of a message from Dr.

Henríquez y Carbajal in Washington saying that he expected to obtain the withdrawal of the proclamation.

Since it was now too late to make adequate preparations, the military governor was authorized to announce on July 27 that the election set for August 13 would be indefinitely postponed, but to say that the American government's plan had been carefully considered and would not be changed. The deadlock that ensued lasted for several months. Admiral Robison continued to talk with individual Dominicans, who maintained their opposition to a military mission. At Washington, Welles talked with Henríquez y Carbajal, who had now apparently abandoned his contention that he should be reinstated as president. Dr. Henríquez was willing to support the American government's plan if the provision for a military mission could be made more acceptable, but the State Department did not feel that any of his proposals gave enough assurance that the Dominicans could maintain order after the American forces left.

The Dominicans were probably less willing to make substantial concessions because they were hoping for support from a United States Senate committee which was investigating the situation in the Republic and in Haiti. The committee had been appointed in July 1921, primarily to look into stories of atrocities alleged to have been committed by American forces in the two countries. The Dominicans hoped that its findings would discredit the occupation and make it harder for the State Department to resist their demands for an immediate, unconditional withdrawal. They were aided by North American anti-imperialist organizations in gathering and presenting evidence at the hearings which the committee held at Santo Domingo and elsewhere in November. The committee, however, was inclined to support the State Department's policy. Its chairman, Medill McCormick, had promised before leaving Washington to try to persuade the Dominican leaders to accept the plan of evacuation.[3] When he found that there was little hope for a settlement based on the plan, he wrote Hughes that the occupation would have to continue, possibly for another three years, and that in the meantime an effort should be made to train and promote Dominican officers so that they could eventually take over command of the constabulary.[4] In its report to the Senate, the committee made recommendations about pol-

[3] See S. Johnson's memorandum of Dec. 8, 1921, 839.51/2237.
[4] McCormick to Hughes, Dec. 16, 1921, 839.00/2456.

icy in Haiti but said that it would defer its report on the Dominican Republic pending negotiations for the withdrawal of the American occupation.[5]

In his letter to Hughes in December McCormick stressed the need to do something about the military government's financial problems. In the first part of 1921 all of the public schools were closed and most government employees were compelled to take twenty days' leave without pay each month. A sudden suspension of the public works program left thousands of men unemployed. Many of the higher officials drew salaries as American naval or marine officers but the government received practically no other financial help from the United States.

A few months earlier, in June 1921, the State Department had consented to a loan of $2,500,000 to make possible the continuation of some public works, but this had given only temporary relief and it had been an unfortunate operation from a financial point of view. The terms on which Speyer and Company bought the republic's four-year 8% bonds were unfavorable even for a time when interest rates on foreign bonds were unusually high. The bonds were redeemable by drawings every six months at 105% of their face value, so that a holder who was lucky in the first drawing would get 18.9% on his investment. Those whose bonds were drawn subsequently would receive less, but even an investor who was not paid until maturity could count on a return of 9.07%. The bankers, who paid 96½ for the bonds and sold them at par, perhaps felt they could not sell them at all on less attractive terms, but the transaction exposed both the military government and the United States government to criticism. The State Department apparently was not consulted about the details of the contract, and when the facts were brought to Hughes' attention by Henríquez y Carbajal's American lawyer Hughes wrote the Secretary of the Navy expressing surprise and suggesting that the American government had a duty to the Dominican people to see that the terms of any such transaction were fair.[6]

The high amortization charge on the 1921 loan imposed a heavy burden on the Dominican Treasury, especially as an earlier loan issued in 1918 also involved heavy charges. In both cases the bonds were secured by the customs receipts and it had been

[5] "Inquiry into the Occupation and Administration of Haiti and the Dominican Republic," *Senate Report no. 794*, 67th Congress, 2nd Session.
[6] Hughes to Denby, July 11, 1921, 839.51/2197.

necessary to provide for their retirement before 1926 because it seemed likely that the customs receivership would end before then with the final retirement of the bonds issued under the treaty of 1907. Senator McCormick proposed that a new loan be floated to refund both issues on terms which would permit a more gradual repayment and also to provide money to complete the much needed north-south highway.

The military government desperately wanted a loan, but the Dominican leaders opposed any further borrowing because they knew that a new loan would make it still more difficult for the United States to relax its control of the Dominican government's finances. In the State Department, where I was temporarily in charge of the Latin American division, we were reluctant, for the same reason, to consent to a loan. The department felt compelled to let the military government borrow another $500,000 in January 1922, but any substantial long-term loan would require an extension of the life of the customs receivership. This could only be done by a formal agreement between the two governments, and it did not seem proper for the United States to make such an agreement with the military government. Furthermore, the Department felt that there had been an implied promise in the June proclamation that no further loans would be contracted pending the withdrawal of the occupation.

It was hardly possible, however, to permit the existing situation to continue. The American government wanted to withdraw from the Dominican Republic, but only under conditions which would give the new Dominican government a reasonable chance to survive. The Dominican leaders' attitude seemed to make any agreement on such conditions impossible. Meanwhile the military government's inability to pay its employees or keep the schools open was hurting the Dominican people and cast discredit on the United States. A loan would relieve the situation. The completion of the partly built main highways would be of inestimable economic value and would make it easier for any new government to maintain order. It was also necessary to complete the training of the new constabulary, which had been set back by lack of funds.

Secretary Hughes consequently reluctantly approved a new approach to the problem when Admiral Robison and Minister Russell came to Washington for a conference in January 1922. The admiral and the minister were authorized to tell the Dominican leaders that the proclamation of June 14, 1921 would be withdrawn if they did not immediately ask that elections be held and agree to have their followers participate. The United States would then continue to govern the country until the most urgent public works had been completed and until an adequate Dominican constabulary was functioning. The American representatives were to explain that the officials who would supervise the proposed elections would not necessarily be members of the American military forces, but might well be Dominicans recommended by the political leaders. They were to say that the United States was ready, as a "final concession," to give up its requirement that American officers continue in the constabulary until its training was completed. Instead there would be an understanding that a legation guard of American marines would stay at Santo Domingo until both governments agreed that the constabulary could maintain order. The members of the guard might serve under an informal agreement as instructors for the constabulary. At the same time Robison and Russell were to say that the military government would be authorized to contract a new loan. They were to explain that a loan was indispensable whether the military government continued or a Dominican government was set up, and that it would necessarily entail an extension of the life of the customs receivership.

This message was conveyed to the Dominican leaders at a meeting in the archbishop's palace in Santo Domingo on February 23. They were told that not more than two years would probably be needed to finish the north-south and east-west highways and the training of the constabulary. The only response was an immediate and flat rejection, and on March 6 Robison issued a "Proclamation . . . Providing for the Continuance of Military Occupation until approximately July 1, 1924." He said that the military government would continue its program of public works and public education and would continue the organization and training of a military force which would be capable of maintaining order without help from the United States. It would negotiate a loan for these purposes. When the public works program was completed and the military force trained, the United States would consider the complete withdrawal of its forces from the Republic.

Five New York banking houses submitted bids for the loan. The market had improved, and Lee Higginson and Company, the successful bidder, agreed to buy $6,700,000 twenty-year, 5½% bonds at 90½% of their face value. The proceeds took care of the military government's most pressing debts and refunded the 1921 bonds, but not the 1918 issue. There was enough additional money to build up the constabulary and to continue work at least on the north-south highway. The loan was part of an authorized loan of $10,000,000, the balance of which was to be issued only after agreement between the two governments. To avoid the need for a treaty extending the life of the customs receivership, the contract provided that the revenues pledged for the service of the loan would be collected by officials appointed by the president of the United States, after the expiration of the treaty of 1907. The military government guaranteed that any future Dominican government would accept this arrangement, a commitment which it was permitted to make because the State Department considered the ratification of all the obligations assumed by the military government on behalf of the Dominican Republic an essential condition for any withdrawal. To avoid imposing too heavy a burden on the Dominican Treasury, the amortization of the loan would not begin until 1930, when it was thought that the bonds issued in 1908 would be fully retired.

The American officials at Santo Domingo were pleased at the prospect of continuing to rule the country for what seemed likely to be a considerable time,[7] but the State Department still hoped that an agreement could be reached with the Dominican leaders. When he informed President Harding about the loan, Hughes wrote that he had not agreed to a larger amount, or agreed to commit the United States to any public works beyond the completion of the north-south highway, because he wanted to be able to withdraw at any time. He said that there were indications that the Dominican leaders might now be more willing to cooperate. They were still unalterably opposed to the continued maintenance of American forces in the republic, but the secretary thought that the need for American forces might disappear if the Dominicans tried wholeheartedly to assure peace. The one object of the United States, he wrote, was to withdraw as soon as a native government capable of maintaining order could be established.[8]

[7] I was convinced of this after taking part in the conference with them.
[8] Hughes to Harding, March 30, 1922, 839.00/2503.

Hughes' optimism was based chiefly on conversations which he and other officials of the department had been having with Dr. Francisco Peynado, an eminent lawyer from Santo Domingo. Peynado had been a member of the advisory commission appointed in 1921 to draft new legislation. He had also been one of the leaders with whom the military governor had conferred during the effort to obtain acceptance of the State Department's plan for withdrawal, and had opposed the plan, as the other leaders did. He came to Washington in March 1922, apparently on his own initiative and because he thought that further negotiations with the military governor would accomplish nothing. He told the State Department that the Dominicans objected to any blanket ratification of the acts of the military government, but he thought that they would agree to the validation of specific acts which had created rights and obligations. This was essentially what the State Department wanted. He also thought that there would be no strong objection to the continuance of the customs receivership, which had been in existence long before the American intervention. He protested against the recent loan, but said that this was a *fait accompli*, which the Dominicans would have to accept. He was emphatic in his opposition to a military mission or a legation guard, but Hughes was disposed to make concessions on this point in order to reach an agreement. The problem of maintaining order after the American withdrawal looked somewhat less formidable after several of the bandit leaders who had been operating in a small way in the eastern end of the island surrendered in April and May. The economic situation was also improving and the road work was progressing so well that the north-south highway was opened to traffic on May 6.

By the end of May 1922, the informal talks with Peynado had reached a point where it seemed likely to be profitable to make another attempt at an agreement with the Dominican leaders. It seemed better, however, not to leave the negotiations in the hands of the admiral and the minister. The secretary consequently asked Sumner Welles, who had recently resigned as chief of the Latin American division, to take on the task as American commissioner at Santo Domingo. Before Welles left Washington, Horacio Vásquez and Federico Velásquez and Elías Brache, who between them represented most of the political groups in the Dominican Republic, came to the United States, and they and Peynado agreed with Welles on a tentative plan of evacuation which Welles took with him when he went to the island early in July.

Under the plan, a provisional president and a cabinet would be chosen by a majority vote of a commission composed of the four Dominicans who had signed the plan and Monseñor Adolfo Nouel, the archbishop of Santo Domingo, who was one of the country's most influential citizens. The provisional administration would at once take over the executive departments. It would continue to have the assistance of the officers who had been in charge of the executive departments under the military government, and it would make no changes in personnel except for due cause. Expenditures not authorized by the budget would be made only with the consent of the military governor, who would remain in control of the forces of occupation but would delegate to the provisional government the powers necessary to carry out the plan. The American forces would be concentrated in not more than three places, and the Dominican constabulary would take over the maintenance of order except in case of serious disturbances. The provisional president would reorganize the provincial and communal governments and would arrange for the election of a congress and a constitutional convention to enact the legislation that would be needed. This would include a law ratifying the acts of the military government. After the legislation had been passed and the judiciary had been reorganized, a constitutional president would be elected.

The American forces would leave the country after the constitutional president had been inaugurated and had signed a convention of ratification negotiated with the United States by the provisional government. In this, the Dominican government would recognize the validity of all executive and departmental orders of the military government which had levied taxes, authorized expenditures, or established rights on behalf of third persons, and the validity of all legally made government contracts. These orders and contracts were to be listed individually in the convention. The orders were to be recognized as laws of the republic until they were lawfully abrogated and the Dominican government would agree to take no action that would impair rights acquired under them. It would specifically recognize the validity of the bond issues of 1918 and 1922 and agree that the treaty of 1907, which set up the customs receivership, would remain in force until these loans had been repaid.

The State Department gave the press a summary of the plan of evacuation on July 11, but indicated that the plan would be put into effect only if it was clearly acceptable to a majority of the Dominican people. Hughes had been very reluctant to agree to the selection of a provisional president by a small group of politicians who had no clear mandate from the voters, and he had accepted the arrangement, tentatively, only because it seemed the only course which the Dominicans would accept. Welles' first task after he reached Santo Domingo was to find out what the Dominican people thought of the plan. There had been some opposition when the plan was first announced, but the leaders who had signed it had been able to overcome some of this feeling and Welles' explanation of the program, when he visited most of the principal towns, seemed to convince many people that the plan would really lead to the restoration of Dominican independence.[9] After his tour, Welles reported that an overwhelming majority of the Dominican people approved the plan, and that the four leaders who had signed it unquestionably represented an immense majority of the voters. He consequently recommended that these leaders and Archbishop Nouel be permitted to elect a provisional president and that he be authorized to publish the plan officially when he considered it advisable to do so. The State Department approved both recommendations.

The principal opposition to the plan came from the military governor, who had not been consulted and had apparently not even been kept informed about the recent discussions in Washington. The admiral thought that it would be impracticable to have the military government and a provisional Dominican administration functioning side by side over a considerable period of time, and he thought that the police force was far from ready to assume responsibility for the maintenance of order when the provisional government took office. He consequently urged the Navy Department to insist on several changes in the plan. Welles offered to discuss some of these changes informally with the Dominican leaders, but he pointed out that the United States could not insist on them without exposing itself to charges of bad faith. The State Department supported Welles and asked the Navy to instruct the admiral to cooperate. It said that changes in the plan

[9] Sumner Welles, *Naboth's Vineyard, The Dominican Republic, 1844-1924* (New York, 1928), Vol. II, pp. 859ff.

would be made only by Welles in consultation with the Dominican leaders.

During August and September, Welles had almost daily conferences with the Dominican leaders about the plan and its application. Publication of the text was delayed because the military government took some weeks to compile a list of the acts
that were to be ratified by the proposed convention. Several
changes were agreed on, most of them intended to make the plan
more palatable to persons who opposed any recognition of the
legality of the military government.

The State Department objected to one proposal, which would
have left controversies in connection with validated acts of the
military government to be dealt with solely by the Dominican
courts, and it was finally agreed that such controversies, where
they affected American interests, should be settled by arbitration.
Another question which the Dominicans raised was settled when
Hughes authorized Welles to say that the United States would
withdraw its forces, if the Dominicans carried out their part of
the plan, even though the United States Senate might not approve the proposed treaty of evacuation. The plan, in its final
form, was published on September 23, 1922.

Meanwhile, Welles and the military governor reached an
agreement with the commission about training the Dominican
police. The Dominicans had taken a strong stand in public
against any continuing American military influence, but they
knew that the position of the new Dominican government would
be precarious if the American officers in the police could not be
replaced by competent Dominicans, and that the number of
trained Dominican officers was only half of what would be
needed. At Washington, Vásquez and Velásquez and Peynado
had told the State Department that they would agree that the
provisional government should employ American officers under
contract to complete the training of the police.[10] Under the final
agreement, American officers would withdraw from the force
when the provisional government took office, but the training of
recruits and officers would remain under the jurisdiction of the
military government. To replace the American officers in the
operating police force, the provisional government would temporarily appoint Dominicans who had had military experience

[10] White to Welles, personal, Aug. 17, 1922, 839.00/2982.

before the occupation. It was hoped that enough new officers could be trained during the life of the provisional government to replace these.

As chief of police, the commission agreed on General Buenaventura Cabral, who was serving under the military government as governor of Azua Province and was not affiliated with any political party. Welles considered the choice an excellent one, and the military governor agreed to give Cabral every opportunity to become familiar with the work of the police force before his formal assumption of command. The admiral, who still disapproved of the State Department's plan, thought that the arrangements for training and officering the police were as satisfactory as any that were possible under the plan. His still strong objection to the provision that the American forces be concentrated in not more than three places during the life of the provisional government was partly met when the commission, at Welles' suggestion, asked that one company of cavalry remain in Seibo Province to keep banditry in check until the Dominican police was able to deal with the situation.

The commission, under Welles' guidance, worked surprisingly well during the summer months, despite the fact that three of its members were party leaders, each of them eager to seek any possible advantage in the electoral campaign which would soon begin. Before the American intervention, there had been two important political parties, headed by Juan Isidro Jimenes and Horacio Vásquez, and a third group, with less following, headed by Federico Velásquez. Vásquez and Velásquez were members of the commission. Jimenes had died and his party, now called the liberals, was represented by Brache. It was not certain, however, that Brache would be the liberal candidate, and a delicate situation developed when it began to appear that the party might nominate Peynado. This could give the liberals two votes on the commission. Vásquez and Velásquez were disturbed because the commission would not only select the provisional president but would have to draft the electoral law and other important legislation and would have a hand in other preparations for the election. A crisis was averted, for the time being, when Peynado gave assurances that he had no understanding with any candidate and no desire to be a candidate. He promised that he would resign from the commission if he should become a candidate.

58

On October 2, 1922, the commission chose Juan Bautista Vicini Burgos as provisional president. Vicini Burgos was a wealthy businessman with a reputation for honesty and no political ties. José del Carmen Ariza, another politically independent businessman, was named by the commission as minister of the interior. The other members of the cabinet, two from each party, were selected by the provisional president from lists submitted by the party leaders. The inauguration of the new government was delayed until October 21, to give time to reorganize the police under the new Dominican officers.

At the suggestion of the State Department, Admiral Robison left Santo Domingo two days before the inauguration. He had frequently disagreed with what Welles was doing and he was especially displeased when the Dominican commission with Welles' approval asked that the American marines not on duty be kept in their camps on the day when the Dominicans would vote for a permanent president. The commissioners wanted to make it clear that the Americans were not supervising or even observing the elections, and hoped to avoid unpleasant incidents at a time when the populace would be excited. Robison considered the proposal an insult to the marines, but his objection was overruled after a conference between Secretary Hughes and the secretary of the navy.

At the same time Hughes asked that the military governor be ordered to suspend punitive measures against several newspapers and not to order further suspensions of newspapers without Welles' approval. The censorship of the press had been abolished early in 1920, under pressure from the State Department, but the military government continued to imprison or fine agitators whose utterances it considered dangerously subversive or intolerably insulting. The State Department often hesitated to interfere because it knew that incendiary attacks could be a danger to public order, but after Welles' arrival at Santo Domingo it insisted on a more liberal policy. It did, however, acquiesce in the continued suspension of *La Información* of Santiago, which had published defamatory articles about the relations between the military government and two prominent Dominicans, because Welles thought that the paper should not be allowed to resume publication until it published a retraction.[11]

[11] Welles to Hughes, Aug. 19, 1922, 839.918/20.

Brigadier General Harry Lee of the marine corps became acting military governor. The provisional president and his cabinet
took over most of the functions of the government, but the American commander still had authority to stop any expenditure not
provided for in the budget which the military government had
promulgated. He would also have to maintain order if the Dominican police could not do so. Fortunately, General Lee, who
was appointed military governor in April 1923, got on well with
the Dominicans. When Welles returned to the United States, he
reported that all problems connected with the plan of evacuation
had been settled and that no further difficulties should arise in
the near future. He suggested, however, that it might be well for
him to return to Santo Domingo later, and the provisional president and the members of the commission urged the American
government to continue his mission until the inauguration of a
constitutional president.

Welles' forecast of smooth sailing proved overoptimistic. It is
hard to believe that he failed to realize that the rivalry between
the political parties would threaten the success of the plan for
withdrawal when he was no longer present. The provisional president immediately ran into trouble with his cabinet. The American officials in the Treasury Department all resigned because they
could not work with the minister of finance, and the minister
himself had to be removed because he permitted improper use of
funds for the benefit of Velásquez' party. The minister of health
was removed for somewhat similar misconduct, and the minister
of the interior, who was the one non-partisan in the cabinet, resigned after a disagreement with the provisional president.[12]

The work of the commission was also affected by partisan
rivalry. The members who represented political parties rarely
found time to attend meetings. They did not seem to realize that
their failure to complete the drafts of the electoral law and the
laws reorganizing the provincial and municipal governments,
which had been almost ready for promulgation when Welles left
in October, would inevitably delay the holding of the election
and the withdrawal of the American forces. The American minister, whose already none-too-great prestige had naturally been diminished by Welles' appointment, could do little to speed up
their work, and in fact gave the State Department little informa-

[12] Welles, *op. cit.*, Vol. II, pp. 879ff. See also Russell's dispatch of Nov.
12, 1922, 839.51/2334.

tion about what was going on. Even after the electoral law was finally promulgated, on March 9, 1923, the commission seemed to take little interest in setting up the electoral machinery and making other preparations for registration and voting. It became clear that it would not be possible to install a constitutional government on August 16, 1923, which was the date tentatively agreed on before Welles' departure.

There was a change in the personnel of the commission in January 1923, when Peynado resigned after rather reluctantly accepting the presidential nomination of a part of the old Jimenista party, which now called itself the "coalition." His successor was Manuel de Jesús Troncoso de la Concha, the president of the superior land court. Peynado's opponents charged that he was a candidate of the American sugar companies, an allegation which perhaps contributed to a growing antagonism toward Americans that caused the military governor some concern.

The prospect for an election brightened when Welles returned in April 1923 and insisted that the commission pay more attention to its work. The central electoral board, composed of three eminent jurists, was installed on April 10. It was more difficult to find suitable members for the provincial and municipal electoral boards, though the law imposed heavy penalties for refusal to serve, but on May 17 Welles reported that everything was ready for the registration of voters and that he was leaving for the United States. Again he was overoptimistic, for various problems delayed the beginning of registration until June. Meanwhile animosities between the parties were growing more violent and there were persistent reports that arms were being smuggled into the country. The race narrowed down to two candidates in August, when Velásquez agreed to support Vásquez in return for the promise of the vice presidency and the right to name a third of the congressional candidates. A little later Peynado made a deal with Desiderio Arias, the leader of another faction of the liberal party. This disturbed the State Department, because Arias had been a notorious troublemaker before 1916, but Peynado, in response to Welles' cable expressing thinly veiled disapproval, denied that he had made any promises to Arias.[13]

The increasing violence of the campaign made the prospect for a satisfactory election less and less bright. The commission,

[13] Hughes to Russell, Oct. 5, 1923, 839.00/2743a and Russell to Hughes, Oct. 10, 839.00/2746.

which should have exercised a restraining influence, ceased to meet because of the bitter feeling between its members. The provisional president tried to be impartial but it was hard for him to control his cabinet, where the "alliance," as the union between Vásquez and Velásquez was called, now had four members while the coalition had only two. On the other hand, the central electoral board seemed partial to Peynado. The alliance was outraged in September when the board refused to accept its nominations in the important province of La Vega on the ground that they had been submitted in an original and a certified copy instead of in duplicate as the law required, and they paralyzed the board by bringing impeachment proceedings against two of its members. On October 17 Russell reported that it was probable that the election would again have to be postponed.

Welles, who had been trying with little success to guide the electoral procedure through cabled instructions which he suggested to the State Department, returned to Santo Domingo on November 3. He told the party leaders that their failure to hold an election would leave the United States free to reconsider its whole policy. If there were to be an election, each party must abandon obstructive policies and give up the undue advantages which it had obtained: the coalition by the decision of the electoral board, and the alliance because its leaders had delayed the announcement of their agreement until after each had obtained its share of the offices in the provisional government and its separate representation on the local electoral boards. Welles suggested a new start: the elections would be postponed and would be held under an amended law with new electoral boards. The Dominican leaders agreed to this proposal, after several days of angry discussion, and on November 12 the provisional president issued a decree indefinitely postponing the elections.

Welles with some difficulty persuaded Peynado to give up a demand that a new provisional president be appointed. He agreed, however, that there should be a redistribution of government jobs to give the coalition more adequate representation. The coalition wanted 50% of the government employees from the provisional president's private secretary to the janitor in the national palace. Welles saw no need for changes in positions that could not really influence the conduct of the election,[14]

[14] Welles to Hughes, Nov. 27, 1923, 839.00/2765. A part of this telegram is printed in *Foreign Relations, 1923*, Vol. I, p. 914.

but the coalition was given an additional post in the cabinet and many changes were made among the provincial governors and in the courts. A new, supposedly impartial, minister of the interior was also appointed. The other coalition leaders were not satisfied with these changes, and talked of withdrawing from the election, but Peynado insisted on continuing to cooperate in the execution of the plan of evacuation.[15]

The Dominican leaders' evident willingness to accept an indefinite continuance of the occupation if the alternative were a government controlled by their enemies led Welles to doubt whether either Vásquez or Peynado could carry out a constructive program if elected. Either would be hampered by the fact that he was supported by a coalition in which there were other powerful leaders, and also by the slim majority in Congress which the system of proportional representation seemed to assure. Welles was also disturbed by the low caliber of most of the politicians who were running for office. When he went over the list of congressional candidates he found few who were considered honest and almost none who were sufficiently intelligent to draft a law. Many had criminal records. The candidates for governorships in the provinces seemed even worse. Welles consequently attempted to persuade Vásquez and Peynado to drop their own slates of candidates and to agree on one good man for each position. He also suggested that they pledge themselves to maintain the civil service law, to keep the administration of the police and public health and education out of politics, and to appoint the best men, regardless of political affiliation, to the cabinet. Both leaders professed hearty approval of these proposals. Each one publicly promised to keep the police force out of politics. Neither, however, was really willing or able to withdraw support from party followers on whose loyalty the outcome of the election might depend, and very few candidates of either party were actually replaced as the result of Welles' efforts.[16]

By February 1924, it was clear that the alliance would win the election, and Peynado, who had spent all his personal fortune in the campaign, wished to abandon the contest. He asked Welles to "force" Vásquez to withdraw in favor of a compromise candi-

---

[15] Luis F. Mejía, *De Lilís a Trujillo, Historia Contemporánea da la República Dominicana* (Caracas, 1944), p. 196.

[16] Welles to Hughes, Dec. 7, 1923, 839.00/2775; Welles to White, Jan. 26, 1924, 839.00/2991.

date, or at least to agree to a postponement of the election. Welles of course refused and indicated that he would consider the election valid even if only one party participated. Peynado continued as a candidate and the election was held on March 15 in a relatively orderly way. Out of more than 100,000 votes, a far larger number than in any previous election, Vásquez received more than 71,000. Velásquez was elected to the vice presidency, though this office would not exist until a constitutional amendment created it. Contrary to expectations, the alliance obtained large majorities in both houses of Congress. The prospect for the future seemed brighter when Peynado congratulated the president-elect and promised to cooperate with him.

On June 12 Vásquez and Velásquez and Peynado, as the Dominican plenipotentiaries, and Minister Russell for the United States, signed the convention of evacuation, which listed some hundreds of acts of the military government which were to be recognized as valid. Vásquez was inaugurated as president a month later, and on September 18 Russell reported that the provisions of the plan of evacuation had been fully carried out and all of the forces of occupation had left the country.

The new president was sixty-four. He had begun his political career as one of the leaders of the group that assassinated the dictator Heureaux in 1899 and was provisional president for a short time thereafter. In 1902 he became president, after one of the frequent revolutions that marked the first years of the century, but was soon ousted by another revolution. His followers, the *Horacistas*, controlled the government during most of the period between 1902 and 1916, but he had not again been president, partly because other leaders in the party were more aggressive and ambitious. He had relatively little formal education and little administrative experience, but he had a good reputation for honesty and for common sense.

In June, shortly before he took office, Vásquez visited Washington, where he and Welles discussed with the State Department the ways in which the United States could help his government. He especially wanted to obtain a loan from American bankers, under a new treaty which would replace the 1907 convention, and he indicated that he would agree that the American legation should exercise some supervision over the expenditure of the proceeds and that an American engineer should continue to direct the public works department. He also seemed disposed to ask that American marines continue to instruct new recruits and officers for the police. It looked as though he would voluntarily accept the sort of help that he and other Dominican leaders had rejected when it was proposed as a condition for the withdrawal of the American forces. After his inauguration, however, the hope for this sort of cooperation between the two governments evaporated. There was still strong public opposition to anything that suggested a continuance of American control, and Vásquez himself was unwilling to give foreigners any authority that would restrict his freedom of action. Many of the Americans who were still working for the Dominican government left when they found that their work was hampered by political interference.

The plan for completing the training of the police had to be abandoned. Under the provisional government officers and recruits for the police had passed through training centers directed by American marines before being assigned for regular duty, and had taken a second course in the centers after some experience in active service. The arrangement had worked well, and Vásquez had agreed in Washington to retain several marine officers under contract to continue it. He said that he wished Colonel Cutts, who was in charge of the training centers, to continue to direct the program. When he returned from Washington, however, he refused to give the American officers the independent authority which Cutts considered indispensable or to employ as many officers and enlisted men as Cutts wanted. Welles urged Cutts to try to meet the president's wishes, but the colonel replied that the marine officers would not remain in Santo Domingo under the conditions on which the government insisted. The negotiations broke down and all the American officers left. Fortunately, the training of the police had already reached a point where the force was very much more efficient than any armed force which the republic had had before the occupation and the maintenance of order was not a serious problem after the marines withdrew.[17]

Another activity in which Welles had hoped that Vásquez would accept American help was the public works administration. This had been directed by a foreign engineer-in-chief ever since the 1908 loan had made a modest sum available for its work. At first the engineers were selected by the Dominican gov-

[17] The correspondence about the police is in file 839.1051.

ernment itself, but in 1912 the State Department persuaded the government to agree very informally that the United States should recommend a competent man for the job. A. J. Collett, the first man appointed under this arrangement, continued to serve under the military government until he was replaced by John H. Caton III in 1921. Vásquez, before he left for Washington in June 1924, told both Welles and Caton that he wished the latter to continue as engineer-in-chief. He would not promise the independent authority and control over appointments which Caton and Welles thought desirable, but Welles was convinced of the president-elect's good intentions and sure that no difficulty would arise.

After his inauguration Vásquez did nothing about renewing Caton's contract, and insisted that Caton make several political appointments which impaired the efficiency of the service. Russell thought that the State Department should withhold approval of the loan which the government was about to obtain until there was some assurance that the situation would be corrected. The department was unwilling to go so far as this. It told the minister to say to Vásquez that the question of retaining Caton was one for the Dominican government to decide, but that the United States would be lacking in candor if it did not point out the importance of maintaining the efficiency of the public works organization. Both the United States and the bankers, Hughes said, would be influenced in their decisions about the proposed loan by their confidence in the way in which the proceeds would be used. The minister was to emphasize that this was merely "friendly advice." Caton's contract was renewed on November 6, but his situation continued to be unsatisfactory and he was finally dismissed in March 1925. The State Department gave him little support because it desired, as it cabled Russell, that the Dominican government should "exercise as far as possible complete and untrammeled authority consistent with its obligations."[18]

There was less difficulty about the project for a new loan. The country had begun to recover from the post-war depression, but the provisional government had been unable to collect enough in taxes to meet its expenses and it was evident that the constitutional government must have help if it was to get off to a good start. A plan for a short-term loan to provide for immediate needs and to make it possible to continue the public works pro-

[18] Grew to Russell, Oct. 31, 1924, 839.15/185. Most of the correspondence about the public works administration is in file 839.15.

gram had been worked out during Vásquez' visit to Washington, and at the same time there had been a tentative agreement on the terms of a new convention which would replace the treaty of 1907 and would make it possible to reduce the unreasonably large proportion of the customs revenues that had to be applied to debt amortization under the old treaty. To meet immediate needs, Lee Higginson and Company lent the government $2,500,000 at 5½%, to be repaid within two years from the proceeds of a larger loan, collecting a commission of 1½% on the transaction.

The new convention, signed at Washington December 27, 1924, was very similar to the 1907 treaty, except that where the latter required that half of the amount by which the customs revenues exceeded $3,000,000 in one year should be added to the contractual payments for amortization of the outstanding bonds, the new arrangement called for the use of only 10% of any surplus over $4,000,000 for this purpose. The new treaty also had a provision for the arbitration of controversies between the signatories. There was no change in the two articles which had caused the most controversy before the American occupation: the provision regarding appointments in the customs service and the commitment of the Dominican government not to increase its debt without the prior consent of the United States.

The signature of the new convention seemed to indicate that much of the anti-American feeling that had existed during the occupation had disappeared. There was some opposition, but this was caused largely by dissension within the government's coalition, which was beginning to break up. Velásquez tried to prevent ratification, but the president finally obtained a majority in Congress by the use of patronage and, it was suspected, by bribery.[19] Several questions which were raised in the Congress about the interpretation of the new treaty were dealt with in notes exchanged between the two governments when ratifications were exchanged in October 1925. It should be noted that the new convention did not actually extend the life of the customs receivership. Under the terms of the convention of evacuation, this had to continue until the retirement of the 1922 loan, which would mature in 1942, and the two governments intended that any bonds issued under the new arrangement should also mature in that year.

[19] See Welles' memorandum of June 17, 1925, 839.00/3895.

In connection with the short-term loan, the State Department was able to bring about the settlement of another matter that had been causing it embarrassment for some years. The case of the Santo Domingo Water, Light and Power Company was an example of the sort of problems that arose when the American government's duty to its own citizens conflicted with the responsibilities which it assumed by intervening in another country. Under a concession obtained in 1912, a group of Americans had invested about $900,000 in a steam generating plant which provided electric light for Santiago and Puerta Plata, and in a water supply system for Santiago. The frequent revolutions before 1916 and the high price of fuel during the world war made the venture unprofitable, and the company asserted that the military government, by insisting that it pay the land tax, despite the exemption from taxes which it claimed under its concession, injured its credit and made it impossible to raise needed funds. In February 1921, after the municipalities of Santiago and Puerto Plata refused to agree to an increase in the already high rate of 20 cents per kilowatt hour for electricity, the company suspended service, leaving both cities without electric light and one of them with no water except what could be carried from a river by hand or by pack animals.

In April 1921 the two municipalities agreed to buy the company's plants for about half of their estimated value, but there was a dispute about the terms of payment, and Congressman Wason of New Hampshire, who was personally interested in the company, asked that the State Department intervene. The military government and the Latin American division in the State Department did not think that the United States should intervene under the circumstances, but the solicitor, who usually handled such cases, insisted that Russell be instructed to urge the military government to "take active measures" to persuade the cities to go through with the purchase agreement. The military government promised to do what it could, but neither it nor the State Department wanted to attempt to coerce the cities during the negotiations for American withdrawal. The dispute dragged on until September 1924, when the State Department apparently intimated that it would withhold its consent to the short-term loan until there was a settlement. On the same day that the United States gave its consent to the loan, the Dominican government agreed to buy the company's properties for $100,000 in cash and $300,000 in two-year 5½% notes.[20]

So long as Welles retained his position as commissioner, it was impracticable to appoint a new minister and Russell remained at his post. Welles, who left Santo Domingo before Vásquez' inauguration, planned to return in the summer of 1925, and he hoped that he would be able to persuade the president and other Dominican leaders to revive the program of cooperation which he had discussed with them earlier. He urged the State Department to retain enough control over the proposed new loan to ensure proper expenditure of the money and to enable it to insist on an efficient organization in the public works administration, and he thought that Vásquez might agree to the appointment of American experts to draw up a comprehensive agricultural program and to help reorganize the treasury department. He also wished to revive the training program for the Dominican police, under a new plan more modest than that which Colonel Cutts had thought necessary. Secretary Kellogg approved these ideas early in June.[21] Before Welles returned to Santo Domingo, however, President Coolidge abruptly terminated his appointment and he left the government service.

There is little reason to suppose that the Dominicans would have accepted Welles' program if he had continued as commissioner. Welles had been remarkably successful in obtaining the Dominicans' cooperation in carrying out the plan of withdrawal, during the periods when he was actually in Santo Domingo, but it was easier to convince them when they knew that a refusal to cooperate would delay or prevent the withdrawal of the occupation. The plan which he now suggested would have met with strong nationalistic opposition, and would have been incompatible with the president's need to build up his following by the use of patronage and government funds. Whatever he said in Washington, Vásquez probably never really intended to give a foreigner control of the public works administration or to let the police force be commanded by officers who were not devoted to his own political fortunes. He certainly would have objected to any foreign interference with the use of government funds. Welles, in fact, had never obtained from him any definite com-

[20] The correspondence about this matter is in file 839.6463.
[21] See Welles' memorandum of June 2, 1925, 839.51/2627.

mitments which the State Department could have invoked if it had wished to carry out the program.

The State Department showed no interest in the program after Welles retired. The sort of control which the proposals envisaged was hardly consistent with the policy of non-interference which was taking shape by 1925. The department made no further suggestions about the training of the police or the retention of an American as head of the public works department. When the Dominican government obtained loans in New York—$3,300,000 in 1926, $5,000,000 in 1927, and $5,000,000 in 1928—the United States did not attempt to control the expenditure of the proceeds. The Dominican government early in 1926 asked the State Department to suggest the name of a competent engineer to study its ports and make plans for improvements to be effected with the proceeds of the expected loans, and J. W. Beardsley, who was recommended by the chief of the bureau of insular affairs, was employed, but he acted merely as an adviser to the Dominican government and the public works department. An agricultural expert obtained through Welles' efforts had to leave the country soon after his arrival because his health broke down. Welles himself continued to keep in touch with his Dominican friends and to give them advice, sometimes in a way that irritated the American legation, but he had little further contact with the State Department. The prestige and influence of the American legation became much greater after Evan Young, a career diplomat of long experience, became minister in 1925.

Chapter Four

THE TREATY REGIME IN HAITI

Haiti, like the Dominican Republic, was occupied by American forces during the Wilson administration, but in Haiti a native government was left in office and its relations with the United States were governed by a treaty signed in 1915. Haiti was different in many respects from its neighbor. In the eighteenth century the western end of Hispaniola was a rich French colony where hundreds of thousands of Negro slaves worked on the sugar and coffee plantations owned by white settlers. France lost control and all of the whites were killed or driven out during a long period of turmoil which began with a slave revolt in 1791 and culminated in the declaration of Haiti's independence in 1804. Thereafter, the black peasants, speaking a part-French, part-African creole and practicing a mixture of African religions called voudou, had little further contact with western civilization. The mulattoes in Port au Prince and a few smaller towns, speaking French and priding themselves on their French culture, became a new aristocracy. They were a relatively small part of the population, for great numbers of them were massacred by black leaders during the war for independence, but they usually held most of the positions in the government because they could read and write. Sometimes the "elite," as they called themselves, controlled the government, but frequently they had to submit to the rule of the black military leaders who had more following among the peasants and in the army. Governments were normally set up and changed by military force and the rulers were usually too preoccupied with mere survival to devote attention to constructive activities. Haiti was probably the most backward country in the Americas in the first years of the twentieth century.

There were few North Americans in the republic before 1915, but a considerable number of French and Germans. French bankers had floated government loans and had established a national bank which acted as the government's treasury and disbursing agent. Nearly all of the priests in the Catholic church, to which most of the elite belonged, were French, and the best schools were run by French religious orders. The Germans, on the other hand, went into business. One German group controlled the electric light plants at Port au Prince and Cape Haitian, the wharf at Port au Prince, and the P.C.S. Railroad, which served the country around the capital. Others were engaged in trade and in the first years of the century some of them made a lucrative business out of financing revolutions. German activity in Haiti aroused some disquiet in the State Department.

It was a project sponsored by French and German interests that first caused the United States to become involved in Haiti's internal affairs. In 1910 the Haitian government accepted a proposal from a Franco-German group for the reorganization of the National Bank of Haiti and for a substantial loan. The United States objected to the arrangement because it did not wish to have European interests take over the important functions which the bank would have in connection with the government's finances and the reform of the currency. It withdrew its opposition when several American banks were given a share in the business under conditions that assured a 50% American control. The National City Bank of New York, as the leader of the American group, shared the management of the national bank with representatives of the French stockholders during the next few years, but the loan was floated in France, which at the time offered the only market for Haitian bonds.

After 1910 the National City Bank also acquired an interest in the National Railroad of Haiti, which an American promoter was trying to build. Both the national bank and the railroad were involved in continual controversies with the short-lived revolutionary governments that succeeded one another with increasing frequency after 1911, and the State Department repeatedly had to intervene diplomatically in usually unsuccessful attempts to prevent violations of their rights or confiscation of their property. The irritation caused by these incidents probably helped to convince the Wilson administration that it must make the same sort of effort to restore order in Haiti that it and its predecessors had been making in other Caribbean countries. Efforts to persuade the Haitians to accept help were futile, and in 1915, when organized government seemed temporarily to have disappeared, President Wilson ordered the military occupation of the country.

A government set up under the protection of American marines agreed to a treaty which gave American officials control of many of the Haitian government's most important functions: the financial administration, the organization and training of a new police force, and the execution of "such measures as in the opinion of the high contracting parties may be necessary for the sanitation and public improvement of the Republic." The treaty was to be in force for ten years, but in 1917, in the hope of making possible the flotation of a long-term loan, the two governments agreed that it should remain in force until 1936. In 1918 a new constitution, drawn up with the assistance of the American legation and the marine commander in Haiti, and revised by the State and Navy Departments at Washington, was approved by a "plebiscite." This did away with the longstanding prohibition against land ownership by foreigners and temporarily entrusted the legislative power to an appointed council of state which hopefully would cooperate with the occupation better than an elected congress. After the ratification of the treaty, in 1916, five "treaty services" were established: the customs receivership, the office of the financial adviser, the *gendarmerie* or police, the public works administration, and the health service. All of these were directed and partly staffed by Americans nominated by the president of the United States and appointed by the president of Haiti, and each was attached to one of the ministries of the Haitian government. The general receiver of customs and the financial adviser were American civilians. Marines trained and commanded the *gendarmerie*, and civil engineers from the navy and navy doctors headed the public works administration and the health service. The rather general language adopted in an effort to avoid offense to Haitian pride left room for argument about the interpretation of some provisions of the treaty of 1915, but the State Department insisted from the start that the treaty officials must have full control of the services which they headed, including the right to appoint and remove all of their subordinates.

The results of the American effort, before 1921, were somewhat disappointing. The American marines and the native constabulary which they organized restored order in most of the country, but in 1918 there was a peasant uprising in the hilly regions of eastern and northeastern Haiti where revolutionary armies had often been recruited before 1915. This was suppressed only after more than a year of guerrilla fighting in which

1,500 Haitians were thought to have been killed. Relatively little could be done about the "public improvement" contemplated by the treaty because first the war in Europe and then quarrels between Haitian and American officials prevented the flotation of a loan to provide the necessary money. There had, however, been some work on roads and irrigation projects, and most notably a great improvement in sanitary conditions in the towns. The *gendarmerie* had thoroughly reformed the Haitian prisons and had improved local government throughout the country by having its police officers act as advisers to the communal authorities.

More might have been accomplished had it not been for the poor organization of the American establishment. There was no centralized direction of the treaty services. In Washington, responsibility for Haitian affairs was divided between the State Department, which supervised the customs service and the financial adviser, and the Navy Department, which furnished personnel for the other services. The brigade commander, who had responsibility for maintaining order and general authority over the police force, reported directly to the Navy Department. Neither he nor the American legation had any clear authority over the public works and health services, which were, however, dependent on the financial adviser for funds. This situation led to friction between the treaty services and at times encouraged the Haitian government to play off one against the other, with bad results for American prestige. The State Department, which thought that it should control American policy in Haiti, attempted to improve the situation by insisting that all of the American officials meet regularly at the legation under the chairmanship of the minister to discuss and coordinate their work, but this was only partly successful. Arthur Bailly-Blanchard, the American minister, was an elderly gentleman from Louisiana who had served most of his life as a secretary in large embassies where he obtained no experience that would fit him for work in Haiti. He had been at Port au Prince since 1914, but he had little contact with Haitians and he gave the State Department little information about what was going on. His influence was overshadowed by that of the brigade commander, who often seemed to take more interest in constructive projects than the legation did.

The work of the treaty officials had also been hindered by friction between American and Haitian officials. Many of the elite

74

seemed at first to regard the intervention as a lesser evil than the anarchy which preceded it, and Sudre Dartiguenave, who became president in 1915, seemed to welcome American support. When he accepted the treaty of 1915, however, he had apparently hoped that the officials appointed under it would serve as advisers to his ministers and that the military control which the marines had imposed would be modified when the treaty went into effect. He protested vigorously when he found that the treaty officials expected to dictate the policy of their services and to control all appointments in them. In 1920 he provoked a conflict with the American legation and the financial adviser by promulgating several laws to which the legation had objected and by refusing to approve a new charter for the national bank. The National City Bank of New York had recently become sole owner of the national bank, and the draft charter recognized this and contained several provisions on which the State Department had insisted because it thought that they would be beneficial to Haiti. To force Dartiguenave to change his attitude, John A. McIlhenny, the financial adviser, suspended payment of the salaries of the president and his cabinet and the council of state, which had voted the objectionable laws. The State Department disapproved his action, and the payment of salaries was soon resumed, though the Haitian government did not change its position. The resultant bad feeling made further cooperation between McIlhenny and the president impossible and seriously damaged the relations between the Haitian government and the American minister.

In Haiti, as in the Dominican Republic, Harding's statements during the presidential campaign had raised hopes for a change of policy under the new administration. Dartiguenave set forth his ideas about the direction which the change should take in a letter which he addressed to the president on the day of his inauguration. He did not ask that the treaty of 1915 be abrogated or modified but simply that it be given "a thorough and loyal execution." He urged that the training of the *gendarmerie* be completed as soon as possible, so that the military occupation might be withdrawn. In the meantime the occupation should not intervene in administrative or judicial matters and the American military courts should not exercise jurisdiction over Haitians. The *gendarmerie* should keep out of politics, especially during the campaign for the election of a new Haitian president, which was about to begin. He charged that the American officials in Haiti showed no understanding of Haitian needs and no desire to co-operate with Haitian officials and had done nothing for the country's economic development.

The letter apparently impressed Harding, who wrote Hughes that he would like a picture of the relationship between Haiti and the United States, and recommendations for changes which would be a "reflex of the high purpose we wish to pursue in exercising our peculiar relationship to the Haitian Republic." The president's reply to Dartiguenave, which was drafted in the State Department, was nevertheless non-commital. The Latin American division was already working on plans for the reorganization of the American representation in Haiti, but with the idea of strengthening rather than weakening American control.

In Haiti it would have been difficult to carry out a plan of withdrawal like that which was adopted in the Dominican Republic. In the latter country, where the people all spoke Spanish and there were organized political parties, it was possible to hope that a government chosen in a free election might be relatively stable after the marines were withdrawn. In the case of Haiti, even some of the anti-imperialists who had most urgently demanded the evacuation of the Dominican Republic thought that a cessation of American control would simply bring back the anarchy that had prevailed before 1915.[1] There was little political organization, even among the small upper class, and there was very little communication between the elite and the peasants. Elections, when they were held at all, were a farce, because 95% of the voters were illiterate and completely ignorant about governmental affairs. The position of the United States was more defensible in Haiti because relations were governed by a treaty which neither party wanted to abrogate.

Some months elapsed, however, before the new administration decided what it should do. In the meantime there was increasing evidence of wide-spread hostility to the American occupation and also of political opposition to Dartiguenave. A group which

[1] In August 1921, Oswald Garrison Villard, speaking as representative of the *Union Patriotique* of Haiti, The National Association for the Advancement of Colored People, and the Haiti and Santo Domingo Independence Society, told a Senate committee that an immediate withdrawal would be a disaster, but urged that the state of military occupation should be terminated. *New York Times*, Aug. 4, 1921.

76

called itself the *Union Patriotique* was carrying on a campaign of public speeches and newspaper articles which was arousing public opinion to a dangerous pitch of excitement. Both Dartiguenave and Colonel John H. Russell, the brigade commander, thought that something should be done to check the agitation before it led to disturbances in the streets, and Russell asked permission to impose some form of censorship. The State Department refused to approve any censorship; but as the situation got worse and Dartiguenave again asked Russell to act, the Navy authorized Russell to issue a proclamation under authority of martial law prohibiting articles or speeches of an incendiary nature or tending to stir up agitation against American officials. Two journalists were arrested two days later. One of them was Jolibois *fils*, who was to achieve prominence by repeated arrests for press offenses in the years to come.[2]

Sumner Welles, who was irritated by the Navy's acting without consulting the State Department, urged the need for an immediate decision as to the new administration's policy in Haiti, and in July 1921 Secretary Hughes took the matter up with the president. "We cannot leave Haiti at the present time," he wrote, "and I conceive it to be the duty of the administration to do its utmost to perfect the methods of administration and to make our occupation of the greatest benefit to the inhabitants of Haiti." He thought that it might be desirable to negotiate a new treaty, but not immediately, and that in the meantime a foreign loan should be obtained and the *gendarmerie* should be improved. He also recommended that a marine officer be named as the president's personal representative in Haiti, to coordinate the activities of all the treaty officials. The president approved this program on August 15.[3]

The president's decision made it possible to deal with Haitian matters on which action had been delayed until the basic question, whether to continue or to withdraw the American intervention, had been resolved. One of the most pressing was to decide what position the American government should take with regard

[2] This account is based on several papers in the first part of file 838.918, and on Welles' memorandum of June 15, 1921 to Fletcher, 711.38/180 and Russell's telegram of May 28, 1921 to the Navy Department, 838.00/1778.

[3] Hughes to Harding, July 19, 1921, 711.38/147a, and Harding to Hughes, Aug. 15, 1921, 711.38/148.

to the election of a new president in Haiti. The constitution of 1918 provided that the president should be named by congress, and that the first congressional election should take place in January of an even-numbered year. The president was to decide which year this should be, and in the meantime the legislative power would be exercised by a council of state of 21 members appointed by the president. There had been no congress since 1917, for no election had been held in 1920. It would be more difficult to avoid holding one in 1922 because Dartiguenave's term would expire in May of that year and provision must be made for the choice of his successor.

Dartiguenave wanted to be reelected, but he knew that most of the other political leaders would oppose him and that he would not be able to control a new congress unless the *gendarmerie* cooperated with him to assure the victory of his candidates in a popular election. In elections before the intervention, only soldiers and a few friends of the leader who had military control voted, and when the congress chose a president its members either sold their votes or acted under compulsion from the army. In 1917, in the only congressional election held since the intervention, the American marines had maintained order but had not helped the government's candidates, and the result had been a congress which obstructed what the administration and the occupation were trying to do and which was forcibly dissolved in a few months. Dartiguenave took up the electoral problem with the State Department in a note delivered by the Haitian minister on July 2, 1921, pointing out the importance of having a congress "composed of men animated by the desire to effect a peaceful transfer of power, and not of professional politicians who afford no guarantee of morality or patriotism." He said that the government had a "sacred duty" to assist the proper sort of candidates, and that the American government should cooperate with him in this effort instead of ignoring or opposing the government's friends as the American officials had done in 1917.

The State Department did not reply until September 2 when it informed the Haitian minister that the United States could not countenance elections in which the will of the voters was not freely expressed. The next day, however, Hughes wrote Bailly-Blanchard that he recognized that the ignorance and illiteracy of the majority of the Haitian voters would make it improbable that truly free elections could be held. Furthermore, he said, elections which were not unduly influenced by the government would probably result in the choice of an anti-American congress which would impede American efforts to cooperate with Haiti in any constructive policy. The State Department would not therefore advise the president to hold elections in 1922 and would interpose no objection to the election of the new president by the council of state. Bailly-Blanchard reported that Dartiguenave was "very much pleased" with the secretary's reply.

This action set a precedent which was followed until the United States changed its policy in Haiti in 1930. The State Department was never happy with a situation where it was compelled to countenance the appointment of the legislative body by the president and the election of the president by the same small group, but it was not willing to face the complications that would inevitably have followed the installation of a freely elected congress. It could not agree to the Haitian government's proposal that it help to control the election, and the department's legal advisers thought that the position which it did take was defensible from a constitutional point of view.[4] After 1922, however, it was difficult to maintain the fiction that the government of Haiti represented the Haitian people or to reply to critics who accused the United States of preventing rather than promoting the development of democratic institutions in Haiti. The State Department could only argue that there could in fact be no stable, democratic government in Haiti until conditions had been completely changed by a program like that which the United States was endeavoring to carry out.

The decision to remain in Haiti also made it possible for the financial adviser to resume efforts to obtain a foreign loan. Aside from the need for money for roads and irrigation and other necessary public works, a general refunding of existing debts was a prerequisite for any efficient management of the government's finances. Before 1915, buyers of the government's bonds and contractors and other creditors who could not be paid immediately had frequently been given "affectations," or liens on specific items of government revenue, and the national bank, which received and disbursed the government's funds, was required to set aside the amounts due to each creditor each month before turning over the balance to the government. Meanwhile the government had to borrow from the national bank each month to meet its current

[4] Solicitor's memorandum of March 25, 1921, 838.00/1798.

expenses. This arrangement was profitable to the bank and protected the government's creditors, but it broke down when a revolutionary regime took the treasury from the bank early in 1915. The financial adviser continued to disregard the affectations after the intervention, but they were contractual obligations which could not be ignored indefinitely. Since they were usually liens on specific sources of income, it would be hard to revise the tax system without discharging them. The American financial officials were especially anxious to revise the antiquated customs tariff.

The State Department was also interested in refunding Haiti's bonded foreign debt, most of which was held in France. Quarrels over foreign debts had frequently led to threats of European intervention in Haiti and other Caribbean states, and the substitution of American for European financial influence had been an important objective of American Caribbean policy since 1909. Haiti had obtained three loans in France, in 1875, 1896, and 1910. Service on these, suspended after the intervention, had been resumed in 1920. The financial adviser wanted to refund the bonds as soon as possible, because the depreciation of the franc, which was assumed to be temporary, would make it profitable to do so. The total amount outstanding was approximately 90,000,000 francs.

There were many other unpaid claims against the treasury. The Haitian government was liable, as guarantor, for approximately $3,544,000 of bonds issued to finance the building of the National Railroad of Haiti. These had been sold in France, though the railroad was an American company. There was also an interest guarantee of $41,280 per annum on the bonds of the P.C.S. Railroad, which had been taken over during the world war by American interests, and there were internal bonds, issued between 1912 and 1914, to the amount of $2,868,000. Haiti owed the national bank about $1,800,000, chiefly on account of advances to cover budget deficits before the intervention. There were also a great number of miscellaneous claims of natives and foreigners.

Haiti and the United States had agreed in 1919 on a protocol which provided for a $40,000,000, thirty-year loan to pay the French bonds and the railroad guarantees and the awards of a mixed claims commission which was to be set up. The new bonds were to be secured by liens on the republic's customs and inter-

80

nal revenues, and it was agreed that these revenues would continue to be collected by officials nominated by the president of the United States during the life of the loan after the expiration of the treaty of 1915. McIlhenny, the financial adviser, had gone to New York in October 1920, to discuss the proposed loan with American bankers, but he had found the bankers unwilling to consider the business until the new administration should have decided its policy in Haiti. They showed more interest after they were assured that the United States did not contemplate any immediate relaxation of American control. McIlhenny talked with several bankers, in the hope of obtaining tentative bids from them and then working out the details with the institution that seemed disposed to offer the best terms.

On August 12, 1921, the National City Bank of New York wrote the State Department that it was interested in the proposed loan but would have to be able to give prospective purchasers of the bonds strong and definite assurances that the United States would continue to control Haiti's finances until all of the bonds had been paid. After consulting President Harding, Hughes replied on August 22 that the United States would continue to exercise all of the powers which it enjoyed under its agreements with Haiti with respect to the collection and application of Haitian revenues and that American troops would not be withdrawn during the life of the treaty so long as their retention was necessary to assure peace and tranquility. On September 24, again with the approval of the president, Hughes said that his letter might be shown to any properly interested party, and that excerpts from the treaty of 1915 and the protocol of 1919 might be printed in any prospectus which might be issued. Letters similar to that of August 22 were later sent to other bankers with whom McIlhenny talked. The bankers would probably not have gone ahead with the loan, or would have made a much less favorable offer, if they had not received definite assurances of this sort, but the commitment made by the secretary was troublesome when the American government wished to change its policy in Haiti eight years later.[5]

On October 18, the State Department informed the chargé d'affaires at Port au Prince that the National City Bank had offered to take $14,000,000 in ten-year, 7½% notes at 92, whereas Speyer and Company and Blair and Company, working together,

---

[5] For these letters see 838.51/1129, 1132, 1133, 1139a, 1147a.

had offered 94. In both cases the bankers asked the deposit of a larger amount of thirty-year, 6% bonds, as collateral. The department recommended that the Haitian government accept the Speyer-Blair offer, but on November 14 it cabled that Lee Higginson and Company would purchase $16,000,000 in thirty-year, 6% bonds at 85 and that it considered this the best of the proposals. It urged that the Haitian government accept one of these offers immediately.

Dartiguenave wanted a loan but he did not want one negotiated by McIlhenny. He had resented the financial adviser's high-handed action in suspending government salaries and he felt that McIlhenny had treated him with gross discourtesy on other occasions. On November 16, in a letter to President Harding, he asked that another financial adviser be appointed. This communication was filed without reply after the State Department failed to persuade the Haitian minister to have it withdrawn.[6] The department was troubled by McIlhenny's tactless conduct, but it felt that it would destroy the influence of all the treaty officials if it removed one of them because the Haitian government objected to his official actions. In a reply to the State Department's cable recommending the Lee Higginson proposal, Dartiguenave asserted that the protocol of 1919 had lapsed, because it contemplated a loan to be made within two years after its signature, and said that the government would not agree to tie up all its revenues for thirty years for a loan which would produce only $14,000,000. The State Department denied the validity of these arguments, and attempted to exert pressure by instructing the general receiver of customs to apply a larger proportion of the customs receipts to debt payment, reducing the amount available to the Haitian government,[7] but Dartiguenave was adamant in his refusal to authorize McIlhenny to sign any loan contract. The loan negotiations had to be suspended for the time being.

One reason for Dartiguenave's stubbornness was a general expectation in Haiti that the Senate committee which was investigating charges of abuses in Haiti and the Dominican Republic would recommend a change in American policy. The committee held hearings in Haiti in the latter part of November 1921. Mr.

---

[6] S. Johnson's memorandum of Nov. 16, 1921, 838.51/1262.

[7] The department's motives are explained in a Latin American division memorandum of Jan. 23, 1922, 838.51/1189.

Ernest Angell, representing the *Union Patriotique* of Haiti as well as the Haiti-Santo Domingo Independence Society and the National Association for the Advancement of Colored People in the United States, presented most of the witnesses and helped to question them. The committee's conclusion, after hearing a great amount of testimony, was that the American marines, in general, had done a good job under difficult conditions. Its findings tended to discredit some of the lurid stories that had been published in the United States.[8]

The committee's unanimous report gave the president and Secretary Hughes strong bi-partisan support for the Haitian policy on which they had already decided. It stressed Haiti's need for continuing help from the United States and urged that this help be broadened to include education and the improvement of the administration of justice. It recommended the conclusion of the proposed loan. The committee hoped for an early reduction of the marine forces in Haiti but did not suggest that the American intervention could be terminated at an early date. The report was not published until June 1922, because the committee held further hearings in Washington after its return from Haiti. In December 1921, however, Senator McCormick, its chairman, told the press that the committee would not recommend any immediate reduction of American forces in Haiti and that it would urge the flotation of a loan and the appointment of a high commissioner to coordinate the work of the American officials there.

The proposal to appoint a high commissioner had been approved by the president in August 1921 but it had seemed better to defer action until the Senate committee had visited Haiti. From the beginning it seems to have been assumed that the post would go to a marine officer. The State Department would probably have preferred to entrust the job to a civilian diplomat, but it knew that Bailly-Blanchard was unequal to the task and it did not want to remove him because he had spent most of his life in the career foreign service but would have no pension if he retired. The appointment of a civilian high commissioner from outside of the regular diplomatic establishment would have required legislation which the administration could not request without

---

[8] For the testimony before the committee see "Hearings before a Select Committee on Haiti and Santo Domingo," *U.S. Senate*, 67th Congress, First and Second Sessions Pursuant to S. Res. 112. Washington, 1922. The committee report is S.R. 79, 67th Congress, 2nd Session.

provoking an unwelcome debate on its whole Haitian policy. Senator McCormick later asserted that his committee would have preferred the appointment of a civilian, but in discussing the matter with the State and Navy Departments he urged that a marine officer be chosen because only a military man would be able to exercise the necessary authority over the treaty officials who came from the navy and the marine corps.[9]

The Navy's candidate was General Smedley Butler, who had served brilliantly as chief of the *gendarmerie* during the first years of the occupation. General Butler, however, had a reputation for vigorous and resourceful but not always discreet action, and both the Senate committee and the Latin American division in the State Department thought it would be better to have a high commissioner who could be expected to rely on persuasion rather than coercion to obtain cooperation from the Haitians and whose appointment would arouse less opposition in Haiti.[10] The Navy's next choice was Colonel John H. Russell, the brigade commander at Port au Prince. Russell was promoted to brigadier general in January 1922, and was appointed high commissioner, with the rank of ambassador, in February. Bailly-Blanchard, still nominally minister to Haiti, was assigned to duty in the State Department, where he spent the few remaining years of his life in innocuous pursuits.

The choice was a good one. General Russell was level-headed and tactful and had the combination of flexibility and firmness which his delicate task required. Though he had been brigade commander during the period of bitter controversy before 1921 and had occasionally had to coerce the Haitian government by invoking the authority of military occupation, his relations with the Haitian leaders were apparently better than those of other principal American officials. His ideas about economic and social development were somewhat unsophisticated, but he was genuinely interested in the welfare of the Haitian people. He gave the treaty services a leadership and a sense of purpose which hitherto had been lacking.

Russell's instructions, which Hughes signed on Feburary 11, 1922, authorized the high commissioner to coordinate and direct

[9] McCormick made this statement at a conference at which I was present in Dec. 1921.

[10] See the Latin American division's memorandum of Jan. 5, 1922, 711.38/175.

the work of all the treaty officials. He was told that his first objectives should be the stabilization of the government's finances, the flotation of the proposed loan, and the improvement of the *gendarmerie* so that the forces of occupation could be gradually withdrawn. He was also to urge reforms in the Haitian judiciary and to endeavor to persuade the Haitian government to agree to amend the treaty of 1915 to place the educational system under an American official. He was to "bear in mind at all times that the sole desire of the Government of the United States in its relations with the Republic of Haiti is to advance the welfare, both moral and material, of the Haitian people, with the hope that the assistance which the United States is enabled to bring them will enable them, at no distant date, to undertake the task of maintaining a National Government, with no further interference on the part of this Government in their domestic affairs." "Whatever measures you may urge that government to take," the secretary wrote, "should conform to the customs, habits, and even to the prejudices of the Haitian people, so far as may be consistent with the accomplishment of the indispensable requisites of stable and efficient government."

The State Department now assumed control of the American effort in Haiti. The marine brigade, with some 500 to 800 officers and men, was concentrated at Port au Prince and Cape Haitian and normally took no part in policing the country. The brigade commander continued to report to the Navy Department, but Russell, as senior officer present, was expected to see that military policy conformed to the policy laid down by the secretary of state. The high commissioner directed the *gendarmerie* and all of the other treaty services and he was the principal American diplomatic representative, though the legation, under a chargé d'affaires, dealt with some routine matters. The individual treaty officials continued to work with the ministries to which they were attached, but when disputes occurred they were usually settled by the high commissioner and the president of Haiti.

Many anti-imperialists criticized the appointment of a high commissioner, and the United States Senate, on February 23, asked the president for information about it. Some weeks later, Senator King of Utah, always one of the most active critics of the State Department's Caribbean policy, requested an investigation of the president's authority to appoint an ambassador to Haiti without the Senate's approval. Hughes told the Senate, rather

85

legalistically, that Russell was not an ambassador, either in name or in fact, though he would hold the personal rank where diplomatic precedence was involved. Much of the criticism centered on the fact that a military officer, rather than a civilian, had been appointed.

Russell, who came to Washington to receive his instructions, returned to Haiti in March 1922, not long before the time when the council of state would elect a new president. Dartiguenave seemed to have few political friends, and there was talk of popular resistance if the council should name him. All of the contending groups sought Russell's support, but the high commissioner tried to make it clear that he would be absolutely neutral. On April 8 he told the press:

> It is my desire that you publish in your papers an earnest request to the people that during the coming election they conduct themselves in an orderly manner.
>
> The people must learn that they must abide by the laws and the Constitution of their country and that a violation of the laws is not only not in the interests of their country but not in their own interests.
>
> It is my hope that the moment the election is over we will all put our shoulder to the wheel and push together for the development of Haiti. "Push for Haiti" should be the slogan, the watchword of all.
>
> If such is done in a short time Haiti will become a land of happiness and prosperity.
>
> In the coming election, I espouse the cause of no candidate. The obligations contained in the Treaty of 1915 between the Republic of Haiti and the United States must, naturally, be carried out to their fullest extent.

Dartiguenave replaced several members of the council of state with men who could be expected to vote for his reelection,[11] but early in April he discovered that nearly all of the councillors had turned against him. He could not legally dismiss any of them while the council was in session. He consequently withdrew his candidacy at the last minute and Louis Borno was elected president. Russell, who had apparently not even known that Borno was a leading candidate,[12] did nothing to influence the council's

[11] Russell referred to this in his dispatch of Feb. 17, 1926, 838.00/2195.
[12] On the day of the election, Russell wrote the State Department that

choice. It was later reported that the election had cost Borno $16,000, a sum which presumably had to be divided between several of the twenty-one members of the council of state.[13] The new president, who took office in May, was one of the ablest lawyers in Port au Prince. He had held high positions in Dartiguenave's administration and had been a determined and effective supporter of the Haitian point of view in conflicts with the occupation. In 1918 his obstructive attitude led Bailly-Blanchard and Russell, who was then brigade commander, to demand and obtain his removal as minister of finance. There was some doubt about his constitutional eligibility, because his father was alleged to have been a French citizen, but the chief justice of Haiti's highest court told Russell that the decision of the council of state on this matter was final, and Russell recommended that Borno be recognized immediately as president-elect. McIlhenny and some other officers who had served in Haiti opposed recognition[14] but the State Department followed Russell's advice.

Neither Russell nor the State Department foresaw that Borno would abandon his predecessor's obstructive policy and work effectively with the high commissioner during the next eight years. The new president had a real interest in Haiti's economic and social development and realized how much the treaty services could contribute to this. He also seemed to realize how much more real authority he would exercise if he worked with the treaty services instead of obstructing them. His freedom of action was greatly limited by the treaty of 1915, but he was far from being a puppet of the United States. He had definite views about questions of policy and his views often prevailed in cases where there were differences of opinion. As time went on his relations with Russell became close and cordial. The two men liked and trusted each other, and the differences of opinion that inevitably arose only occasionally reached a point where they were even reported to the State Department.

Before Borno took office, he assured Russell that he would go ahead with the proposed loan. He insisted, however, that the financial adviser obtain bids from several bankers instead of con-

---

Stephen Archer, the president of the council of state, would probably be elected. *Foreign Relations, 1922*, Vol. II, p. 468.

[13] Merrell to Kellogg, Aug. 28, 1925, 838.002/110.

[14] This matter was discussed at a conference in which I participated.

cluding the negotiations with Lee Higginson and Company. Mc-Ilhenny objected, because he had committed himself to Lee Higginson after deciding that theirs was the best of the preliminary proposals. The State Department, which had approved his action but which realized that competitive bidding might produce a better offer, would have been in an embarrassing position if Lee Higginson had not voluntarily relinquished any claim to preferential treatment. The department, after some argument, gave in to Borno's wishes on several other points, and on June 28 Russell jubilantly reported that the council of state had passed a law authorizing the loan. Interested bankers were invited to submit bids for $16,000,000 of thirty-year, 6% bonds, which were to form Series A of the $40,000,000 loan authorized by the protocol of 1919.

When the bids were opened it appeared that the National City Bank offered to buy the bonds at 92.137% of their face value, as against Lee Higginson's offer of 90.427% and a lower bid from the Speyer-Blair group. Apparently the National City Bank was willing to risk a loss on the transaction in order to maintain its position as Haiti's banker. The loan contract was signed on October 6, 1922, and on the seventh the United States gave the formal approval required by the treaty of 1915. With President Harding's authorization, Hughes renewed his assurance that agents appointed by the president of the United States would collect and allocate the revenue pledged for the service of the bonds after the expiration of the treaty of 1915.[15]

On October 11, McIlhenny resigned. Borno had made it clear that his return to Haiti would be unwelcome, and Russell and members of the Senate committee had urged that he be replaced.[16] Sumner Welles, who thought that some of the charges against the financial adviser were unfair, had insisted that the change be delayed until the loan negotiations were over. As early as April 1922, however, the State Department had selected John S. Hord as McIlhenny's successor. Hord had had experience as a tax expert in Puerto Rico and the Philippines, and he had recently been in Cuba with General Crowder, who spoke highly of him. He had been in Washington for several months preparing himself for his new position.

[15] 838.51/1397a.
[16] See Welles' memorandum of March 14, 1922, 838.51/1324.

The greater part of the proceeds of the loan was used to re-fund or reduce the Haitian government's debts. Approximately $6,000,000 went to purchase francs for the retirement of the French bonds, and somewhat over $2,000,000 was set aside for the arrears of interest and amortization on the national railroad bonds. The national bank received $1,733,000 to cancel its long-standing debt. Part of the remainder was held for the payment of claims to be adjudicated by the proposed claims commission. Only $2,000,000 to $2,500,000 was available for public works. This was not enough for any very ambitious development program, but it was perhaps as much as the treaty services were equipped to use profitably for the time being.

A dispute arose when some holders of the French bonds of 1910 demanded that they be paid in gold rather than in francs. The word "gold" had been used in the caption of the bonds, apparently because the revenues pledged for their service were to be collected in "gold," meaning dollars, rather than in Haitian *gourdes*, but there was no provision in the bonds or in the loan contract for the payment of interest or amortization in anything but French francs. The State Department supported the Haitian government in rejecting the French government's demand that the question be arbitrated. The dispute dragged on until 1938, when Haiti agreed to give each holder of a 500-franc bond $25 in scrip payable over a period of fifteen years, in addition to his 500-franc principal.[17]

One of the purposes of the treaty of 1915 and of the protocol of 1919 had been the establishment of a commission to pass on outstanding claims of natives and foreigners against the Haitian government. The original plan, to pay all of the awards of the commission from the New York loan, had been abandoned because the bankers thought that a large loan would be hard to market, and also because the Haitian government objected to "exteriorizing" its internal debts. The proceeds of the A bonds would make it possible to pay a portion of the awards in cash and the balance was to be paid in internal bonds issued as Series B of the loan authorized by the protocol.[18]

[17] *Association Nationale des Porteurs de Valeurs Mobilières*, Report for 1938, p. 28. Apparently payments on the scrip were delayed, for the Association's report for 1965 stated that the final distribution was made in that year.

[18] See McIlhenny's statement to the Senate committee, March 15, 1922, *Hearings*, Vol. II, p. 1394.

The protocol provided that the Haitian government should appoint a commission of three members: one nominated by the minister of finance, one by the secretary of state of the United States, and a third, who should not be a citizen either of Haiti or the United States, by the financial adviser. To encourage the acceptance of the awards by European claimants, the State Department had arranged in 1920 that the governments whose nationals had important claims should select the person who was to sit on the commission as the financial adviser's nominee while their claims were being considered. The State Department had been unable to persuade Dartiguenave to appoint the commission but after Borno took office the council of state passed the necessary legislation and the commission started work in April 1923. Hector Saavedra, a Cuban recommended by General Crowder, sat as the third member of the commission while American and Haitian claims were being considered.

The protocol required that the work of the commission be completed within two years, but a dispute with the French government, which insisted that a claims convention signed in 1913 entitled its nationals and *protégés* to special treatment, delayed the consideration of French claims. The dispute was settled in 1926, after long negotiations at Port au Prince and at Washington. The claims commission ended its work the same year. It passed on more than 70,000 claims, most of which had already been examined by earlier claims commissions but had not been paid. Only 157 were presented by Americans and about 1,000 by Europeans. The vast majority represented small debts owed by the Haitian government to its own people, and it was Haitians who benefited most from the commission's work. Out of a total amount of $3,526,170 awarded, Americans received $455,000, French claimants $756,000, Germans $500,000, and Haitians more than $1,500,000. The commission's awards were paid one-third in cash and two-thirds in Series B bonds, which were similar to those of Series A except that they were payable only in Haiti and were subject to a 10% Haitian income tax.

Series B bonds were also given to the holders of the internal bonds issued by the Haitian government in 1912, 1913, and 1914. These had been sold originally to local investors at discounts ranging from 11% and 13% of their face value in the case of the 1912 and 1913 issues to 36%, 44%, and 53% for the three issues of 1914. Under the protocol of 1919 these bonds would have been settled by the claims commission, which presumably would have treated them with little generosity. Since many of them were held by people who had political influence, Dartiguenave insisted that they be exempted from the commission's jurisdiction, and McIlhenny agreed. In December 1922, the holders were offered a settlement which more than 90% of them promptly accepted. The interest was paid in full at the contract rates up to the end of 1922 and the holders were given B bonds at the rate of 100% of their holdings in the case of the 1912 issue, 95% in the case of the 1913 bonds, and 85%, 80%, and 75%, respectively, in the case of the three 1914 issues.

Series C of the loan authorized by the protocol was issued to refund the bonds of the National Railroad of Haiti, for which the Haitian government was responsible as guarantor. The national railroad had obtained a concession in 1910 to build a line from Port au Prince to Cape Haitian, but revolutions and constant quarrels with the Haitian government had slowed construction so that only three unconnected sections, totalling about 100 miles, had been built by 1915. The work had been financed by the issue of bonds at the rate of $20,000 per kilometer of completed track, and the Haitian government had agreed to pay the interest and sinking fund on these if the railroad company was unable to do so. Of a total of $3,544,548.74 bonds outstanding in 1922, two-thirds had been sold in France. Most of the remainder was being held as collateral for loans to the railroad company by the National City Bank and other American firms.[19] The Haitian government had defaulted on its interest guarantee before the American intervention, and the protocol of 1919 provided that the arrears of service should be paid in cash out of the proposed loan.

Russell thought that it would be better to use some of this cash for further construction which might make the railroad more useful to the country. There was little traffic on the existing lines, but there might be more if the lines could be extended into the Artibonite Valley and other productive regions.[20] A plan to give the bondholders new bonds for a part of their claims was consequently worked out early in 1923, and Roger L. Farnham, who had been appointed receiver of the railroad company by a New York court in 1920, was asked to discuss it with the bondholders.

[19] Latin American division memorandum of Jan. 16, 1924, 838.77/288.

[20] *Second Annual Report of the American High Commissioner at Port au Prince, 1923*, pp. 2, 3.

91

Farnham persuaded nearly all of the French holders to accept a new Haitian government bond for $72.29, plus $35.75 cash, in exchange for each 500-franc ($96.53) railroad bond with its back interest and to agree to the use of the rest of the available money for new construction. The National City Bank also accepted, but reluctantly because it feared that the issue of new bonds would affect the price of the A bonds in the New York market. The Haitian government consequently authorized the issue of $2,660,000 in Series C bonds to provide for the exchange. $600,000 was made available for new construction, and the government agreed that it would provide further funds, by another bond issue, when the financial adviser thought that the government's financial situation permitted such action. The railroad company agreed to assume the service of the C bonds if and as its revenues permitted, and to give the government cumulative, non-voting, preferred stock in return for the bonds to be issued later. The arrangement seemed fair to all concerned. The Haitian government saved a substantial amount by reducing the principal of the debt, and the bondholders received a well-secured obligation in place of one which might have no protection if the United States should modify its control over Haiti's finances. The railroad company's debt was reduced and it obtained funds for new construction.

There was one other major item in the State Department's program for the financial rehabilitation of Haiti. The product of the various internal taxes was deposited in the national bank like other government funds, and its expenditure was controlled by the financial adviser, but the amount that reached the bank was very small because the tax laws were antiquated and they were administered by Haitian officials. The financial adviser thought that the internal revenues could become an important source of much needed income if the tax laws could be revised and if the administration were taken over by his office. Neither the treaty of 1915, nor the protocol of 1919, however, specifically obligated the Haitian government to turn over the collection of the internal revenue before 1936, and Dartiguenave had refused to consider any change in the existing situation. Early in 1924 Borno agreed to the establishment of an *Administration Générale des Contributions* under the direction of officials chosen by agreement between the minister of finance and the general receiver of customs, and in June of that year William E. Dunn was appointed to head the new service. In the same month the council of state passed a new internal revenue law. During the next five years the annual receipts from internal taxes, which had been little more than $150,000 during the first years of the occupation and only $400,000 in 1923, increased to $1,200,000.

One of Russell's first objectives was the establishment of a new treaty service to deal with education and agriculture, and particularly to improve the situation of the peasants who formed the great majority of the Haitian people. The typical peasant had little land and few tools, and cultivated the land he did have in a very inefficient way. The chief money crop was coffee, which grew half-wild in the places where French settlers had once had plantations. There were very few large or well-cultivated farms, for those members of the elite who owned land had little interest in developing it and preferred to live in the cities, where government jobs or trade offered a more attractive livelihood. The Americans hoped that the establishment of order and removal of the restrictions on foreign landownership might encourage the development of large plantations financed by foreign capital, but this would be only a partial answer. The main problem was to make the Haitian peasant more productive: to show him how to be a better farmer, and to reduce the illiteracy and superstition which made him a prey to many kinds of exploitation. This would require a program of education for which the treaty of 1915 made no explicit provision.

The relatively few schools that existed were attended chiefly by children of the mulatto upper class. The best of them were run by French religious orders in the larger towns. The budget provided for public schools throughout the country, but it was estimated in 1921 that only about 14,000 children actually received instruction in them. Most of the money appropriated for them was stolen or diverted to other uses. Many of the American officials had been troubled by this situation, and in 1917 the brigade commander, Colonel Eli K. Cole, persuaded Dartiguenave to employ L. J. Bourgeois of Louisiana as superintendent of public instruction. Bourgeois could accomplish very little, and when he was discharged by the Haitian government in 1920 Russell, who was then brigade commander, recommended that the occupation take control of the educational system. The State Department suggested to Dartiguenave that a joint commission be appointed to study the problem, but the Haitian president replied that the American government's only responsibility with respect to education in Haiti was to see that adequate funds were provided.

Borno was more receptive when Russell suggested in 1922 that the two governments do something about education. He welcomed a suggestion by Senator McCormick that Dr. Robert R. Moton of Tuskegee be asked to make a study of Haiti's educational problems, and in December 1922, Dr. Moton sent Mr. W.T.B. Williams to make a preliminary survey. Meanwhile Russell and Borno discussed what the two governments could do. Borno thought that it would be politically unwise to place the existing school system under American control, but he was willing to accept American help in a new program of agricultural and technical education to be carried out under Article XIII of the treaty of 1915, which provided for the appointment of engineers to carry out projects for the "public improvement" of Haiti. An agreement for the appointment of an "agricultural engineer" and an "assistant agricultural engineer" was signed in April 1923. A few days later Dr. George F. Freeman, who seemed to be one of the very few Americans qualified by training and experience to direct an agricultural development program in a tropical country, was nominated to head the *Service Technique de l'Agriculture et de l'Enseignement Professionel*. The new treaty service was to institute programs of agricultural and vocational education and a broad program for the increase of agricultural production. Dr. Carl Colvin, who was to have charge of the vocational and professional schools, was appointed as assistant agricultural engineer a year later.

It was hoped that the *Service Technique*'s schools would create a whole new class of productive citizens: farmers who were more efficient and prosperous and had a stake in the stability of the government, and artisans in the cities with skills that would make them useful in the development of new industries. Russell thought that the "classical" education offered in the existing Haitian schools guided the pupils *from* rather than *toward* productive industry,[21] preparing young people for the professions or for clerical work, but inculcating a distaste for manual labor. Under the new program, the chief emphasis was on the establishment of farm schools where peasant children could be given the rudiments of an education and taught better farming methods.

[21] *Annual Report of the High Commissioner for 1925*, p. 6.

94

A central school of agriculture, which could train Haitians as teachers for these, opened in June 1924. In 1925, ten rural farm schools were established with a total enrollment of 642 and by 1930 the number had increased to sixty-five, with 7,493 pupils.[22] Even these provided instruction for an insignificant proportion of the peasant children, especially as many of those enrolled attended irregularly. Many parents were at first suspicious of a program which put the children to work in the school gardens rather than in their own, but they became more interested in the schools as time went on.

The central school also trained teachers for the new industrial schools and trained Haitians to take part in the *Service Technique*'s programs for the control of plant and animal diseases and its demonstration and experimental work. In addition it offered courses in engineering and other technical subjects to prepare young men for positions in government departments or in private enterprise. In 1929 it had 207 regular students and 447 enrolled in a summer school for teachers. Eight industrial schools were set up in Port au Prince and five in other towns, with a total enrollment which reached 4,000 in 1928-29.

Though Russell reported in 1928 that all of the *Service Technique*'s schools were "filled to overflowing" as soon as they opened,[23] the program encountered much hostile criticism. It was unpopular with the elite, who disliked what seemed to be an effort to change their traditional educational system, and who had no interest in the welfare of the peasants and the urban proletariat. The elite were cool to the idea of building up a middle class which might challenge their own political and social ascendency. Some of the criticism, unfortunately, was justified. The course work at the central school suffered from the fact that few of the American teachers spoke French. It was difficult to recruit teachers for the farm schools, because few peasant children could read and write and few boys in the towns had any desire to live and work in the country. Each year fifty students were given scholarships of $20 per month in return for a promise to teach in the farm schools after graduation, but the results were not entirely satisfactory. The *Service Technique*'s educational program, and its efforts to help Haitian farmers in other ways, could have done much for Haiti if there had been time to develop

[22] *Annual Report for 1929*, p. 39.   [23] *Annual Report for 1927*, p. 6.

them more fully and to correct some of the early shortcomings, but it was still the most vulnerable part of the American treaty organization when nationalist resistance to the occupation became violent in 1929-1930.

Rather large expenditures on the *Service Technique* cut down the amount of money available for the older treaty services, but coordination under the direction of the high commissioner and diminishing friction with Haitian officials made their work more efficient. The Americans who held the higher positions in these treaty services were for the most part competent and genuinely interested in their work. In choosing civilian appointees Hughes and his successors were able to resist the political pressures which had led to unfortunate appointments in the Dominican Republic and in a few cases in Haiti during the Wilson administration.

The most important civilian appointee was the financial adviser. Hord, who succeeded McIlhenny, suddenly resigned to accept another position in July 1923, and W. W. Cumberland, who had been foreign trade adviser in the State Department and later adviser to the reserve bank of Peru, took his place in December 1923. Cumberland became both financial adviser and collector general of customs, an arrangement which the Haitian government had urged and which made for economy and efficiency. He made some enemies by his aggressive defense of the Haitian government's interests, but he gave the financial services a vigorous leadership which they had lacked under his immediate predecessors. When he resigned in 1927 to go into private business, Arthur C. Millspaugh, who had also been foreign trade adviser in the State Department, and more recently financial adviser to Persia, succeeded him. Millspaugh left Haiti in 1929, after a series of disagreements with General Russell. Sydney de la Rue, who took his place, stayed at Port au Prince until the United States ceased to have any responsibility for Haiti's finances.

The *Service Technique* was also staffed by civilians, but the Americans in the other treaty services were for the most part from the navy or the marine corps. Nearly all the officers in the *gendarmerie* were marines: officers who were given a higher rank in the police than they held in the marine corps, or noncommissioned officers who served as lieutenants or captains. There were several civil engineers from the United States Navy in the public works administration, and several navy doctors in the health service.

The older treaty services continued the programs which they had started before Russell's appointment. By 1923 roads connecting Port au Prince with most of the other principal towns had been made passable for automobiles, though they had been built as rapidly and cheaply as possible and required constant maintenance and improvement. The public works administration also improved communications with towns which were not on the main roads and with the countless small communities which had no connection with the outside world except by unimproved bridle paths or footpaths. After 1927 it devoted increasing attention to the construction of trails, usable by motor vehicles during the dry season but primarily designed for pack animals and for the peasant women who carried much of the country's commerce on their heads. It also rehabilitated and extended some of the irrigation systems which the French had built in colonial times but which the peasant farmers had been unable to keep up.

The *Service d'Hygiène*, the health service, considerably expanded its work. In 1926 the Haitian government turned over to it the administration of the national medical school at Port au Prince. Most of the Haitian faculty were retained, and a grant from the Rockefeller Foundation provided new teaching equipment and made it possible to send several Haitian doctors to study in France and the United States. The health service continued its programs of sanitation and mosquito control and had hospitals in the principal towns. Its rural clinics, which gave a total of 1,431,000 treatments in 1929, reached the peasants in all parts of the country. The three serious diseases which were most prevalent among the country people—yaws, malaria, and intestinal parasites—were all easily diagnosed and responded well to treatment, and the peasants were quick to appreciate the benefits which the clinics brought them. The health service was the most popular part of the American establishment.

Nearly all of the work of the treaty services had to be carried on with the Haitian government's own very limited resources. The United States paid the regular salaries of the marines and naval personnel assigned to the services, but each individual also received additional pay from the Haitian government. The Haitian government paid all of the salaries in the financial service and the *Service Technique*. Since only a small balance remained from the 1922 loan after the debts had been refunded, and since the Haitian government's total income was not more than $8,000,000 to $10,000,000 each year, the amount available for schools and roads and sanitation was pitifully small. The history of the occupation might have been quite different if it had been politically possible in 1922 to ask the United States Congress to appropriate money for foreign aid; but in the 1920's the payment of the salaries of the marine and naval officers working for the Haitian government, which amounted to about $500,000 each year,[24] was regarded as generous.

The amount of money available for public works was made smaller by the fact that Cumberland, while he was financial adviser, insisted on maintaining a large surplus in the treasury and on reducing the foreign debt more rapidly than the contracts required. Cumberland thought that large development programs should be delayed until the treaty services had built up trained staffs to deal with them efficiently and until there was assurance that funds would be available to maintain good roads and other projects after they had been completed. A policy of rapid loan repayment would strengthen the government's credit and make it easier to borrow more money when it could be used effectively. Cumberland thought, too, that real economic progress could come only with substantial investments of foreign capital.[25]

Most of the American officials who dealt with Haiti believed that the establishment of plantations financed by foreign capital would help to promote the economic development which was a chief purpose of the treaty of 1915. There seemed to be no other quick way to increase production and provide employment for the great numbers of Haitians who were always eager to work even at the prevailing wage of 20 cents per day. It was in the hope of encouraging foreign investment that the United States had insisted on a provision authorizing the ownership of land by foreigners when the Haitian constitution was revised in 1918. The change was unpopular in Haiti, where foreign landownership had always been thought of as a danger to the country's independence; and one of the chief causes of the controversy between Dartiguenave and the American officials in 1920 had been the

[24] Russell to Kellogg, Feb. 10, 1926, 838.51/1868.

[25] Cumberland expressed these ideas in conversations with me. For his views about foreign capital, see the financial program which he submitted to Russell in 1924. Russell to Hughes, Nov. 20, 1924, 838.51/1733.

passage of a law making the acquisition of land by foreigners more difficult. This law was superseded in 1925 by one which gave foreigners and foreign corporations the right to own land for residential, agricultural, commercial, industrial, or educational purposes.

The establishment of foreign agricultural enterprises was still made difficult by the chaotic state of land titles. After independence, the government claimed the ownership of all lands which had belonged to the French colonists, but since then much of the government's property had been taken over, legally or illegally, by private individuals and much had been occupied by peasant squatters. No one knew how much the government still owned because the domanial records had been destroyed in a fire in 1888. There was no system for determining or registering land titles.

The American treaty officials thought that it was imperative to set up a system, not only to encourage agricultural development but to increase the very small amount of revenue which the government was receiving in rents for the land that still belonged to the state. General Russell and his advisers prepared a project for a cadastral law in 1927, but the State Department did not approve it because it foresaw appalling possibilities of abuse if land titles were settled by Haitian courts. Judge Robert C. Round, the author of the Dominican Republic's land registration law, was employed to draw up a new project but in the end no action was ever taken. One formidable obstacle to a cadastral law was the expense of the survey which would be necessary. The Haitian government could hardly afford to assume it, and it seemed inadvisable to compel the peasants to pay for their titles.[26]

Very little land in Haiti actually passed into foreign hands. In the first years of the occupation there were a few efforts to establish foreign plantations. The Haitian American Corporation started its large sugar plantation near Port au Prince, which later became profitable, but other foreign ventures were unsuccessful. The West Indies Trading Company acquired some land near St. Michel in 1919 to raise castor beans for airplane lubricants. It later planted 4,000 acres in long staple cotton, but this was destroyed by a fungus disease and the company went out of busi-

---

[26] Millspaugh, Arthur C., *Haiti Under American Control, 1915-1930* (Boston, 1931), p. 170. The correspondence about the cadastral law is in file 838.32.

ness. Potential investors showed more interest in Haiti after 1921, when it appeared that the American occupation would continue, but they wanted tax exemptions and other special privileges to offset the risks involved in a new venture in a strange country, and they found it difficult to obtain them. Each proposal for a concession had to be negotiated with the American treaty officials, who tried to make sure that the Haitian government would derive the maximum benefit from the deal, and also with the State Department, which was equally careful to eliminate any monopolistic or unduly favorable provisions. The State Department was inclined to be especially cautious, and sometimes rather uncooperative, in several cases where congressmen or other politically influential people seemed to have a personal interest in the proposed concessions. After spending months or years in the effort to frame proposals which the American government would support, the promoters then had to obtain the approval of Borno and the council of state. In some cases, at least, this involved the payment of bribes.

One of the few enterprises that were established was the Haitian Pineapple Company. In 1922 the California Packing Corporation approached the treaty officials with a proposal to grow pineapples in Haiti. It asked for the exclusive right to export pineapples from the republic, arguing that the smooth cayenne plants, which it would have to import, could easily be stolen by other persons who might wish to export the fruit. Russell refused to approve a monopoly, and he and the treaty officials proposed instead that the one percent income tax which the company would pay should be halved if similar privileges were granted to anyone within twenty years and that the company should be exempt from most other Haitian taxes. The company did not accept this and enlisted the help of Congressman Knutson of Minnesota and ex-Congressman Rodenberg of Illinois in an effort to get better terms through the State Department. After two months of discussion, in which Russell took part, the department approved a new project which was more acceptable to the company in some respects, though it gave it no monopoly and cut the term of the proposed concession from 99 to 50 years. The company then obtained the approval of the Haitian government, after reportedly paying $45,000 in graft.[27] It started work in 1923

[27] See Assistant Secretary Harrison's memorandum of a conversation with Mr. Heroy of the Sinclair Oil Company, Nov. 14, 1923, 838.63/58.

on 5,000 acres of leased land near Cape Haitian, but a disease which attacked the new plantings made the venture a failure.[28]

Congressman Knutson was also active in an effort by the New York firm of Flynn, Marbourg and Flynn to obtain a monopoly of the export of logwood from Haiti. McIlhenny, to whom the project was submitted in January 1921, favored it because he thought that it promised a fairer return to the peasants and more revenue to the government than either received under existing conditions. He was ready to give the monopoly to Flynn, Marbourg and Flynn without competitive bidding because it was the only American firm exclusively engaged in the logwood business in Haiti. The proposal was discussed for more than a year by various offices of the State Department, but in July 1922 Secretary Hughes turned it down on the ground that the award of exclusive privileges to an American firm without giving other companies, American and foreign, a chance to bid on it would be inconsistent with the American government's open-door policy. Six months later Flynn, Marbourg and Flynn suggested that the Haitian government ask for competitive bids, but Russell recommended that no action be taken pending the arrival of the agricultural expert who was to head the *Service Technique*. Though the company continued to press the matter, and Knutson threatened to make trouble for the State Department in Congress, no further action was taken.[29]

Ex-Congressman Rodenberg and two or three other Republican politicians were the promoters of another project, to irrigate the valley of the Artibonite River. Russell had estimated that from 80,000 to 100,000 acres of land in this valley could be made productive if water were brought to them, and he thought that the development of this region was the most important economic problem that confronted the Haitian government.[30] Since the Haitian government could not do the necessary work with its own resources, he and the treaty officials were disposed to welcome a proposal which would make capital available for the work under satisfactory conditions. It proved very difficult, however, to reconcile the promoter's desire for terms which would encourage the investment of capital with the treaty officials' desire to protect Haitian interests. The promoters hoped to make their

[28] The correspondence about the pineapple concession is in file 838.6159.
[29] The correspondence about the logwood concession is in file 838.602 F 67.
[30] See his annual report for 1923, p. 10 and the report for 1924, p. 3.

profit from the cultivation of bananas and other products on large tracts of land which they would lease or purchase and from the sale of water to other landholders in each irrigation district, and there was a long argument over 'the rentals to be paid for government lands and especially over the rates which the company might charge for water and the treatment of peasants who could not or would not pay for water when the company made it available. Neither Russell nor the State Department wished to have the treaty officials accused of forcing the Haitians off their land for the benefit of an American company. At Secretary Kellogg's request, Dr. Elwood Meade, the United States commissioner of reclamation, looked into the matter, and on his advice the company decided to confine its efforts principally to the irrigation of land which it would itself acquire and cultivate. A concession was approved by the Haitian council of state in 1927, but the promoters could not raise the capital which they needed, and the concession was cancelled by the Haitian government in 1931.

The one important new source of income that was developed by American capital, aside from sugar, was sisal. The *Service Technique* demonstrated the feasibility of sisal production in Haiti, by making experimental plantings and procuring decorticating machinery. In 1927 De Coppet and Doremus, an American company, negotiated a contract to lease up to 8,000 hectares of land from the Haitian government for sisal production at a rent equal to 6% of the land's appraised value. The government agreed not to increase the existing export duties on the fiber which the company produced. The company established plantations near Fort Liberté on the north coast, chiefly on land which was of little value for other crops. Its product soon became one of Haiti's principal exports.

In 1930 American companies owned only 5,291 hectares in Haiti, of which the sugar company had 3,034. 14,479 hectares were leased, mostly from private Haitian owners. The total was less than two percent of the estimated amount of land in the Haitian plains, where most of the country's arable land was situated.[31]

The treaty officials' determination to protect the interests of the Haitian government also led to controversies with American com-

[31] Memorandum submitted by the financial adviser to the Forbes Commission, March 12, 1930, 838.51A/174½.

panies which were already established in Haiti. The most important of these was the National City Bank of New York, which before the occupation was part owner of the National Bank of Haiti and had an interest in the national railroad. Some critics of American policy alleged that the purpose of the intervention was to protect these interests. It is true that the State Department had often supported the National City Bank in its disputes with the Haitian government before 1915, and that these disputes probably helped to convince the Wilson administration that intervention was necessary, but the situation changed after the American government took over responsibility for Haiti's financial administration. The State Department insisted on changes in the contractual provisions for a reform of the currency to make the plan sounder and less profitable to the bank, and when the National City Bank bought out the other stockholders and became sole owner of the national bank in 1920, the department withheld its approval until the national bank agreed to a substantial reduction in the commissions which it received on all receipts and payments on government account. The State Department also proposed that the bank be required to pay interest on the government's deposits, but President Dartiguenave refused to agree, apparently because he thought that the government's funds should be held intact in the bank's vaults and not used in business transactions. The National City Bank was unhappy about the State Department's policy and its president complained to Hughes in 1922 about the treatment which the bank had received from the officials in the department who dealt with Haitian affairs.[32] The bank obtained the contract for the Haitian government's loan of 1922, but only because it submitted the best bid.

The failure to receive interest on deposits became more costly after the 1922 loan gave the government a considerable amount of money which would not be spent for some months or years. The financial adviser consequently transferred $3,000,000 of the loan proceeds and customs receipts to New York. The National City Bank paid interest on it, but Cumberland insisted on better terms and threatened to remove the funds to another bank which offered a higher rate. The State Department urged caution. It thought that the national bank's contractual right to serve as sole depositary for all Haitian government funds might be upheld if

[32] Mitchell to Hughes, June 7, 1922, 838.51/1285.

the matter were submitted to arbitration, as the bank's concession required, and that in that case the Haitian government might receive no interest at all. After some further argument, however, the bank finally agreed to pay Haiti the same interest which it paid on other foreign deposits.

The changes on which the State Department and the treaty officials insisted made the national bank's concession less onerous to the Haitian government and less profitable to the bank, but it did not make the bank's operations unprofitable. Its stockholders received dividends of 10% in 1927, 12% in 1928, 14% in 1929, and 14% in 1930.[33] This was not, however, an unconscionable return on an investment in a country where the future was so uncertain.

There were still more unpleasant controversies with the American corporation which owned the P.C.S. Railroad, the tramway at Port au Prince, the electric light companies at Port au Prince and Cape Haitian, and the wharf at Port au Prince, as well as the large sugar mill and plantations near the capital. All of these enterprises, except the sugar company, had formerly belonged to a group of Germans and German-Americans, who sold them during the world war to some American investors from the Middle West. After the company went through bankruptcy in 1921, it was reorganized as the Haitian Corporation of America. It began to make profits a few years later, partly because tariff protection enabled it to sell its sugar at high prices in Haiti. In 1925 it reported an investment of nearly $8,000,000, most of it in Hasco, as the sugar company was called, and in the P.C.S. Railroad.

Some of the concessions under which the corporation's older subsidiaries were doing business contained provisions which the American treaty officials considered objectionable, and efforts to change these and disputes about their interpretation gave rise to much bad feeling. The disputes put the State Department in a difficult position. It sympathized with the treaty officials' determination to protect Haiti's interests but could not permit them to treat an American company unfairly. It could have withheld protection if it had been convinced that the company's claims were unconscionable, but it was hard to say that privileges granted before the intervention, to induce investment in a country where the risks were so great, had been unreasonable. Frequently, too, there was room for doubt about the legal questions involved. In

[33] Armour to Stimson, Nov. 19, 1932, 838.51/2562.

some cases the company had favorable decisions from the Haitian courts, which were always ready to decide against the treaty officials.

The most serious dispute related to the claims of the P.C.S. Railroad, the *Chemin de Fer de la Plaine du Cul de Sac*, which operated two short lines from Port au Prince to Lake Saumâtre and to Leogane. The first of these had been built under a concession which guaranteed the company a subvention in the absence of profits, and there had been a longstanding dispute about the amount due; the government maintained that its obligation was limited to a payment of 6% on the invested capital, while the company asserted that the government had guaranteed a 6% return on this capital so that it should also make up any deficit incurred in the operation of the line. The claims commission rejected the company's claim for past deficits in 1925, but the company maintained that this decision did not settle the matter.

The American treaty officials doubted whether the railroad should receive any subvention at all. They estimated that the Lake Saumâtre line could not have cost more than $327,000, whereas the subvention was based on an alleged expenditure of $688,000, and they had information indicating that the company had in fact had substantial profits in some years when it claimed a deficit. After 1922 the company's lines carried little freight except cane for the Hasco mill and it carried this at low rates which assured a deficit. In December 1925, the financial adviser refused to approve the usual annual payment of $41,280 for the interest guarantee unless the company surrendered its claim for past operating deficits. The State Department, however, thought that this action was unjustified and ordered that the payment be made.

Meanwhile, the Haitian Corporation of America had been quarrelling with the treaty officials about other matters. The corporation claimed that the customs service was collecting import duties from its sugar company and its electric light plants in violation of their concessions and without regard for decisions in favor of the company in the Haitian courts. It refused to accept the State Department's offer to arbitrate the dispute. The State Department's solicitor nevertheless studied the matter and expressed the opinion that the sugar company's claim for $23,858 should be paid, but that the electric light company's claim for

$12,958 had less merit. The financial adviser, after some protest, consequently paid the sugar company's claim in March 1929.

There was another controversy over the payment of dues for the use of the wharf at Port au Prince. Under a concession obtained in 1906, the wharf company collected one dollar per ton on all merchandise imported or exported at Port au Prince, even when the goods did not pass over its wharf. The treaty officials considered this an unjustifiable privilege which discouraged trade. The customs service nevertheless collected the wharf dues for the company until 1926. A law passed in that year turned the collection over to the company, but this arrangement was soon discontinued because the payments which the company exacted, especially in the case of flour imports, caused loud complaints. The company contested the legality of the change and began to sue importers in the Haitian courts for dues which they had already paid to the government. When the Haitian Supreme Court decided in favor of the company, the State Department ordered the financial adviser to accept the decision.

The dispute about the P.C.S. interest guarantee was revived at the end of 1927 when President Borno flatly refused to approve the annual payment and brought suit in the Haitian courts to have the railroad's concession annulled on the ground that it was no longer a public utility but merely a subsidiary of the sugar company. The State Department urged Borno to make the payment, but he refused, and the negotiations which followed merely intensified the bitter feeling between the Haitian Corporation of America on the one hand and President Borno and the treaty officials on the other. In the summer of 1928 the corporation approached the republican national committee with threats to publish damaging statements about the situation in Haiti during the presidential campaign. A year later, however, it changed its attitude and offered to discuss a compromise settlement along lines which the State Department had suggested some months earlier. General Russell and Sidney de la Rue, the financial adviser, came to Washington and in October 1929 they and the representatives of the company agreed on a settlement which was later approved by the Haitian government.

Under the new contract, the railroad became a private line, operated without supervision from the government. The company agreed to remove the tramway tracks from Port au Prince. With the advent of buses and jitneys, the tramway cars, drawn by wood-burning locomotives which belched smoke and sparks through the principal streets, had already ceased to operate. The railroad tracks in the city were to be relocated. The P.C.S. interest guarantee was canceled, but the company received $155,000 for payments already due and an additional $55,000 to cover the cost of track removal and relocation. It was also agreed that the government should purchase the wharf at Port au Prince at a price based on ten times the revenue which the company received from it. All claims of the Haitian Corporation of America and its subsidiaries against the Haitian government were to be considered settled.

There was little change in the political situation in Haiti between 1922 and 1930. Borno and the council of state which he appointed continued to cooperate with the high commissioner. It will be remembered that the council of state was authorized by the constitution of 1918 to perform the functions of a congress until the president of Haiti should see fit to hold elections in an even-numbered year. In 1923, Borno asked the American government's advice about holding a congressional election in 1924. Secretary Hughes replied that the question was one which the Haitian government must decide for itself. If Borno considered an election necessary, the United States would cooperate to maintain order, but if he thought that the continuance of the council of state would facilitate action on such matters as the internal revenue law, the combination of the offices of the financial adviser and the general receiver, and the reorganization of the national railroad, the United States would not object. Borno was delaying action on these matters at the time, because he resented the American government's failure to support him in repressing hostile criticism. Hughes said that the continuance of the existing situation could not be contemplated as a permanent policy, but it might be justified as a temporary measure to facilitate reforms necessary for the realization of the objects of the 1915 treaty.[34]

The officers who dealt with Haitian affairs in the State Department did not feel that they could support Borno in holding an election in the usual Haitian style, and the alternative was to permit the election of a hostile Congress which might cause incalculable difficulties for Borno and for the treaty services. Borno was not so unpopular in 1923 as he became later, but in Haiti the political leaders tended to oppose any president, after he took of-

[34] Hughes to Dunn, Sept. 29, 1923, 817.00/1967.

fice, if only because the choice of a new president offered them the opportunity for personal profit. In the Latin American division, we fully intended at this time to insist on an election in 1926, when Borno's term was to end.

As 1926 approached, however, the prospect of having an elected congress seemed just as unattractive as in 1923. When Borno told Russell in February 1925 that the Haitian government did not think that an election should be held, Russell was instructed to say that the United States would not object if the president in his own discretion decided that a popular election was inadvisable. The State Department went on to say, however, that the American government felt obligated under the treaty of 1915 to help Haiti develop a satisfactory electoral system, which was indispensable to stability in a country whose constitution was based on republican principles. Russell was asked to prepare an electoral law which could be applied in the communal elections of January 1926 and which would make possible national elections when it seemed advisable to hold them. Russell presented a draft electoral law to the State Department in June 1925, but the department was doubtful about some of its provisions and especially about one which would have legislated political parties into existence. It suggested that an expert be sent to Haiti to study the problem, but Russell thought that neither Borno nor the opposition leaders would agree to this. The idea of reforming the electoral system then seems to have been dropped.

On October 8, 1925 Borno published a long statement explaining his decision not to hold legislative elections in 1926. The masses of peasants, he said, were still incapable of exercising the right to vote, and most of the townspeople, disgusted with immoral maneuvers and insolent frauds, were not interested in voting. For democratic suffrage there must be organized parties with platforms, and these did not exist. The government was preparing an electoral law which would make possible the creation of parties and the constitution of an intelligent electoral body, and it intended to have legislative elections when the time was appropriate. The statement did not seem to evoke any great outburst of popular indignation in Haiti.

When the time for communal elections came, in January 1926, none were held in the entire department of Port au Prince or in several important towns in other departments. When the State Department expressed concern about this, Borno asserted that in most cases the local politicians had prevented elections by stealing registration books or by other tricks. It seemed more probable, however, that the Haitian government itself, in many cases at least, had ordered that there be no voting, because it wished to keep the municipal administrations in the hands of its friends.[35]

As the end of Borno's term approached, there was a marked resurgence of hostility to him and to the occupation. American warships kept out of Haitian waters during the electoral period at Borno's request, because the opposition was circulating rumors about a secret treaty giving the United States a naval base in Haiti. The opposition did not seem to be very well organized, for Russell listed twenty-five men as the "most prominent" of the announced candidates for the presidency.[36] Their hope of defeating Borno, in a vote in his handpicked council of state, was less fantastic than one might suppose. There was reason to doubt the loyalty even of some members of the president's cabinet, and it was impossible to be sure that Borno's appointees on the council of state would not turn against him at the last minute as the councillors had turned against Dartiguenave in 1922. When the council met for the election, however, Borno was in full control. The diplomatic corps and many of the candidates were present, and the proceedings were orderly. The councillors were not searched for weapons before entering the hall, as they had been in 1922, but at Russell's special request they left their arms in the anteroom. In June 1926, after being inaugurated for his second term, Borno visited the United States and was entertained at the White House.

There was no serious disorder in Haiti between 1921 and 1929. The *gendarmerie*, renamed the *Garde d'Haiti* in 1928, took over most of the police work and did it well. The marine brigade was concentrated at Port au Prince and Cape Haitian. The technical state of martial law, proclaimed in 1915, still existed. It had little practical effect, but it permitted the brigade's provost courts to deal with offenses against the marines and with any activities which the American military authorities considered dangerous to public order. Although the State Department thought that martial law must be maintained, for the protection of the marines.

---

[35] Kellogg to Russell, Feb. 1, and Russell to Kellogg, Jan. 26, Feb. 3, 1926, 838.00/2189, 2190, 2191.

[36] *General Conditions Report*, April 8, 1926, 838.00/2221.

It did not like to have Haitians punished by the brigade courts, especially in cases where the offenses were motivated by opposition to the Haitian government or the occupation. In August 1922, when Russell ordered that three newspapermen be brought before a provost court for publishing intemperate attacks on President Borno, he was instructed to rescind the order if he could do so without serious injury to American prestige. Russell released the prisoners, but he said that Borno, who had ordered the arrests, was much disturbed. Russell pointed out that the American forces in Haiti would have little protection if they had to look to the Haitian courts to punish actions that endangered them.[37] The State Department replied that it recognized that provost courts must be used in aggravated cases to protect the American forces and treaty officials, but said that they should rarely if ever be employed to protect Haitian officials or individuals, or to punish newspaper attacks on them, except perhaps in cases where the suppression of newspaper propaganda was manifestly necessary to maintain the peace. The obvious way to check abuses by the press was to enact adequate laws, and to reform the judiciary so that the Haitian government could enforce the laws through its own courts. The department realized that this would take time, and that meanwhile provost courts might have to be used in exceptional cases; but it pointed out that the trial of Haitians by provost courts embarrassed it and might subject its policy to serious criticism.

Apparently as a result of the State Department's suggestion, Borno promulgated a new press law in December 1922. He must have discussed it with Russell, but the State Department knew nothing about it until after it was in force. The law set heavy penalties for insults, outrages, or defamations committed through the press against officials of the government or foreign diplomats, and forbade the courts to grant bail to persons accused of such offenses. No periodical might be published without the authorization of the secretary of the interior.[38] These provisions would enable the government to prevent the publication of opposition newspapers and to deal harshly with unfriendly critics. The State Department did not feel that it should demand the repeal of the measure, but it asked Russell to use his influence to see that the

[37] Russell to Hughes, Sept. 6, 1922, 838.00/1904. A part of this dispatch is printed in *Foreign Relations, 1922*, Vol. II, p. 555.
[38] Russell sent the text in his dispatch of Dec. 20, 1922, 838.91.

law was not enforced in a way likely to arouse criticism or to make martyrs of offending newspapermen.[39]

Borno and Russell thought that the department did not appreciate the importance of checking the violent press campaign which the government's opponents were carrying on. The nationalist newspapers, and especially the *Courrier Haitien* edited by Jolibois *fils*, were publishing scurrilous attacks on the president and the treaty officials, apparently trying to see how far they could go before the government or the marines felt compelled to react. Russell knew that there was real danger that their incendiary articles might lead to rioting or inspire violent attacks on individuals. The *gendarmerie*, or as a last resort the marines, could probably control any disorder that occurred, but it would be better to suppress disorderly tendencies before they led to bloodshed. He said that the new press law was not entirely satisfactory, because the Haitian courts usually refused to convict persons arrested under it. Offenders could be held for long periods without bail and without trial, but this exposed the government and also the *gendarmerie* to justified criticism. Russell still felt that he should be authorized to use provost courts when he considered it necessary.

Borno was so resentful about what he considered the American government's failure to support him that he suspended action on several matters in which the State Department was interested and asked Russell to discuss the situation with the State Department when the High Commissioner visited Washington in the summer of 1923. The department did not change its position. Russell was authorized to assure Borno that the American government appreciated the dangerous character of the recent press attacks and would support any proper measures to control them. Control, however, should be exercised under Haitian law and through Haitian courts. The American government did not want provost courts to be used, except possibly in cases where their use was urgently required for the maintenance of order, and then only on specific instructions from the State Department. They should not be used simply because the Haitian courts refused to act, for the Haitian government should be able to correct deficiencies in its own courts. If treaty officials were subjected to newspaper attacks which could not be ignored without hurting their prestige, Russell might ask the Haitian government to act

[39] Harrison to Russell, Aug. 21, 1923, 338.3821 Jolibois *fils*.

111

through its own courts, and the government would have a duty to do so. Wherever possible, however, criticism of treaty officials should be ignored.[40]

Russell thought that the department's attitude was unrealistic. A few weeks after he received the secretary's instruction, the *gendarmerie* broke up a nationalist meeting at Cape Haitian and arrested Jolibois and two companions, who were urging the audience to work for Haiti's independence. The high commissioner thought that agitation of this sort could only lead to bloodshed, and since the prisoners would certainly be released if they were brought before a Haitian court he recommended that they be tried by a provost court. The State Department did not approve and the arrested nationalists were released without being brought to trial at all. Soon afterward, however, Borno, at Russell's request, ordered the arrest of Jolibois and four colleagues for publishing an article defaming the *gendarmerie*. They were held without bail for several months, until the court of *cassation* ordered their release. During the next few years, newspapermen and nationalist propagandists were repeatedly imprisoned for varying periods, under the press law, without bail and without trial. By August 1926, Jolibois had been jailed fourteen times for a total of thirty-four months, though he was actually convicted only once.[41] He became a national hero and an international celebrity through the publicity which he received from the anti-imperialist press abroad.

The high commissioner and the *gendarmerie*, and consequently the American government, shared the responsibility for this rather questionable policy of repression. The State Department did not like it but it hesitated to forbid actions which Russell and Borno considered necessary for the preservation of order. Its policy did almost stop the trial of Haitians by provost courts, and martial law became little more than a technicality. Senator McCormick, in January 1924, urged that martial law be abolished altogether, but Hughes pointed out that the usefulness of the marine brigade would depend on its ability to exercise the authority of an occupying force in case of necessity, and that the marines could not be protected without this authority.[42]

40 Hughes to Russell, Sept. 29, 1923, 838.00/1964.
41 Merrell to Kellogg, Aug. 2, 1926, 838.00/2267.
42 McCormick to Coolidge, Jan. 13, Jan. 19; Hughes to McCormick, Feb. 6, 1924, 838.00/1997, 1998, 2000.

The judiciary was unquestionably the weakest branch of the Haitian government. Except for the *Cour de Cassation*, the highest tribunal, the courts had always been almost incredibly venal and irresponsible. The impossibility of obtaining justice from them made it difficult both for natives and for foreigners to do business in Haiti, and their hostility to the occupation created troublesome problems. The police complained that they could rarely get convictions of arrested criminals, and civil suits involving the treaty services were almost invariably decided against them. The treaty officials regularly refused to recognize the validity of decisions which would hamper their work or which would require expenditures that the financial adviser did not approve.

The president of Haiti had little control over the courts because the judges were in office for life. In an effort to correct the situation, a transitory provision suspending the irremovability of judges for a period of six months had been incorporated in the constitution of 1918, but this brought about little if any improvement. Russell from the time of his appointment looked on reform of the judiciary as one of his most important objectives. The State Department was also interested, especially as it realized that without reform it would be difficult to avoid the use of provost courts. In September 1922, it asked Judge Richard U. Strong, the legal adviser to the military governor at Santo Domingo, to go to Haiti as legal adviser to General Russell, especially to prepare a plan for judicial reform. Strong made several recommendations, which Secretary Hughes approved after examining them himself, but Borno was reluctant to adopt most of them. A law passed early in 1925 cut down the number of judges somewhat and increased their salaries, but Russell reported that this did little good.[43] It seemed clear that what was needed was a constitutional amendment which would change the whole system.

Russell discussed the question with Borno, and in April 1927, the president came forward with a project for a number of constitutional amendments, dealing not only with the judiciary but with several other matters. The proposal would have made possible Borno's reelection for a six-year term in 1930. When Russell discussed Borno's draft in the State Department, during a short visit in May, some of the officers there raised objections to the re-

[43] The correspondence about Strong's project is in file 838.04.

113

election provision and some other features of the draft, but they apparently did not make themselves entirely clear. When Russell returned to Port au Prince, he gave Borno to understand that his proposals were approved. Russell then left for a vacation in Europe. Borno submitted the proposed amendments to the council of state and made them public, and he was indignant when the State Department sent word that some of them, including the re-election provision, were unacceptable. After some discussion, the State Department agreed to most of the proposed amendments, including the increase in the presidential term, but Borno promised that he would not seek reelection in 1930.

The most important of the amendments authorized the president to make changes in the personnel of the courts during a period of twelve months. Another limited the terms of the judges of the court of *cassation* to ten years and those of other judges to seven years. An amendment to which Russell attached much importance did away with jury trials in cases involving offenses by the press. Another proposal which would have deprived the court of *cassation* of its authority to pass on the constitutionality of acts of Congress was abandoned because the State Department refused to approve it. The changes in the constitution were approved in January 1928, by a plebiscite in which 177,436 citizens voted "yes" and 3,799, "no." The *gendarmerie* was instructed to take no part in the election except to maintain order, but the Haitian government appointed temporary *conseillers d'agriculture* to assist in the electoral process. After the plebiscite, Borno called a special session of the council of state to consider laws reorganizing the courts and increasing judges' salaries. A new court of *cassation* was appointed and a fine palace of justice was erected in Port au Prince. In his annual report for the year 1929, however, General Russell could only say, "There has been no material change in the status of the judiciary during the year under review. The problem of the reform of the judiciary is of absolutely fundamental importance for Haitian development."

In the first months of 1929 the American officials in Haiti and the officials who dealt with Haitian matters in the State Department were fairly optimistic about the future of the American experiment there. The treaty services were proud of what they had achieved and looked forward to more constructive work in the years to come. The government's finances were being efficiently and honestly administered. The *garde* had made life and property safe throughout the republic and had improved government at the local level. The new roads had improved communication between the various sections of the country and had encouraged internal commerce. Haitian towns were pleasant and safe places to live in and a great deal had been done to reduce the prevalence of disease in rural areas. The *Service d'Hygiène* was the one treaty service which was rarely criticized even by the nationalists. The *Service Technique* had accomplished less, partly because it had been set up more recently, but there was reason to hope that its educational work and its programs to help farmers and stockraisers would produce benefits in the future. Agricultural production had increased substantially, though not spectacularly, since 1923.

The masses of the people were still poor but the peasants no longer had to fear the periodic destruction of their crops and houses by revolutionary armies, and the *garde* prevented some of the many sorts of oppression from which they had suffered. So far as a foreign visitor could see, they seemed to appreciate what had been done for them. Most of the American officials felt that it was the peasants for whom they were working and thought that much of the hostility to the treaty regime among the elite arose from resentment at the use of the government's resources in projects that would benefit the common people rather than the upper class. They did not take too seriously the increasing nationalist opposition to Borno and to the American occupation because they knew that any Haitian president, once in office, was likely to be attacked by all of the other political leaders. Among the public in general, there was probably less discontent early in 1929, when the country was relatively prosperous, than later in the year when the effects of the depression began to be felt, and when disorders in Port au Prince forced the United States to reconsider its Haitian policy.

Chapter Five

CENTRAL AMERICAN PROBLEMS

The chief obstacle to peace and stable government in Central America had been the constant interference by the governments in one another's internal affairs. Guatemala, El Salvador, Honduras, Nicaragua, and Costa Rica set up a federal republic after they became independent in 1821, but the union disintegrated after several years of civil strife and a number of efforts to revive it were defeated by local jealousies and factional rivalries. In most of the states, however, the political parties which fought to control the government of the federal republic continued to exist. Liberals and conservatives in each country regarded their former associates in neighboring countries as allies and helped them in revolutions against governments controlled by the other party. No president felt entirely secure if he had unfriendly neighbors. Frequently this situation led to international wars in which three or four states were likely to become involved. Only Costa Rica, which developed more stable institutions, was usually able to stay aloof from such conflicts.

In 1907 the United States and Mexico invited the Central American states to a conference in Washington, where representatives of the five governments signed a series of treaties designed to put an end to the chronic disorder which had discouraged any sort of progress in the isthmus. They agreed to submit all disputes between them to a permanent Central American court of justice, and promised not to interfere in one another's internal politics and not to permit the use of their territory as a base for revolutionary activities against other states. All promised to respect the neutrality of Honduras, whose weakness and central position had frequently invited aggression. After 1907 the main effort of American diplomacy in Central America was to persuade or compel the five governments to live up to these agreements.

The principal troublemaker was President José Santos Zelaya of Nicaragua, who opposed American interference in Central

America and continued his efforts to increase his own influence by subverting the governments of his neighbors. After several unpleasant episodes, involving American interests in Nicaragua as well as acts of aggression against other states, the State Department made no attempt to conceal its sympathy with a revolution which began on the east coast of Nicaragua in October 1909. When Zelaya ordered the execution of two American soldiers of fortune who had been serving in the revolutionary army, Secretary Knox publicly denounced him and gave the revolution his moral support. Zelaya's followers continued to resist, but the revolutionists entered Managua and took over the government in August 1910.

It seemed doubtful whether the new administration, controlled by an unstable coalition of conservatives and dissident liberals, could long maintain itself. Secretary Knox and his advisers thought that the best way to help it would be to set up an American customs collectorship and arrange for a foreign loan. They believed that the customs collectorship was responsible for the stability which the Dominican Republic had enjoyed since 1907— a stability which was to end abruptly in 1911—and they were at this time working on a plan for a collectorship and a loan in Honduras, which also seemed to need help. By a treaty signed June 6, 1911, Nicaragua agreed to seek a loan and to entrust the collection of customs to an official nominated by the fiscal agent of the loan and approved by the president of the United States.

When this treaty and a similar treaty with Honduras reached the United States Senate, opposition developed and after some months it became clear that neither would be ratified. Meanwhile, however, the Nicaraguan government signed a tentative loan contract with Brown Brothers and Company and J. and W. Seligman and Company of New York, and pending the flotation of the loan the bankers advanced $1,500,000 to make possible the establishment of a national bank and the reform of the depreciated paper currency. A customs collectorship like that contemplated in the treaty was set up to assure payment. This was the beginning of a series of transactions that involved the bankers and the State Department in Nicaragua's financial affairs between 1911 and 1920, despite the fact that the proposed large loan never materialized. The American government also became deeply involved in the republic's political affairs. It intervened by force to put down a revolt which threatened to bring Zelaya's

117

followers back to power in 1912, and thereafter it maintained a legation guard of about 100 marines at Managua as evidence of its determination to prevent another civil war. This enabled the conservative party to retain control of the government for several years despite the liberals' apparent numerical superiority.

What happened to Zelaya and to the Nicaraguan liberals in 1912 made other Central American political leaders more circumspect about violating the 1907 treaties, and the United States' moral support of constituted governments, frequently indicated by visits of warships where trouble seemed likely, further discouraged revolutions. Between 1911 and 1917 no Central American government was overturned by force. It was not possible, however, to prevent revolutions permanently in countries where the opposition had no other way to obtain control. In 1917, Tinoco, the minister of war in Costa Rica, seized power by a coup d'etat. President Wilson refused to recognize him but at the same time he discouraged attempts at counterrevolution, and Tinoco stayed in power for two years, without recognition, before he was overthrown. In 1919 President Bertrand provoked a civil war in Honduras by attempting to impose an unpopular candidate as his successor. When the United States urged a free election, and threatened to intervene to assure one, Bertrand resigned. Soon afterward the revolutionary army took Tegucigalpa and its leader, General López Gutiérrez, controlled the ensuing election and became president. He was promptly recognized by the United States. In 1920 the American government was compelled to accept the result of a popular uprising which overthrew the dictator Estrada Cabrera in Guatemala.

The American government had also impaired the effectiveness of the 1907 treaties by its own acts. In the Bryan-Chamorro treaty, signed in 1914, Nicaragua gave the United States an option to build an interoceanic canal by way of the San Juan River, part of which formed the boundary between Nicaragua and Costa Rica, and to establish a naval base in the Gulf of Fonseca, in which El Salvador claimed rights. Costa Rica and El Salvador complained to the Central American Court of Justice, which upheld their claims. Neither Nicaragua nor the United States accepted the decision, and Nicaragua denounced the treaty under which the court functioned, so that the tribunal went out of existence in March 1918. Its disappearance raised questions about the continued validity of the principal agreement signed at the 1907 conference, the General Treaty of Peace and Amity, which provided that all disputes not settled by diplomacy should be submitted to the court. The United States nevertheless continued to insist that the other provisions of the general treaty, and especially its prohibition of assistance to revolutions, must be respected.

Many Central American leaders were disturbed about the deterioration of political conditions in the isthmus, and in June 1920, the government of El Salvador proposed that the five states hold a conference to revise the 1907 treaties and to consider steps toward a Central American union. The restoration of the federal republic had always been an aspiration of Central American patriotism and the prospect for success seemed brighter than on previous occasions because a party which advocated the union had just come into power in Guatemala, which was the most powerful of the five states. The conference met at San José, Costa Rica, in December 1920, and drew up a treaty for the establishment of a federal government. Nicaragua, however, withdrew from the meeting after a dispute about the validity of the Bryan-Chamorro treaty, and Costa Rica, though her delegates signed the treaty of union, did not ratify it. Guatemala, Honduras, and El Salvador went ahead with the project. A provisional federal council, with one member from each state, was installed at Tegucigalpa in June 1921, and a constituent assembly met there in July.

When El Salvador first proposed a conference for the establishment of a federal government, Sumner Welles urged that the United States invite the Central American states to hold it in Washington, or at least be represented at the meeting in San José. He thought that a union would promote peace and would be a barrier to Mexican influence in the isthmus. President Wilson, however, refused to encourage the union. Welles understood that the president thought that the United States could exercise more influence in Central America if it were dealing with five independent governments,[1] but it is also possible that Wilson knew something of the unhappy history of previous attempts at union. After the change in administration Welles was apparently able to persuade Secretary Hughes to take a more favorable attitude.

[1] See Welles' memorandum to Hughes, Oct. 22, 1921, 813.00/1136a.

119

Hughes expressed a warm interest in the project in a speech at a luncheon in honor of the Nicaraguan minister of foreign affairs in June 1921.

The assembly at Tegucigalpa produced a federal constitution early in September 1921, and on October 1 the federal government was inaugurated, under the direction of a provisional federal council. For the time being, since the provisional council had no money and no administrative machinery, the state governments continued to function as they had before the union, except that the government of Honduras began to move to the inaccessible little town of Comayagua to permit Tegucigalpa to become the federal district. The people of each state were asked to elect members of a federal congress, which was to meet in January 1922, and one delegate to the permanent federal council which would take office in February 1. There was apparently a relatively free election in Honduras, but in El Salvador the government chose the candidates and did not permit a so-called unionist party to oppose them.[2]

The Central American union was one of the first important matters that I had to deal with after I was detailed to the Latin American division and assigned to the Central American desk in 1921. One of the first acts of the provisional federal council was to send representatives to Washington to ask the moral support of the United States. Many people in Central America and some officials in Washington thought that the attitude of the United States would determine the success or failure of the union, and that we should support it. Others, of whom I was one, feared that success would be unlikely, even with American support, and thought that we should be cautious in dealing with a project which might well end in civil or international war. Early in November Hughes recommended to the president that the United States let it be known that a union established with the consent of the peoples and governments of Guatemala, El Salvador, and Honduras would have the friendly support of the United States. A few days later, however, he sent the president a memorandum by me recommending that the United States do nothing to discourage the union and that the federal government be recognized when it was firmly established, but describing the failure of past attempts at union and discussing the prospect for the suc-

[2] Wilson to Hughes from Tegucigalpa, Nov. 4, 1921, 813.00/1146; Schuyler to Hughes, from San Salvador, Oct. 28, 1921, 813.00/1141.

cess of the current effort. The obstacles to success: the absence of the respect for law and the ability to compromise which were needed to make a federal system work; the difficulties that would arise in connection with the elections; and the failure of the recently drafted constitution to give the federal government adequate power, seemed grave if not insuperable.[3] The idea of an early statement of support for the union was dropped.

When the Central American delegates arrived, they were received by Hughes on November 26 and then had several informal talks with Welles and with me. The results were not encouraging. The delegates could give us little information about the policies which the federal government would follow or even about the concrete steps which it would take to establish its authority. They did not press for immediate recognition. They asked for a public statement of the American government's support of the union, but we indicated that we would want more information about their plans before considering what could be said.[4] The conversations were still going on when President Herrera and the Unionist party were overthrown by a military revolt in Guatemala on December 6.

It was obvious that the attempt at union was ending in the same way that several previous attempts had ended. The new rulers of Guatemala belonged to the liberal party, which traditionally at least had a sentimental interest in union, and they pretended to want to preserve the federal government, but it seemed unlikely that they could work harmoniously with the political groups in El Salvador and Honduras who had been friendly with their predecessors. Many supporters of the federal government, in fact, were urging that El Salvador and Honduras intervene in Guatemala to restore the unionists to power. If they did so, or if Guatemala took the offensive to forestall their intervention, there would be a general Central American war. The danger evaporated, however, when Hughes told each of the Central American governments that the United States would view with the greatest concern any interference by one of them in the affairs of another. He said that no lasting union could be imposed by force. The embryonic federal government at Tegucigalpa disbanded after a

[3] Hughes to Harding, Nov. 2, 1921, 813.00/1136a; Hughes to Harding, Nov. 17, 1921, 813.00/1145a, transmitting my memorandum of Nov. 17, 813.00/1184.

[4] See my memorandum of Dec. 14, 1921, 813.00/1186.

futile attempt to reach an agreement with the new authorities in Guatemala.

There were critics who thought that the Central American union might have succeeded if the United States had given it more support. This criticism reflected an exaggerated idea of what American diplomacy could reasonably be expected to accomplish. It is conceivable that enthusiastic support from Washington and energetic diplomacy might have induced the Central Americans to set up a more effective central government and might for a time have discouraged efforts to overturn it. It could not have changed the basic obstacles to the establishment of a stable union: the political backwardness which made the holding of free elections impossible in most of the five countries, the unwillingness of the groups in power in individual states to give up any of their power, and the other factors which made for instability in the separate states and would be no less troublesome under a federal system. If the United States could not prevent civil wars in the separate states, it could hardly expect to prevent the quarrels and disorders which would break out under a federal government. Any effort to do so would have involved us in constant interference and probably occasional armed intervention in Central American affairs. By 1921 the experience which we had had with intervention in the Caribbean made the idea of assuming new responsibilities unattractive.

Some Central American governments, in fact, were being accused of underhand attempts to foment trouble in neighboring countries even while they were trying to set up the union. In May 1921 an American warship was sent to Amapala at the request of the president of Honduras, who said that he expected an invasion from El Salvador.[5] In August and again in October the Nicaraguan government complained that revolutionary bands were operating near its northern frontier with help from Honduran officials and perhaps from El Salvador. The State Department made representations to both of the accused governments, and asked the War Department to sell a quantity of arms and ammunition to Nicaragua on easy terms to enable that government to defend itself. In January 1922, when the federation was breaking up, there were reports that the Cuyamel Fruit Company, which had aided revolutions in the past, was sending arms to the

[5] Spencer to Hughes, May 2, and Hughes to Spencer, May 4, 1921, 815.00/2253.

north coast of Honduras and that Guatemala and El Salvador and Nicaragua were about to support a revolution there. Investigation at New Orleans and Puerto Cortés did not substantiate the accusation against the fruit company and Honduras' neighbors apparently gave up any plans which they might have had when the United States made vigorous representations to them. The State Department pointed out to Nicaragua that the United States had supplied that government with arms on the assumption that they would be used to maintain peace.[6] Not long afterward the department remonstrated vigorously with President Orellana of Guatemala, who was apparently planning to join with Honduras in fomenting a revolution in El Salvador.

The situation along the border between Nicaragua and Honduras was especially bad, with frequent reports of impending invasions from one side or the other and occasional clashes between the troops of the two governments. It was strongly suspected that Carlos Lagos, the Honduran minister of war, was deliberately making it worse. Neither government wanted war, and in August 1922 the presidents of Nicaragua and Honduras agreed to meet on the U.S.S. *Tacoma* in the Gulf of Fonseca to discuss the situation. At their invitation the president of El Salvador also attended and the American ministers to the three countries were present as observers. On August 20 the three presidents signed an agreement pledging each government to prevent anyone in its territory from fomenting revolution in a neighboring state. They also proposed that a general Central American conference be held in December to discuss measures to improve relations between the five states.

At Washington we welcomed this proposal because we had already decided that a conference ought to be convened to revise and strengthen the 1907 treaties; and in October 1922 the United States invited the Central American governments to meet in Washington to discuss ways to make the 1907 treaties more effective. The proposed agenda included measures for the limitation of armaments and a plan for "tribunals of inquiry" to obtain the facts in disputed situations. To allay misgivings in some quarters in Central America, discussion of a Central American union or a revival of the Central American court was specifically ruled out. The American government offered to participate through

[6] For the correspondence about these events see file 815.00, enclosures 2281 ff.

123

delegates, or merely to extend friendly help outside of the meetings, as the Central American states might desire. Costa Rica thought it would be more appropriate for the United States not to participate formally, but withdrew its suggestion when the other countries did not agree, and Secretary Hughes and Sumner Welles, who had returned to the United States after completing the first phase of his work in the Dominican Republic, were appointed as the American delegates. The conference met in December 1922.

Hughes naturally could not attend many of the meetings, but Welles, apparently without arousing resentment, skillfully steered the conference's work. He was able to obtain the adoption of the greater part of a series of draft treaties which I had prepared to be presented as informal suggestions but not as proposals by the United States. A new General Treaty of Peace and Amity reaffirmed the pledge to settle all disputes peacefully and the requirement that each government prevent anyone in its territory from giving aid to a revolution in a neighboring state. A new court, consisting of a panel of jurists from which the parties could select judges to deal with each dispute which they could not settle otherwise, replaced the old court with its politically appointed members. To some critics this seemed a step backward, but it was an arrangement which promised to be more workable. In a region where there was little tradition of judicial independence, it had been difficult for judges appointed by the governments and serving, in practice, at the pleasure of the party in power, to maintain the independence which an international tribunal should have.

A new convention provided for the establishment of commissions of inquiry to ascertain the facts in cases where violations of the treaties were alleged. We were interested in this because our efforts to maintain peace had often been hampered by the impossibility of finding out what was happening or who was at fault. Frequently the Central American governments themselves did not have the facts. The presidents could not always prevent local officials from surreptitiously aiding would-be revolutionists in a neighboring country, and it was difficult for the weak and inefficient military forces to patrol the national frontiers. We thought that the commissions, to be fully effective, should have American members. There was some opposition to this, but those who raised them were satisfied when the United States agreed to become a party to the convention.

In the 1907 treaties, the signatory states agreed not to recognize a government coming into power in a Central American country by coup d'etat or revolution until the country had been constitutionally reorganized by a free election. Neither the Central American states nor the United States had paid much attention to this provision, though the general practice of the United States was in accord with it. Article II of the new general treaty barred recognition, even after a free election, if the head of a revolutionary government was one of the leaders of the revolt or a close relative of one of the leaders, or if he had been a cabinet officer or had held a high military command at the time of the revolt, or the subsequent election, or within six months preceding the revolt or the election. Furthermore, no government would be recognized if its head were a person expressly disqualified for the presidency or vice-presidency by his country's constitution. Some of us had grave doubts about the wisdom of such a stringent prohibition, but the Central American delegates wanted it and Welles did not think it advisable to oppose them.

Our proposal for a convention for the limitation of armaments aroused no enthusiasm. We had hoped that the success of the recent Washington conference for the limitation of naval armaments might encourage the Central American states to reduce their own expensive but inefficient armies and we had hoped especially to persuade some of the governments to replace at least a part of their armed forces with constabularies trained by foreign instructors. The Central American governments accepted limitation in principle, but each insisted on a maximum number of men under arms considerably larger than the number in its existing forces. The idea of establishing constabularies was accepted in principle, but with obvious reluctance.

On the whole, we were well pleased with the work of the conference. We realized that some of the new treaties would meet with opposition in Central America, and the American ministers in the isthmus were instructed to use their influence to obtain ratification and to see that the agreements were implemented after they had been ratified. The department indicated that it attached special importance to the general treaty, to the conventions dealing with commissions of inquiry, the Central American tribunal, and the limitation of armaments, and to a convention in which the governments had agreed to consider reforms in their electoral laws. By the middle of 1925 most of the new treaties had been ratified by all of the signatories. El Salvador rejected the convention for the Central American tribunal and a part of Article II of the general treaty dealing with recognition. The conference ended in February 1923.

Within a few weeks of the adjournment of the conference, it became evident that a civil war in Honduras might provide the first test of the efficacy of the new treaties. Honduras was the weakest and in many ways the most backward of the Central American states, with a population estimated at about 630,000. The most important region, economically, was the north coast where American fruit companies, the Cuyamel around Puerto Cortés, Vaccaro Brothers at La Ceiba, and the United Fruit at other ports, had plantations which were beginning to make the country the world's greatest exporter of bananas. The companies dominated the economic life of the coast and the customs duties which they paid formed a considerable part of the government's revenue. Much of the work done on the plantations was done by Negroes from the British and French West Indies. Most native Hondurans lived in the scattered valleys of the mountainous interior, in villages or small towns which had changed little since colonial times. Tegucigalpa, the capital, was connected with tidewater on the Gulf of Fonseca by one of the first automobile roads in Central America, but in general travel was by horse- or muleback. Aside from a small silver mine near Tegucigalpa, controlled by American capital, there was little economic activity except cattle raising and small-scale agriculture.

Since independence, Honduras had been a battleground for her stronger neighbors. Rulers in Guatemala and El Salvador and Nicaragua had repeatedly sought to dominate the government, if only to prevent a rival dictator from establishing control there. The neutralization of the country by the 1907 treaties had little practical effect. Constant disorder had discouraged economic progress. Like politicians in most of the Central American states, the Honduran leaders were "liberals" or "conservatives," but the parties tended to split into factions around individual *caudillos* who often had their main support in one locality.

The American government had been trying for many years to persuade the other Central American states to respect Honduras' neutrality and to help the government to remedy the chaotic state of its finances. The Taft administration had insisted that the Honduran government sign a treaty placing its customs under American control and providing for a loan from American bankers to refund the long unpaid British debt. The treaty was rejected both by the Honduran Congress and by the United States Senate, but the State Department continued to be interested in Honduras' financial problem. In 1920 it persuaded President López Gutiérrez to employ Arthur Young, one of the department's ablest economists, as financial adviser. Young accomplished some useful reforms, but honest financial administration was unwelcome to many of the politicians, and in August 1921, despite a rather threatening remonstrance from the State Department, López Gutiérrez terminated Young's contract.

It became clear early in 1923 that there might be trouble in connection with the presidential election to be held in October of that year. Conservatives, with the help of conservative officials in Nicaragua, were already making incursions along the frontier, and several leaders of the president's own liberal party were opposing the efforts of Carlos Lagos, the president's brother-in-law, to control the selection of the liberal candidate. Lagos was no longer minister of war, but he exercised much influence through his sister. There was a political crisis in February, when the president appointed several of Lagos' adherents to his cabinet. The State Department was disturbed because a civil war in Honduras would discredit the new Central American treaties before they were even ratified. Franklin Morales, the new minister at Tegucigalpa, was consequently instructed to remind López Gutiérrez that he had promised to hold a free election, and to say that the evident attempt of one political group to control the election machinery was a threat to the peace of Honduras and of Central America.[7]

Morales was a political appointee from Atlantic City, who had had no diplomatic experience. He delivered the message, but López Gutiérrez merely defended his recent appointments, and Morales was convinced that the president was dominated by his wife and brother-in-law. There seemed to be nothing that the State Department could helpfully do for the time being.

The situation in the liberal party seemed to be the chief danger

---

[7] Hughes to Morales, Feb. 26, 1923, 815.00/2529. For the background, see my memorandum of Feb. 19, 1923, *ibid.*

127

to peace. If there was more than one liberal candidate, and no candidate received a majority, the decision would go to Congress and there was a general belief that this would mean civil war. At Morales' suggestion, López Gutiérrez tried to bring about an agreement between the liberal leaders, but with no success. The State Department was doubtful about the propriety of seeming to interfere in the internal affairs of one party, especially as President Orellana of Guatemala was also trying to encourage the liberals to unite in order to assure the election of a liberal, pro-Guatemalan administration, but it authorized Morales to explore the possibility of finding a compromise candidate acceptable to all parties.[8] As White pointed out, this would mean that the president of Honduras was chosen by a small group of politicians rather than by an election, but free elections seemed impossible. He thought that they might eventually become possible with peace and economic progress.[9] Morales was able to persuade all the candidates to come to a meeting on May 7, but none would withdraw.

Morales continued to work for peace, sometimes with more zeal than wisdom. The State Department felt compelled to caution him when he said that the American government considered one candidate enough for each party and that it would not countenance a revolution. The department continued to hope for the selection of a compromise candidate, and on June 30 it told Morales to issue a public statement emphasizing the gravity of the situation that would ensue if the effort for an agreement between the presidential candidates failed. It said that the American government's attitude with respect to the recognition of any new government would be consonant with the provisions of Article II of the recently signed Treaty of Peace and Amity. This declaration that no one could expect recognition by the United States if he seized power by force enunciated a policy which was to have important consequences, both good and bad, during the next ten years. The State Department was somewhat concerned when it learned that Morales was telling the Hondurans that the statement meant that the United States would not recognize a government imposed by official pressure. The department was not prepared to accept a principle which would make it hard to

[8] Hughes to Morales, April 28, 1923. This telegram, like much of the correspondence on Honduras, was published in *Foreign Relations, 1923*, Vol. II.
[9] White to Phillips, April 26, 1923, 815.00/2630.

maintain relations with most Central American governments, and it warned Morales not to commit it to a policy which it had not announced.[10]

On July 12 the Guatemalan minister suggested to Hughes that the other Central American governments should offer their good offices for a peace in Honduras, working in conjunction with the American minister in Tegucigalpa. This seemed a dangerous proposition. Guatemala had been taking what the department considered an unhealthy interest in the Honduran presidential contest and was undoubtedly seeking to make sure that the liberals stayed in power. Nicaragua, on the other hand, had repeatedly been accused of aiding conservative raids across the frontier. In El Salvador, the historic political parties did not mean so much, but the government apparently wished to avoid the installation of an unfriendly administration in Honduras and the State Department had had to remind it occasionally of its neutral obligations. White advised against acceptance of the Guatemalan proposal, because he thought that each government would simply work for its own friends and the conference would be a failure.[11]

As election day approached, tension increased. Tiburcio Carías, the conservative candidate, claiming that the government was mistreating him and his supporters, threatened to revolt even if it should mean that he would not be recognized if he became president. The division in the liberal party continued. López Gutiérrez was now supporting the veteran liberal leader Policarpo Bonilla, while Lagos had come out for Juan Angel Arias. At the end of September López Gutiérrez asked that an American warship be sent to Amapala on a courtesy visit. He was told that the government would not need moral support of this nature if it conducted the election fairly, and that the United States would not want to extend moral support if the elections were not fair.

López Gutiérrez seems to have made a real effort to assure fair play. He ordered all officials to be neutral and on October 11 he replaced three *comandantes* against whose conduct Carías had protested. He could not entirely prevent Lagos and Angel Zuñiga Huete, the minister of government, from giving improper help to Arias, but both Bonilla and Carías expressed themselves as

[10] Hughes to Morales, Aug. 4, 1923, 815.00/2609.
[11] Memorandum to Hughes, July 12, 1923, 815.00/2623.

fairly well satisfied with the outlook on the eve of the election. The voting began October 28 and went on for three days. On the first day Carías had a small majority, but on the second and third days many Cariistas were forcibly prevented from casting their ballots. Three persons were killed and twenty-two wounded at Tegucigalpa when the police fired into a line of conservatives who were waiting to vote. Fifteen persons were reported killed elsewhere. Morales thought that intimidation and violence prevented Carías from receiving a majority of at least 30,000.[12] As it was he had about 47,000 votes, while Bonilla had 33,000 and Arias 18,000. This meant that the election would go to Congress.

Carías, who insisted that he should have had a majority, refused to consider any arrangement that did not give him the presidency. The conservatives were able to prevent the Congress from acting because the liberals, though they had a majority there, did not have the two-thirds required for a quorum. The Honduran minister at Washington suggested that the United States might exert pressure for a peaceful settlement, but the State Department thought that the Congress should settle the matter in accord with the constitution.[13] It warned Morales not to get involved in any negotiations or intrigues, though he might exert a proper influence, very impartially, to discourage the use of force. On December 15, when Morales reported that Carías was about to revolt, allegedly with help from the United Fruit Company, the minister was authorized to tell all concerned that the United States' attitude with respect to recognition of revolutionary governments had not changed, and that it would be especially difficult to recognize a government controlled by a faction which resorted to revolution without awaiting the outcome of constitutional procedures.

A few days later, when López Gutiérrez suddenly declared martial law throughout Honduras and ordered the arrest of more than 200 prominent Cariistas, the State Department realized that its non-recognition policy might do more harm than good if it encouraged governments in office to impose their successors by force or fraud.[14] Morales was instructed to tell the president that the United States would find it as difficult to recognize an administration placed in office by oppressive governmental action as if

[12] Morales to Hughes, Nov. 1, 1923, 815.00/2752.
[13] See White's memorandum of Nov. 6, 1923, 815.00/2738.
[14] See my memorandum of Dec. 21, 1923, 815.00/2810.

it came to power by any other unconstitutional procedure. It became increasingly clear, however, that Lagos and Arias intended to control the action of Congress by force. One Cariista deputy was murdered and another imprisoned, and on January 2 armed pro-Arias deputies and their followers forcibly prevented other conservatives from taking their seats. Morales, with the State Department's approval, again attempted to bring about an agreement for a coalition government, but could only obtain a promise from all of the candidates that none of them would start a revolution before the end of López Gutiérrez' term on February 1.

On January 12, Morales cabled that Carías suggested that the State Department select a *designado* who would take over the presidency and hold a new election. The minister said Arias also favored this plan. The department considered the proposal for several days, but finally replied that it felt that the *designado* should be chosen entirely by Honduraneans. It thought, however, that new elections under a new president would be a satisfactory solution and it authorized Morales to use his good offices to bring this about. In the latter part of January, when López Gutiérrez asked what the attitude of the United States would be if he stayed in power as dictator after the end of his constitutional term, the State Department replied that it might maintain relations with the government temporarily if the president gave written assurance that he would immediately hold new elections and adopt a series of specified measures to assure fair play. López Gutiérrez agreed, but Carías and his followers said that they would have no confidence in elections controlled by the existing government, and on January 30 Carías left Tegucigalpa with a force of armed men and proclaimed himself president.

The State Department still hoped that the plan which it had proposed might prevent a civil war. On February 1, in a telegram to the American legations in Guatemala, El Salvador, and Nicaragua it expressed disappointment at Carías' action and strongly urged that none of the neighboring governments give him any help. It was disturbed, however, when López Gutiérrez announced that he would call for elections to a constituent assembly, rather than for a new president, and it soon realized that the president could not free himself from the influence of subordinates who were determined to maintain control of the government. On February 9 the United States formally withdrew recognition from the liberal administration.

arías moved toward the frontier to join a force which had
n organized in Nicaragua and had apparently been supplied
n arms by the Nicaraguan government. The State Department
remonstrated with Martínez, the president of Nicaragua, and
made representations to Guatemala and El Salvador, which were
thought to be helping Lagos and Arias, but there was now little
hope for peace. The situation became worse when Gregorio Ferrera, a veteran liberal revolutionist who had a large following
among the Indians in the mountainous country along the Guatemalan frontier, started a revolution on his own account.

Americans and other foreigners were in greater danger than
they had been in any Central American country for several years.
The contending armies, the "reds" or government troops and the
"blues," as the revolutionists called themselves, were made up of
undisciplined recruits under officers who were often as ignorant
and irresponsible as their men. The situation was especially
alarming on the north coast, where there was much hostile feeling toward Americans and even more toward the British West
Indians who worked for the fruit companies. Early in February,
in response to an urgent plea from the American consul, the State
Department asked the navy to send a warship to La Ceiba, but
asked that there be no landing of marines or interference in the
political situation, except in a serious emergency, without consultation with the secretary of state.[15] The U.S.S. *Rochester*, and
later other vessels of the special service squadron, were sent to
north coast ports. Their presence undoubtedly saved many lives,
especially at La Ceiba where a landing party set up a neutral
zone in which Americans and other non-combatants took refuge
during the savage fighting that raged through the rest of the city
for several days. Neutral zones were also set up at Tela and
Puerto Cortés when fighting seemed imminent. In each case this
action was taken with the approval of both sides.[16] By the middle
of March, Ferrera's lieutenant General Vicente Tosta had taken
control of the north coast and things were quieter.

There was less fighting in the interior. Both Carías and Ferrera
were near Tegucigalpa, but both were short of ammunition and
neither seemed to be in a hurry to risk an attack on the city. Arias

[15] Secretary of state to secretary of the navy, Feb. 5, 1924, 815.00/2855a.
[16] Secretary of the navy to secretary of state, April 17, 1924, transmitting
a report from Admiral Dayton, commander of the special services squadron,
815.00/3103.

132

was now in full control there, and he continued in control after López Gutiérrez died on March 10 and the cabinet assumed the executive power. The diplomatic corps, at Morales' suggestion, tried to find a way to stop the war, but with no success. In this situation, despite the misgivings which it had had earlier, the State Department warmly supported a Guatemalan proposal for mediation by Honduras' neighbors. Ferrera agreed to a three-day armistice to give time for a peace mission to arrive, but disagreements between Guatemala and El Salvador delayed the arrival and Ferrera, who feared that Carías would attack Tegucigalpa before he did, resumed fighting.

In Tegucigalpa, meanwhile, conditions were becoming intolerable. All civilians, and especially foreigners, were terrorized and subjected to extortion by the government's troops. Morales himself was in danger because his resistance to the exaction of forced loans from Americans had angered the liberal officials. In view of the legation's reports, the State Department authorized the minister to ask for a landing force from the U.S.S. *Milwaukee*, which was at Amapala, if he thought that the danger to American lives made this imperative. Morales did so when soldiers in the city began an orgy of looting stores and homes and killing those who opposed them. On March 19, 176 bluejackets reached the city and took up their duties as a legation guard. The *de facto* authorities protested but the diplomatic representatives of all of the other Central American countries warmly approved. The presence of the guard made all foreigners feel more secure. In other respects, however, the situation in the city continued to grow worse. There was little food, and typhoid and dysentery were epidemic. There seemed to be little hope for any improvement. Carías, Tosta, and Ferrera, who controlled most of the country outside of the capital, had agreed to work together, but each was still suspicious of the others; and they apparently did not have enough ammunition to take Tegucigalpa and end the war.

The State Department felt that it must make an effort to prevent Honduras from sinking into anarchy, and on April 8 Hughes asked Sumner Welles, who was at Santo Domingo, to go to Honduras to see what could be done. Welles was told that the United States wished to use its good offices for peace, either alone or if practicable in cooperation with Guatemala, El Salvador, and Nicaragua. He was given virtually a free hand to do what he saw fit,

133

but was told that the United States wanted a government in Honduras which it could recognize consistently with the provisions of the 1923 treaties. He reached the neighborhood of Tegucigalpa after a hurried voyage on a destroyer and a difficult and dangerous trip overland on April 14. He talked with Carías and Tosta at their headquarters outside of the city and they accepted a plan for the choice of a provisional president by the various factions. The council of ministers and Ferrera were less easily persuaded, but after some days of discussion and argument all factions agreed to send representatives to a conference on the U.S.S. *Milwaukee* at Amapala. Hostilities would be suspended after the conference chose a provisional president, and a more comprehensive agreement would then be negotiated with the mediation of the United States and the other Central American states. Welles did not propose an immediate armistice because the armistice arranged by the diplomatic corps in March had been violated, with damage to the prestige of the mediators.

The conference met on the *Milwaukee* on April 23. For several days, no one would make any concessions. On April 28, however, Welles told Arias' representatives that he had received news that the provisional government's forces had been defeated and that Tegucigalpa was about to fall. The "red" delegates then agreed to accept General Tosta as provisional president to govern with a cabinet representing all political parties. Welles seems to have withheld the news of the revolutionists' victory from the delegates of Carías and Ferrera, who had no means of communication except through the *Milwaukee*'s radio, and they also agreed on the selection of Tosta. When the revolutionary leaders learned that Tegucigalpa had fallen, some of them felt that they had been tricked and questioned whether they were bound by the document that they had just signed. Carías, Tosta, and Ferrera had agreed previously that Fausto Dávila, a prominent and respected civilian, should become provisional president when the revolution triumphed and many of the revolutionists would have preferred Dávila to Tosta. Welles, however, insisted that the recently signed pact be carried out. He thought that it would be difficult for the United States to recognize Dávila, without departing from the principles of the Central American treaty, whereas the recognition of Tosta could be defended because it was alleged that he had not joined the revolution until there was no longer a constitutional government at Tegucigalpa.

134

When Tosta took office, on April 30, the American government promised him its moral support. The American landing force left Tegucigalpa without having fired a shot during its forty-two days in the city. A final agreement between the political groups was signed at Amapala on May 5, in the presence of representatives of all of the Central American states. A constituent assembly was to meet within ninety days to provide for the restoration of constitutional government. Tosta would continue as provisional president until a constitutional president, chosen at a free popular election, took office. He would not himself be a candidate. All political parties would be represented in the provisional government, and there would be a general amnesty and full guarantees for the defeated "reds." The delegates from the other Central American states promised the new government their moral support and passed a vote of thanks to Welles.

While the American and Central American delegates were still at Amapala, Tosta, in Tegucigalpa, appointed a cabinet in which Carías was minister of government and Cariistas held most of the other posts. Morales had apparently acquiesced in these appointments, but Welles wrote the provisional president that he could expect no support from the United States until he complied with the peace agreement. Welles also asked the delegates from the other Central American states to ask their governments to withhold recognition of Tosta. Tosta rectified his error on May 8, by appointing a cabinet representing all parties, and on May 16, having waited to give the other Central American governments a chance to act at the same time, the State Department instructed Morales to express the American government's gratification at the end of the war and to promise moral support and assistance to the provisional government. Welles had left Honduras some days earlier.[17]

In his final report to the Secretary of State, Welles laid much of the blame for the trouble in Honduras on the American fruit companies.[18] American officials had made similar charges against the companies on several occasions in the past fifteen years. It seems clear that the United Fruit Company openly helped the

[17] Most of the correspondence about Welles' mission is printed in *Foreign Relations, 1924,* Vol. II. Apparently no one in the State Department knew until later of Welles' action in withholding information about the situation at Tegucigalpa from the delegates.

[18] Report of June 2, 1924, 815.00/3185.

Cariistas during the electoral campaign of 1923, and that the Cuyamel Fruit Company, which had conflicting interests, helped Ferrera and Tosta during the war. Both companies apparently furnished funds for the purchase of the arms which reached the revolutionists in April 1924 and enabled them to take Tegucigalpa. The United States placed an embargo on the shipment of arms to Honduras on May 15, but the Cuyamel Fruit Company evaded it by shipping the arms through Cabo Gracias, Nicaragua, with the connivance of the local officials there.[19] The State Department thought that there had been a conspiracy to violate United States law, but it was difficult to get concrete evidence. The Cuyamel Company was relatively frank in explaining what it had done, and even in attempting to justify its actions on the ground of business necessity, but the United Fruit Company was not. It seemed unfortunate that American warships should have to be sent to Honduran ports to protect people who were at least partly responsible for the disturbances that endangered them.

The situation at Tegucigalpa was still uncertain. It could hardly be supposed that a group of successful revolutionary generals, each with his own personal army, would really leave the selection of the constitutional president to the free choice of the voters. Only a few days after Welles' departure, Morales cabled that Tosta was supporting Carías candidacy, and that Ferrera, who supported Fausto Dávila for the presidency, might revolt. The State Department authorized Morales to say informally, as an expression of his own opinion, that the United States would probably find it very difficult to recognize Carías as president, but he was warned not to commit the United States to non-recognition, either in the case of Carías or in that of Dávila, who also seemed likely to be ineligible.[20]

On June 5 Morales reported that Tosta, Carías, and Ferrera had agreed that José María Casco, a prominent attorney, would be the "national party's" candidate. Morales said that he had achieved this result by using the department's recent telegram about the probable ineligibility of Carías. Welles, who was in Washington for a few days, dictated the State Department's reply, vigorously disapproving of Tosta's participation in the agree-

[19] For the information about this arms shipment see Morales' dispatch of June 18, 1924, 815.00/3198 and a letter from Montgomery of the Cuyamel Fruit Company to Welles, dated July 14, 1924, 815.00/3223.

[20] Hughes to Morales, May 23, 1924, 815.00/3172.

ment and threatening the withdrawal of moral support if the provisional president did not at once make it clear that he did not
support any candidate. Morales replied rather lamely that the
agreement was secret and that it seemed the only way to avoid
a civil war. It did not bar other candidates, and Tosta said that
he would not impose Casco. The State Department was somewhat reassured when Tosta issued orders that seemed to assure
freedom in the election of the constituent assembly, to take place
at the end of June.

The Honduran leaders realized of course that the State Department had not approved what Morales had done, and the incident presumably made them less disposed to take seriously the
minister's statement, expressed as a personal opinion, that the
United States would probably not recognize Carías if he were
elected president. It soon became evident that the department
would have to make its position clearer. On July 2 Morales was
authorized to deliver a note repeating the statement made on
June 30, 1923, that the American government's attitude toward
the recognition of a new government in Honduras would be consonant with the provisions of the Central American treaty. He
was to say that the department could not understand Carías'
continued presence in the ministry of government and to demand
a definite statement of the provisional president's intentions.
When this message seemed to have little effect, Morales was instructed to summon all of the "blue" leaders to a conference to
tell them that the United States would not recognize as president
of Honduras any leader of a revolution against a recognized government, and that this applied to Carías. When the conference
met, Carías was urged by all present, including Tosta, to withdraw his candidacy but he refused to do so. The State Department then made public the fact that it had warned Tosta that no
revolutionary leader would be recognized as president, and
Guatemala, El Salvador, and Nicaragua, at the department's suggestion, told Tosta that they too would be guided by the provisions of the Central American treaty. Costa Rica did not join
them, and El Salvador, which did go along with the State Department's policy, expressed the opinion that the policy was
wrong because Carías had been cheated out of the election in
1923 and would have at least 75% of the votes in a new election.

The State Department knew that Carías would probably win
in a free election, but it felt that it had to maintain the non-recog-

nition policy, to which it had so definitely committed itself, and that it must insist on the fulfilment of the Amapala agreement which Tosta was violating by his support of Carías. It knew too that Ferrera would probably revolt and would probably be joined by the recently defeated liberals, unless the provisional president changed his conduct. A revolution seemed in fact to be starting when Ferrera's lieutenant Fonseca, the chief of police of Tegucigalpa, left the city on July 23 with 120 armed men. Morales persuaded Carías and Ferrera and Martínez Funes, another powerful "blue" leader, to sign a statement that none of them would be a candidate, but the statement was not published and no one seemed to take it very seriously. Ferrera continued to complain about Tosta and Carías, and on August 6 he left Tegucigalpa with 500 followers, each carrying three extra rifles. Since the United States embargo had made it difficult for anyone to obtain arms in Honduras, the loss of so many weapons put Tosta in a difficult position. He asked permission to import some rifles and ammunition, but the State Department replied that the provisional government had forfeited any right to moral support by its violations of the Amapala agreement. Tosta nevertheless prepared to fight, imprisoning the principal liberal leaders and appointing a new, predominantly Cariísta cabinet.

The State Department was by this time convinced that it must have more effective diplomatic representation in Honduras. The accessible records do not show just what happened, but in July Stokeley Morgan, the senior secretary of the legation in Panama, was ordered to Tegucigalpa to help the minister; and on August 7 Morales telegraphed that the group in power were hostile to him because they thought him responsible for the State Department's policy and that he thought that another representative might be in a better position to bring about a settlement. The State Department at once authorized him to turn over the legation to Morgan and Morales left Tegucigalpa on August 19.

On August 22 Morgan was instructed to tell all of the political leaders that the American government urged that Tosta reorganize his cabinet in a way which would assure a free election. The chargé was to say to Ferrera and his associates that they would be responsible for a national disaster if Tosta did this and the rebels refused to cooperate. Morgan obtained a letter from Tosta promising free elections and a letter from Carías saying that he would not be a candidate for the presidency, but when he telegraphed Ferrera the latter replied that he had just won an important battle and would go on fighting. Ferrera rebuffed a further effort for peace when Morgan and representatives of Tosta went to talk with him early in September, and paid little attention to the State Department's warning that it would not recognize any government he set up.

The renewal of the civil war alarmed the Americans on the north coast, who had hardly recovered from the terrifying experiences of the preceding year. The consuls at Puerto Cortés and La Ceiba asked for warships, and marines were landed for a short time at La Ceiba. The landing was probably necessary, but the State Department was becoming increasingly reluctant to resort to shows of force and it was concerned because consuls too frequently asked the commander of the special service squadron for a ship, without consulting the department, when the need for one was not clear. It consequently attempted to lay down a general policy to cover such cases. On September 4, the legation and the consuls in Honduras were instructed that requests for the presence of a warship should ordinarily be made through the State Department, and only in cases where there was need to protect American lives. This was designed to discourage the consuls from communicating directly with vessels of the special service squadron, except in a real emergency. The instruction said that men might be landed in coast towns in a very serious emergency actually and imminently imperiling American lives. The landing parties should avoid any action which could be regarded as partial to one faction. Their primary object was to protect American lives, but American property should also receive such protection as was practicable without unduly expanding the sphere of operations and without interfering with any of the contending factions. The American representatives were told to make very energetic representations if there was any willful or unnecessary damage to American property and particularly if there was any effort to exact forced loans from Americans. They might use their informal good offices to protect the lives and property of other foreigners where this was practicable.[21]

Ferrera's revolt was suppressed in October, after Tosta personally took command of the government's forces. This left the Cariistas in full control, and the State Department realized that the Amapala agreement, with its provision for a free election

[21] 815.00/3317a.

under a coalition cabinet, was no longer workable. It still insisted, however, that it would not recognize any government that did not meet the requirements of the Central American treaty. By this time some of us wished that we had not committed ourselves so definitely to the principles laid down in the treaty, but if we retreated no one in Central America would take the American government's warnings seriously when the next crisis arose. Furthermore, we were at the time trying to dissuade President Martínez of Nicaragua from persisting in an unconstitutional candidacy for reelection, and we did not wish him to think that a threat of non-recognition was a bluff.[22]

The prospect was not encouraging. Carías, despite his assurances that he would not be a candidate, was still determined to be president, and he had the enthusiastic support of the triumphant "blue" party and probably the support of a majority of the voters. He was apparently not convinced that the American government would refuse to recognize him if it were confronted with a *fait accompli*. Morgan, however, was vigorous and persistent. He got the representatives of Guatemala, El Salvador, and Nicaragua to talk with the "blue" leaders, and he obtained some rather half-hearted support from Tosta and Martínez Funes. He also asked the American fruit companies to withhold loans which the Honduran government wanted. On December 6, in response to his request for a categorical statement that would disabuse the political leaders of the idea that the United States was simply bluffing, the State Department authorized him to say that the American government was following with sympathetic interest the preparations to establish a constitutional government and hoped to cooperate with the new administration in the rehabilitation of the country, but it was constrained to reiterate in the most positive manner its earlier statements that it could not recognize an administration headed by anyone disqualified by the Central American treaty. It would regret the disastrous economic consequences that would follow the establishment of a government that could not enjoy normal relations with the United States and its Central American neighbors.[23] This statement was not, however, communicated formally to the Honduran leaders because the State Department asked Morgan to withhold it for a few

[22] See my memoranda of Oct. 23, and Dec. 5, 1924, 815.00/3424 and 3477.
[23] 815.00/3473.

days, if he could, to give time for similar action by the other Central American states. While the department was obtaining their agreement, Carías decided to withdraw his candidacy. Morgan nevertheless told the provisional government that he had such a statement, to prevent any last-minute changes of mind.

On December 9, 1924, the government party nominated Miguel Paz Barahona as its presidential candidate. Paz, who had run for vice president on Carías' ticket in 1923, was a civilian with a good reputation, and Morgan thought he was as good a choice as could be expected under the circumstances. There was no reason to question his eligibility under the Central American treaty. The election was set for December 28, which left the liberals little time to campaign. Some of them asked through the American legation at San Salvador that the State Department insist on a postponement, but they were told that their party had forfeited any right to make such a request by its conduct since the Amapala agreement.[24] This was of course a reference to Ferrera's revolt. The liberals consequently refused to take part in the election, and Paz Barahona received nearly all of the votes cast. He was inaugurated on February 1, 1925, and immediately recognized by the United States.

The State Department regarded the election of Paz Barahona as a satisfactory ending to a troublesome situation, but it could hardly feel that its policy in Honduras had been a success. It had been unable to prevent two civil wars. Very possibly no effort by an outside power, short of forceful coercion, could have restrained the combativeness and the selfish ambition of the Honduran leaders, but the efforts which the American government did make might have been more effective if the United States had been better represented at Tegucigalpa. Morales worked hard and courageously for peace, but his inexperience and lack of training led him into errors of judgment which made it difficult for the State Department to give him full support and hurt his standing in Honduras. Such influence as he had was probably lost when Welles was sent to Honduras to do what the legation should have been doing.

One may of course question the wisdom of the policies which the State Department asked the minister to carry out. The effort to obtain agreement on a compromise candidate for the presidency, before the first revolution started, had little chance of suc-

---

[24] Hughes to Schuyler, Dec. 18, 1924, 815.00/3493.

141

cess, but seemed worth trying. The plan embodied in the Amapala agreement, to hold a free election under a provisional president with a cabinet representing all parties, turned out to be unrealistic, but it would have been unreasonable for the State Department not to support it after it had been agreed on by all factions in Honduras. The wisdom of the State Department's insistence on the withdrawal of Carías' presidential candidacy is perhaps more doubtful. The hope was that no leader would start a revolution if he knew in advance that he would not be recognized as president. The policy did not prevent the revolutions of 1923-1924, apparently because the leaders were not convinced that the American government, which had too often made threats in the past without following them up, really meant what it said. What happened to Carías seemed to show that the United States was not bluffing, and the belief that no revolutionary leader would be recognized as president was unquestionably one of the reasons why Honduras enjoyed eight years of relative tranquillity after 1925.

When Paz Barahona took office, the outlook was not encouraging. The treasury was empty and government salaries were in arrears. Carías, who still dominated the conservative party, was angered by the president's effort to conciliate the liberals and withdrew his support. In April 1925, Ferrera started a revolution but was defeated by government forces under Tosta. Ferrera continued to threaten the peace, but his efforts were ineffective after the State Department made strong representations to the government of Guatemala, which had been helping him. There was also a bad situation on the north coast, where the anti-foreign attitude of General Filiberto Díaz Zelaya, the military commander, caused much trouble. There was a small liberal uprising near La Ceiba and marines were landed to prevent fighting in the fruit company compound.

Though it was increasingly anxious to keep out of the internal politics of the Central American states, the American government gave Paz a considerable amount of moral support. It sold the new government arms and ammunition to reequip its army, and Lawrence Dennis, who succeeded Morgan as chargé d'affaires, tried to persuade the other "blue" leaders to cooperate with Paz. In November 1925, however, when Paz asked whether the United States would land marines, if necessary, to back up his effort to oust insubordinate officials on the north coast, Dennis replied

142

that the United States should not be asked to use force to support a government which could not solve its own problems. The State Department "highly" approved this reply, saying that the Honduran leaders should be told that they were responsible for their government; that "the center of Honduran political activities is in Honduras and not in Washington, and that regeneration must come from within."[25] This instruction, drafted by Francis White, was evidence of the change which was taking place in White's attitude and in the department's attitude toward Caribbean political problems.

After 1925 the political situation gradually improved. Carías continued to be unfriendly, but the president built up more support in his own party, and most of the liberals accepted the regime. The north coast was more tranquil after Díaz Zelaya was bribed to resign and go abroad. George T. Summerlin, a career diplomat who was sent to Tegucigalpa as American minister in November 1925, did much unobtrusively and through his personal influence to keep things on an even keel.

One of the principal events of Paz Barahona's administration was the final settlement of the longstanding problem of the British debt. The State Department had been interested in this problem since Secretary Knox made it one of the chief objectives of his "dollar diplomacy" in 1909, but several efforts by the Taft and Wilson administrations to arrange for a refunding loan had failed. The debt arose from three loans which had been contracted in London between 1867 and 1870, with bankers who were evidently irresponsible and crooked. Bonds totaling more than £5,000,000 were issued, ostensibly to finance the construction of a railroad from the north coast to the Gulf of Fonseca, but very little of the money ever reached Honduras. The bonds soon went into default. By 1921, with unpaid interest, the government owed the bondholders the equivalent of more than $125,000,000. No one supposed that Honduras, with total revenues of six or seven million dollars in a good year, could pay this amount, but the British government insisted that a reasonable settlement must be made.

In 1922 the Pan American Development Syndicate, headed by Congressman Louis T. McFadden, the chairman of the House of Representatives' committee on banking and currency, proposed

[25] Dennis to Kellogg, Nov. 20, 1925, 815.00/3913; Kellogg to Summerlin, Dec. 22, *Foreign Relations, 1925*, Vol. II, p. 337.

to lend Honduras $5,000,000. The Syndicate would use part of this amount to buy up the outstanding British bonds and would keep the balance for itself; and it would organize a "Honduras Trust Company," which would collect all of the government's revenues, charging a commission of 7½%. The trust company would issue bank notes and coin money, and would have a first option on all concessions which the government might grant. The Honduran government does not seem to have shown much interest in this plan, but the sponsors insistently urged that the State Department support it. Secretary Hughes emphatically refused. The plan would have given the proposed bank unreasonable monopolistic privileges and would have been excessively profitable to the syndicate, because the British bonds could probably have been bought up for not more than $2,000,000. During the next three or four years the sponsors tried from time to time to persuade the State Department to approve a modified plan, but with no success.

Meanwhile the British government and the Council of Foreign Bondholders were making efforts to obtain a settlement. Early in 1923 the López Gutiérrez administration agreed to an arrangement which would discharge the debt by payments totaling £1,200,000 spread over thirty years, but the Honduran Congress rejected it. A similar arrangement was negotiated with Paz Barahona in 1925. At the request of the British embassy, the American legation at Tegucigalpa was instructed to do what it could informally to see that the Congress approved the agreement, which the Congress did in 1926. The government promised thirty annual payments of £40,000 each, which would make possible the redemption of the bonds at 20% of their principal amount, with no accrued interest, during the first fifteen years, and at 25% during the last fifteen years of the period when the payments were being made. As security, the government agreed that a 3% consular tax on goods being shipped to Honduras would be paid exclusively in stamps. These would be sold to exporters by the National City Bank of New York, which would turn over the proceeds to the Council of Foreign Bondholders.[26]

Except for what happened in Nicaragua, which will be dealt with in Chapters VI and VII, the events discussed in this chapter

[26] Part of this correspondence is printed in *Foreign Relations, 1925,* Vol. II. See also the British embassy's "Aide Memoire" of Jan. 18, 1926, and Kellogg to Summerlin, Jan. 21, 1926, both in 815.51/626.

were the most important matters with which the State Department had to deal in Central America between 1921 and 1929. It was also involved throughout the period in efforts to settle the boundary disputes between Guatemala and Honduras and Nicaragua and Honduras, but these efforts were confined to friendly mediation and it seems unnecessary to go into their rather tedious history. There were no serious political disorders in Costa Rica, which had a truly democratic government, or in Guatemala and El Salvador, where the governments were stable but not democratic. The State Department occasionally had to warn El Salvador and Guatemala about their obligations under the Central American treaties, but it had little occasion to interfere in their internal political affairs. In both countries, however, it became involved to some extent in loan negotiations with American bankers.

In the case of the loan to El Salvador the American government assumed responsibilities reminiscent of the era of dollar diplomacy. El Salvador, like the other Central American states, had been affected by the post-war depression, and in the first months of 1921 payments on the foreign debt were suspended and salaries of government officials fell several months in arrears. In June 1921, President Jorge Meléndez asked Minor C. Keith to obtain a foreign loan for him. Keith, who was president of the International Railways of Central America, was interested in the proposal because the government owed his company money and especially because a loan might enable El Salvador to finance the building of a branch of the International Railways between El Salvador and Guatemala. He consequently accepted a sixty-day option to arrange a loan of $10-20,000,000, which would take care of the government's most pressing debts and provide money for paving, sewers, and water supply in San Salvador as well as for the proposed railway construction. The outstanding British bonds were to be refunded if possible. To secure the new bonds, the republic's customs service was to be administered by two directors, one appointed by the bankers from a list submitted by the government and the other to be appointed by the government from a list submitted by the bankers. As an additional safeguard, the contract would provide for the submission of any dispute to the chief justice of the United States for decision.

Keith's relations with the State Department had not been cordial. American officials had often been critical of the actions of

145

the United Fruit Company while he was in charge of its Central American operations, and in 1917-1919 he had infuriated President Wilson by openly supporting Tinoco in Costa Rica when the American government refused to recognize the revolutionary government. This affair, however, seemed to be regarded as ancient history, and Messrs. Lansing and Woolsey, who had been secretary of state and solicitor when the State Department was trying to find grounds to prosecute Keith in 1917-1918, now represented him in laying his plans before the department. The department was interested in a proposal which seemed likely to improve a bad situation in El Salvador, especially after the new American minister, Montgomery Schuyler, cabled that the government would probably fall if it did not receive the loan and that it had asked him to help in arranging it. Undersecretary Fletcher wrote Lansing and Woolsey that the department did not like the provision for two customs collectors, but would be glad to see the loan arranged if provision were made for a single collector general of customs to be chosen by the government from a list of five names submitted by the bankers and approved by the secretary of state.[27] Welles, in a personal letter to Schuyler, wrote that the department would endeavor in every possible way to assist Keith.[28] The Latin American division arranged informally for the Department of Commerce to put Keith in touch with bankers in New York. When Keith found that he would need more than ninety days to arrange the financing of the loan, he asked the State Department to support his request for an extension of the option. Woolsey told Welles that a German firm was promising to obtain a loan for El Salvador in Hamburg if Keith failed. Schuyler was instructed "in view of the Department's interest in seeing American bankers secure the larger loan" to try informally to have the option extended.

The State Department again intervened when Benjamin Bloom, an American banker at San Salvador, joined with the Anglo and London Paris National Bank of San Francisco in an effort to defeat Keith's project by submitting a loan proposal which would not involve control of the customs except in case of default. Bloom and other local bankers had long made a profitable business of lending the government money on exorbitant

[27] Fletcher to Lansing and Woolsey, Aug. 1, 1921, 816.51/74.
[28] Welles to Schuyler, Aug. 3, 1921, 816.51/83.

terms or in return for special favors,[29] and they had no desire to see the government's finances rehabilitated. Bloom and the San Francisco bank offered to take 8% bonds at 80. Schuyler was instructed on September 3 to tell President Meléndez that Bloom's proposition was "unduly onerous and likely to perpetuate the financial evils which have hitherto afflicted the Salvadorean government," and that it seemed unwise to enter into such a transaction when a more beneficial project was pending. The minister was to say also that Keith had arranged for a temporary loan of $250,000 to meet the government's immediate needs. After these representations, Keith's option was extended for five months.

Officers in the State Department informally told several bankers in New York of the department's interest in Keith's project but the bankers were reluctant to consider a loan unless the United States was associated in some way with the proposed customs control. The National City Bank of New York, with which Keith was negotiating, suggested that this be accomplished by an exchange of notes between the two governments. The State Department was reluctant to agree to this, but in October 1921, when it appeared that there would be no loan unless the American government assumed some responsibility in connection with it, it decided to help. Schuyler was told of the department's earlier suggestion to Keith that there might be a single collector of customs, nominated by the bankers and approved by the secretary of state. This had not been incorporated in Keith's proposal, but the minister was authorized to use his good offices to have Keith's option amended to include it. The minister was told confidentially that the United States was disposed to agree to an exchange of notes providing for the American government's participation in the arrangement, but he was to take no initiative in this connection until the Salvadorean government approached him.

The Salvadorean government did not like the proposed change in the organization of the customs collectorship but Schuyler in-

[29] On Sept. 29, 1909, the American chargé d'affaires at San Salvador wrote:

It is a matter of regret also that the two men most responsible for debauching the governments of this country from the time of Regalado [President from 1898 until 1903] to the present day are both Americans, Mr. David Bloom, a naturalized and Mr. Benjamin Bloom, a native-born citizen. State Department file, numerical case 4598/104.

147

sisted rather vigorously that it be accepted.[30] On October 20, he received from the Foreign Office a note in which El Salvador assured the United States that the government would comply with the loan contract's provisions about the customs collectorship and would submit all disputes to the chief justice of the United States for final decision. The contemplated arrangement would be very similar to that in Nicaragua. Schuyler was told to withhold a reply to the note until Keith's negotiations with the First National City Company were farther advanced.

In February 1922, the department was given copies of the proposed loan contract. It suggested a few changes, which the bankers accepted, and on February 28 Schuyler was authorized to reply to the Salvadorean government's note, saying that the United States would carry out those stipulations of the loan contract which applied to it. Meanwhile, with the State Department's approval, the bankers selected William W. Renwick as interim collector of customs.[31] When the contents of the contracts became known in San Salvador, however, there was violent opposition to any foreign control of the customs, and the president asserted that his representative in New York had exceeded his instructions. Both Bloom and the Mexican minister assured the government that they could get money for it under better conditions.[32] Schuyler was indignant and the State Department had to warn him not to give the impression that the United States had any interest in the matter except to help El Salvador to get a loan on conditions acceptable to the government.[33]

On April 5 the Salvadorean government proposed to Keith that the loan be secured by only 50% of the customs revenues and that this money be collected through the sale of customs warrants by a "fiscal agent" appointed by the bankers. The fiscal agent would also have broad but vague powers to supervise the operation of the customs service. The National City Bank showed no interest in this proposal. The State Department tried very cautiously to persuade El Salvador to make a better one, but it could accom-

[30] See the portion of his dispatch of Oct. 21 which was not printed in *Foreign Relations*, 816.51/107.
[31] National City Company to Hughes, Feb. 8; Fletcher to National City Company, Feb. 16, 1922, 816.51/132.
[32] Schuyler to Hughes, March 15, 1922, 816.51/138.
[33] Schuyler to Hughes, March 16, and Hughes to Schuyler, March 20, 1922, 816.51/139.

plish nothing through Schuyler, whose relations with the government were by this time very strained. In June 1922, the National City Company made it clear that it would drop the matter unless El Salvador accepted the original plan.

Keith, however, decided to endeavor to arrange a loan on conditions which the government would accept, and on June 24 he signed a contract with the government for a loan to be secured by 70% of the customs receipts. These would be collected by a fiscal agent through the sale of warrants to be used in the payment of customs duties. The bankers would take control of the customhouses only in case of default. The Salvadorean Congress approved the new contract without a dissenting vote, and the State Department agreed that the exchange of notes should apply to the new transaction. The department expressed a friendly interest in the loan when it was consulted by bankers in New York, and it authorized the embassy in London to let the British bondholders know that it looked with favor on the refunding plan which the new agreement contemplated. Keith found it difficult to persuade other bankers to join him in underwriting the bonds, but after two or three groups had considered the business and dropped it, F. J. Lisman agreed in December to take charge of the sale of the bonds. The Metropolitan Trust Company of New York was to be fiscal agent for the loan.

In drawing up the fiscal agency contract, the Metropolitan Trust Company insisted on a full disclosure of some aspects of the project which had not previously been revealed. It now appeared that Keith himself would make a profit of more than $200,000 from the transaction, from payments for expenses, profit from the refunding of the sterling bonds, and in other ways,[34] and that $6,000,000 of the bonds were to be taken by the underwriters at 88 and sold to the public at 99, a spread that seemed unreasonably large. When Hughes learned of this, he was inclined to withdraw from any connection with the loan. He thought that Keith's expenses and profits should at least be paid out of the spread, but Lisman refused to consider this, emphasizing the high cost of selling bonds of a country like El Salvador, especially at a time when market conditions were not very favorable. Keith said that he wanted to go forward with the loan even

[34] This was Keith's own estimate in his letter of Dec. 18 to the secretary of state, 816.51/233. There was some reason to think that the profit might be considerably greater.

149

if he received no profit, but he thought that he ought to receive some remuneration after he and his staff had devoted most of their time for eighteen months to the loan negotiations. He pointed out that he had helped El Salvador to obtain $2,200,000 in short-term loans while the negotiations were in progress. The case which Keith and his associates presented, and especially a telegram from the minister of finance of El Salvador saying that the government agreed to Keith's profits, finally convinced the secretary that the arrangement was not indefensible. On January 6, 1923, Keith's representative was told that the State Department did not wish to stand in the way of the loan, though it thought the transaction costly to El Salvador.[35]

The secretary stated his position more definitely when Mr. Hecht, the president of the Hibernia Bank and Trust Company of New Orleans, called at the department to ask what protection his bank could expect if it participated in the loan syndicate. Hughes said that the department would do exactly what was stipulated in the loan contract. He could give no general assurances and could not bind his successors. He pointed out that the department had to consider the attitude of two groups in the United States: those who wanted intervention to promote financial reforms and safeguard investments, and those who thought that the American government was already going too far. He could not guarantee that the loan would be paid or promise to bring pressure to this end. Personally he thought that the high cost of the operation made provision for the risks involved, and that it would be too much of a good thing if the American government took a position that practically did away with the risks.[36]

The loan was to be issued in three series: $6,000,000 of 8% "A" bonds to be sold to the public; £1,050,000 6% "B" bonds to be exchanged for the outstanding sterling bonds; and $10,500,000 7% "C" bonds to be given to other creditors in El Salvador and abroad. It proved difficult to find underwriting for the A bonds. Lisman, who had undertaken to sell them, underwrote less than $500,000 himself, and no one seemed willing to underwrite the rest. Apparently Keith finally persuaded the sterling bondholders to accept $1,000,000 in A bonds instead of the cash which they

[35] The above account is based partly on my own recollection and partly on correspondence in decimal file 816.51, particularly on enclosures 231 to 234 inclusive.

[36] Young's memorandum of Jan. 27, 1923, 816.51/241.

had expected to get on account of back interest, and Keith's company, the International Railways of Central America, not only took bonds in lieu of cash which it should have received but borrowed money on its own credit to underwrite more bonds. Keith personally underwrote the rest of the issue.

The National Assembly of El Salvador approved the final contracts for the loan in August 1923. Renwick, who had been asked by the local authorities to stay in El Salvador after the breakdown of the negotiations with the National City Bank, was appointed representative of the fiscal agent under the new contract, to sell the certificates which importers and exporters had to present in payment of 70% of the customs duties. He also supervised the operation of the customs service, with representatives in the customhouses who had a right to inspect merchandise and documents and to participate in the settlement of disputes about the payment of duties.

The marketing of the A bonds in the United States led to an unpleasant incident. The State Department had repeatedly told the bankers that the text of the exchange of notes, though it might be shown to prospective purchasers of the bonds, must be treated as confidential and that any advertising matter mentioning the American government's connection with the loan must be confined to the bare facts. It was indignant when it learned that Lisman was using advertisements that not only quoted the text of the notes but asserted that the notes meant that a warship would immediately appear off El Salvador's coast if there were a default. The department issued a press release denying the accuracy of the advertisements. It said that the secretary of state had consented to use his good offices in referring controversies to the chief justice or another federal judge because it was clearly desirable to have an appropriate means for settlement, and had agreed to assist in the selection of a collector of customs in case of default simply to facilitate the choice of a competent and disinterested person. The government of the United States had no other relation to the loan.[37] The department also sent a harsh letter to F. J. Lisman and Company.[38] Lisman promptly apologized and both Lansing and Woolsey and the Metropolitan Trust Company said that they had not known about the advertisements and were much embarrassed. Nevertheless,

[37] State Department press release of Oct. 18, 1923.
[38] Harrison to F. J. Lisman and Company, Oct. 23, 1923, 816.51/311.

when the Metropolitan Trust Company asked that the legation at San Salvador inform the government that Renwick had been appointed fiscal representative under the loan contract the State Department refused to act. It referred again to the inaccurate and misleading advertising matter and said that it wished to have no relation to the loan except as set forth in the exchange of notes.[39]

The loan seems to have been good on the whole for El Salvador. Most of the cash proceeds went to repay the advances which Keith had obtained for the government from time to time during the negotiations, but these advances had helped the government to weather a critical period. The refunding of the sterling debt and the repayment of most of the internal debt were advantageous. Renwick, by sound and tactful advice, was able to bring about a considerable improvement in the customs service and in the government's financial administration generally, but the government had no occasion to feel that the loan contract seriously affected its autonomy.

In the case of Guatemala very little of practical importance resulted from the State Department's participation in loan negotiations. Guatemala's worst financial problems arose from the state of the paper currency. In 1898, in return for loans, the Guatemalan government relieved the local banks of their obligation to redeem their notes in silver on demand and at the same time permitted large new issues. The banknotes soon drove other forms of money out of circulation, and by 1921 the paper *peso* was worth little more than two cents in gold. Most of the notes were so dilapidated that pasting them together was a regular expense in any office where quantities of them were used. In 1919, at the State Department's suggestion, President Estrada Cabrera employed Professor Kemmerer of Princeton University to draw up a plan for currency reform. Neither Estrada nor his successor Carlos Herrera did anything to implement the plan, but the government which took power after the revolution of December 1921 immediately began to negotiate for a loan which would make a reform possible.

In May 1922 Blair and Company of New York told the State Department that they had tentatively agreed to lend Guatemala $15,000,000, of which $2,500,000 would be used for the stabiliza-

[39] Harrison to the Metropolitan Trust Company, Nov. 1, 1923, 816.51/323.

tion of the currency and the remainder would be invested in securities in the United States and held as a reserve to assure service of the bonds. The bankers would set up a new national bank, controlled by themselves, which would issue notes to replace the outstanding banknotes and also $5,500,000 in new money to pay Guatemala's internal debt and to provide funds for public works. The bank would collect the government's revenues by selling certificates for the payment of customs duties and taxes.[40]

The State Department thought that this proposal would be unfair to Guatemala and extremely profitable to the bankers. It would not provide a sound currency reform, but would in fact bring about further inflation. The department's insistence on changes and the opposition which developed in Guatemala when the plan was published discouraged the bankers and they dropped the matter. A few months later, when the Guatemalan minister of finance came to the United States in a further effort to get a loan, the State Department tried to help him by giving the Guatemalan legation a note expressing interest in the stabilization of the currency and the refunding of the internal debt, but no bankers seemed willing to consider the business.

In October 1923, the State Department learned that a contract for a loan and currency reform had been negotiated with the Guatemalan government by Lionel Stahl, an American connected with one of the local banks in Guatemala City. Stahl represented a group headed by the Anglo and London Paris National Bank of San Francisco, which had been involved a year earlier in efforts by local bankers in San Salvador to defeat Keith's loan project there. Guatemala was to issue $8,000,000 in 7%, twenty-year bonds, which the bankers would pay for, not in cash but in notes issued by a reserve bank which they would set up and manage. These notes, which would be backed by a 33⅓% reserve held in New York, would be exchanged for the existing currency. The reserve bank would collect all of the government's revenues, and the bonds would be secured by a first lien on 50% of the coffee export tax and 75% of the import duties. The bankers would thus get $8,000,000 in bonds and would apparently put up in return only $2,500,000 for the reserve fund and $1,000,000 capital for the reserve bank. It was not clear that even these sums would

---

[40] Coudert Brothers to the secretary of state, May 10, 1922, 814.51/379. See also Young's memorandum of May 13, 814.51/384.

become the property of the government. The State Department instructed the American legation in Guatemala to tell the bankers and the officials of the Guatemalan government that it considered the proposed contract "fundamentally objectionable," and to remind the bankers that the department, in March 1922, had asked that all American bankers consult it before concluding loan agreements with foreign governments.[41]

The bankers made a number of changes in their plan but the State Department thought that these made the arrangement only a little less unfair and unsound. Stahl and his associates were still discussing the matter in Washington, in February 1924, when a group of French, British, American, and Spanish bankers came forward with a rival proposal for the establishment of a bank of issue. The Stahl group pointed out that foreigners would undoubtedly get the business if an American did not. The State Department replied that it was ready to advise against any disadvantageous project, but it told Minister Geissler in Guatemala that it was suspending judgment on the Stahl contract while the bankers considered whether they could make further changes. It said that it did not want to see a foreign-controlled central bank of issue in Guatemala, especially if it acted as depository for the government's revenues. When the American bankers interested in the new project asked about its attitude, they were told that the American government would not give them any help in connection with such a bank.[42]

Meanwhile, Minor Keith, who wanted to make sure that any loan to Guatemala provided for the payment of the government's debt to his International Railways, had arranged to have Professor Kemmerer go to Guatemala to work out a sounder plan for currency reform. Kemmerer's recommendations were the basis of a proposal which Keith submitted for the State Department's consideration in the autumn of 1924. A loan, secured by an arrangement much like that in El Salvador, would make possible the establishment of a national bank which would exchange its own adequately secured notes for the outstanding paper money. All of the government's debts except the sterling bonds would be refunded. As in El Salvador, the secretary of state would be asked to take part in the selection of a customs expert who would

[41] Hughes to Geissler, Nov. 8, 1923, 814.51 An 4/3.
[42] Hughes to Geissler, April 5, 1924, 814.516/49a.

see that the customs revenues were properly collected. Disputes about the contract would be submitted to an American judge for decision.

The plan seemed sound technically, and after one or two changes suggested by officers in the State Department it did not seem likely to be unreasonably profitable to the bankers. The State Department hesitated to give it active support while a rival American group was still urging its own project; but on January 9, 1925, it authorized Geissler to say that it had been consulted about the plan and had expressed no objection to it. The secretary of state would agree to participate in the selection of a custom expert or in the submission of disputes to an American judge only if the Guatemalan government asked him to do so. Geissler was to make it clear that the United States was not urging the adoption of any particular project, because it must be impartial if other American groups offered a satisfactory competing plan. It had in the past objected to plans which it considered unsound or unfair, and impartiality did not mean that the American government had no preference between good and bad plans.[43] This message was never conveyed to the Guatemalan government because Keith, discouraged by the government's attitude, never formally presented his plan. The Guatemalan government did, however, issue 8% bonds in 1927 to discharge its debt of $2,515,000 to the International Railways.

The State Department made no further effort to push loan projects in Guatemala, and it told Geissler not to urge the advisability of a loan, even in a personal way, unless his advice was asked. It thought that a loan would almost inevitably involve some form of financial control, and that to advocate one might arouse suspicion of the American government's motives.[44] The Guatemalan government had by this time apparently decided to get along without a loan. Its financial situation had improved, with a rise in the price of coffee, and it seemed possible that it could reform the currency without resort to borrowing. In 1923, when the exchange rate had risen to 63 to the dollar, the government had set aside specific revenues to build up an exchange fund and had created a *Caja Reguladora* to administer the fund. The *Caja* had been able to stabilize the *peso* at 60 to the dollar.

[43] Hughes to Geissler, Jan. 9, 1925, 814.51/481.
[44] Hughes to Geissler, Jan. 23, 1925, 814.51/486.

In 1926, when the exchange fund reached 40% of the amount of paper money in circulation, it was turned over to a Central Bank which was given the exclusive right to issue currency. The *quetzal*, worth one dollar, became the monetary unit. Since that time Guatemala has had one of the most stable currencies in the hemisphere.

Chapter Six

GETTING THE MARINES OUT
OF NICARAGUA

In 1921 Nicaragua had about 600,000 inhabitants. Most of them lived in the low, hot lake region on the Pacific side of the isthmus, cut off from the Atlantic coast by a broad strip of jungle, and eighteen to twenty days from New York by any usual means of transport. There was a one-track railway which connected the towns of the lake region with one another and with the Pacific port of Corinto, and there were a few small steamers on Lake Nicaragua. Otherwise travel was by oxcart or by horse- or mule-back as it had been in colonial days. Automobiles were just beginning to appear in the largest towns. The capital, Managua, with some 40,000 inhabitants, had few buildings of more than one story, and its unpaved, badly drained streets made it appallingly dusty most of the year. The American legation, which was one of the finest houses, had no glass windows and was dimly lit by unshielded electric bulbs hanging from high ceilings. There were few official representatives of other countries and few resident foreign business or professional people. In such a community the conduct of diplomatic relations was quite different from the more formal procedures of a larger capital.

The Nicaraguans were notably intelligent and enterprising but more of their interest and energy had been focused on partisan politics than on economic development. The traditional hostility between "conservatives" and "liberals" was more intense than in any other Central American state. Every Nicaraguan was born into one party or the other, and politics was largely a matter of geography. Granada, the conservative center, was the home of a number of wealthy families who owned cattle ranches and other properties in the eastern part of the lake district, while most of the liberal leaders lived in the larger city of León in the west. Managua lay between them. It had been a small town when it was made the capital in 1852, but by 1921 it had become larger than Granada and was the home of important political figures in each party.

The United States had discouraged revolutions in Nicaragua since 1912 by maintaining a legation guard of about 100 marines at Managua. The State Department and two New York banking firms, Brown Brothers and J. and W. Seligman, exercised a limited and rather ineffective control over Nicaragua's finances. After the United States Senate failed to approve the loan treaty signed in 1911, the bankers could not recover the small amounts which they had already advanced to the government and had to make further advances to keep the government from collapsing. In 1913 they bought 51% of the stock of the Pacific Railroad of Nicaragua, and 51% of the stock of the national bank which they had helped the government to establish. The customs receivership which they had set up to secure their loans continued, and in 1912 the bankers negotiated for the government an agreement by which the holders of Nicaragua's sterling bonds consented to a reduction of the rate of interest in recognition of the better security which the receivership gave them.

In 1914, to help the government to meet the financial crisis caused by the outbreak of war in Europe, the bankers and the British bondholders waived temporarily the payments which they should have received from the customs, in return for a promise that they would be repaid when the government received $3,000,000 under the canal option treaty which was awaiting approval by the United States Senate. Secretary of State Bryan agreed to this arrangement, but when the treaty fund became available, in 1916, there was much pressure from Nicaragua's other creditors and Secretary Lansing insisted that a substantial part of the money be used to pay them and especially to pay the awards of a joint claims commission which the two governments had set up several years earlier. This led to an acrimonious conflict between the State Department and the bankers, which was finally settled when all concerned agreed to the financial plan of 1917.

Under this plan, Nicaragua undertook to pay the bankers and the British bondholders out of current revenues over a period of years, and to make this possible the government agreed to restrict its ordinary expenditures to $95,000 each month. It might spend an additional amount of $26,666.66 with the approval of a "high commission" composed of the Nicaraguan minister of finance, a resident American member appointed by the secretary of state of the United States, and an umpire, also appointed by the secretary of state. Other claims against Nicaragua would be adjudicated by a new claims commission and would be paid partly in cash from the treaty fund, and partly in new "guaranteed customs bonds," secured by the customs revenues. The high commission would be the fiscal agent for these. All of the government's revenues, under the plan, would be deposited in the national bank, which was managed by the New York bankers, and would be withdrawn only in payment of items authorized in the financial plan and the budget. It was hoped that the high commission's control of a portion of the government's budget would enable the resident American member to exercise a helpful influence on the government's general financial policy.

Nicaragua was prosperous during the last years of the world war, and by 1920 the government had paid off the debt to the bankers and the arrears on the British bonds and had accumulated a surplus of $1,000,000, which was earmarked under the financial plan for public works. It might now have freed itself from the restrictions of the financial plan, but it decided instead to use the machinery of the plan to obtain funds to build a railroad connecting the towns of the interior with the Atlantic coast. Conditions in the bond market were unfavorable, but Brown Brothers and Seligman agreed to help the government set up a plan under which a loan could be obtained when the market improved. They insisted however that the government must first buy back their stock in the Pacific railroad, which would presumably become less valuable if the Atlantic line were built. They had paid $1,000,000 for 51% of the railroad company's stock in 1913, but the line had become more profitable under their management, and they now asked $1,750,000. The government agreed to pay this: $300,000 in cash and the balance in 9% treasury bills to be paid out of surplus revenues under a new financial plan. The financial plan of 1920 was very similar to that of 1917 except that it increased the government's budgetary allowance from $95,000 to $105,000 per month.

When the new administration took office in Washington in 1921, the bankers still managed the railroad, pending the payment of the 1920 treasury bills, and managed the national bank, in which they owned 51% of the stock. The bank was the depositary for all government funds and was responsible for the country's currency. Both the railroad and the bank were incorporated in the United States with boards of directors in New York. The

159

Nicaraguan government, which now owned all of the railroad company's stock and 49% of the bank's stock, had a minority representation on each board, and the secretary of state at Washington, under an arrangement made by Secretary Bryan in 1913, named one director of each company, who was also supposed to act as examiner. The State Department thus had some responsibility for the conduct of both companies, and some responsibility for the collector general of customs, who was nominated by the bankers but approved by the State Department before appointment. It was more immediately responsible for the high commission, where the secretary of state appointed two of the three members. All of this involved an interference in Nicaragua's affairs which was incompatible with the American government's general policy in the Caribbean as it evolved after 1921, and it was a connection which from the State Department's point of view was certainly more troublesome than profitable. It was difficult to discontinue it, however, because a great number of the Nicaraguan government's creditors, American and European as well as Nicaraguan, had accepted the guaranteed customs bonds in payment of claims in reliance on the American government's relationship to the customs receivership and the high commission.

The new administration made no changes in the personnel of either organization. Colonel Clifford D. Ham, who had been collector general of customs since 1911, and Roscoe R. Hill, a former officer in the State Department who had become resident member of the high commission in 1920, continued in office. So also did Professor Jeremiah W. Jenks of New York University, who was the umpire of the high commission and the State Department's nominee on the boards of directors of the national bank and the railroad. The State Department as a rule made little effort to supervise the work of the customs service or the high commission and gave Dr. Jenks no instructions in connection with the bank or the railroad. It could not, however, avoid being drawn into the disputes which occasionally arose between the American officials or the bankers on the one hand and the Nicaraguan government on the other.

One such dispute was in progress in 1921. The Nicaraguan government had accepted the financial plan of 1920 in the expectation that a loan for the Atlantic railway could soon be arranged. When it found that the bankers were unwilling to make the loan on conditions which it considered acceptable, it accused them of bad faith and appealed to the State Department for help. The department had been involved to a very limited extent in the 1920 negotiations, but it tried informally to bring about an agreement. It could not however urge the bankers to make a loan which they considered unwise. The loan was never made and relations between the Nicaraguan government and the bankers were for a time rather strained.

The most unsatisfactory feature of our relations with Nicaragua was the continued presence at Managua of the legation guard which had kept the conservative party in power since 1912. Since the marines were regarded as a symbol of the American government's determination to prevent a revolution, the liberals did not dare to revolt. The conservatives gave them no opportunity to win elections. I was especially interested in this situation because I had worked in Nicaragua as a graduate student and was convinced of the unfairness and unwisdom of the American government's policy. In 1920, as a very junior officer in the State Department, I had persuaded some of my superiors that the department ought to insist on a fair presidential election, but the venerable Alvee A. Adee, the second assistant secretary of state, had vetoed what he said would be an improper intervention in Nicaragua's internal affairs. The department did, however, send an observer to see how the election was conducted, and in view of the observer's report it extracted a promise from General Emiliano Chamorro, the outgoing president, that an American expert would be employed to draft a law which would make possible a fairer election in 1924.

Probably neither President Harding nor Secretary Hughes knew anything about the situation in Nicaragua when they first took office. Certainly their choice of a new American minister showed no realization of the delicacy of the task that lay before him. John E. Ramer was apparently an important figure in the republican party in Colorado, but he was totally unqualified for diplomacy. During his instruction period in the department, when he showed no desire to learn anything about the problems that awaited him, it became evident that he was probably the worst of several incompetent political appointees who were being sent to replace the equally incompetent democratic political appointees in Latin America. The Latin American division could do little or nothing about diplomatic appointments at the beginning of an administration.

In the Latin American division we felt that the first objective of our policy in Nicaragua must be to create a situation where the legation guard could be safely withdrawn. An immediate, unconditional withdrawal could only be regarded by the liberals as an invitation to revolt. We had no desire to see a civil war which could undo the rather modest progress which had been made since 1909 with the American government's help, but we thought that we could extricate ourselves from a situation which was increasingly embarrassing if we could bring about the election in 1924 of a government which had real popular support. The liberals, who would presumably take over, would probably make trouble for the customs receivership and the New York bankers, but I do not remember that we were particularly concerned about this aspect of the situation. I imagine that we assumed that the American government would still have enough influence to see that any new Nicaraguan administration honored its contractual obligations. Hughes, when he went into the matter, approved the idea of endeavoring to see that Nicaragua had a better election in 1924, and as a first step the Nicaraguan government was persuaded to employ Dr. Harold W. Dodds, then secretary of the national municipal league in New York, to draft a new electoral law.

A series of incidents in 1921-1922 made the withdrawal of the legation guard seem more urgent. The Navy Department had been complaining for some time that it was hard to maintain the guard's morale and efficiency because its quarters were unsatisfactory and few diversions were available. The seriousness of the situation became evident in February 1921, when more than twenty marines destroyed the plant of a newspaper which had published an insulting article, and again in December when forty marines deliberately planned an attack on the Managua police and killed three men. Later four marines who expected to be arrested in connection with the attack deserted and killed two more police before one marine was killed and the others captured. Most of the men involved in these affairs were court-martialed and sent to prison, and in February 1922, the Navy Department told the State Department that the entire commissioned and enlisted personnel of the legation guard was being replaced.

Both the chargé d'affaires at Managua and the consul at Corinto pointed out that such incidents were likely to occur so long as the American marines remained in Nicaragua, and expressed the opinion that their presence was unnecessary.[1] Shortly afterward, however, Ramer, who had just arrived, strongly recommended that the marines not be withdrawn. The persons whom he consulted thought that a revolution would start within forty-eight hours of their departure, with grave danger to American interests in Nicaragua. He said that the gradual reduction in the strength of the guard, which the State Department had suggested as a possibility, was impracticable.[2]

The immediate withdrawal of the guard seemed less advisable because the political situation in Nicaragua was deteriorating. President Diego Manuel Chamorro had little administrative ability and little personal following. The country was feeling the effects of the world-wide depression, and there had been a poor coffee crop in 1921-1922. There were frequent minor disturbances along the frontier with Honduras, and even after the United States sold the Nicaraguan government arms and ammunition to enable it to protect itself there was a general feeling of insecurity. In April 1922, the conservative authorities arrested thirty to forty persons accused of plotting to kill the president. A month later a group of dissatisfied conservatives seized the Loma, the fortified hill which dominates Managua. It was suspected that ex-President Emiliano Chamorro, who was still the chief leader of the conservative party and was in Washington as Nicaraguan minister, had ordered the uprising, to warn the president against attempting to act independently. The president and his cabinet and most of the American colony gathered in the marine camp for protection, and Major Marston, the marine commander, warned the rebels that the legation guard would intervene if there was any firing on the camp or on the city. Ramer emphatically told the rebels that the United States would not permit a revolution and persuaded them to evacuate the Loma in return for a promise of lenient treatment.

The State Department approved Ramer's action, but we had misgivings when we received more complete information about some of the statements and threats which the minister had made. In August, when the minister wrote that he planned to take the same action if there were another revolt, he was warned by cable

---

[1] See Goold's dispatch of Dec. 16, 1921, 124.1718/39; and Playter's report of Dec. 18, 124.1718/40.

[2] Fletcher to Ramer, Jan. 20, 1922; Ramer to Hughes, March 15, 1922, 124.1718/39, 52.

163

that the legation guard should not intervene in internal disturbances without definite instructions from the State Department, except in a situation actually threatening the safety of the legation or the lives of members of the guard. He was told that it might be proper to prevent fighting in the quarter of the city where the legation or the guard was located, or to prevent rebels firing from the Loma into the city; but such action must be solely for the protection of the legation and not for the purpose of intervening in local politics. Members of the government might be granted asylum in the marine camp but in no circumstances should they be permitted to conduct the government or direct military operations from there. The minister must use his discretion in handling any sudden emergency, but the department did not wish the guard to intervene by force in local political affairs except where such action was unavoidable in self-protection.[3]

After this incident, the early withdrawal of the legation guard seemed more important than ever. For ten years the Nicaraguans had supposed that the guard would prevent any forcible overthrow of the conservative government. There were only approximately 100 marines, but 100 well-armed disciplined men were a formidable force in a country where a few hundred, untrained, poorly armed recruits might suffice for a revolution. There had been no occasion since 1912 for the guard to take any military action, and the State Department had apparently not attempted to lay down a policy for it to follow in case of disorder. At an earlier date it might have been willing to contemplate intervention by the guard to prevent a revolution against the constituted government. In 1922 the department was trying to avoid intervention of this sort. The instruction to Ramer showed that the presence of the guard at Managua was little more than a bluff, which might be called at any time with embarrassing consequences.

By this time, under the leadership of Francis White, the Latin American division had formulated a more definite plan for dealing with the Nicaraguan problem. We still felt that the legation guard might safely be withdrawn if the election of 1924 produced a government that had real popular support. It was obvious that the election would not be satisfactory if it were run by the Nicaraguan government. In the congressional and municipal elections in 1922, the conservative candidates won in practically

[3] Ramer to Hughes, Aug. 4, 1922, 817.00/2883. The reply is printed in *Foreign Relations, 1922,* Vol. II, p. 750.

164

every district, including the overwhelmingly liberal city of León. We intended to see that the presidential election in 1924 was fairer. Harold Dodds visited Nicaragua in 1922 and drew up a simple, workable electoral law which seemed likely to assure fair play if it were properly administered. The Nicaraguan Congress approved the law in March 1923, and we planned to have Dodds return to Nicaragua the next year to help with the registration of voters and then with the election itself. We knew that the Nicaraguan government would object to any effective supervision, but we thought that it could not resist if the United States insisted. The conservative leaders had welcomed Dodds politely and had not opposed the enactment of his electoral law. The liberals had received him enthusiastically.

We also planned to urge the Nicaraguan government to establish a constabulary to be trained and for a time at least to be commanded by Americans. We had the Nicaraguan situation in mind when we suggested that the Central American conference of 1922-1923 adopt the convention for the limitation of armaments, with its pledge to consider the creation of new police forces. For many years the State Department had thought that the elimination of the graft-ridden, unreliable armies would be a long step toward stable government in the more disorderly Caribbean states, and the success of the constabularies in Haiti and the Dominican Republic had encouraged us to press the idea on other countries. In Nicaragua, a police force under nonpartisan control would prevent violence and intimidation during the election and would prevent persecution of the defeated party afterward. It would also presumably strengthen the position of the incoming administration.

We felt that the execution of this program was too important a matter to be left entirely to Ramer. We had no confidence in the minister's judgment or in the accuracy of the information which he sent us. We consequently arranged to have Walter Thurston, who was one of the ablest younger officers in the career service, sent to Managua as secretary of the legation, with instructions to report directly to the department on all matters connected with the election. This was the sort of arrangement to which the State Department sometimes had to resort where the chief of mission was a political appointee. It created a bad situation in the legation and hurt American prestige, but at least it made it possible to know what was going on.

165

Our opinion of the minister sank lower when he showed poor judgment in dealing with a dispute between the collector general of customs and President Diego Manuel Chamorro early in 1923. The questions involved were unimportant, relating to the timing of remittances for the service of the foreign debt and the handling of some small trust funds, and they could probably have been settled rather easily with a little good will and common sense. Ramer, instead of trying to find a solution, advised Colonel Ham to yield to the government's demands. The matter became serious when the president allegedly threatened to use force to prevent Ham from entering his own office. Neither the bankers nor the State Department agreed wholly with Ham on the questions involved in the dispute, but it was impossible to acquiesce in an effort to coerce an official whose usefulness depended on his independence from government control. Fortunately some of the president's wiser advisers worked out an agreement that restored good relations before the State Department, which had been unable to obtain much information about the dispute from Ramer, had to take any definite action.

Ramer's failure to support Ham apparently encouraged the Nicaraguan government to attack Hill, the resident American member of the high commission. President Chamorro was angry because Hill, after agreeing to the expenditure of $446 for refreshments at a large reception in the presidential palace, had refused to approve payment of the bill from the funds controlled by the high commission. Hill had attended the reception, and after investigation in the kitchen, had discovered that only two cases of champagne were being served.[4] In March 1923, the Nicaraguan government demanded that the resident commissioner be removed, accusing him of exceeding his authority under the financial plan and of offensive conduct toward Nicaraguan officials. The State Department, whatever its doubts about Hill's conduct, had to insist on his freedom to make decisions that might be objectionable to Nicaraguan officials. It explained this to the Nicaraguan government and said that any disputes between the resident members of the high commission should be submitted to the umpire.[5]

In October 1923, after working on it for some months, the

[4] Ramer to Hughes, March 8, 1923, 817.51/1412, gives an account of this incident. I also heard the story from Hill.
[5] Note to the Nicaraguan minister, March 23, 1923, 817.51/1403.

Latin American division laid before the secretary a statement of policy on Nicaragua, embodying the plans for American assistance in the 1924 election and the proposal for a constabulary. Before reaching a decision, Hughes discussed the matter with General Chamorro, the Nicaraguan minister, with whom we had already discussed it informally. Chamorro objected to the plan for the election, arguing that any appearance of supervision would hurt the prestige of the conservative party and cost it thousands of votes. He also objected to the proposal for a constabulary. Nevertheless the secretary on October 8 sent Ramer by mail the text of a note to be delivered to the Nicaraguan government informing it of the department's plan. The note said that the United States thought that the holding of a free presidential election would make the further presence of the legation guard unnecessary, and that the marines would be withdrawn when the new government was installed on January 1, 1925. They would remain until then only if the Nicaraguan government thought that their presence would help to assure freedom in the election. The American government would be glad to ask Dodds or another expert, with any needed assistants, to go to Nicaragua some months before the election to help administer the new electoral law and would also be glad to help in the organization and training of a constabulary. The new government should be in a strong position, especially if the recently signed Central American treaties were ratified so that potential revolutionists would know that they would not be recognized by the other Central American governments if they obtained control. In any case the policy of the United States, as it had indicated in connection with the recent revolution in Honduras, would follow the principles laid down in the Treaty of Peace and Amity.

In 1923 mail to Nicaragua took nearly three weeks, and while the department's instruction was on the way President Diego Manuel Chamorro died suddenly on October 12. Bartolomé Martínez, who took over as vice president, was a man of Indian descent and limited education who had been put on the conservative ticket in 1920 as representative of a group which opposed the domination of the Granada aristocracy. For a time his influence in the government seemed to be overshadowed by that of Emiliano Chamorro, who returned from Washington and resumed the leadership of the conservative party. Chamorro's prestige was enhanced by the fact that Secretary Hughes, without

167

realizing what it could mean, had arranged for him to travel from Panama to Corinto on an American warship.[6]

Chamorro undoubtedly intended at this time to return to the presidency in 1925, but he knew that his election would be difficult without Martínez' support. He and his associates consequently promised to support Martínez for reelection. Presumably they were confident that the United States would not permit the president to be a candidate, because Article 104 of the Nicaraguan constitution specifically prohibited the election as president or vice president of a person who had held the office at any time during the preceding presidential term. Chamorro had had to give up his own candidacy for reelection in 1920 because the American government disapproved of it. At the same time the conservatives invited the liberals to join with them in establishing a "national government" with Martínez at its head. The liberals, who were divided and seemed to have no strong leaders, were glad to discuss the idea. Though they were confident of their numerical majority, they were not at all sure that the United States could or would assure a free election. After some three weeks of negotiation, the representatives of the two parties reported that they could not agree on a common ticket but they promised nevertheless to carry on the electoral campaign with moderation and mutual respect and agreed that the winning party would give its opponents representation in the new administration. The question of the constitutionality of Martínez' candidacy seemed to have been deliberately ignored.[7]

In the meantime the conservative leaders had been discussing the note about the withdrawal of the legation guard, which Ramer delivered on November 14. Some of them, including General Chamorro, apparently wanted the marines to leave immediately, but many others were disturbed at the idea that the guard should be withdrawn at any time. The Nicaraguan government's reply, dated December 13, asked that the guard remain at least until the inauguration of the new administration on January 1, 1925. It expressed a willingness to have Dodds come to Nicaragua, with not more than two or three assistants, some months

---

[6] When I remonstrated with Mr. Hughes he expressed regret but said that he had acceded to Chamorro's request, without knowing that I had already turned it down, because the Minister was "such a nice fellow." We all liked Chamorro.

[7] Ramer to Hughes, Dec. 10, 1923, 817.00/3007.

before the election, but said that lack of funds would make it impossible to ask him to stay for any considerable amount of time and would also make impossible the immediate organization of a constabulary. The note thus rejected the essential features of the State Department's plan. The Nicaraguan government asserted its determination to guarantee the freedom of the 1924 election without interference from the United States.[8]

Early in November, while the negotiations for a coalition government were still going on, Ramer asked what position he should take with regard to the constitutionality of Martínez' reelection. It seemed probable that this inquiry had been instigated by the other conservative leaders, who were still ostensibly supporting Martínez' candidacy, and we were reluctant to answer it. There could be little doubt about what the constitution meant, and what the conservatives were really asking was what the United States would do if the constitution were violated. We wanted to avoid interference, so far as we could, and we wanted to discourage the Central Americans from bringing their problems to Washington for settlement. On the other hand, after the position which it had taken on Chamorro's candidacy in 1920, and after it had committed itself so definitely to a recognition policy based on the Central American treaty, it would be extremely difficult for the American government to recognize Martínez if he were elected. If we could not recognize the next president of Nicaragua, our whole plan for the peaceful withdrawal of the legation guard would be unworkable. I personally thought that we should tell Martínez that he could not constitutionally be elected, before he formally announced his candidacy, but I was overruled. Ramer's inquiry went unanswered. When he cabled on December 8 that the conservatives were awaiting the department's reply before deciding on a presidential candidate, he was told that the department would not express an opinion unless it was officially asked to do so by the Nicaraguan government.[9]

During the next few weeks Chamorro's friends, through Ramer, tried repeatedly to obtain a ruling from the State Department, while Martínez and his associates tried to create the impression in Nicaragua that the department did not oppose him. Since Señor Zavala, the Nicaraguan chargé d'affaires, was a

[8] Ramer to Hughes, Dec. 17, 1923, 817.1051/35.
[9] Ramer to Hughes, Dec. 8, and Hughes to Ramer, Dec. 10, 1923, 817.00/2994.

Chamorrista, Martínez sent Toribio Tijerino, the consul general at New York, to talk with the department. When Zavala and Tijerino came to my office, Tijerino discussed the Nicaraguan political situation in very general terms, without asking or receiving any expression of opinion about the constitutional question. Afterward, without consulting Zavala, he signed the chargé's name to a cable reporting that I had expressed sympathy with Martínez' candidacy and that the State Department did not intend to interfere. Much the same thing happened after two or three subsequent meetings. Tijerino argued eloquently that the constitution should not be an obstacle to something which the Nicaraguan people desired, but did not officially ask for an opinion. We attempted to correct Tijerino's misstatements in cables to Ramer, but the minister apparently only grew more confused about what the department's position was.

In January 1924 Ramer reported that the minister for foreign affairs had asked for a ruling by the State Department and that an immediate statement was necessary because the situation in Nicaragua was grave. We supposed that this was the official request on which we had been insisting. We replied by quoting the text of Article 104 of the Nicaraguan constitution, saying that the department did not feel that the American government should make suggestions about its interpretation, especially as it did not see that the provision left any room for interpretation.[10] Martínez replied that he had already been informed of the State Department's attitude, and that he was submitting the question to Congress. Both communications were made public in Nicaragua.

The department's statement did not settle anything, because Ramer still could not understand the department's position. This was partly our fault, because we had no confidence in the minister's discretion and we had not attempted to explain why the department was reluctant to say flatly that Martínez would not be recognized if he were elected. It is hard to understand, however, why the minister failed to grasp the meaning of the statement made in January. His continuing uncertainty about his government's attitude naturally encouraged Martínez to disregard what the American government had said. He persisted in his intention to be a candidate and in his efforts to obtain the State Department's consent. The Nicaraguan Congress, in the meantime, decided that it had no authority to interpret the constitution.

[10] Phillips to Ramer, Jan. 24, 1924, 817.00/3015.

Under the new electoral law, the registration of voters took place in March 1924. Harold Dodds went to Nicaragua with three assistants to help with it and it went off remarkably well. There was some wilful obstruction, chiefly from followers of Chamorro, but not enough to affect the result. Dodds' experience, however, convinced him that the election in October would not be free unless there were effective American supervision, especially as the registration showed that the two parties were more nearly equal numerically than most observers had thought.[11] At his suggestion the State Department obtained Martínez' consent to having one of his American assistants remain in Nicaragua to see that adequate preparations for the election were made. The department planned to keep track of these preparations through Thurston, who was instructed in February to give all of his time to electoral matters and authorized to confer with the minister for foreign affairs and other Nicaraguan officials as he saw fit.

By this time it was obvious that we could hardly hope to carry out our program in Nicaragua if Ramer continued as minister there. He was not only incompetent but dangerously indiscreet. It was always very difficult, however, to bring about the removal of a political appointee who had strong support in his own state. Ramer might have stayed in Managua indefinitely if he had not decided to make up for his failure to keep the department informed by writing two dispatches in April. To avoid letting Thurston or the legation clerk see them, he wrote these in longhand and gave them to a marine typist, who faithfully followed the Minister's spelling and grammar. Many proper names and Spanish phrases were barely recognizable and the literary style was quite unlike that to which the department was accustomed. Ramer discussed the political activities of the "heavy politicals" (the *jefes políticos* or provincial governors) and thought that there would be no fair election unless the State Department "intercedes and sends in one hundred and fifty or two hundred Navy officials from Panama to assist at the polls if it can be done. We have the law adopted by Congress, why not enforce it?" He thought that it would be "a good idea" to double the number of marines at Managua, "just for show, as it would make them set up and take notice." In the other dispatch he reported that he had sent word to Martínez, through the president's niece, that the State Department would "protest" the appointment of

[11] Dodds to Munro, May 21, 1924, 817.00/3075.

Toribio Tijerino as minister of finance because Tijerino was "anti in spirit and praises bolshevism."[12]

These dispatches provided the final bit of evidence which convinced the secretary that Ramer must leave Nicaragua. The minister was rebuked for interfering in the appointment of members of the Nicaraguan cabinet and soon afterward he was ordered to Washington for "consultation." Because the administration did not wish to offend his friends in Colorado, he was not told until after the election in the United States in November that he would not be permitted to return. Even some of the people who had been anxious to bring about his recall felt that this treatment was outrageous, because Ramer was given no indication that he would have more than a short stay in Washington and he consequently left his family in Managua for several months before he was permitted to return for them.

Walter Thurston took charge of the legation at Managua. The political situation was still uncertain. Chamorro had broken with Martínez, but the president still seemed to hope that he could be reelected with the help of the anti-Chamorro conservatives and the liberals. In May 1924, when the conservative convention nominated Chamorro for the presidency and the liberals nominated Juan Bautista Sacasa, Martínez seemed to be left with the support of only a small group of dissenting conservatives. This did not seem to discourage him because lack of popular support did not necessarily mean that an official candidate would lose an election.

The State Department finally realized that it must take a more definite position about Martínez' candidacy. It would be in a ridiculous situation if its efforts for a free election resulted in the election of a president whom it could not recognize. It withheld action until Ramer left Managua and then told Thurston to tell Martínez that the American government would have to decide when the time came whether it could recognize the new president of Nicaragua and that it felt constrained to say that Martínez' election would be unconstitutional. The president was inclined to argue, but when the State Department said that it would be "highly indisposed" to recognize him, and then permitted Thurston to publish a letter stating its position, he gave up the idea of being a candidate. In July he made a deal with the liberals to support Carlos Solórzano, his minister of finance, for

[12] Dispatches of Feb. 20, and March 3, 1924, 817.00/3054, 3055.

the presidency and Dr. Sacasa for the vice presidency. Only a few conservatives followed Martínez in this coalition, and liberals took over many of the more important administrative and military positions.

The American government of course had no interest in any political grouping or any particular candidate. When the minister of foreign affairs asked Thurston whether the State Department would view the new coalition ticket with favor, the department declined to express an opinion, saying that it felt that "the transference of the center of political activity of Nicaragua to Washington would be detrimental to that Government's interests" and that it would recognize any candidate not excluded by the 1923 treaty and fairly and constitutionally elected. The department made it clear that it still wanted to see a free and fair election. The complicated political situation that had developed since President Diego Manuel Chamorro's death did not seem likely to make the holding of a free election any easier. The coalition would have control of the army and the police, and of the national treasury, which was an important asset in an election, but the Chamorrista conservatives, who were now the opposition party, controlled the Congress and the courts. Thurston learned in July that the administration was arranging a public demonstration to demand a constitutional convention, which would make it possible for the president to get control of all branches of the government. He told Martínez that any such action would have disastrous consequences; and when some adherents of the coalition did stage a demonstration Martínez told them that he agreed with them but that Nicaragua did not enjoy full sovereign rights because there was a foreign power that interfered more than it should in the country's internal affairs.[13]

In the summer of 1924 the Nicaraguan government completed payments for the Pacific railroad stock and became free to run the railroad as it saw fit and to dispose of all of its revenues except the amounts withheld by the customs receivership for the service of the bonded debt. It completed its emancipation from the bankers' control by buying the bankers' stock in the national bank. The bank was now affiliated with the Mercantile Bank of the Americas, which had taken over the bank stock formerly owned by Brown Brothers and Seligman. The purchase did not entirely terminate the bankers' relationship with Nicaragua, for

[13] Thurston to Hughes, July 26, 1924, 817.00/3140.

they still had a responsibility in connection with the customs receivership, which had to continue to provide for the service of the
British bonds and the guaranteed customs bonds. Brown Brothers ceased to have any connection with Nicaraguan affairs but
the Guaranty Trust Company of New York, which was interested
in the Mercantile Bank of the Americas, had for some time been
associated with Seligman in the management of the national bank
and the railroad.

The sale of the bank stock was profitable to the Mercantile
Bank, which received $300,000 for stock carried on its books for
little more than half that amount, and which insisted that the
government as part of the deal buy for $300,000 another sub-
sidiary, the *Compañia Comercial de Ultramar*, whose assets were
apparently worth far less than that. The State Department
doubted whether the transaction was wise from Nicaragua's
point of view but it did not want to oppose a step which would
give the government financial independence. Many Nicaraguans
and most of the Americans in Nicaragua opposed the purchase
of the bank because they feared that government management
would imperil the currency system. President Martínez, however,
gave positive public assurances that the stability of the currency
would be maintained and for the time being he made no important changes in the way in which the bank and the railroad were
run. Both companies remained under the control of boards of
directors sitting in New York with a substantial North American
membership, including representatives of the bankers. The
J. G. White Management Corporation, which had been operating
the railroad for the bankers, continued to manage it, and the
bank continued to be directed by an officer selected by Seligman
and the Guaranty Trust Company.

The payment of Nicaragua's debt to the bankers raised questions about the continued validity of the financial plan. The State
Department wanted to give up any financial control in Nicaragua
if it could properly do so,[14] but when the Nicaraguan government suggested that the financial plan would come to an end with
the payment of the treasury bills the solicitor of the department
decided that it would have to continue because the holders of the
sterling bonds of 1909 and the guaranteed customs bonds of 1918,
which had been given to Nicaraguans and foreigners in payment

[14] See my memorandum of Sept. 30, 1924, 817.51/1520, which was approved by Francis White and the secretary.

of claims, had contractual rights under it.[15] It was clear, however, that the restriction of the government's budget to $105,000 per month would mean little when the government could dispose as it saw fit of all of its revenues, and that the high commission's control of the additional allowance of $26,666.66 would mean even less. In September 1924 the Nicaraguan government, which was again displeased with Hill, pointed this out and urged that Hill's functions be turned over to the collector general of customs. The State Department did not feel that the complaints against Hill justified his abrupt removal, but it told him that it was planning to combine the two offices in the near future. Hill nevertheless continued at his post until 1928, partly because the political situation in Nicaragua made a change seem inadvisable.

Dodds, though other commitments made it very inconvenient, had promised the State Department that he would return to Nicaragua in September 1924 to supervise the election to be held on October 5. He had arranged to take with him thirteen assistants to provide chairmen for the departmental electoral boards. He had recommended the employment of a large number of impartial precinct watchers, but the State Department had considered this impracticable. After the success of the registration, we thought that supervision with a relatively small staff would give reasonable assurance of a fair election. The administration's control of the army and the police would be offset to some extent by the fact that most of the members of the electoral boards, which had been chosen before Martínez' alliance with the liberals, were Chamorristas. Martínez was apparently willing to have Dodds come and had in fact said that the Nicaraguan government would pay his expenses in order to avoid the appearance of American intervention. Thurston was consequently instructed on July 16 to suggest that Martínez invite the electoral mission to come to Nicaragua in the middle of September. He was told, for his information and discreet use, that the department would consider sending Dodds to observe the election even if the Nicaraguan government did not accept his services, because the American government would need his report in order to decide whether the new administration had been constitutionally elected.[16] Secretary Hughes was away when this instruction was

[15] Hughes to Thurston, June 30, 1924, 817.51/1494.
[16] When part of this instruction was printed in *Foreign Relations*, the threat to send Dodds if the Nicaraguan government did not employ him was omitted.

175

sent, but Francis White, who had discussed the matter with the secretary some weeks earlier, had understood that he approved the proposed course of action.[17]

Martínez and his cabinet at first felt that they would have to agree to the State Department's proposal, but Toribio Tijerino, whom Ramer had so well described as "anti in spirit," persuaded them to reject it. Thurston was informed that the government could guarantee a free election. It thought that the proposed supervision would be inadequate and would give merely the appearance of fairness. What the president's advisers apparently had in mind in this latter statement was the probability that the conservatives would misuse their control of the electoral boards and the courts if American supervision made it hard for the government to use extra-legal means to coerce them. Thurston was at first told that this reply was not necessarily final, but when the State Department asked that it be reconsidered, Martinez said defiantly that his government would "assume the attitude . . . which best serves the interests of Nicaragua" if civilians or marines came without invitation. Hughes felt that the United States could not impose supervision of the elections if the Nicaraguan government resisted it, and the plan to send Dodds to Nicaragua had to be given up. The failure of the program on which we had been working for more than two years would have seemed more unfortunate had it not been for the recent changes in Nicaragua. One of the principal arguments for supervision of the elections had disappeared when the liberals, who had been kept out of office by the presence of the legation guard, took control of the government through their alliance with Martínez.

Despite their defiant attitude, Martínez and his friends realized that it was important to make the elections seem free and fair. Since some American labor leaders had been sympathetic to the liberals' complaints about their exclusion from the government in the past, some of the liberals asked the Pan American Federation of Labor to send a delegation to observe the election. Samuel Gompers, who was president of the Pan American Federation, showed some interest, but dropped the idea when the State Department explained the situation to him.[18] Later Martí-

[17] See my memorandum to the acting secretary, Aug. 14, 1924, 817.00/-3170.

[18] Gompers to Hughes, Aug. 21, and Hughes to Gompers, Sept. 2, 1924, 817.00/3143. See also my memorandum of Sept. 2, 817.00/3192.

nez suggested that American marines observe the voting and examine the returns before the official count. Both Thurston and
the State Department were doubtful about permitting marines
to do this without adequate training, and when Martínez said
that the marines must go in civilian dress, and simply as observers, his proposal was rejected.

Chamorro and his followers carried on a vigorous campaign
and were probably allowed more freedom of action than the liberals had had in elections under the conservative regime. The
Chamorristas complained that they were often denied permits
for meetings and that their partisans were not allowed to carry
even machetes, while the government's friends carried revolvers;
but on the other hand the coalition complained about the conduct of the electoral boards and the courts, which the Chamorristas controlled. The State Department and the legation did
what they could to prevent abuses. When Martínez threatened
to force the national electoral board to put his "republican conservative" party on the ballot, in addition to the liberal party, the
State Department warned him against any attempt at coercion;
but, at the same time, it told Thurston to impress on Chamorro
the fact that the American government was watching the performance of the electoral boards and the courts and that any un-
lawful procedure by them would make it hard to consider the
results of the election as an expression of the wishes of the people.[19] Three days before the election, the conservative leaders
told Thurston that they would withdraw from the contest unless
the American government announced that the result of the election would not be recognized if the government resorted to coercion.[20] The State Department refused to issue a statement, but it
told Thurston to present a note recounting its efforts to bring
about a free election and reaffirming its intention to withdraw the
legation guard on January 1.

Just before the election, Martínez issued decrees making
changes in the personnel of the electoral boards and creating a
special force of armed police to be present in each polling place.
The Supreme Court upheld the national electoral board when it
protested against these actions, but the government rejected the
court's decision. Election day, October 5, was relatively quiet,
though the government imposed a state of siege late in the after-

[19] Hughes to Thurston, Sept. 2, 1924, 817.00/3145.
[20] Thurston to Hughes, Oct. 2, 1924, 817.00/3164.

noon because of minor disorders in the conservative department of Chontales. The coalition candidates were reported to have won by a substantial margin.

The conservatives had many complaints about the way in which the voting was conducted, and Thurston, after a careful inquiry, reported that the election "was preceded by such sustained governmental pressure and violence, was effected under such drastic governmental control, especially in the departments of Estelí, Rivas, Chontales, Carazo, Masaya, Granada and Matagalpa, and was exposed to such fraudulent alteration of the returns through the possession by unauthorized persons of the urns and ballots for several days after the election during the state of siege, as to render the published statements of the result unworthy of acceptance."[21] Suspicions about the counting of the votes were the more justified because the conservative members of many departmental and district boards were excluded from the proceedings by force. In November the conservative majority on the national board of elections declared that the board could not make the final canvas of the vote because some of the returns had not been received, but the liberal member of the board completed the canvas by himself. The government announced that slightly more than two-thirds of those registered had voted, and that Solórzano had received 48,000 votes and Chamorro 28,000.

The outlook for the new government was unpromising. The liberals seemed to have few able and experienced leaders, and they would have to work with a conservative president who had little prestige and little proven ability. The defeated conservatives, on the other hand, had in Emiliano Chamorro a leader who had great prestige as a soldier and statesman and who commanded the enthusiastic loyalty of the rank and file of the party. They were indignant about the treatment which they had received in the election, and their representatives told Thurston that they would not press appeals under the electoral law because they thought that any new elections would be held under still worse conditions. It seemed unlikely that they would settle down peacefully under the new administration.

Just before the result of the election was announced, Martínez told Thurston that he would imprison some of the conservative leaders unless Chamorro publicly promised not to attempt an up-

[21] Thurston to Hughes, Oct. 28, 1924, 817.00/3196.

rising. Chamorro was willing to assure the American legation in writing that he would not revolt, but he refused to make a public statement. The State Department instructed Thurston to obtain a written promise from Chamorro, and then to tell Martínez that he had it and that the American government would be most unfavorably impressed by political imprisonments or unusual military measures in the absence of an armed revolt. Chamorro and two other principal conservative leaders, Adolfo Díaz and Carlos Cuadra Pasos, assured the legation that they were not engaged in any revolutionary activities, but Chamorro made it clear that the statement was valid only for the time being.[22] Meanwhile Solórzano, the president-elect, had been worrying not only about a possible Chamorrista revolt but also lest Martínez use the uncertain situation as a pretext for remaining in power after the end of his term on January 1. The agreement which he and Martínez had signed promised the liberals at least two cabinet posts and five provincial governments and half of the appointments in the courts, but this left Solórzano free to fill many other positions as he saw fit. He secretly offered to give some of them to the conservative leaders if they would recognize his election[23] but Chamorro refused to negotiate on this basis.

The State Department did not decide what to do about recognizing the new government until it received Thurston's detailed report on the election[24] and a cable sent on November 28 giving his recommendations.[25] Thurston thought that the new government would certainly be overthrown if the United States recognized it without taking any further steps to support it, or if the United States withheld recognition. He thought that the American government had two possible courses of action: to accept the result of the election in return for formal assurances that the 1928 election would be supervised by the United States, that there would be a genuine coalition government in the meantime, and that the maintenance of order would be turned over to a foreign-controlled police force; or, as an alternative, to insist on and supervise a new election. He pointed out that the second course would require at least a show of force. To us in the State Depart-

[22] Thurston to Hughes, Nov. 20, and Hughes to Thurston, Nov. 26, 1924, 817.00/3217; Thurston to Hughes, Dec. 2, 817.00/3226.

[23] Thurston to Hughes, Nov. 20, 1924, 817.00/3216.

[24] Thurston to Hughes, Nov. 5, 1924, 817.00/3222.

[25] Thurston to Hughes, Nov. 28, 1924, 817.00/3216.

ment neither alternative seemed practicable. The secretary could hardly commit his successor to supervise an election in 1928, especially as by that time, with the withdrawal of the legation guard, there would presumably be no more reason to supervise an election in Nicaragua than in any other country. Furthermore, we thought that a coalition government would not work. To insist on a new election did not seem feasible. As the department told Thurston, the election would be of no value without close supervision, "which would also mean armed intervention which is not to be contemplated." The least objectionable course seemed to be to recognize the Solórzano administration just as the American government regularly recognized new governments after even worse elections in other Central American states. If this involved a loss of face, it also had the merit of fairness: it gave the liberals the benefit of the same tolerance shown the conservatives after the elections of 1912, 1916, and 1920. It would help to dissipate the idea that the United States was partial to the conservatives.[26]

Thurston was consequently told, on December 10, that the State Department was "disposed to raise no question regarding the validity of the elections and to continue normal diplomatic relations" with Solórzano after his inauguration. Without telling Solórzano of this decision, however, Thurston was to say, as an expression of his own personal opinion, that a "definite, formal, written engagement" to begin immediately the formation of a constabulary with American help, to take adequate measures, in which the United States could cooperate, for the solution of economic problems, and to assure fairness in the 1928 elections, might prove the deciding element in determining the American government to raise no question about the recent election. The economic problems to which the department referred had arisen because the government, in order to buy the national bank from the New York bankers, had stripped the bank of its reserves, and the bank's inability to finance the current coffee crop was causing an economic crisis which threatened to make the political situation worse. In addition to suggesting that Solórzano give these assurances, Thurston was to suggest that the president-elect try to obtain the cooperation of other political groups. The department did not feel that a coalition cabinet, imposed by pressure,

[26] For the Latin American division's views, see my memorandum of Dec. 3 and White's memorandum of Dec. 6, 1924, 817.00/3222.

would work well, but it was willing to have Thurston use his good offices to bring about a conciliation with the conservatives if his help were desired. After Solórzano gave the required assurances, the department would instruct Thurston to warn Chamorro against any attempt at revolution.

Solórzano gave the required assurances in a statement signed on December 13. Thurston then held several conferences with the conservative leaders, but his efforts to persuade them to cooperate with the incoming administration were fruitless. Martínez made matters worse when he prevented a number of conservative senators and deputies, including some who had been certified as elected in October, from taking their seats when Congress met. The State Department emphatically expressed its disapproval, but to no effect. The department, meanwhile, did not inform Solórzano of its decision to recognize him. The elections in Honduras were to be held in the last days of December, and in view of our efforts to persuade Carías not to be a candidate we did not want the Hondurans to get the idea that we had been obliged to accept a *fait accompli* in Nicaragua. The United States simply continued to maintain normal relations with Nicaragua after Solórzano was inaugurated on January 1, 1925.

In his inaugural address the new president emphasized his desire for friendly relations with the United States. He said that he hoped for American cooperation in preparing for the next presidential election and in organizing a constabulary. In conversation with Thurston he asked the chargé to give him a plan for the constabulary, suggesting that it be placed under the direction of Major Keyser, the commander of the legation guard. He expressed the hope that the guard would remain at Managua.

On January 3 Secretary Hughes asked the navy to withdraw the legation guard at the earliest possible moment, and a few days later the marines began to prepare to leave. There was consternation in government circles and among the foreigners in Nicaragua, for no one seems to have taken very seriously the American government's statement that the guard would be withdrawn after the new government took office. The government asked that the guard remain until an efficient constabulary could be established, saying that an immediate withdrawal would have dangerous economic and political consequences and would compel Nicaragua to build up an expensive army. Most of the Ameri-

181

cans in Nicaragua, including those in the financial services, sent word through the legation that the withdrawal might lead to revolution and urged that it be postponed.

Thurston thought that there might be a revolution when the marines left, and he recommended that the American government announce publicly its recognition and its moral support of the Solórzano administration, to show that the withdrawal was not intended as an invitation to revolt. He was authorized on January 7 to make it clear that the continuance of diplomatic relations implied formal recognition. He might also tell the party leaders, orally, that the United States would give moral support to the new administration in maintaining the constitutional order and that it would be glad to cooperate with Solórzano in carrying out the program outlined in his inaugural address. The State Department pointed out, however, that the Nicaraguan government had known for a year that the marines would be withdrawn and had had before it during that time the offer of help in training a constabulary. The department said that the marines would leave about February 9. After receiving the text of the Nicaraguan government's plea for delay, however, the department said that it would permit the legation guard to remain at Managua until September 1 if the Nicaraguan government would go forward energetically with the organization of the constabulary. It felt that it was not quite fair to hold Solórzano responsible for his predecessor's failure to act. The new administration assured Thurston that it would proceed with the constabulary at once.

The State Department had some time since asked the legation at Managua to prepare a plan for a constabulary and it had been trying to obtain legislation from Congress to permit members of the armed forces of the United States to assist other Latin American governments as they were already assisting Haiti and the Dominican Republic. Meanwhile it hoped to have members of the legation guard help informally in training the Nicaraguan police force while they remained at Managua, and it thought that civilian instructors could be employed under contract after the guard left if the hoped-for legislation was not approved. Major Keyser of the legation guard had prepared a plan which was designed to avoid so far as possible the appearance of foreign control. Under this proposal, American instructors would not command the constabulary in its ordinary operations, but would have full authority over the "training branch," whose commander would draw up rules and regulations for the whole force and would control finances and supplies. He would also have authority to order the return to the training branch of any officer or enlisted man in the constabulary. The new force, with 23 officers and 392 enlisted men, would replace the existing army and police. To prepare for its training, the navy had already detailed to the legation guard several marines who spoke Spanish or had had experience in constabulary work in other countries.

On February 10 the legation was authorized to present this plan to the Nicaraguan government. Unfortunately, the instruction went to Minister Ramer, who had been permitted to return to Nicaragua temporarily to get his family and personal possessions. Ramer simply handed the plan, in an unsigned memorandum, to the minister of government, and apparently deliberately encouraged the Nicaraguan officials to think that they could delay or prevent the withdrawal of the legation guard by delaying action on the constabulary. After Thurston again took charge of the legation on March 4 the Nicaraguan government showed no eagerness to go ahead with the plan, until Thurston intimated that the marines would leave before September if their help in training the constabulary was not needed. The government then submitted the plan to the Nicaraguan Congress, which made changes reducing the authority which the American officers would have and providing that the constabulary would cooperate with but not replace the army.

Thurston urged that the legation guard be withdrawn without further delay, but the State Department wanted to give the Nicaraguan government every possible chance to maintain peace. It told the navy that it would have no objection to the withdrawal of the guard in the first part of August, but it asked that officers be designated to start the training of the constabulary in the meantime if the Nicaraguan government asked for them.

Since there was as yet no legal authorization for American officers to accept regular employment in the new force, the State Department had looked into the possibility of finding civilians who could serve under contract, and it had already put the Nicaraguan legation in Washington in touch with Major Calvin B. Carter, who had many years of experience in the Philippine constabulary. On June 10 Carter signed a one-year contract with the Nicaraguan government to serve as chief of the proposed constabulary. In telling Thurston about the contract the State Department emphasized that it had been made directly between Carter and the Nicaraguan legation and that Carter and his four American assistants should be regarded as Nicaraguan employees with no connection with the United States government. Thurston was told, however, to give them all proper assistance. Carter arrived in Managua early in July and at once began to train a number of men who had already been recruited for the new force.

Just before Carter's arrival it became known in Managua that the marines would leave early in August. This apparently took Solórzano and his associates by surprise, for Ramer had been writing them from Washington that the president and the secretary of state expected the guard to remain in Nicaragua until the new constabulary had been organized.[27] In an obvious attempt to obtain a further delay, the government on July 2 asked that members of the legation guard begin to train the constabulary, but the State Department rather curtly replied that this would now be impracticable, referring to the fact that the Nicaraguan government had shown no interest in offers of help which the American government had been making during the past six months. On July 17 the minister for foreign affairs opposed the withdrawal in a formal note, citing the assurances which the government had received from Ramer. President Solórzano disavowed this communication when he learned of it, but on July 27 his minister at Washington told the State Department that his government feared there might be disorders when the guard was withdrawn. He asked that the United States issue a statement saying that it disapproved of any revolutionary activities and would refuse to recognize any administration coming into power by force. The department, which was irritated by Solórzano's failure to take action in some recent cases where marines off duty had been attacked by Nicaraguans, as well as by his procrastination in connection with the constabulary, refused to do so.[28]

The marines left Managua on August 1. The Nicaraguan newspapers treated the withdrawal as an occasion for national rejoicing. The presence of the legation guard at Managua had perhaps

[27] Thurston to Kellogg, July 18, 1925, 124.1718/136.

[28] See Morgan's memorandum of conversation with the Nicaraguan minister, July 27, and White's memorandum to the secretary, July 28, 1925, 817.00/3296. Stokeley Morgan had recently replaced me as assistant chief of the Latin American division.

been more disturbing and distasteful to the people of the other Central American states than to the Nicaraguans, who had benefited from the period of peace which had followed the American intervention, but most Nicaraguans were probably glad to see the marines go.

The situation was quite different from that which the State Department had envisaged when it announced the plan for withdrawal in October 1923. At that time we felt that we had a right to insist that the conservatives, whom the American government had kept in power for thirteen years, should agree to effective supervision of the election of 1924. We thought that both parties should welcome the organization of an American-trained constabulary, the liberals because it would help to assure a free election, and the conservatives because it would protect them if the liberals won. We hoped that the institution of a government which had the support of a majority of the people, and the support of an efficient police force, would create a situation where the marines could be withdrawn without serious danger of revolution. We knew that it might be necessary to exert strong diplomatic pressure and perhaps a threat of force to persuade the Nicaraguan government to accept electoral supervision, but we thought that this sort of intervention would be preferable to the continuance of the indefensible situation that existed or to the civil war which would follow if we simply withdrew the marines. The death of President Diego Manuel Chamorro and the defection of Martínez from the conservative party completely changed the picture. It could no longer be said that the legation guard was keeping a minority government in power. Some of us still felt that a continued insistence on a free election and on the creation of a constabulary would offer the only hope for the establishment of a situation where the marines could be withdrawn without a revolution, but under the changed conditions Secretary Hughes was probably right in refusing to consider the use of coercion.

Secretary Kellogg, after his painful experience with the second intervention in Nicaragua, thought that the withdrawal of the marines in 1925 was premature and ill-advised.[29] In the light of hindsight, it is possible to argue that the disastrous events which followed their withdrawal might have been avoided if the guard

[29] He said this to me.

had remained at Managua for another year or more. It seems more likely, however, that the weak, internally divided coalition government would have broken down even if the guard had remained, and that the American government would then have faced much the same situation which confronted it in 1926-1927. In any event it would have been difficult to justify the continuance of the sort of interference in Nicaragua's affairs which the presence of the guard represented.

Chapter Seven

THE SECOND INTERVENTION
IN NICARAGUA

Within four weeks after the withdrawal of the legation guard the weak coalition regime at Managua began to break down. The State Department soon found itself dealing with a usurping conservative government, which it could not recognize without abandoning the principles laid down in the Central American treaties, and at the same time trying, unsuccessfully, to dissuade the liberals from attempting to regain power by force. Before a government which could be recognized had been established, one of the most destructive civil wars in the country's history had begun and the marines had returned to Nicaragua. To end the war, the United States had to promise to disarm the armies on both sides, to assume responsibility for the maintenance of order, and to supervise a presidential election. I was stationed at Panama while these events were occurring, and the account which follows is based on the official record and on what I learned after I took charge of the legation at Managua in 1927. Like other observers, I found it difficult at the time to understand how the American government could become involved in a course of action so inconsistent with the policy which the State Department had been attempting to follow since 1921.

The United States was represented at Managua, after August 1925, by Charles C. Eberhardt, who was one of the first officers from the consular branch of the foreign service to be appointed as minister after the reorganization of the service under the Rogers Act. Mr. Eberhardt had been a highly respected consular inspector, but had little experience in political affairs. At Managua he was confronted by exasperatingly difficult problems unlike any that he had encountered in his previous service. He was further handicapped by the State Department's failure to give him an adequate staff. One diplomatic secretary after another was sent to Managua but each soon found some excuse to leave, and much of the time he had only one clerk to assist him. Such

187

situations were not uncommon in the 1920's, when the foreign service was smaller and less well trained than it is today, but in this case it was particularly unfortunate. The minister was energetic and courageous, and he spoke Spanish fluently, but he frequently showed poor judgment in crises.

Trouble started almost immediately after Eberhardt's arrival. Solórzano had appointed liberals to many of the most important positions in the coalition government, but a conservative, the president's brother-in-law Alfredo Rivas, was in command on the fortified hill of La Loma, which dominates Managua. On August 28, 1925, most of the prominent people of the capital, including the diplomatic corps, were at a reception at the International Club in honor of Leonardo Argüello, the liberal minister of public instruction. The president was there, but left early, and shortly after his departure a group of armed men invaded the hall shouting that they had been sent by Rivas to free the president from "liberal domination." The terrified guests were kept in the hall for about an hour while the invaders seized and carried off the minister of finance and several other liberal officials and newspapermen, and Eberhardt had a disagreeable experience when one of the liberals, in an effort to avoid capture, seized him around the waist and had to be forcibly detached. The prisoners were released the next day, but only after the president agreed to replace many of the liberals in the government with conservatives whom Rivas designated.

The affair at the club demonstrated the hopeless weakness of Solórzano's government. Eberhardt reported that the president was vacillating between resigning or ousting Rivas. He did not wish to repudiate altogether his obligations to the liberals, some of whom were still in the government, or to throw himself into the arms of the Chamorrista conservatives, who were thought to have inspired the coup. It was difficult, however, to get rid of Rivas, who was supported by Mrs. Solórzano and the other ladies of the family, and who arrogantly brought fifty men and two machine guns with him when he called at the palace. Rivas gave up his command on La Loma on September 9 in return for $4,500 and the promise of the Nicaraguan consulate at Los Angeles, but he stayed in Managua and continued to exercise a powerful influence through his sister.

The new constabulary which Major Carter was training was still too weak numerically to give the government effective support. Carter had to discharge 80 of the 200 men who had been recruited before his arrival and he had little cooperation from the government. The president seemed reluctant to give him money or supplies, and especially reluctant to give him any considerable amount of ammunition. He had nevertheless done a good job with the men that he had, and after the affair at the club the constabulary took over the guard at the president's house and the policing of Managua. The liberals asked that it take over the Loma but Solórzano's conservative supporters successfully opposed this.[1]

Emiliano Chamorro was perhaps not responsible for Rivas' coup, but immediately after the coup he began to plan to complete the destruction of the coalition government. As the outstanding leader of the conservative party, he had more influence with the conservative officers of the garrison at Managua than did the conservative republicans who supported Solórzano. On the early morning of October 25, 1925, he seized command of the fort on La Loma, while armed bands of his followers moved into the streets of the capital, and were soon involved in fighting with Carter's constabulary. Carter offered to retake the Loma and restore order if the president would give him ammunition and some machine guns, and Eberhardt supported him in his request, but Solórzano, after some vacillation, declined to encourage any resistance. By noon the Chamorristas were in full control of the city. The constabulary, which had lost two men killed and had killed fifteen of the rebels, was surrounded in its camp and might have been annihilated if Chamorro had not intervened to protect it.

Chamorro told Eberhardt that his purpose was to drive the liberals from the government. He wished Solórzano to continue as president, while he himself controlled the armed forces. Eberhardt warned him that the legation must support the constituted government and that no regime taking power by force would be recognized by the United States—a statement which the State Department promptly approved—but on October 26 Solórzano yielded to Chamorro's demands. The conservative leader was appointed commander-in-chief of the army and got $10,000 from the treasury to cover the expenses of his coup. The liberals were

---

[1] For the state of the constabulary at this time see Eberhardt's dispatch of Oct. 2, 1925, 817.1051/87 and C. B. Carter, "The Kentucky Feud in Nicaragua," *World's Work*, Vol. 54 (July, 1927), p. 312.

ousted from the government. Vice President Sacasa went into hiding in León, but Chamorro's forces put so much pressure on his friends, by forced loans and other abuses, that Sacasa left Nicaragua early in November.

In the vice president's absence a *designado* elected by Congress would become president if Solórzano should resign or be removed, and it seemed certain that Chamorro could control the election because the conservative republicans elected in 1924 could be expected to vote with the Chamorristas now that their coalition with the liberals was dissolved. Congress was summoned to meet on December 15. Meanwhile the conservative leaders tried to find out from Eberhardt what position the American government would take. They were anxious to avoid a course which might lead to non-recognition. Many of them thought that the 1924 elections should be annulled and new ones held. Eberhardt told them that he did not know what the State Department's attitude would be and asked for instructions.

The minister had thus far seen no reason to object to what the conservatives were doing. He had reported that Chamrorro had kept within the letter of the constitution, and that the country, under his control, was more orderly that it had been for some time. Most of the Americans in Nicaragua, he said, were hoping for a Chamorro government.[2] At the State Department there was evidently no desire to become involved if interference could be avoided. So long as Solórzano was president the United States could maintain normal relations with him, but if Solórzano should resign, either voluntarily or under compulsion, the department would have to consider its position in the light of its commitment to the principles laid down in the Central American treaties. After its very recent vigorous opposition to Carías' candidacy in Honduras, it could hardly recognize a revolutionary government in Nicaragua. Eberhardt was consequently authorized to say that the United States would recognize any constitutionally elected or appointed successor if Solórzano resigned, but that it would not recognize any government that had come into power by violent or unconstitutional means. The nullification of the 1924 elections, under existing circumstances, would be a course of very doubtful legality and one which the State Department could not approve. The department reiterated its adher-

[2] Eberhardt to Kellogg, Oct. 31, 1925, 817.00/3336.

ence to the principles set forth in the Central American treaties and instructed Eberhardt to make sure that all concerned understood its attitude.

This statement apparently put an end to talk about annulling the 1924 election but it did not answer some of the other questions which the Nicaraguan politicians were putting to Eberhardt and which the minister, rather unwisely, was trying to answer. Some of them wanted to know, for example, whether the United States would support Sacasa if he claimed the presidency in the event of Solórzano's resignation. The minister told them that the United States, as a "mark of courtesy," might possibly bring Sacasa back to Nicaragua on a gunboat, but he tried to discourage the idea that the United States might install him in the presidency by force. When he reported this, the State Department replied that it did not consider it wise to return Sacasa on a war vessel and that it would not install him in the presidency by force. While it would not recognize a usurping government, it was under no obligation to oppose such a regime by force or to put a constitutional government in office. The department cautioned the minister not to say anything which might encourage the Chamorristas to seize control. He was advised to refuse to answer hypothetical questions.

Chamorro, meanwhile, was going forward with his own plans. When the Congress met, it disqualified eleven liberal and conservative republican members on the ground that they had been seated by force by the Martínez government, as in fact they apparently had been. It also ordered Sacasa to return to Nicaragua within twenty-five days to answer trumped-up charges of conspiracy. Eberhardt expressed disapproval of these actions, and the State Department approved his position, saying that the disqualification of the congressmen might make doubtful the validity of the election of *designados.* On the other hand, it advised the minister that it had told Sacasa that the American government would not support him by force. It said that any regeneration of Nicaragua must come from within. There would be no stability in Central America so long as the people there felt that the last word came from the Department of State. The American government's unwillingness to take responsibility for Nicaragua's internal political problems was again emphasized in a mail instruction sent to Managua on December 23 in which Eberhardt was exhorted to take every opportunity to impress on the Nicaraguans their responsibility and the fact that the center of Nicaraguan political activity was in Nicaragua, not in Washington.[3]

Secretary Kellogg and his advisers were undoubtedly sincere in their desire to avoid involvement. They had maintained relations with Solórzano after Chamorro's coup and they had apparently accepted tacitly the plan to elect a *designado* despite the violent measures which had made it possible to put a conservative in the presidency in this way. They had to take a more definite stand, however, when Eberhardt reported on December 24 that the *designado* would be Chamorro. The minister warned the conservatives that the United States would almost certainly refuse to recognize a government headed by Chamorro, but this did not deter them, and the minister asked for a direct statement from the State Department. Kellogg replied on January 2, 1926, that "this government would not extend recognition to any government which came into power through violent or unconstitutional means." This left some room for interpretation and apparently did not entirely convince the conservative leaders; but on January 6, after Eberhardt reported a plan to elect another *designado* who would be replaced later by Chamorro, Kellogg cabled that the United States would not recognize "any government headed by General Chamorro." He said that he realized that the consequences might be serious but felt that a principle was at stake which must be maintained. If the Nicaraguan leaders followed a course leading to non-recognition the responsibility was theirs.[4] On the following day the American legations in the other Central American capitals were instructed to urge the governments to tell Chamorro that they would not recognize him if he assumed the presidency. All of them did so, more or less willingly.

Chamorro, nevertheless, had himself elected first *designado* and on January 13 the Congress impeached Vice President Sacasa, on flimsy and ridiculous charges, and banished him from Nicaragua for two years. It did not refer the charges to the Supreme Court, as the constitution required.[5] The Congress then gave Solórzano

---

[3] Kellogg to Eberhardt, Dec. 23, 1925, 817.00/3358.

[4] Kellogg to Eberhardt, Jan. 2, 1926, 817.00/3364; Eberhardt to Kellogg, Jan. 2, and Kellogg to Eberhardt, Jan. 6, 1926, 817.00/3376.

[5] See articles 84 and 123. Morgan pointed this out in his memorandum of March 29, 1926, 817.00/3508.

leave of absence but refused to permit him to resign, presumably to hold him in reserve if the United States should support Sacasa's claim to the presidency. Chamorro took over the presidency on January 16. On January 22, Secretary Kellogg told the Nicaraguan minister at Washington that the United States did not and would not recognize the new regime.

Chamorro's decision to assume the presidency was disastrous for Nicaragua and for the United States. If a moderate conservative had taken Solórzano's place, the civil war and the American intervention might have been avoided. The advent of a president whom the American government publicly denounced as a usurper and who was feared and hated by the liberals because of his recent rough treatment of the people of León, made a revolt practically inevitable. Chamorro later said that he might have acted differently if he had been told of the American government's attitude before he publicly committed himself.[6] It is true that the State Department, as was often the case, had for a time seemed reluctant to say what it meant explicitly and unequivocally, but it had certainly made clear its disapproval of any course of action that would put Chamorro in the presidency. Evidently Chamorro simply did not believe that the United States would withhold recognition for any considerable period if it had no alternative except to countenance a revolution. He said as much to Eberhardt on several occasions.[7]

The next eleven months gave the State Department one of its unhappiest experiences with the use of non-recognition as an instrument of policy. It could not abandon its position without giving up principles which it had pledged itself to maintain, but non-recognition inevitably increased the probability of a revolt by the liberals, which the department did not want. The American government, in the early months of 1926, would have been glad to see Sacasa take over the presidency if he could have done so peacefully. When Sacasa called at the Latin American division in January, Stokeley Morgan told him that the United States would undoubtedly regard him as the constitutional president of Nicaragua if Solórzano should resign, but would be extremely reluctant to intervene again by force in Nicaragua and would not feel that it was obligated to use force to install a constitutional

---

[6] He said this in a letter to Alejandro César, a copy of which is in the State Department's files, 817.00/4877.

[7] Eberhardt to Kellogg, Jan. 5, 1926, 817.00/3381.

government. Later, on at least two occasions, Morgan told Sacasa that the United States would disapprove of any revolution, and would disapprove any intervention in Nicaragua by governments friendly to the liberals. He urged the liberals to be patient while the United States and the Central American governments tried to bring about a return to constitutional government by moral pressure.[8] When the Guatemalan government suggested that the other Central American states should help the liberals to oust Chamorro by force, Kellogg pointed out that this would be a violation of the Central American treaties.[9]

For several months, moral pressure seemed to accomplish nothing. Chamorro knew that the United States was opposing any effort to oust him by force. He was encouraged by his friends in Washington, and especially by Chandler Anderson, who had been his legal adviser there, to think that the United States would soon have to recognize him. He paid little attention to what Eberhardt said. At Washington Secretary Kellogg and other officials talked forcefully to Salvador Castrillo, the Nicaraguan minister, but Chamorro had no confidence in Castrillo. He was encouraged in his resistance by the fact that the Americans in the customs and the national bank, and even the resident American member of the high commission, who was an appointee of the secretary of state, continued to cooperate with his government. These officials, meeting at the American legation, had decided to remain at their posts, and the State Department had approved their decision.[10] It evidently was reluctant to destroy the results of many years of effort to strengthen Nicaragua's economy and it had to consider the interests of the bondholders and other creditors who had relied on promises that the customs would remain under American direction and that the high commission would see to the service of the guaranteed customs bonds. Most of the resident Americans were friendly to Chamorro and seem to have hoped and expected that American policy would soon change.

The State Department's efforts were less convincing because it had no practical course of action to propose. When Dr. Carlos

[8] Morgan's memoranda of Jan. 9, March 2, and March 16, 1926, 817.00/3405, 3490, 3506.
[9] Geissler to Kellogg, Feb. 7, and Kellogg to Geissler, Feb. 10, 1926, 817.00/3453.
[10] Kellogg to Eberhardt, Jan. 23, 1926, 817.00/3412.

Cuadra Pasos, who had apparently come to Washington as an unofficial representative of the conservative party, asked on February 26 what solution the United States suggested, Francis White told him that the Nicaraguans must solve their own problems, adding that the United States supported constitutional government and law and order and the 1923 treaties. In March Morgan told Castrillo and Cuadra Pasos that he thought that Solórzano should be reinstated, saying that Chamorro could continue as a cabinet officer or adviser and that he would probably be recognized as president if he were fairly elected at the end of Solórzano's term. On March 11 Eberhardt was instructed to say, if his opinion were asked, that the State Department had all along felt that the only possible and legal solution was for Chamorro to withdraw and permit Solórzano to return to the presidency.[11] In view of Solórzano's incompetence and the conservatives' lack of confidence in him it is not surprising that this suggestion had little appeal.

The conservatives were already taking steps to eliminate the possibility of Solórzano's return. The titular president had been compelled by threats and pressure to sign a resignation on January 14, but the Congress, instead of accepting it, compelled him to take a leave of absence. He was promised his salary, but apparently did not receive it. On March 13 the Congress accepted the resignation. As he left Nicaragua on March 25, Solórzano told Eberhardt that he hoped that the United States would restore him to the presidency. The Congress decreed that Chamorro should be president until January 1929. In April it arbitrarily removed three liberal judges and one conservative republican judge from the Supreme Court. Similar changes made soon afterward in the appellate courts deprived the liberals of nearly all of the positions which they held under the coalition.

Early in April Morgan informally suggested to Sacasa and to Castrillo, the Nicaraguan minister, the possibility of naming an impartial provisional president who would immediately hold elections in which Chamorro would not be a candidate.[12] Sacasa seemed receptive to the idea but it was apparently not seriously

---

[11] Grew to Eberhardt, March 11, 1926, 817.00/3497a. For what White and Morgan said to the Nicaraguan representatives, see Grew to Eberhardt, March 4, 1926, 817.00/3485a and Morgan's memoranda of March 10, and March 11, 1926, 817.00/3493, 3502.

[12] Morgan's memorandum of April 2, 1926, 817.00/3532.

considered by the conservatives. It could now hardly be expected that the liberals would not resort to armed revolt. Many of their leaders were in exile and those who remained in Nicaragua were being subjected to the persecution which was always the lot of the opposition in a Central American country where political conditions were disturbed. Despite the State Department's warnings against revolution, which were not very convincing in the light of its disclaimer of any intent to intervene in Nicaragua, they would probably have revolted earlier if they had had more aggressive leadership. Neither Sacasa, who was one of the most respected physicians in Central America, nor his chief associates were the sort of people who might be expected to organize a revolution.

The principal liberal leaders, in fact, were apparently not prepared for a revolution when a group of their followers seized Bluefields on May 2, 1926, and from there took control of the entire east coast. Sacasa assumed the leadership of the movement, but did not go to Nicaragua, and the liberals got little support in western Nicaragua, where there were only small, easily suppressed uprisings. The United States maintained a position of strict neutrality. The captain of the U.S.S. *Cleveland*, which was sent to Bluefields to protect American lives and property, declared the city a neutral zone and forbade fighting there, but he was ordered not to hinder the military operations of either side unless the need to protect American lives and property made interference necessary. Neither side was to be prevented from exercising civil jurisdiction in the areas that it occupied. The American consul reported that the revolutionists welcomed the establishment of the neutral zone, which made it unnecessary for them to protect the city.[13] The revolutionists caused the State Department some embarrassment, however, when they removed the American customs collector at Bluefields because he refused to promise to deliver to them a shipment of arms which they expected from the United States. The department was reluctant to appear to help Chamorro, but it could not very well countenance a flagrant violation of the financial plan of 1920 and it consequently instructed the American consul to demand that the collector be reinstated.[14] This matter was still pending when the revolution collapsed.

[13] McConnico to the secretary of state, May 13, 1926, 817.00/3579.
[14] Kellogg to McConnico, May 20, 1926, 817.51/1641.

The new constabulary played a major role in the revolution's defeat. Major Carter and his assistants had continued to serve the Nicaraguan government, with the acquiescence of the American legation and the State Department, and Chamorro had built the force up almost to full strength and had supplied it with arms. At Eberhardt's suggestion, it had been sent to León after Sacasa's flight to replace the conservative soldiers who had been brutally mistreating the liberals there. Later it had policed Managua. Most of the liberals in its ranks had been discharged, at their own request. The American officers took no part in the fighting, for Carter had gone to the United States on sick leave and his assistant, Major Rodríguez, stayed in Managua when 250 men of the constabulary were sent to the east coast in May. This small force lost fourteen men killed and twelve wounded, and it seems to have been chiefly responsible for a government victory at Rama on May 19 which destroyed the rebel army. The American marines were withdrawn from the neutral zone but at Consul McConnico's suggestion the *Cleveland*, and later the U.S.S. *Tulsa*, was kept at Bluefields for some weeks to prevent reprisals against the defeated party.

In June 1926, Eberhardt went on leave and Lawrence Dennis, the junior secretary who had recently been in charge in Honduras, took charge of the legation at Managua. Dennis at once began to send cables urging a more vigorous attitude toward Chamorro. He reported that the minister's efforts to make the American government's policy understood had been "utterly ineffective" and recommended that the department make it clear that the minister's departure did not mean that the policy would be changed. Kellogg consequently issued a press statement on June 8, saying that the United States would maintain its policy of non-recognition and hoped that the Nicaraguan people would return to a constitutional form of government which would make recognition possible. At the same time he warned Dennis not to put himself in an untenable position and not to do anything that might encourage the liberals to revolt.[15]

Dennis' vigorous and sometimes unorthodox efforts to persuade Chamorro that he must withdraw and to persuade the other conservatives that they must force him out caused the State

---

[15] Dennis to Kellogg, June 7, 1926 (two telegrams) 817.00/3607, 3609, and Kellogg to Dennis, June 9, 817.00/3609. The press statement is printed in *Foreign Relations, 1926*, Vol. II, p. 787.

department some uneasiness. On June 14 the secretary warned him not to expose himself to charges of undue interference in Nicaragua's affairs and to confine himself, in answering inquiries, to the "fundamental fact" that the United States would not recognize any regime that had come into power by unconstitutional means. At the same time he should make it clear that the United States would not look with favor on a revolution. When the chargé pointed out that the cooperation of the American officials in the financial services and of former United States Army officers in the constabulary gave the impression that the United States was not serious about non-recognition, and urged that the American government prevent the national bank from turning over half a million dollars in surplus revenues at the end of June, Kellogg himself dictated the reply. He told Dennis to examine the bankers' agreement of 1911 and the financial plan of 1920. If the Americans in the bank refused to turn over the surplus, they might be forcibly removed, for the bank was the property of the Nicaraguan government. He told Dennis, however, to urge the American officials to be neutral, and to say to the constabulary officers that they could not expect protection from the United States if they took an active part in political affairs.[16]

It was increasingly difficult to persist in a policy which seemed to offer little hope for success. Chamorro tried to counter Dennis' activity by telling friends in the United States about the chargé's meddling in Nicaraguan politics, and his accusation aroused the interest of the anti-imperialists. Senator Borah, the chairman of the Senate Foreign Relations Committee, expressed concern about what Dennis was doing, and the acting editor of the *Nation* asked whether it was true that Dennis was encouraging revolution in Nicaragua.[17] The other Central American governments were also unhappy about the State Department's policy, because they found it troublesome to be cut off from normal relations with a close neighbor. In July President Orellana of Guatemala again urged joint "fraternal" action by the other states to restore constitutional government in Nicaragua, but Kellogg replied that the 1923 treaties did not sanction interference by one country in the affairs of another and that the State Department was con-

---

[16] Dennis to Kellogg, June 9, and Kellogg to Dennis, June 12, 1926, 817.00/3616.

[17] Borah to Kellogg, June 14, 1926, 817.00/3638½; Gannett to Grew, June 23, 1926, 817.00/3651.

vinced that the proposed action would have no good result. Geissler, the minister to Guatemala, was told confidentially that the department still hoped to find a solution that would avoid the danger of embroiling Central America in hostilities.[18]

The State Department was working on a new plan. In June Chamorro had sent word that he would transfer the presidency to a *designado* elected by Congress if the American government would state publicly that it would have no objection to Chamorro's subsequent election as president and if the other conservative leaders would guarantee that he would be the party's only candidate. The election would be supervised by the United States. In the meantime, Chamorro would be commander-in-chief of the army. This proposal seemed unacceptable, especially as the solicitor's office expressed the opinion that Chamorro's election would be illegal because Article 104 of the Nicaraguan constitution prohibited the election as president of anyone who had served as president at any time during the preceding term.[19] On August 11, however, Herbert Stabler, who had succeeded Francis White as chief of the Latin American division, recommended that Chamorro be urged to turn over the presidency to a man acceptable to all parties in Nicaragua and that he be told that there would be no objection to his election as president in 1928. Using a new and somewhat questionable translation of Article 104 of the Nicaraguan constitution, Stabler argued that Chamorro could be considered eligible in 1928. In the meantime Chamorro would be permitted to remain in the cabinet, but would not be commander-in-chief of the army. The constabulary would be reorganized by an American military mission to facilitate American supervision of the election.[20] Dennis, when his views were asked, thought that the best opinion in Nicaragua held that Chamorro would not be eligible in 1928 but that the question was "academic" because the president was rapidly losing the support of the conservative party. The chargé thought that a coalition government would not work but that it might be

[18] Geissler to Kellogg, July 27, 1926, 817.00/3692; Geissler to Kellogg, Aug. 9, and Kellogg to Geissler, Aug. 12, 1926, 817.00/3699.
[19] Solicitor's office memorandum of July 30, 1926, 817.00/3701. For other correspondence about the proposal see 817.00/3673, 3676, 3677, 3685, 3708.
[20] Stabler to Kellogg, Aug. 11, 1926, 817.00/4823. Art. 104 provided, in part, that anyone who exercised the presidency *"en propriedad o accidentalmente"* was ineligible for election for the next term. Stabler held that *"accidentalmente"* should be translated "by succession."

possible to carry out the plan under a non-military conservative like Adolfo Díaz or Martín Benard. He thought that most of the liberals would rather accept a compromise than make a revolution.[21] On this last point he was wrong, for a revolution was already beginning.

Sacasa had gone to Mexico in May to obtain the Mexican government's support in another attempt to oust Chamorro by force. President Calles promised to supply arms and men for an uprising, and Sacasa in return allegedly agreed to introduce an agrarian reform and other radical measures, and to abrogate the canal treaty with the United States, if he became president of Nicaragua. He would also cooperate in plans to set up a Central American union which would be dominated by Mexico.[22] In August the liberals revolted in the country around León and Chinandega and on the east coast. In the West, the movement soon collapsed, chiefly because President Quiñonez of El Salvador detained the steamer *El Tropical*, which was bringing arms furnished by the Mexican government, and interned several hundred Nicaraguan liberals. On the isolated east coast the insurgents had better luck. In July Sacasa's representative Seydel Vaca bought the steamer *Foam* in New York and sent her to Puerto México with a crew of Americans who later asserted that they had been misled about the object of the voyage. At Puerto México, Mexican soldiers loaded the ship with arms, and a number of Nicaraguans, commanded by General José María Moncada, came on board. Moncada was to be the principal leader of the revolution. The *Foam* proceeded to Nicaragua, where Moncada took Río Grande and Bragman's Bluff. Other vessels brought arms from Mexico during the next few weeks and the rebels seized several east coast towns and prepared to attack Bluefields, which was the capital of the east coast province.

Sacasa's negotiations in Mexico had been reported to the Nicaraguan government by a member of the liberal revolutionary committee who did not approve of the vice president's commitments, and had been reported to the State Department by Cuadra Pasos, but the officials in the Department had been skeptical about the story. The liberal leaders in Managua assured Dennis that their party would have nothing to do with the Mexi-

[21] Dennis to Kellogg, Aug. 19, 1926, 817.00/3720.
[22] J. Edgar Hoover's memorandum of Feb. 21, 1927, 817.00/4604½, gives the story of Sacasa's arrangement with Calles.

can government. The revolt consequently seems to have taken the American government by surprise. When it started, warships were sent to both coasts to protect Americans and the U.S.S. *Galveston* landed marines at Bluefields and declared the city a neutral zone.

The American government's first reaction was to increase its pressure on Chamorro. When the fighting started, Dennis urged that Chamorro be told firmly that he must reach a peaceful settlement with the liberals to avoid the "ruin" of Nicaragua. The State Department consequently authorized him on August 27 to re-affirm its determination not to recognize the *de facto* regime and to say that the situation threatened to endanger American and other foreign lives and property and might force the United States to take measures for their protection. The department said that interference with the financial plan had already caused the United States government considerable anxiety. Further blood-shed could be avoided only through the withdrawal of Chamorro and a return to constitutional government. The department thought that the first step would be a conference attended by members of all parties.

After strong pressure from Dennis and some pressure from other conservative leaders, Chamorro finally asked Dennis on September 9 to arrange a conference with the liberals and prom-ised that he would withdraw from the presidency after the con-ference even if no agreement about a new president was reached. Just as Dennis was achieving this result, Kellogg suddenly be-came alarmed about the extent of the legation's participation in the effort for a settlement. In a "rush, double priority" telegram which he dictated himself, he told Dennis that peace proposals should not be addressed to the legation and that Dennis should not issue invitations to the proposed conference because this might be construed as making the United States responsible for a settlement or as an undue interference in Nicaragua's domestic affairs. He outlined again the policy of the United States with regard to recognition and said that the American government would protect Americans and their property and would try with-in reason to protect the financial plan; but he said, "it is evident that if you take any steps which will be construed as a demand for his [Chamorro's] resignation or as an ultimatum and appear to align yourself with any one group or political faction, we are liable to be more deeply involved than if we pursue our consistent policy." A more cautious chargé d'affaires might have been reduced to impotence by an implied rebuke of this sort, but Dennis merely replied that he had said what he was instructed to say and that he was not responsible if these statements were construed as something more than suggestions. He had in fact just sent off a cable of his own complaining that his efforts to convince Chamorro were continually being frustrated by reports from people in Washington who had been talking with the State Department.[23]

Despite the secretary's misgivings, the State Department did what it could to make sure that the conference took place. Dennis was told to make it clear to the liberals that he was merely using his good offices for the establishment of peace and could not be a party to any agreements that were reached, but he was authorized to help with the arrangements for the meeting. The commander of the special service squadron, which had ships at Corinto and Bluefields, was ordered to try to persuade the liberal military leaders to accept a truce,[24] and the legation at Guatemala was instructed to transmit invitations to attend the conference to Sacasa and other liberal leaders who were in that city. Dennis was authorized to intimate to any liberals who opposed the peace plan that the question of recognizing any new government might have to be considered in its relationship to the establishment of peace and order in Nicaragua, a veiled threat that the United States might recognize a conservative government if the conference failed.[25]

On September 15 the president of the United States imposed an embargo on the shipment of arms to either party in Nicaragua. The State Department had considered this in January, but Eberhardt had pointed out that the embargo would help Chamorro, who still had the arms bought from the United States in 1921, and might be interpreted as a step toward recognition.[26] Presumably the same considerations deterred the department from imposing an embargo during the May revolution, when it was trying to maintain a conspicuous neutrality. In September, the conservatives' agreement to a peace conference made the sit-

[23] Kellogg to Dennis, Sept. 9, 1926, 817.00/3767, and Dennis to Kellogg, Sept. 10, 817.00/3778, and Sept. 9, 1926, 817.00/3774.
[24] Secretary of navy to secretary of state, Sept. 18, 1926, 817.00/3811.
[25] Kellogg to Dennis, Sept. 13, 1926, 817.111a.
[26] Eberhardt to Kellogg, Jan. 21, 1926, 817.00/3412.

uation different. An embargo might help to prevent bloodshed, and it put the American government in a better position to urge that the other Central American states and Mexico stop the shipment of arms to either party.

Arranging the conference required negotiations with Sacasa in Guatemala and the military leaders on the east coast and the liberals at Managua. Chargé d'Affaires Ellis reported from Guatemala that Sacasa and his friends welcomed mediation but insisted that any settlement be based on the recognition of the constitutional regime in Nicaragua. Their attitude apparently strengthened the State Department's doubts about the propriety of a plan of settlement which involved the choice of a new president by the party leaders, and on September 25 the department suggested to Dennis that Solórzano, who still claimed that his resignation was invalid, should be reinstated at least for a short time to call a special session of Congress to elect as *designado* the person who might be agreed on. Dennis replied that Solórzano's weakness and incompetence made this idea impractical,[27] and the idea was dropped. Sacasa also proposed that the other Central American states be invited to the conference, but the State Department thought that the other states were too partial to one side or the other to be helpful. While Sacasa was still considering what he should do, the American consul at Bluefields reported that the military leaders had agreed to a fifteen-day truce under which the conservative forces would withdraw to Rama and the liberals to Pearl Lagoon, leaving Bluefields as a neutral zone controlled by American naval forces. Soon afterward a delegation of liberals from western Nicaragua went to Guatemala, traveling on an American warship, to talk with Sacasa. By the middle of October arrangements for the conference were completed.

Dennis had told the State Department earlier that he realized that the settlement which he was trying to negotiate would leave the conservatives in power because the Congress, where they had a majority, would have to elect Chamorro's successor. He said that he would not recommend such a settlement if he thought that the United States was prepared to compel the holding of a fair election, or that the liberals could reestablish the constitutional order without a civil war. He thought, he said, that a bad peace was better than a good revolution. Dennis was worried,

---

[27] Kellogg to Dennis, Sept. 25, 1926, 817.00/3832, and Dennis to Kellogg, Sept. 29, 817.00/3831.

however, about the possibility that Chamorro might be able to bring about the selection of one of his own lieutenants as provisional president and that this might make it impossible for the American government to recognize the new regime. When he consulted the State Department he was told that the United States would not recognize any government that did not meet the requirements of Article II of the Central American treaty of 1923, but that it might be willing to give moral support during a transition period to a government which it could not recognize *de jure*. The department did not want to offer any suggestions about specific candidates, and it hoped that patriotic Nicaraguans would make their influence felt and compel the choice of a suitable man. It relied on Dennis' efforts to help the Nicaraguans through the exercise of good offices.[28] It would hardly have been practicable for the State Department to insist on the choice of a provisional president who fully met the requirements of the 1923 treaty because so many of the conservative leaders had been involved in Chamorro's coup.

The conference met on October 16 at Corinto, where the American naval commander set up a temporary neutral zone for the protection of the delegates. The sessions were held on the U.S.S. *Denver*, with Dennis presiding. At first the delegates seemed conciliatory and friendly. The conservatives, who had now agreed on Adolfo Díaz as Chamorro's successor, offered the liberals participation in the Congress and the higher courts and the diplomatic service, but insisted that the new provisional president be a conservative. The liberals at first insisted that Sacasa must be recognized as president and said that they would continue the revolution with aid from Mexico and other governments if he were not. Dennis thought that the American government should make a forceful statement to "smash the doctrine of constitutional restoration by means of foreign aid and revolution" but the State Department thought that the threat of renewed hostilities aided by Mexico would make the conservatives more reasonable and hesitated to make a statement which would encourage Chamorro in an intransigent attitude. Later the liberals proposed to submit to arbitration by the other Central American governments the question whether a settlement based on the Nicaraguan constitution and the Central American treaty would require the installation of Sacasa as president. Dennis op-

28 Kellogg to Dennis, Oct. 5, and Oct. 13, 1926, 817.00/3882, 3909.

posed the idea and the conservatives rejected it. The conservatives also rejected the liberals' offer to have Sacasa resign in favor of some prominent citizen not closely connected with either party. The conference closed on October 24 with what was apparently an almost friendly agreement to disagree.

Evidently each party preferred to continue the civil war rather than submit to being ruled by the other. Each still felt confident that it could win the war. The conservatives had had the best of such fighting as had thus far occurred, and they expected to have the moral support of the United States once Chamorro had been eliminated and a new government had been set up. The liberals, on the other hand, felt that Sacasa had a clear right to the presidency and that they could win the civil war with Mexico's help. They had thus far been able to count on the neutrality of the United States. Some of them were doubtless unhappy about the implications of Mexican support and uneasy about the attitude which the American government might assume; and it was probably for this reason that they had made a real effort for a settlement by proposing Sacasa's withdrawal in favor of a non-partisan president.

If the United States had persuaded the conservatives to accept this proposal, it is possible that the civil war might have ended and that the disastrous events of the subsequent American intervention might have been avoided. A provisional president chosen by agreement might have been able to maintain order if the United States had given him adequate support and had agreed to supervise the election of his successor. This, however, would have involved a more extensive interference in Nicaragua's internal affairs than the American government was at the time prepared to undertake. After the State Department's insistence that the two parties must settle their problems by themselves, Secretary Kellogg would hardly have wanted to exert the strong pressure on the conservatives that would have been necessary to persuade them to relinquish control of the government. He would also have been reluctant to undertake to give the provisional government the sort of support that it would need during the two years that would elapse before the presidential election.

The statements which the liberals made at the conference about the help that they were receiving from Mexico perhaps made the State Department more willing to see the conservatives remain in power. Until October 1926, the department seems to have been genuinely impartial in its attitude toward the two parties in Nicaragua. After the conference, its sympathies were clearly with the conservatives. Relations between the United States and Mexico had been very strained for some months because of Mexico's oil and land legislation, and Secretary Kellogg was convinced that the Mexican government's policies showed that there was a bond of sympathy if not a definite understanding between Mexico and Soviet Russia. The Mexican intervention in Nicaragua thus seemed to have sinister implications not only for Nicaragua but for all Central America. The secretary was perhaps more alarmed than were some of his associates, but even those who did not see Mexican intervention as part of a communist plot felt that the extension of Mexican influence in Central America would endanger American interests there.

The State Department, however, could hardly give the conservative regime at Managua any support until Chamorro was out and a government with some claim to constitutionality had been set up. Under pressure from Dennis, Chamorro reluctantly complied with his promise to withdraw. He turned over the presidency to Sebastián Uriza, the second *designado*, on October 30. The conservative leaders had agreed that Adolfo Díaz should be chosen as provisional president when Congress met, and Dennis had told them that he thought Díaz would be recognized. On November 2, the State Department told Dennis that it felt that the United States, in view of Chamorro's withdrawal and in the absence of Solórzano and Sacasa, might properly recognize *de jure* a *designado* elected by Congress, provided that the Congress contained the members elected in 1924. The department went on to say that it did not suggest or favor any candidate but that Díaz, if designated, would be a wise choice: honest, capable, and with the necessary firmness of character. It did not consider him debarred by the 1923 treaty. It would be loath to see the election of an incompetent or weak *designado*, under whom the situation would go from bad to worse. Dennis was authorized to make use of these comments in informal discussions, but not to make a public statement; and he was to use the utmost care to avoid any criticism that the government of the United States was endeavoring to direct Nicaraguan internal politics. The State Department did not agree with Dennis' view that Uriza should have all possible moral support until Congress met, and when Dennis insisted that Nicaragua would be "Mexicanized" if the United

States continued a policy of "laissez faire" it told him that the department knew best what its policy should be. It said, however, that if Sacasa should subsequently set up a government in Nicaragua, "the department could not consider him other than a revolutionist."

To comply with the State Department's demands, the members of Congress who had been expelled by Chamorro were invited to resume their seats. This left the conservatives with a majority, because most of the conservative republicans elected in 1924 had returned to the party. When the Congress met in joint session on November 11, 53 members were present, out of a total of 67, and 44 voted for Díaz as first *designado*. Dennis was instructed to attend Díaz' inauguration on November 14, and on the 17th the State Department announced the formal recognition of the new government. This action, in my opinion, was proper. In the absence of the president and the vice president, neither of whom were in Nicaragua, the Nicaraguan constitution required that the Congress elect a *designado* who would become provisional president. The establishment of an administration to which the American government could give moral support seemed to offer the best prospect for a peaceful solution on terms which the United States could accept. Continued non-recognition would probably have meant a liberal victory, with Mexican support, but only after a bloody civil war. The conservatives, who would still have had Chamorro as their military leader, could have put up a desperate fight.

The recognition of Díaz, however, aroused much criticism. All of the other Central American states had followed the American government's lead in refusing recognition to Chamorro, but only El Salvador and Honduras recognized Díaz when he was inaugurated. The Guatemalan government openly sympathized with the liberals, and the president of Costa Rica said that he considered Díaz' election unconstitutional. As time went on resentment in Central America seemed to increase. There was also criticism in the United States. American newspapers had shown relatively little interest in Nicaraguan affairs before December 1926. When Chamorro appealed to the League of Nations against Mexico's intervention, there had been more discussion of the possible implications of the league's interference in Latin American than in the implications of Mexican intervention in Nicaragua. The controversy about the recognition of Díaz received more attention.

207

The State Department was accused of trying to keep control of Nicaragua through the conservative party for the benefit of the New York bankers. It was asserted that Sacasa was the rightful president of Nicaragua and that the revolution was an effort to free the country from American domination.

The State Department answered its critics by demonstrating the constitutionality of Díaz' election, but for some time it did not think it wise to say anything publicly about the Mexican intervention. In November 1926, it had only a part of the evidence that was later available about Mexico's shipment of arms to the rebels, and some of the evidence that it had could not be used without endangering the sources from which it was obtained. Kellogg had merely referred to "interference from outside sources" when he announced Díaz' recognition. On November 18 the State Department apparently inspired a story sent out by the Associated Press describing the concern felt in official circles in Washington about Mexico's efforts to spread bolshevism throughout Central America, but this surreptitious effort to impress public opinion, though it created a sensation, did little to strengthen the department's position. Some newspapers expressed alarm but pointed out that the report was not substantiated by evidence. Others suspected that its publication was either an effort to provoke war with Mexico over the oil question, or part of a plot by American bankers to get control of the bank and the railroad in Nicaragua.

Adolfo Díaz, the new provisional president, did not have the strong personal following which Chamorro had in the conservative party, but he had fewer enemies. His reputation for fairness and moderation probably made him as acceptable as any conservative could have been to the liberals, who had received comparatively fair treatment during his earlier period as president. He was genuinely friendly to the United States, which had intervened by force to keep him in office in 1912, and most of the Americans who worked in Nicaragua liked and trusted him. During his earlier administration, he had proposed that provisions like those of the Cuban Platt amendment be incorporated in the canal option treaty, but the Wilson administration, after accepting the idea, gave it up because of opposition in the United States Senate. The State Department in 1926 certainly had no thought of reviving the proposal for a protectorate, which would have been totally inconsistent with its whole Caribbean policy, but it was undoubtedly glad to have a president in Nicaragua who had a record of friendly cooperation with the United States.

In explaining the recognition of the new administration, Kellogg emphasized his expectation that it would make peace proposals and offer the liberals a participation in the government. Díaz thus had some justification for assuming that the United States would support him in an effort to stop the war. Soon after his inauguration he asked the American government to do something to prevent further Mexican intervention, and to authorize the legation and the American naval commander to act as intermediaries to bring about an informal peace conference. He declared his willingness to withdraw his troops from León and other western districts where the liberals were in the majority if his opponents would agree to discontinue hostilities in western Nicaragua. He was ready to offer Moncada $50,000 to pay off his army and would promise the liberals a generous participation in his government if peace could be established.[29] A few days later he asked that the United States send a military mission to reorganize the Nicaraguan army. He did not expect the mission to arrive before the war ended, but he thought that an announcement that one would be sent would help his peace efforts and would also make it easier to remove Chamorro from the command of the army, which the ex-president was reluctant to give up. To make his peace offer more convincing and also because of acute financial difficulties, Díaz demobilized about half of the 8,000 men that the conservatives had under arms.

The State Department was willing to convey Díaz' peace proposal to the liberals but it responded rather coldly to his other requests. Kellogg apparently did not intend to give the Nicaraguan government the sort of active support which Díaz seemed to expect, and the State Department had been disappointed when Díaz permitted Chamorro to continue in command of the army and retained most of the members of his predecessor's cabinet. It said that it would consider sending a military mission after the revolution was over. It refused to sell arms to Díaz, but said that it would consider issuing licenses for export by private dealers. On December 8 Kellogg cabled Dennis that the State Department "has perceived with regret that there appears to be

[29] Dennis to Kellogg, Nov. 15, 1926, 817.00/4063. Dennis transmitted a copy of Díaz' letter with his dispatch of Nov. 20, 817.00/4207.

a tendency on the part of the Díaz administration to rely upon the Government of the United States to protect it against the activities of the revolutionists by physical means." Dennis was to make it clear that recognition implied no obligation to extend armed assistance. The American government was ready to lend the encouragement and moral support which it generally accorded to friendly constitutional governments when they were threatened by revolution, but it was not prepared to go farther.

The peace effort failed. Dennis discussed Díaz' proposals with the liberals in Managua, who seemed anxious for a settlement, and he asked Admiral Latimer, the commander of the special service squadron, to take them up with General José María Moncada, the commander of the liberal army on the east coast. Moncada referred them to Sacasa, who rejected them. The prospect for peace seemed less bright after Sacasa, apparently with some reluctance, joined the liberal forces on the east coast late in November and was inaugurated by them as president of Nicaragua on December 1. He was promptly recognized by Mexico but he received no reply to his request for recognition by the United States. In view of the liberals' attitude, Díaz held up any further demobilization of the conservative forces.

Chamorro, meanwhile, was insisting that he would not give up the command of the conservative army unless the United States promised to support the new government against the revolution. Díaz told Dennis that he might resign if Chamorro did not withdraw, but he apparently did not feel strong enough to remove him. Dennis informally urged the general to give up his post, and early in December Chamorro complained to the State Department that the chargé was trying to force him to resign. The State Department, in a rather far-fetched effort to avoid the appearance of interference, replied that it did not understand that Dennis had demanded Chamorro's withdrawal, and that its own views would be communicated through Minister Eberhardt, who was about to return to Managua. Eberhardt was told to say, if Chamorro asked him, that the American government did not demand his withdrawal, but to suggest that Chamorro accede to the wishes of his own family and party, who thought that his resignation would facilitate a peaceful settlement.[30] Chamorro did not wait to hear the department's views, for he resigned his com-

[30] Kellogg to Dennis, Dec. 8, 1926, 817.00/4227a.

mand on December 8, just before Eberhardt arrived, and accepted a diplomatic post in Europe.

The minister's return did not signify any change in policy, but it changed the way in which the State Department's policy was carried out by the legation. Dennis, with all his brashness and occasional excess of zeal, had been an effective representative, who had kept the department well informed about what was going on. Eberhardt did not always have a clear understanding of the department's purposes or of the problems with which he was dealing and he often failed to give the department the information which it should have had. His superiors were perhaps not unwilling to see the legation in the hands of someone who would be less insistent on taking action which the local situation seemed to demand and less critical of the department's occasional timidity and indecisiveness, but it was unfortunate that the American government was not better represented in a situation which turned out so disastrously for Nicaragua and for the United States.

The civil war, when Díaz took office, seemed to have reached something like a stalemate. The liberals held the smaller east coast ports, but Bluefields, which was by far the most important place on the coast, was controlled by the United States Navy. The conservatives administered civil affairs there, and they had a military base at Rama. They thus controlled the Escondido River, which was the principal means of travel across the broad band of jungle which separated the east coast from the interior. The conservatives controlled western Nicaragua, where most of the country's people lived. There had been little actual fighting in either region. The State Department still hoped that Díaz, with its moral support, would be able to bring about a peace agreement. The legation's reports about the peace negotiations had been rather inadequate, and the department did not realize for some time that they had failed.

The department was consequently unpleasantly surprised when Eberhardt cabled on December 13 that most people in Nicaragua believed that the government would be overthrown by a general uprising as soon as it became clear that the United States would do nothing to help it. Díaz, two days later, urgently asked for help to protect foreigners and restore peace, saying that the government would fall if Mexican aid to the revolution

211

was not checked and that he authorized in advance any measures which the United States might take. Kellogg expressed his astonishment in a cable to Eberhardt, pointing out that the legation had given the department the impression that Díaz had the support of a substantial majority of the people. He said that Eberhardt must realize that "the Government of the United States cannot take any steps which would be considered as American armed intervention." The State Department would, however, issue licenses for the export of arms, if Díaz asked this, and the United States Navy would take all proper steps to protect American lives and property on the east coast. To protect the Americans, the secretary asked the navy to land marines at such places on the east coast as Latimer might think advisable. This meant that American forces would take control of several places which were held by the revolutionists.

The secretary apparently did not intend that the marines should interfere with the liberals' military operations. The naval forces at Bluefields and Corinto had endeavored to avoid any action that might help either side. Both parties had agreed to the establishment of a neutral zone at Bluefields, and neither had been allowed to interfere with foreign shipping there. The State Department had told the liberals that it expected them to respect the financial plan and not to change the personnel in the customhouses in the ports which they occupied, but it told Latimer in October that he should not use force to collect revenues for Chamorro. Díaz had complained that the naval forces on the east coast were partial to the liberals, but Dennis thought that this charge was unfounded.

When Kellogg asked that additional marines be sent to the east coast, however, Stabler, who had succeeded Francis White as chief of the Latin American division, suggested informally to the navy that the neutral zones might be established in places where they would control the liberal bases and cut off their supplies from Mexico. This suggestion was passed on to Admiral Latimer. When American forces landed at Río Grande and Sacasa's capital at Puerto Cabezas, they seized the arms which the liberals had in those ports and imposed a censorship on the radio station at Puerto Cabezas which prevented the revolutionary government from communicating with its forces along the coast. Kellogg was disturbed when he learned of this, and asked that the admiral be told to confine his activities to protecting the lives and property of Americans and foreigners where they were in danger and where there was no other assurance of protection. He thought that American forces should be landed only where such protection was necessary, and that they should not try to control the importation of arms except where the arms had been shipped from the United States in violation of the American government's embargo. Kellogg said that it was not the policy of the United States to intervene by force in Nicaragua's affairs and that "great care should be exercised by the American forces in Nicaragua to preserve the strictest neutrality between the revolutionists and the constitutional authorities."

Admiral Latimer consequently returned the arms, except for some which were said to have been accidently destroyed, and at least modified the radio censorship. Thereafter, the neutral zones did not seem to interfere greatly with either side's military operations. In most cases the zones extended about one mile from the foreign properties which they were intended to protect. The revolutionary government at Puerto Cabezas at first protested against what it termed an infringement of Nicaraguan sovereignty, but as time went on it seemed happy to carry on under the protection of the marines. General Moncada, though he complained about the seizure of the arms, wrote the consul at Bluefields that he thought it would be desirable to neutralize the entire east coast to protect commerce and foreign interests.[31]

The Mexican government continued to send arms to the revolutionists, and, to judge from reports of the American consular officers in Mexico, made little effort to conceal what it was doing. On December 3 the steamer *Superior*, which had been loaded with material from the Mexican army's warehouse at Puerto México, sailed from Vera Cruz for Nicaragua, reportedly escorted by a Mexican warship. On her return, according to a story heard by the American embassy in Mexico, she brought a letter from Sacasa to President Calles asking for further help. Calles gave the captain $50,000 to take to Nicaragua on his next trip, but the trip was delayed when the captain disappeared with the money. A more tragic episode occurred when the sloop *Carmelita*, carrying arms from Mexico, took refuge from a storm at Bonacca Island in Honduras and the local *commandante* and

[31] McConnico to the secretary of state, Dec. 31, 1926, 817.00/4386.

213

four soldiers were killed by machine-gun fire when they attempted to board her.[32] Several other vessels were engaged in the traffic. With these arms, the liberals defeated Díaz' forces at Pearl Lagoon on December 23 and 24, in a battle in which about 1,400 men took part on each side. The conservatives thereupon withdrew their forces from the east coast to avoid further conflict. There was now little hope for an early suppression of the revolution. The government still controlled western Nicaragua, but there were mounting fears of a Mexican-aided invasion from the Pacific.

On December 29 Díaz made another urgent appeal for help and intimated that he would surrender unless the United States did something to stop Mexican intervention. Eberhardt thought that the government would collapse if no help came. There were rumors that a large vessel was approaching the Pacific coast from the north and the minister said that Díaz could not guarantee protection to foreigners if there were an attack. The British and Italian chargés d'affaires also thought that their nationals were in imminent peril and asked for American protection.[33]

Eberhardt's report, based primarily on what Díaz told him, probably exaggerated the seriousness of the situation, but it convinced Kellogg that the United States would have to take further steps to protect foreigners in Nicaragua and to prevent a collapse of the Díaz government. On January 6, 1927, 160 marines were sent to Managua as a legation guard. Latimer was authorized to seize arms or ammunition landed by unauthorized persons if the president of Nicaragua asked him to do so, and neutral zones were set up at practically all of the east coast ports where they were not already established. The admiral's new instructions would seemingly have made it possible to cut the liberals off from their foreign supplies, but no large shipments were intercepted, possibly because none were sent.

The reestablishment of the legation guard and the creation of new neutral zones, followed shortly by an announcement that six additional warships and 600 more marines were being sent to Nicaragua, called forth a wave of criticism in Latin America and

[32] On the *Superior*, see Sheffield's telegrams of Dec. 30, and Dec. 31, 1926, 817.00/4329, 4333. The story about the *Carmelita* was reported by Admiral Latimer. Secretary of navy to secretary of state, Dec. 22, 1926, 817.00/-4292.

[33] Eberhardt to Kellogg, Dec. 29, 1926, 817.00/4326.

in the United States. The State Department could hardly continue to maintain that its policy was one of non-interference and neutrality. In explaining what it was doing, it asserted that it was supporting a friendly, constitutional government against a revolution backed by a foreign power, in a country where the United States had special interests. On January 7 the State Department and the White House gave the press what the *New York Times* described as the first authoritative statement about Mexico's connection with the revolution. This seemed to show that the Nicaraguan imbroglio was only a part of the controversy that threatened a break in diplomatic relations between Mexico and the United States, and American liberals who were already criticizing the government's efforts to help property owners in Mexico were not impressed by the allegation that Mexico was trying to spread communism through Latin America. This was evident on January 8 when there was a concerted attack on the administration's Mexican and Nicaraguan policies in both houses of Congress.

Two days later President Coolidge sent to Congress what was described as "an unexpected and dramatic message."[34] Discussing the situation created by Mexico's intervention in Nicaragua, he emphasized the special interest of the United States in Nicaragua growing out of the Bryan-Chamorro treaty and the American government's connection with the financial plan. It would be inconsistent, he said, for the United States not to support a government recognized by it while the revolutionists were receiving arms and munitions from abroad. "The proprietary rights of the United States in the Nicaraguan canal route, with the necessary implications growing out of it affecting the Panama Canal, together with the obligations flowing from the investments of all classes of our citizens in Nicaragua, place us in a position of peculiar responsibility." In this situation the United States must take such steps as might be needed to protect American interests.

The tone of this message seemed somewhat inconsistent with the less "imperialistic" policy toward which the State Department had been moving during the past four or five years. The president's emphasis on the support of American economic interests was surprising, not only because our economic interests in Nicaragua were insignificant but because the State Department for

[34] *New York Times*, Jan. 11, 1927.

215

some years had been acting on the principle that armed intervention could be justified only in cases where American lives were in danger. The president seemed to overemphasize the importance of the United States' canal rights. In the State Department we had tended to look on the canal option as something which the American government had taken in 1914 chiefly as a convenient excuse for giving Nicaragua urgently needed financial help. The American government's subsequent action showed in fact that the message did not signify any real change in policy.

The message did not seem to convince very many of the government's critics. Secretary Kellogg followed it up by giving several hours of testimony at a closed meeting of the Senate Committee on Foreign Relations on January 13, producing documentary evidence about Mexico's intervention and discussing communist activities in Latin America. Nevertheless the attacks in both houses of Congress continued. The State Department was accused of intervening in Nicaragua to collect debts and protect private mining and timber investments and of helping sinister interests which were trying to embroil the United States in war with Mexico. It was asserted that Mexico was doing nothing improper in supporting Sacasa, who was the legitimate president of Nicaragua. Senator Borah was one of the principal critics.

Despite his concern about Mexico's support of the revolution, Kellogg still wanted to see the war ended by an agreement between the two Nicaraguan political parties. On January 10 he told Eberhardt to insist that Díaz explore all possibilities for a settlement and asked the navy to instruct Latimer to help. Díaz responded with a proposal for a new peace conference to be held under the auspices of the United States government. He said that he would insist on remaining in office until December 1928, but would offer the liberals executive and judicial positions and would permit their candidates to be elected to Congress in special elections in two liberal departments. The presidential election in 1928 would be supervised by the United States. Meanwhile a bi-partisan commission would deal with claims for losses during the revolution and the government would purchase the arms held by the liberals. Díaz went on to say that he proposed to ask for an American military mission to train the constabulary, which would be enlarged and would become the sole military force, and that he hoped after the restoration of peace to obtain a large loan for the construction of a railroad to the Atlantic coast and for roads. When Latimer discussed this proposal with Sacasa, the liberal leader refused to consider any arrangement based on Díaz continuing as president, but said that he would favor supervision of the 1928 election by the United States assisted by one or more representatives of the Central and South American republics.

Kellogg told Eberhardt to say that the United States would be glad to supervise the 1928 elections if both parties so desired, and would have no objection to participation in its supervision by the Central American governments. To overcome Sacasa's intransigence about the presidency, Latimer was instructed to tell him that there was not "the slightest possibility" that the United States would recognize his government or any other based on armed force or insurrection even if the revolution were successful. Until new elections were held, it could only recognize the government that it had recognized, and Díaz would get the support "naturally flowing from recognition." This statement was not published, and Eberhardt, who was informed about it, was enjoined not to repeat it to Díaz or anyone else. Sacasa, however, would not abandon his demand that Díaz withdraw, though he was apparently ready to resign in favor of a compromise president if one could be agreed on.

The liberal army was still on the east coast, but small bands of liberals were beginning to operate in western Nicaragua and on February 6 one of these attacked Chinandega. Much of the city was burned in a two-day battle. It is not clear who was responsible but both parties were shocked by the disaster and each blamed the other. Reports that American pilots attached to the constabulary had taken part in the fighting caused the State Department some embarrassment. Major Carter had resigned but the force was commanded by Major Rodríguez, who was a reserve officer in the United States Army. It had apparently taken no part in the recent fighting on the east coast. The department warned the fliers that they could expect no protection from the United States if they participated in hostilities.

Since Chinandega was on the main line of the Pacific railroad, the battle interrupted communications between Corinto and Managua and Latimer asked for reinforcements that would enable him to restore them for the protection of the legation guard at Managua. The Nicaraguan government also asked that the American forces reopen the railroad. The State Department at first

217

insisted that this was the responsibility of the Nicaraguan government. Eberhardt was told to make it clear that the American forces would not under any circumstances fight with the government's troops against the revolution, and Latimer was asked to take every precaution to keep his forces from any direct action against the revolutionists. A few days later, however, on February 14, Kellogg agreed that the admiral should be authorized to keep the railroad open from Corinto to Managua and from there to Granada and to establish such neutral zones along the line as he considered necessary for the protection of Americans and foreigners.[35] Sixteen hundred additional marines and six airplanes were ordered to Nicaragua. Strong detachments were stationed at Chinandega and León and an armed squad with a machine gun traveled on each train between Managua and Corinto. On February 22 the *New York Times* reported that there were 5,414 marines in Nicaragua or en route to the country and eleven cruisers and destroyers at Nicaraguan ports.

The burning of Chinandega and reports that Moncada was bringing his army through the jungle into western Nicaragua seem to have created something like a panic in Managua. Eberhardt thought that the United States should intervene at once to keep the government from collapsing. He and Admiral Latimer had all along been critical of the conservatives' military ineptitude and lack of will to fight, and their low opinion seemed confirmed when the government forces abandoned Matagalpa, which would presumably be the first town attacked. They reoccupied the town when it became clear that Moncada was still far away, but their action frightened the American and British coffee planters in the Matagalpa area. The Europeans in Managua urged that the American government take action to protect all foreigners, and the British government sent a warship to Corinto as a refuge for British subjects in an emergency. On February 19 Díaz proposed that the United States establish a protectorate over Nicaragua, under a treaty which would give the United States the right to intervene to maintain a stable government. He proposed a new financial plan, to make possible a $20,000,000 loan, an American mission to train the constabulary, and American help in a public health program. The State Department told Eberhardt not to encourage any idea that the United States

[35] Secretary of navy to secretary of state, Feb. 14, 1927, 817.00/4584.

might accept such a treaty, but it made no formal reply to the proposal.

Shortly after Díaz made his proposal, however, the American government agreed to sell him 3,000 rifles and 200 machine guns, with ammunition, out of its own stocks, under an arrangement whereby the purchase price, a total of $217,718, would be paid after January 31, 1929, at the rate of $5,000 per month. There were precedents for the sale of arms by the United States government to governments fighting against a revolution—one of them a sale to Mexico in 1923—but the transaction was a further evidence of American support of the conservative government. The State Department also showed an increasing willingness to help Díaz in connection with his financial problems. In December 1926, when Díaz asked the bankers for a loan, Stokeley Morgan had told the bankers that he could not promise them any protection because the State Department itself did not know which side would win the war,[36] and on January 12 the department had told Eberhardt that a loan would be inadvisable until peace was restored. A few weeks later, the department was more sympathetic. In March the Guaranty Trust Company and J. and W. Seligman and Company agreed, with the department's approval, to lend the Nicaraguan government $1,000,000. The bankers had hesitated to make a loan while the American government's policy in Nicaragua was under so much attack, but they changed their attitude when they learned that Rene Keilhauer, who had long been associated with Minor Keith, was ready to lend the government $600,000, apparently with the idea of adding Nicaragua's railroad to Keith's Central American system.

Under the circumstances the terms were reasonable. The bankers received a commission of one percent on the entire amount, and interest at six percent on the amount outstanding at any one time. The term of the loan was one year, but Nicaragua could delay payment of not over 50% of the total amount for a further term of six months. The bankers were given an option on any future Nicaraguan financing. All of the stock of the Pacific railroad and the national bank was pledged as security, and Nicaragua agreed that the bankers should name a majority of the directors of each company so long as the loan remained unpaid. The Nica-

---

[36] Morgan's memorandum of conversation with Tillinghast, Dec. 28, 1926, 817.51/1799.

raguan government, as we have seen, had voluntarily left both institutions under the bankers' management since the government became sole owner of them. The money would cost Nicaragua somewhat more than 7%, because the full amount would not be outstanding at any one time; but the bankers pointed out that Seligman had recently sold Costa Rican bonds at a price that would yield the investor 7.4% and bonds of the Cauca Valley in Colombia on a basis yielding the purchasers about 7.9%. The existence of the customs receivership and the character of the security made a loan to Nicaragua safer than the Costa Rican and Colombian bonds, but on the other hand the general unpopularity of the American government's Nicaraguan policy made a loan to Díaz unattractive to bankers who hoped to do business in other Latin American countries.[37]

After the establishment of neutral zones along the railroad line, American forces were occupying nearly all of Nicaragua's principal towns. They were still under orders not to interfere in the fighting, but it was impossible to suppose that they would not sooner or later get involved. The danger increased after Moncada reached the interior and confronted the government forces in the area between Muy Muy and Matagalpa, north of Managua and the railroad line. There was some bloody but indecisive fighting but neither side seemed able or willing to make an aggressive effort to end the war. Meanwhile, criticism of the American government's policy and suspicion of its motives was becoming louder and more emotional, especially in the other Latin American countries.

A memorandum which Stokeley Morgan wrote on March 18 showed that the State Department was still uncertain about its course of action. The Nicaraguan situation, Morgan said, was unsatisfactory and dangerous. Hitherto the United States had acted solely under its right to protect foreigners, which implied that it would let the parties fight it out with the expectation that the government would win. It had not decided what to do if the revolution won, but it seemed apparent that it could not under any circumstances permit the overthrow of Díaz, which would mean

---

[37] The important correspondence about the loan is printed in *Foreign Relations, 1927*, Vol. III, pp. 421 ff. See also 817.51/1743, 1744, 1750, 1756, 1758, 1759, and 1760. Eberhardt transmitted a copy of the loan contract with his dispatch of April 2, 1927, 817.51/1786.

the end of the 1923 treaties and would encourage revolutions elsewhere. The military situation, he said, was a stalemate, but the revolutionists' morale was higher because the conservatives thought that the United States would support them and could not see why they should get shot unnecessarily. He saw two courses open to the United States: (1) to continue the present policy, which would be all right if Díaz won. If the revolutionists should win, however, the United States would have to intervene, and under very disadvantageous circumstances; (2) to intervene at once, by announcing that the United States would help to put down the revolution. Morgan advocated immediate intervention because it would save lives in Nicaragua, though at the expense of some American lives, and would better protect American interests.[38]

Morgan's superiors were not ready to accept so radical a recommendation, but early in April President Coolidge asked the former Secretary of War Henry L. Stimson to go to Nicaragua to "straighten out the situation." Neither the president nor the secretary of state gave Colonel Stimson any very definite instructions, but they said that the United States must insist on the legitimacy of Díaz' election as president. They thought that the supervision of the 1928 election by the United States, which both parties had accepted in earlier negotiations, offered the best hope for a peaceful solution.[39]

Before Stimson could reach Nicaragua, for the journey even on an American cruiser took more than a week, reports of a decisive conservative victory near Muy Muy gave the State Department the impression that the war was practically over and led Kellogg to send new instructions to be conveyed to Stimson on his arrival. The latter's mission, the secretary said, should not in any sense be an act of mediation and it would be better for Stimson not to take the initiative in consulting with the revolutionary leaders. Kellogg was not inclined to press the government to give up any advantages that it had obtained by the victory, but he thought that Díaz should consider treating the liberals generously and granting an amnesty. The State Department realized that the United States must participate in a permanent arrangement for the establishment of peace. It was prepared to leave a force

[38] 817.00/4849.

[39] See Stimson's undated *Report on Mission to Nicaragua*, 817.00/6181.

221

of marines in Nicaragua if the government so requested, but it hoped that Stimson would discover some way to avoid the responsibility of supervising elections.

When Stimson arrived on April 17 he found that the liberal forces had not been destroyed and that the incompetent conservative generals had not followed up their victory. It seemed clear that no Nicaraguan leader could establish and maintain peace without foreign assistance. He reported that it would probably be necessary for the United States to supervise the 1928 election, and that his mission would be relatively useless if this possibility were excluded. Kellogg replied that the American government would supervise the election, if the Nicaraguan government asked it to, and would be prepared if necessary to leave a force of marines in Nicaragua.

Stimson soon became convinced that any peace settlement must be based on the retention of Díaz as president. The liberals insisted that Díaz withdraw, and Díaz professed a willingness to do so in the interests of peace, but it seemed impossible to find anyone acceptable to both sides to replace him. Since every Nicaraguan of any standing was a member of one party or the other, it would be impracticable to attempt to place a neutral at the head of the government. It would also be impracticable and unjustifiable to insist that the conservative Congress elect a liberal as acting president. Díaz, with his moderate attitude toward opponents and his evident willingness to cooperate in a genuine program of reconciliation, would be as acceptable to the liberals as any real conservative could be. Stimson rejected proposals to place an American at the head of the government, not only because this would violate the Nicaraguan constitution, but because he thought that the president of the United States had no authority to designate such an official.[40]

On April 22 Díaz gave Stimson his proposal for a peace agreement. Both sides would deliver their arms to the American forces and there would be a general amnesty. Representative liberals would be appointed to the cabinet. A non-partisan constabulary would be established under American officers, and presidential elections, not only in 1928 but thereafter, would be supervised by Americans. The effectiveness of the program was to be assured by the continuance in Nicaragua for the time being of a sufficient

[40] Stimson discussed these problems in his *American Policy in Nicaragua* (New York, 1927), pp. 65-70.

force of American marines. Stimson had the Managua liberals transmit these terms to Sacasa by United States naval radio, and invited Sacasa to send a representative to discuss them with him.

Stimson knew that the liberals were unlikely to accept any arrangement that left Díaz in the presidency and he was beginning to feel that the United States might have to use force to stop the war. He was shocked by the outrageous brutality of the fighting. Irregular armed bands from both sides were committing atrocities and depredations in the countryside, and it was clear that there would be a famine if the war continued into the planting season in May and June. The situation became much more alarming when Moncada moved to a position near Tipitapa, on the isthmus between the Nicaraguan lakes, where he could threaten either Managua or Granada. Stimson recommended on April 26 that Admiral Latimer be authorized to prevent the insurgents from advancing beyond the Tipitapa River and that he himself be authorized to intimate to Sacasa that the marines might forcibly disarm the revolutionists if no settlement were reached. This would mean a radical change in policy, but Kellogg authorized him on April 27 to use his discretion with regard to threats of disarmament and with regard to preventing the insurgents from crossing the Tipitapa River.

Three representatives sent by Sacasa reached Managua on April 29, coming from Puerto Cabezas on an American destroyer. They assured Stimson that they had no "hostile understanding" with Mexico and that they desired American aid in reaching a settlement. They were ready to accept all of the terms of the proposed settlement except the retention of Díaz. They said that Sacasa was ready to give up his claim to the presidency, but would not accept a settlement which left Díaz in office. In view of their attitude, Kellogg cabled Stimson on April 30 that he and President Coolidge thought that the substitution of another consitutional president should be considered at least as a possibility. The secretary said that public opinion in the United States, and even newspapers that had opposed the administration's policy, were strongly in favor of a settlement, and that it was important that the negotiations with the liberals should not be permitted to fail. He added, however, that the president gave Stimson the widest discretion in handling the whole problem. Stimson was more than ever convinced that Díaz must remain in office. He pointed out that the president would be a mere figurehead under the proposed settlement, and said that it would be very difficult to find another Nicaraguan who could be trusted to cooperate in carrying out the peace terms. He thought that the only alternative would be the appointment of an American provisional executive.

After two days of conferences, the liberal delegates asked Stimson whether he could arrange for them to confer with General Moncada, who had been almost out of touch with Puerto Cabezas since his march into the interior. Three marine officers carried their message to the revolutionary commander, and a forty-eight-hour truce made possible a conference between the lines at Tipitapa on May 4. Stimson and Eberhardt accompanied the delegates, and after the Nicaraguans had talked with Moncada Stimson took advantage of the opportunity to talk with him alone. Within half an hour the two men reached an agreement that ended the civil war. After reading Díaz' peace terms, Moncada said that he could not consent to Díaz' retention in the presidency, but that he would not resist if the United States insisted on it. He recognized that neither he nor any other Nicaraguan could end the war and pacify the country without the help of the United States. He asked, however, for a letter which he could use in persuading his army to accept the settlement and Stimson immediately dictated and handed him one saying that

> I am authorized to say that the President of the United States intends to accept the request of the Nicaraguan Government to supervise the election of 1928; that the retention of President Díaz during the remainder of his term is regarded as essential to that plan and will be insisted upon; that a general disarmament of the country is also regarded as necessary for the proper and successful conduct of such election; and that the forces of the United States will be authorized to accept the custody of the arms of those willing to lay them down including the government, and to disarm forcibly those who will not do so.

Stimson then made the same statement to Sacasa's delegates, who said that they would advise Sacasa not to attempt to resist the United States.

The war ended at once. Díaz proclaimed a general amnesty on May 5. American marines moved into the Tipitapa area between the two armies and on the same day Latimer and Moncada worked out the details of a plan for disarmament. The admiral announced on May 10 that all arms should be delivered to the nearest detachment of American forces, and that he would take by force arms that were not surrendered. He would receive the government forces' arms in the same proportion as those delivered by the revolutionists, and the Nicaraguan government would pay $10 for each serviceable rifle or machine gun surrendered. Moncada and all but one of his prominent subordinates telegraphed Stimson on May 12 that they would accept the peace arrangement. The exception was General Augusto César Sandino, who told Moncada that he would sign the telegram but then withdrew into the interior with a small group of his men.

Meanwhile, Díaz promised Stimson that he would appoint liberal *jefes políticos*, or governors, in six predominantly liberal departments, and asked the resignations of the judges whom Chamorro had appointed to the Supreme Court, in order to reinstate the former incumbents. He also promised to reinstate members of Congress who had been illegally expelled by Chamorro and to hold congressional elections in districts where they had not been held in 1926. Stimson informed Moncada of all this in a letter which he handed him at a second conference on May 11, saying that the purpose was "so far as possible to restore the political condition as it existed in Nicaragua before the Chamorro *coup d'etat.*" He assured Moncada that the United States would supervise the 1928 election and that American officers would train a non-partisan constabulary to assure fair play. The American government would leave enough marines in Nicaragua to support the constabulary and maintain peace. Before Stimson left Managua on May 16 each side had turned in practically all its arms and the soldiers were hurrying home to plant their crops.

The peace mission made possible the establishment of a democratically elected government which gave the great majority of the Nicaraguan people several years of peace. Most Nicaraguans were glad to see the end of the war, which was causing increasing terror and suffering as it spread to the interior.[41] The success of the mission had been made possible by Stimson's quick grasp of the situation and the confidence which he inspired in those with whom he talked, and especially by the fact that he had been given full authority to act. The settlement was fair to both parties and in the long run acceptable to both, for most of the liberal

[41] I was convinced of this when I went to Nicaragua a few months after the Tipitapa agreement.

leaders who at first objected to it came around after they saw that the American government really intended to hold a free election. There was little doubt that the liberals would win in a free vote. The State Department might perhaps have been expected to be unhappy about this, but Stimson's talks with the liberal leaders had evidently convinced him that their acceptance of Mexican help in the war did not mean that their assumption of power would endanger American interests.

The threat to disarm forces which did not accept the arrangement was criticized in some of the other Central American countries, where sympathy for the liberals had been growing as American interference in Nicaragua increased, but in the United States the settlement seems to have been generally approved. Even Senator Borah rather guardedly praised it. Many who opposed what seemed to be an intervention to help one party in a civil conflict could accept one which was undertaken at the request of both parties. There was a revival of criticism, however, when it became apparent that there were some Nicaraguans who opposed the peace settlement and that the American government's promise to maintain order would involve the marines in armed conflict with them. Stimson and Latimer had foreseen that irregular armed bands might make trouble in remote parts of Nicaragua after the regular armies had accepted a settlement. Latimer pointed out that some of the guerrilla leaders were "better off as insurgents than . . . in time of peace." He specifically mentioned Augusto César Sandino.

Sandino, who had grown up in poverty in a small town in Nicaragua, had gone to Mexico as a boy. On his twenty-first birthday he left Tampico, where he was working for a foreign oil company, to join the revolutionists in Nicaragua. He operated for a time as a guerrilla in the northern provinces, and then joined the main liberal army when Moncada came into western Nicaragua. He wrote Moncada on May 9 that he would accept the peace agreement and disarm his forces, but then marched northward with about 200 men. The American marines might have disarmed him at this time, but they had thus far avoided any actual conflict with Nicaraguans and were reluctant to start one. He soon disappeared into the wild, mountainous country near the Honduran border. For a time he occupied and operated an American-owned gold mine at San Albino where he had once worked. The marines, who were rapidly reducing their forces in Nicaragua, could not immediately organize an expedition to deal with him.

In the early morning of July 16, 1927, Sandino attacked the small town of Ocotal, the capital of Nueva Segovia, with a force far larger than the local garrison of thirty-nine marines and forty-eight Nicaraguan constabulary. The situation was desperate until the marines' five small two-seater planes flew over the town in the middle of the afternoon and drove off the attackers with bombs and machine-gun fire. One marine, but none of the constabulary, was killed. The heroic resistance of the garrison and its dramatic rescue might have made a thrilling story, but the newspaper accounts which were published in the United States and elsewhere gave far more prominence to the marines' foolish boast that they had killed more than three hundred of the rebels. This was a gross exaggeration, for the priest who buried the victims said later that about sixty were killed,[42] but the report made a painful impression in foreign countries. A force of 111 marines and constabulary was sent north to attempt to disarm Sandino, but after one encounter, in which one marine was slightly wounded, the insurgents simply disappeared.

For some weeks thereafter the marines had practically no contact with the Sandinistas or with the other bandit groups which had been operating in the northern jungles. The situation seemed so improved that most of the American forces were withdrawn from Nicaragua on August 27, leaving about 1,200 men under the command of Colonel L. M. Gulick. General Feland, on his way home, was quoted as saying that "the time is past when it is necessary to use armed force to maintain peace in Nicaragua" and that Sandino "is through."[43] Many of the marines who remained in Nicaragua were assigned to the constabulary. An act of Congress, approved May 19, 1926,[44] made it possible, as it had not been in 1925, to assign American officers and enlisted men to train and command the new force, built on what was left of the constabulary organized in 1925 and thenceforth called the *Guardia Nacional*. In August 1927, Colonel Elias R. Beadle was commissioned as general in command of the *Guardia*, succeeding Colonel Robert Rhea who had started to reorganize the force in May.

The provisions of the peace agreement which promised the lib-

[42] See Admiral Sellers' letter of Feb. 18, 1928, 817.00/5412.
[43] *New York Times*, Aug. 28, 1927.   [44] 44 *Stat.* (Part 2) 565.

erals a share in the government gave rise to some controversy. On June 1 Díaz appointed liberals approved by Moncada as *jefes políticos*, or civil governors, in the departments of León, Chinandega, Jinotega, Estelí, Nueva Segovia, and Bluefields, in all of which the majority of the people were liberals, but he rejected Moncada's demand that liberals should be appointed as chiefs of police and collectors of internal revenue in these provinces. Moncada appealed by cable to Stimson, who confirmed Díaz' statement that there had been no specific agreement about the other posts, but thought that Díaz should interpret the Tipitapa agreement generously and that the liberals ought to be given as much control in the departments where they were in the majority as the conservatives had in other departments. Kellogg took the same view and instructed Eberhardt to use his influence "to the utmost" for a generous interpretation of the peace agreement. Eberhardt, however, made little or no effort to persuade Díaz to accept Moncada's demands, and the department dropped the matter because it was working on a plan to place all the internal revenues under American control in connection with a loan which the Nicaraguan government hoped to obtain.

Moncada wanted to control the internal revenue administration in the liberal departments because he feared that discrimination in the collection of taxes would be used for political purposes. Also, the rum in the fiscal warehouses would be an invaluable asset at election time. Eberhardt was probably right, however, in opposing the setting up of what would virtually have been two separate governments in Nicaragua. If the liberals had been given control of the internal revenues in their departments, each party would have regarded them as a political asset. There was less probability of abuse under a centralized administration which could be watched by the high commission and the management of the national bank, where the proceeds of the internal taxes were deposited. Furthermore, it was hardly fair to insist that Díaz make a concession·to which he had clearly not agreed. The suggestion that he interpret the Tipitapa agreement "generously" suggested a failure to realize that neither party, entering a contest in which victory was so important, could be expected to make any unnecessary concessions.

The appointment of liberal *jefes políticos* did the liberals little good because the rest of the administrative machinery remained in the hands of conservatives who took their orders from the president rather than from their nominal superior. The proposal to give the government a bi-partisan character by including liberals in the president's cabinet proved even more impractical. Díaz offered in August to appoint two liberals to the cabinet, but Moncada objected to one of the persons that he selected and it was soon clear that it would be difficult to find candidates acceptable to both parties. The State Department considered urging Díaz to make concessions, but Stimson advised against any action. He said that Díaz was under no obligation to take cabinet ministers whom he did not want.

The effort to reorganize the courts was more successful. Soon after the Tipitapa agreement the members of the Supreme Court whom Chamorro had ousted were restored to their positions, so that the liberals, with the support of one anti-Chamorro conservative, had control of the tribunal. One of the new court's early acts was to order the reinstatement of three liberal judges in the appellate courts at León and Bluefields. Díaz admitted that the judges must be reinstated, but he insisted that they must be reelected by Congress. The dispute dragged on for nearly two months, partly because neither Eberhardt nor the State Department fully understood what it was about, but late in September the legation at Managua worked out a compromise which ensured the reinstatement of the judges but recognized the constitutional right of Congress to elect them.

On July 2, 1927, President Coolidge announced that he would nominate Brigadier General Frank Ross McCoy to be chairman of the commission which would supervise the election of a new Nicaraguan president. General McCoy's military record and his successful handling of assignments of a non-military character— the first of them as a very young officer when he was put in charge of civil affairs on General Wood's staff during the first American occupation of Cuba—made him one of the outstanding officers in the United States Army. The appointment showed the importance which the American government attached to the electoral supervision. It would have been hard to make a better choice for a task that called for wisdom, tact, and firmness of purpose. General McCoy, accompanied by Harold Dodds, made a preliminary trip to Nicaragua at the end of August and spent about a month discussing the electoral problem with party leaders and American officials. One of the matters which he discussed with Eberhardt and with me, for I had just arrived in Nicaragua,

229

was Stimson's proposal that representatives of other American governments be invited to observe the election, to convince both the Nicaraguans and the rest of Latin America of the good faith of the United States. We all felt that the violent feeling which the events of the past year had aroused, particularly in the Central American countries, would make it hard to expect that such observers would be impartial and that the presence of officially appointed observers who were not impartial would complicate the already formidable task of maintaining fair play between the two parties. The proposal was consequently dropped.

I was transferred from Panama to Nicaragua in August 1927 to take charge of the legation while Eberhardt went on leave. The plan at the time, though it was changed later, was to keep the minister away from his post until after the Nicaraguan presidential election in November 1928. During that time the legation's chief task would be to support General McCoy in conducting the election and in general to see that the Tipitapa agreement was faithfully carried out. This involved a great deal of interference in matters of internal administration, ranging from minor police actions to decisions of the Supreme Court. The liberals had objected to the retention of Díaz because they feared that a conservative government would influence the voters by improper use of the courts and the police, the communication system and the funds in the national treasury; and after Stimson insisted that Díaz remain in office the United States had an obligation to see that no such abuses occurred. This involved some friction with the conservative officials. There would have been more if President Díaz had not cooperated loyally in the effort to assure a free election. Díaz was by no means a mere "figurehead" as Stimson thought he would be under the Tipitapa agreement, but in making appointments and using government funds he usually resisted pressure from other conservative leaders to use his authority in unfair ways.

One of our most difficult tasks was to convince both parties that the American government and its representatives were truly impartial. Many Nicaraguans assumed that the United States would decide who the next president would be, and if either party thought that the United States intended the other to win, many of its adherents would lose interest. Both groups were thus sensitive to any expression or action that appeared to show sympathy for either side, and some elements in each frequently tried to place the American officials in a position where they would be compelled to seem to take sides. This was true even in purely social affairs. The liberals complained that American officials attended many governmental social functions, and when we attended a reception in honor of a liberal, the Nicaraguan minister at Washington protested to the State Department. There was a general and not wholly unfounded impression that the personal sympathies of the American minister, who returned in January 1928, were with the conservatives and that some of the marine officers were more friendly to the liberals. It was very difficult for many Nicaraguans to realize that the Americans would not allow personal sympathies to deflect them from a policy of impartiality. Fortunately, General McCoy won the confidence of both parties from the start.

The most troublesome questions were frequently unimportant ones. What was referred to as the "Tipitapa agreement" was really a series of commitments, some of them in writing but others made in conversations between Stimson and the leaders on one side or the other. The general purport was clear. The United States agreed at the request of both parties to supervise the election of 1928. American forces were to disarm both parties and were to maintain order in Nicaragua until a non-partisan constabulary could be trained under the direction of the marines. Meanwhile, Díaz would so far as possible give the liberals the same participation in the government that they had enjoyed before Chamorro's coup d'etat. Many questions, however, were necessarily left unsettled or were dealt with in conversations of which the legation at Managua had no record. This was perhaps inevitable under the circumstances, but it led to frequent disputes in the months that followed. The liberals repeatedly appealed to Colonel Stimson against actions of the government or the legation on the basis of assurances that he had given or was alleged to have given during his talks with Moncada.

An example was the matter of the horses at Boaco. Stimson and General Feland, the marine commander, had told the liberals that each soldier disbanded in the Boaco-Teustepe area might keep one of the horses that Moncada's army had been using during the war. Trouble arose when the conservative police and judges began to return some of the horses to their former owners. Both sides appealed, as they always did, to the legation, which could find no record of any agreement on the subject. The Nicaraguan

231

government maintained that its courts had no alternative but to return the horses when the ownership was clear. The State Department, after consulting Stimson, said that the liberals should keep the horses. They should be considered as having been requisitioned, and the Nicaraguan government should pay the owners. This did not settle the rather numerous cases where it was not clear whether the horse had been taken from its owner before or after the end of the war, but we heard nothing further about the matter after we sent a marine sergeant to Boaco with instructions to deal with each case on its merits. The task of restoring order in Nicaragua would have been far more difficult if it had not been for the resourcefulness and common sense of many of the marine non-commissioned officers who were assigned to tasks of this sort after the peace agreement.[45]

Another incident showed how the courts could be used for political purposes. In September 1927, a liberal political meeting at San Marcos, at which General Moncada was present, grew somewhat boisterous, and when the conservative chief of police attempted to break it up he was stood on his head in the street. There was apparently no bloodshed, but the next morning both General Moncada and Dr. Cuadra Pasos, the minister of foreign affairs, appeared at the legation, each charging that the other's political friends had acted in a way that would make a free election difficult. There seemed to be no occasion for diplomatic intervention, but more than a year later it appeared that orders of arrest, issued by the local conservative judge after the affair, were still outstanding and would disqualify many of the liberals of San Marcos from voting in the presidential election. The legation had to demand that the Supreme Court order the judge to dispose of the cases at once and had to ask President Díaz to see that the judge obeyed the order. On another occasion the legation had to demand the removal of a judge who had ordered the imprisonment of 348 liberals in Nueva Segovia.

The Supreme Court itself misused its power for partisan purposes in a case arising during the municipal elections which were held throughout Nicaragua on November 6, 1927. The United States had no obligation to supervise these elections, but it seemed desirable that they be fair and free both because the possession of the municipal governments would be important during

[45] The above account is based on correspondence in the files, including 817.00/5175, 5183, 5189½, 5203, and 5245, and on my own recollection.

the presidential campaign and because any serious abuses in the way the voting was conducted would tend to lessen confidence in the possibility of a free presidential election. President Díaz agreed to several proposals put forward by the liberals to protect the voters against abuses, and the American marines observed the voting and helped to maintain order. In general, the elections went off relatively well. The liberals were successful in many towns, including Managua where there was a hard-fought contest. In Granada, however, the liberals claimed that the conservative candidate for *alcalde*, or mayor, had not been properly nominated, and appealed to the Supreme Court to declare void all votes cast for him. When it seemed clear that the court would decide in favor of the liberal candidate, I informally pointed out to the chief justice that such a decision would make a very painful impression. The court took no action for the time being.

A few weeks later the conservatives showed still less respect for decency in connection with the election of two members of Congress. Elections had been held on September 4 in several normally liberal districts where the civil war had prevented their being held at the usual time. Except in Bluefields, the liberals won, because the conservatives had promised Stimson that they would not present candidates. In Estelí, however, bandit operations had made voting impossible in many districts, and the liberals asked that a supplementary election be held, so that the conservative-controlled Congress would have no excuse for excluding the senator and deputy from that province. Díaz agreed, but the conservatives now asserted that their promise to Stimson did not apply to Estelí and wished to contest the election. It seemed unreasonable to oppose them because both parties asked that American marines be present to maintain order and assure a free vote.

When the ballots were cast, in November, the marines helped to count them and reported that the liberal candidates, combining the results with those of the September election, had a majority of more than 100. The department electoral board, however, arbitrarily added 100 conservative votes to the tally in each of two precincts and reported 17 conservative and no liberal votes in another precinct where there had been no voting. I warned the government that there would be no further effort to restrain the Supreme Court in the Granada case if the conservatives insisted on stealing this election. The Congress nevertheless admitted the conservative senator and deputy from Estelí, and some time later the liberal candidate, fortunately a highly respected citizen, was installed as *alcalde* in Granada.

What happened in Granada and Estelí showed how complete the American intervention would have to be if a free presidential election were to be held. If either party were in a position to influence the voters by force or fraud, it would certainly do so. Fortunately, the changes provided for by the Tipitapa agreement had already diminished the danger of pressure on the voters by the government. The conservatives controlled most of the municipal police forces, but these were being replaced as rapidly as possible by the national guard under American officers. In the meantime marine detachments in the larger towns discouraged serious abuses. The changes in the courts also helped, or at least gave the liberals a more nearly equal opportunity for the misuse of power. For a time there was a bad situation on the east coast, where it was always difficult for the government to exercise its authority. There were continual quarrels between the liberal *jefe político* and the conservatives who held the other offices, and the guard did not yet have enough men or enough money to take over the police there. Conditions improved, however, after Moncada reluctantly agreed to Díaz' suggestion that ex-president Juan J. Estrada, an old friend of both men, be appointed *jefe político* with authority over the entire administration.

Moncada was still complaining of abuses in the collection of taxes, and General McCoy thought that it would be hard to have a fair election if the internal revenue administration remained in the hands of one party. In an effort to deal with this matter, I made a mistake which caused me much embarrassment. The legation's files, which were in a rather chaotic state, seemed to contain no copy of the financial plan of 1920, but in Colonel Ham's copy, which I borrowed, I found a provision that the collector general of customs might take over the collection of the internal revenues if their yield fell below $225,000 in any period of three consecutive months. Since they had fallen below this amount, I recommended that Ham be instructed to take the action which the plan authorized. Ham was not anxious to take on a disagreeable responsibility but the State Department approved my proposal. I then discovered that the amount had been changed by the Nicaraguan Congress, when it approved the plan, to $200,000 and that the government had collected as much as this in recent months. I consequently had to recommend that nothing be done about the internal revenues until the matter could be dealt with in connection with the loan, which was still under consideration. Díaz was unwilling to surrender control of the internal revenues, except in connection with a loan, because he thought that the effect on the government's prestige would be ruinous.

While the interior provinces were rapidly recovering from the effects of the civil war and the party leaders were devoting their attention almost wholly to the approaching political campaign, it became obvious that the situation in the North was growing worse. There had always been banditry in the Segovias, as the sparsely inhabited provinces along the Honduran frontier were called, and it had naturally increased during the civil war. Sandino's was but one of several groups, some liberal and some conservative, which were robbing and murdering members of the opposite party throughout the region. For a time in the fall of 1927 another liberal named Salgado was almost equally troublesome. The liberals had more support among the country people, who hated the politically powerful conservative Paguagua family, but the conservative bandits, who were no less cruel and rapacious, had many friends among the local officials and judges in Nicaragua, and also in Honduras, where they took refuge when pursuit got too hot. One band had its headquarters on a farm belonging to the *jefe político* of the Honduran department of Choluteca. The mountainous, heavily wooded country was ideal for guerrilla operations. Most of the principal highways were unimproved trails and the telegraph reached only the larger villages.

It was clear that the withdrawal of the greater part of the marines had been a mistake. Those who remained were occupied in training the guard and in maintaining order in the larger towns. The guard was gradually taking over the police work in the interior, but its recruitment was proceeding rather slowly because only a small amount of money was available for it under the tightly restricted Nicaraguan budget. Neither the marine brigade nor the guard could provide any substantial force for operations against the bandits. The marine command announced in September 1927 that it was starting an active campaign against Sandino and Salgado, but the force which it sent north, including a detachment of the guard, was totally inadequate. It could occupy the towns and patrol some of the more important roads, but it

235

had little contact with the bandits except when its patrols, usually dangerously small, were ambushed by superior forces.

It would have been difficult to catch the bandits, even with larger forces. Sandino could recruit three or four hundred men on occasion for an attack on a town or a marine patrol, but most of these hid their arms and returnd to peaceful occupations when they were pursued. The leaders disappeared into the hills with a handful of followers. The marines' intelligence system was woefully inadequate, and the patrol leaders could get little information from the country people, who feared the bandits if they did not sympathize with them. The patrols and the marine aviators had orders not to fire on anyone unless they were clearly being attacked and to take extreme precautions to avoid injury to noncombatants. There were occasions when the marine flyers were compelled by these orders to refrain from bombing or machine gunning what were obviously groups of outlaws.

Partly because of the inadequacy of the forces used, several marines were killed by bandits between September and December 1927. On September 19, 140 of Salgado's followers attacked twenty marines and twenty-five *guardias* at Telpaneca and were driven off with heavy losses after two marines had been killed. Three weeks later a patrol of eighteen men which was attempting to rescue two aviators who had had a forced landing was attacked by 300 bandits and four of the national guard were killed. It was later learned that the two aviators, who had been attempting to escape on foot, had been betrayed by a native guide and killed by the Sandinistas. At the end of December a large patrol was ambushed and five marines and one *guardia* were killed. The Sandinistas continued to attack after the patrol took refuge in the village of Quilalí, but were finally driven off with the help of the marine planes. Some of the more seriously wounded men might have died if First Lieutenant C. F. Schilt had not brought them out in his small plane, landing nine times under fire in the village street.

One of the problems that confronted the marine command was the lack of legal authority to hold such bandits as were captured. It seemed inadvisable to turn them over to the civil courts because any judge who acted against them would be in danger of reprisals. The brigade commander and I thought that the best solution would be to have the Nicaraguan Congress declare martial law in the province of Nueva Segovia to permit the guard to bring prisoners before military tribunals. The State Department, however, feared that the declaration would give Sandino added stature as the leader of an open rebellion, and it did not wish to assume the responsibility involved in permitting American *guardia* officers to hold courts-martial. Though I pressed the matter rather insistently, Secretary Kellogg refused, perhaps wisely, to acquiesce in a measure that seemed necessary to those on the ground.[46] Meanwhile, I had urgently recommended that more marines be sent to Nicaragua. The brigade commander had been reluctant to ask for reinforcements, but it seemed to me that we could hardly assure a free election unless banditry were brought under control. In January 1928, Brigadier General Logan Feland was sent back to Nicaragua with 1,000 marines.

At about the same time, Admiral Sellers, who was now commander of the special service squadron and thus commander of the marines in Nicaragua, wrote personally to Sandino, urging him to accept the Tipitapa agreement to prevent further bloodshed. As in the case of several earlier peace offers, some of them conveyed to the outlaw leader by members of his own family, the reply, addressed to the admiral as "representative of Imperialism in Nicaragua," was a defiant refusal. His revolt, Sandino wrote, was a struggle of the Nicaraguan people to expel foreign invaders. The only way to end it was to withdraw the invading forces, to replace Díaz, and to have elections supervised by Latin American representatives rather than by marines.

Most Nicaraguans were far less interested in what was happening in the North than they were in the presidential election, which was still months away. In the weeks after the Tipitapa agreement there was no clear consensus in either party about the choice of a presidential candidate. Emiliano Chamorro had by far the greatest following in the conservative party, in spite of the unhappy events of the past two years, but he was ineligible under the Nicaraguan constitution and his candidacy was opposed by Díaz and some of the more moderate leaders in Granada. Moncada had represented the liberal party in dealing with questions that arose under the Tipitapa agreement, but his acceptance of the agreement had displeased many of the other liberal leaders and it was not clear that he would have their support.

[46] Munro to Kellogg, Dec. 22, and Kellogg to Munro, Dec. 28, 1927, 817.00/5199; Munro to Kellogg, Jan. 11, and Kellogg to Munro, Jan. 13, 1928, in *Foreign Relations, 1928*, Vol. III, pp. 560-561.

Chamorro returned to Nicaragua in the fall of 1927. On his way home he spent several weeks in Washington endeavoring to persuade the State Department not to raise any objection to his candidacy. The department would have preferred to avoid any appearance of influencing the choice of candidates by either party, but it could not overlook the fact that Chamorro was ineligible for the presidency under the same constitutional provision that ruled out Martínez' candidacy in 1924. It would be rather ridiculous for the American government to supervise an election if it knew in advance that it could not recognize one of the candidates if he were elected, and it was clear from previous experience that Chamorro would persist in his candidacy unless the department expressed its opposition unequivocally. Francis White, who was now assistant secretary in charge of Latin American affairs, consequently handed him a memorandum on October 22 saying that the United States would not recognize him as constitutional president at any time during the term beginning in January 1929. This settled the matter, but it left the conservatives without a candidate and several months passed before they could agree on one. Chamorro continued to be the most influential leader in the party.

Moncada, meanwhile, was obtaining control of the liberal party's machinery. He had much support among the veterans of the revolutionary army, and the fact that the United States treated with him as the spokesman for the party gave him a great advantage. His frequent letters to and from Colonel Stimson, who took a lively interest in the execution of the peace agreement, increased his prestige. The American officials in Managua had to deal with him, because there was no one else who could speak for the party, but they were disturbed at his success in creating the impression that he was the American government's choice for the presidency. Eberhardt suggested on September 8 that he be authorized to dissuade Moncada from making a projected trip to Washington, saying that he and McCoy felt that Moncada had already derived as much political advantage as he should from his relations with the legation and his correspondence with Stimson, and that the courteous reception which he would presumably receive in Washington, in contrast to the reception which the State Department would probably accord Chamorro, could give rise to charges of partiality between the two parties. The State Department, however, did not think it advisable to discourage the visit.[47] When Assistant Secretary White told Stimson of the legation's concern about the situation in the liberal party, Stimson replied that he would "try to watch his step" but pointed out that Moncada owed his advantage to the fact that he was brave enough to show his friendship for the United States when the Sacasa group refused to cooperate.[48]

Part of the liberal opposition to Moncada arose from the feeling that he had given up the prospect of winning the revolution with Mexican support in return for the promise of an election in which the United States might not be able or willing to assure fair play. Much of this feeling evaporated as it became evident that the American government meant to assure a free vote, and when Moncada left for the United States, early in October, he seemed to have the support of a great majority of the party.

One purpose of Moncada's visit, apparently, was to set at rest any doubt about his recognition by the United States if he should be elected president. There was no question about his constitutional eligibility, as there was in the case of Chamorro, but it could well be argued that his case fell within the provisions of the Central American treaty of 1923, which barred the recognition of any of the leaders of a revolution, even after the reorganization of the government by a free election. The American government felt that the treaty would not apply in a situation where a civil war was ended by an agreement that left the constituted government in power. Apparently Kellogg told Moncada, and told the press, that he knew no reason why Moncada should be ineligible for recognition, and Moncada cabled his friends that he had been assured that he would be recognized if elected. When the State Department realized what effect this would have in Nicaragua, it authorized the legation to publish a statement saying that the United States was not going to select any candidate or use its influence to help anyone, but that it would not recognize a president who was ineligible under the Nicaraguan constitution.[49] The Nicaraguan legation at Washington nevertheless

[47] Eberhardt to Kellogg, Sept. 8, and Kellogg to Eberhardt, Sept. 10, 1927, 817.00/5022.

[48] White to Stimson, Sept. 20, 1927, 817.00/5038a, and Stimson to White, Sept. 23, 817.00/5043½.

[49] This statement, which is printed in *Foreign Relations, 1927*, Vol. III, p. 369, purported to contain what the secretary told the press and had

complained that Moncada had derived an unfair advantage from his interview at the State Department and from a friendly telegram sent him by Stimson.

In the first months after the restoration of peace, both political parties seemed disposed to cooperate with the American officials in carrying out the Tipitapa agreement. By December 1927, however, it was becoming evident that many of the conservatives, under Chamorro's leadership, had decided that they would gain more by obstructing the effort to assure a free election. The conservatives had apparently hoped that their control of the government would give them an advantage in the electoral campaign, but the outcome of the municipal elections, especially in Managua, had shown that this advantage was not very great. One of the first indications of the new attitude was an attempt to prevent the ratification of the formal agreement governing the national guard, which had been operating since May under an informal understanding with Díaz. The conservatives evidently hoped to slow down the organization of the new force so as to leave part of the country under the control of the local Nicaraguan police during the electoral campaign.

The *guardia* agreement, signed December 22, 1927, provided that the new constabulary should have a minimum of 93 officers and 1,064 enlisted men, in addition to its band and medical personnel, and a minimum annual budget of $689,132. It was to be the sole military and police force of the republic and would have full control of all arms and military supplies. Its commander would take orders only from the president of Nicaragua. Until enough Nicaraguan officers had completed a course of instruction prescribed by the commander, the president of the United States would nominate officers and enlisted men from the U.S. Navy and Marine Corps to assist in its training. These would be subject to trial only by courts-martial set up under the laws of the

---

told Moncada. The original mimeographed version, which was perhaps used by Kellogg as the basis for an oral statement rather than as a "handout," said that the question of Moncada's eligibility had not been raised and that so far as the secretary knew he was not disqualified, but this sentence was crossed out before the statement was cabled to Managua. (See 817.00/-5099a.) The *New York Times* of Oct. 26 said that Chamorro would not be recognized but Moncada would be, but this statement was not attributed to the State Department.

United States.[50] The agreement was promptly approved by the United States Senate and by the senate in Nicaragua, but the conservatives raised constitutional objections to it in the Nicaraguan chamber of deputies, and it remained unratified throughout the remainder of Díaz' administration. The organization of the guard nevertheless proceeded, and by the end of February 1928, it had 797 enlisted men. It took over more and more of the police work in the cities and at the same time provided forces to operate with the marines against the bandits in the North.

Chamorro's activities made Díaz' position all but intolerable. the president showed no disposition to break the promises that he had made to the liberals and to the United States but it was increasingly difficult for him to control even his own subordinates. He was under terrific pressure from his associates to help his party to avoid defeat. For a time it seemed very possible that he might resign, or at least might accept a Chamorrista suggestion that he make a visit to Washington, leaving a less cooperative *designado* in charge at Managua. When I reported the efforts which I was making to dissuade the president from leaving his post, and suggested that the department support them, Kellogg replied that no one who was interested in carrying out the peace agreement could entertain the idea of a change in the presidency. Díaz rejected the proposal that he visit the United States, but from time to time in the months that followed he threatened to resign and had to be urged to hold on. If he had left, the holding of a fair election would have been infinitely more difficult.

The effort to prevent a free election reached a climax in the Congress' rejection of the new electoral law which the State Department thought necessary if McCoy were to have the powers that he would need. The department's draft was sent to Managua in November. A group of distinguished lawyers, who studied the project at the request of the Nicaraguan government, questioned the constitutionality of its basic features—the appointment of a foreigner as president of the electoral board and the power of the board to make regulations which would have the force of law—but I persuaded Díaz to submit the law to Congress on December 28 without mentioning this opinion. The Nicaraguan senate approved it on January 10, but it met with

[50] For the text, see *Foreign Relations, 1927,* Vol. III, pp. 434ff.

strong opposition in the chamber of deputies, where Chamorro's influence was greater.

Secretary Kellogg, after discussing the matter with General McCoy and the Nicaraguan minister, took the position that the objections to the department's draft were "untenable as a proposition of constitutional law" and that a failure to approve it would be a flagrant breach of faith. Nevertheless, the Chamber of Deputies, on January 17, amended the Senate bill in a way that would have reduced General McCoy and his aides to the position of mere advisers to the Nicaraguan electoral authorities. This of course would have been totally inconsistent with the agreement under which the liberals had laid down their arms, and it seemed imperative to persuade the deputies to reconsider their action. Chamorro, when I talked with him, was defiant, accusing the United States of favoring Moncada and threatening that the conservatives would withdraw from the electoral contest. I thought that Díaz could bring pressure to bear on the deputies and on Chamorro himself by depriving the Chamorristas of some of the jobs and other favors that they enjoyed, but for the first time the president was evasive and uncooperative. He naturally did not want to make a conservative defeat inevitable by breaking up the party and he was probably not unwilling to see the conservatives succeed in their effort to improve the party's chances in the election. He was clearly unhappy and embarrassed about the situation, but he knew that the American government was very anxious that he continue in the presidency and when I pressed him too hard he threatened to resign, and even told the American press correspondents that he was about to do so. The State Department took this threat more seriously than I did, and fear that Díaz might withdraw affected at least the tone of its instructions to the legation during the crisis.

It was harder to convince the conservative leaders because Alejandro César, the Nicaraguan minister at Washington, had been telling them that the United States was not really interested in a free election and that its attitude toward the liberals had been influenced by the recent publication in the Hearst papers of several documents purporting to prove that the Mexican government had supported the liberals during the civil war. These documents, which were later found to be forgeries, had of course no influence on the State Department's attitude, but César's reports about them were shown to the deputies while they were considering the electoral law. Díaz told me about this and said that César was also reporting that Kellogg had given him the impression that the State Department could be convinced that its electoral project was unconstitutional. The president suggested that an explicit statement of the American government's position be handed to César for transmission to Managua.

When I reported this, the State Department authorized me, on January 17, to present a note emphasizing the American government's determination that the Tipitapa agreement be carried out and its conviction that the constitutional objections to the electoral law had no merit. The department said that it would regard a refusal to enact the electoral law as a breach of faith which would compel the American government to consider other measures. It added that it was considering asking César's recall, and that it would make no further important communications through him. This instruction arrived just too late to affect the action of the chamber of deputies, and its usefulness in the negotiations that followed was diminished when it became known that Kellogg, after a talk with César, had decided not to ask his recall. The secretary did not want to do anything to split the conservative party and he thought that the incident was "a good lesson" to César. Its chief result, however, was to create the impression that there was a difference of policy between the State Department and the legation at Managua.

Neither Díaz nor the Chamorrista deputies seemed much interested when I suggested that we explore the possibility of revising the draft electoral law to meet any reasonable constitutional objections without restricting the powers that General McCoy must have, but when the Sixth Pan American Conference met at Habana in January Secretary Kellogg and Francis White revived this idea in talks with Cuadra Pasos and the other Nicaraguan delegates. Cuadra Pasos personally controlled the votes of several deputies, and could probably have brought about the approval of the electoral law if he had been sincere in his professed willingness to support it. On one occasion, in fact, he told me that he would do so if the legation would openly support Díaz and "close its eyes." He did not explain what this meant and I could only reply that I could not close my eyes to any action inconsistent with a free election. At Habana, after vainly endeavoring to convince White of the need for substantial changes in the plan for electoral supervision, Cuadra Pasos came forward on January 26 with a draft of an electoral law which White considered satisfactory. He said that he would make an effort to persuade the conservatives to accept it.

Meanwhile it became known that Eberhardt was returning to his post as American minister. This was a surprise, for I had been told again in December that I would be in charge until after the presidential election.[51] Apparently the State Department had been criticized for leaving a junior officer in charge at Managua when the dispatch of additional marines to Nicaragua and the conservatives' resistance to the electoral law were attracting much attention in the United States. It is possible too that Secretary Kellogg, who had been nervous about Díaz' threats to resign, thought that I had been too vigorous in my efforts to get the law approved. After his return, however, the minister showed little disposition to take over the active direction of the legation's work. He called on President Díaz several times each week, apparently for friendly conversation, but he left the conduct of business almost entirely to me.

The legation had less responsibility for formulating and executing policy after General McCoy returned to Nicaragua in the latter part of January. As the personal representative of the president of the United States McCoy made all decisions in matters connected with the approaching election, and all other American officials, civilian and military, were instructed to assist him. He brought with him a number of assistants, both civilians and army officers. His principal technical adviser was Harold Dodds, who was already familiar with Nicaraguan political problems and whose resourcefulness and common sense did much to make the supervision a success.

McCoy tried to dispel any idea that the United States might compromise on the basic principles of the electoral law, but he took the position that the responsibility for its passage rested on the president and the minister for foreign affairs. His reluctance to discuss the matter with the other conservative leaders gave some of them the impression that the United States was modifying its position. He had to proceed rather cautiously because Secretary Kellogg had exhorted him and Eberhardt to do what they could to keep Díaz from resigning. Díaz and Cuadra Pasos professed to be willing to press for the approval of the Habana com-

[51] White to Munro, Dec. 13, 1927, Francis White papers, Box 5.

promise, but it was clear that their efforts were not wholehearted even after Secretary Kellogg, at the legation's suggestion, sent a strongly worded cable emphasizing the "extreme gravity" of the situation and the American government's determination to carry out its obligations under the Tipitapa agreement.

The Nicaraguan Senate finally passed the Habana redraft of the electoral law on March 7. A few days later Cuadra Pasos told us that he had lined up enough votes to assure its approval by the chamber of deputies, but he urged us to accept some minor amendments, to save Chamorro's face and to avert the breakup of the conservative party. We agreed to some of these, after consulting Moncada, but on March 13 the chamber of deputies rejected the law by a vote of 24 to 18.

Late in the evening of the same day McCoy and Eberhardt and I called on President Díaz to discuss what should be done. We said that the United States would still expect the Congress to pass the electoral law, but that in the meantime preparations for the election must begin. We therefore suggested that the president issue a decree, which might later be ratified by Congress, but which would immediately give McCoy the authority which he had to have. This procedure had at one time been suggested by Cuadra Pasos and also by some of the liberals, and Díaz, who was doubtless glad to be relieved from any obligation to put pressure on the Chamorrista members of Congress, promptly agreed to it. We then consulted the State Department, which approved it, with the stipulation that the validity of the decree should not depend on any future ratification by Congress. There could be some question as to its legality, but it was clear that the American government, to carry out its promise to both parties, had to insist that McCoy have full authority to assure electoral freedom. The State Department had already considered and rejected the alternative of attempting to proceed under the electoral law drafted by Dodds in 1923, because this would not have given the American electoral mission the necessary authority.[52]

Díaz issued the decree on March 21, after the Congress adjourned. It suspended the Dodds law and gave a national board of elections full authority to conduct the election and to prescribe

[52] "S.P." 's (Spencer Phoenix) memorandum to Olds, Feb. 4, 1928, 817.00/5403½; White to Dodds, Feb. 29, 817.00/5435a, and Dodds to White, March 5, 1928, 817.00/5451½. See also Olds' memorandum of March 2, 1928, 817.00/5444.

"with obligatory force" all measures necessary for this purpose. The American chairman of the board, to be elected by the Supreme Court, must concur in all decisions, and could act by himself, without the concurrence of the other members, in case of an emergency. The national board was to organize the departmental and cantonal boards, which like the national board were to have American chairmen and members from each of the political parties. The chairman of the national board was authorized to command the services of the national guard in case of emergency.

After the decree was issued neither party in Nicaragua made any serious effort to obstruct the holding of a free election. Both seemed satisfied with the American government's action, and Chamorro himself told us that he had no objection to it. The Nicaraguan Supreme Court tacitly approved what had been done when it elected McCoy chairman of the national board of elections. The general rapidly established an excellent working relationship with his colleagues on the national board and with the other party leaders. We were all optimistic about the prospects for a satisfactory election and in general about the success of the peace agreement. The country was rapidly recovering from the effects of the civil war. Except in the northern jungles, where the bandits were still eluding the marines and the guard and committing occasional depredations, conditions were generally tranquil.

Even in the North the situation seemed to be improving. In January and February 1928, some of the conservatives had argued that disturbed conditions there would make a free election impossible, and the Chamorristas had persistently spread rumors that disturbances were about to break out in other regions. Sandino, who had been relatively inactive for a time, ambushed a pack train and killed four marines in February, and also staged a foray into the Matagalpa region which did relatively little damage but caused much alarm. After these events, Admiral Sellers recommended that the marine brigade be reinforced. By July 1928, with the addition of a number of officers and men sent to assist in the work of the electoral mission, the American forces in Nicaragua reached a peak of 5,800. The additional men made it possible to patrol the northern provinces more effectively. The worst of the conservative bandits, who had been operating from Honduran territory, were put out of business in March, when President Paz Barahona ordered that their principal leaders be arrested and turned over to the marines at the border. There were Nicaraguans, including some high officials, who suggested that it was hardly fair to suppress the conservative bandits while the liberal bandits remained at large, but the balance between the two parties was not really affected, because it was soon clear that Sandino was as ready to murder liberals who supported Moncada as he was to murder conservatives.

Unfortunately Sandino had only to evade capture and occasionally raid a village or attack a marine patrol to maintain his standing abroad as the symbol of Nicaraguan resistance to North American imperialism. Latin American hostility to the intervention in Nicaragua had been painfully evident at the Sixth Pan American Conference at Habana. In South America propaganda by the communists and also by European business interests, which were trying to regain their pre-war commercial ascendency, made use of the largely mythical war of liberation in Nicaragua to stir up feeling against the United States. There was also communist and anti-imperialist pro-Sandino propaganda in the United States. On January 15, 1928, for example, the "All American Anti-Imperialist League" held a meeting in New York at which the editor of the *Daily Worker* and an associate editor of the *Nation* solicited funds for medical supplies for Sandino. The same organization printed stamps protesting the presence of the marines in Nicaragua and was supported by the American Civil Liberties Union in an unsuccessful attempt to prevent the Post Office Department from barring their use on letters. In a further effort to obtain funds, it circulated pamphlets entitled *Enlist with Sandino* and *Defeat the War Against Nicaragua*, in one of which it urged marines in Nicaragua to mutiny or to desert to Sandino. The American press associations found that there was a good market in the South American press for reports of such activities and reports of anti-imperialist speeches in Congress at Washington; and their dispatches helped to create a distorted picture of what the American government was doing.

Criticism in the United States made it more difficult to arrange the loan which had been under discussion since the time of the peace agreement. While Stimson was in Nicaragua, Fernando Guzmán, the minister of finance, had proposed a loan as a means of bringing about reforms in Nicaragua's financial administration. Many of the Nicaraguan conservatives were not averse to accepting help from the United States in checking graft and increasing the government's revenues, and their willingness increased with the prospect that the liberals might take over the government. After Stimson's return to the United States, he and General McCoy and Francis White discussed Guzmán's letter with J. and W. Seligman and Company. The bankers prepared a proposal which they submitted to the State Department in October 1927, but this was held in abeyance pending the completion of a financial survey of Nicaragua which the State Department had asked W. W. Cumberland to make. Cumberland, who had just resigned as financial adviser to Haiti, spent about three months in Nicaragua studying all aspects of the country's economy. He reported that there was no desperate need for a loan, except as a means for bringing about much needed financial reforms. He proposed a system of financial control much like that in effect in Haiti, and he strongly urged the sale of the national bank to American interests in order to assure the stability of the currency. When he discussed his plan informally with Díaz and Moncada and other Nicaraguan leaders, all expressed approval, though Díaz and Chamorro thought that the changes should not be put into effect immediately.

In the legation we felt that it was imperative to proceed immediately with the proposed loan in order to establish a financial control which would prevent the government from using public funds for electoral purposes. Aside from possible abuses in the administration of the internal revenues, there was the prospect that the bankers' 1927 loan would be paid off in April or May 1928, so that the full amount of the surplus revenues would fall into the government's hands. We pointed out that at least $600,000 would thus be available for political purposes and that this would be enough to hire every registered voter in Nicaragua for one week at current wage rates.[53] We also urged that the State Department support the effort which Díaz was already making to persuade the Guaranty Trust Company and Seligman to buy 51% of the stock of the national bank, in order to remove any temptation to use the bank and especially the currency reserve fund for political purposes. The bankers were managing

[53] See the portion of Eberhardt's dispatch of Feb. 7, 1928, which was not printed in *Foreign Relations*, 817.51/1901.

the bank, but so long as the government owned it they sometimes had to accede to the government's wishes and the bank had recently let the government have a loan of $40,000, part of which had been given to Chamorro for political use. After the repayment of the 1927 loan not only the bank but the railroad company, which had a considerable amount of free money, would be entirely subject to the government's control.

There was much criticism of the loan project from opponents of the intervention in the United States, but on May 23, 1928 Kellogg and other officials of the department met with representatives of the bankers and expressed the hope that a loan could be arranged. In the negotiations that followed between the department and the bankers several differences of opinion developed. The bankers wanted to associate the American government with the loan to an extent which seemed objectionable to the department, and they were not willing to provide as much money for the payment of war claims as the department wanted them to. The bankers contemplated a loan of only $3,500,000 for the time being. Nevertheless on July 23 the State Department cabled the legation the outline of a plan that seemed to have been agreed on. On the same day, however, Kellogg sent word to the bankers that he did not wish the State Department to be associated with the project. This killed it, for the bankers would not go ahead without the American government's support.

During the discussions, the bankers and the State Department had agreed on a change in the existing financial control. Cumberland, in a confidential report, criticized the operation of the customs service and the high commission and recommended that Ham and Hill be replaced. The legation concurred in this recommendation. We felt that Ham had done excellent work in organizing and administering the customs service, but he had been in Nicaragua too long. Hill's tactless and sometimes unwise conduct had caused trouble on several occasions, and the functions of the high commission would be relatively unimportant after the payment of the 1927 loan. The two men consequently resigned, and in June 1928 Irving Lindberg, the deputy collector general of customs, was appointed to both posts.

Fortunately our fear that the government would derive an unfair advantage from its control of the finances proved largely unfounded. We were able to prevent misuse of the surplus revenues

249

by persuading Díaz to turn them over to the guard for its ever-increasing expenses. There was no serious interference with the American managements of the national bank and the railroad, and so far as we knew no serious abuse in the internal revenue administration. Díaz cooperated with General McCoy and the legation in all these matters.

We had always felt that Díaz wished to live up to his promises about the freedom of the election, but there had been times when he seemed unable to resist pressure from other conservative leaders in matters where he was not bound by specific promises. At times he had been so unwilling to risk a break with Emiliano Chamorro that he had let Chamorro dictate appointments and give orders almost as though he were the head of the government. In April 1928, however, he suddenly changed his attitude and gave his support to the presidential candidacy of Dr. Cuadra Pasos, in opposition to Vicente Rapaccioli, who was the candidate of Chamorro and the Granada "oligarchy." Each conservative faction held departmental conventions in April and May, and on May 20 they held separate national conventions, each claiming to represent the party and formally nominating its own candidates.

The split in the conservative party was unwelcome because it seemed important that there be a clear-cut contest between the two traditional Nicaraguan political parties so that the victor would have the unquestioned support of a majority of the voters. The conservatives apparently assumed that the national board of elections would decide which was the legitimate conservative candidate. The Chamorristas were confident that they had the strongest legal case, as they probably did; and the Cuadra Pasos group were confident that McCoy, who would have the deciding vote, would not side with Chamorro against Díaz. McCoy, who was in Washington at the time, had no desire to decide either way. He did not even return to Nicaragua until June 17, and then said that he would consider the matter only in consultation with his colleagues on the electoral board. After hearing both sides, the electoral board decided unanimously on July 6 that neither had demonstrated its right to be recognized to the exclusion of the other. The board offered, however, to consider any plan that would enable the conservative party to participate in the election. At the same time, McCoy issued a statement emphasizing again the fact that neither he nor the State Department favored

250

any particular candidate or party. Díaz and Cuadra Pasos were bitterly disappointed, but both factions realized that they must unite the party if they were to have a chance in the elections.

Ramón Castillo, the conservative member of the electoral board, used his good offices to bring the two groups together, but for some time the negotiations made little progress. Finally Castillo told both factions that General McCoy was threatening to have the board adopt a resolution declaring that the conservative party had ceased to exist. He had no basis whatever for such a statement, but the party leaders were evidently alarmed, and on July 26 we were told that Adolfo Benard and Julio Cardenal had been agreed on as the conservative candidates for the presidency and the vice presidency.[54] Benard was a brother of Martín Benard, who had been the Chamorrista's candidate for the vice presidency. He was one of the most successful businessmen in Nicaragua, but he had never been active in politics and was said to be in poor health. Cardenal was Cuadra Pasos' brother-in-law. The fact that both men were wealthy was one of the considerations emphasized by the conservative newspapers in reporting the nominations.

Moncada had already been nominated for the presidency by a liberal convention in February. His running mate was to have been Judge Medrano of the Supreme Court, but in August 1928, Medrano withdrew because of illness and Dr. Enoch Aguado, who had been serving as the liberal member of the national board of elections, was nominated in his place. On August 20 the conservative member of the national board challenged Moncada's eligibility as a presidential candidate, asserting that Moncada could not be relieved of his position as senator, except to take a position under the executive power, without the permission of two-thirds of the Senate, and also that he had been minister of war in the revolutionary government and was thus barred by the Central American treaty. He further alleged that Moncada, as senator, had collected a fraudulent claim against the government. The board nevertheless accepted Moncada's nomination by a 2-1 vote. McCoy rejected the constitutional argument as untenable and contrary to precedent and held that the 1923 treaty, which would not in any event affect a candidate's eligibility under Nicaraguan law, did not apply where no recognized

[54] The events leading up to the agreement are described in Eberhardt's dispatch of July 27, 1928, 817.00/5913.

government had been overthrown by the revolution. He dismissed the charge of fraud as an informal accusation of which the board could not take cognizance.

Two minor parties sought places on the ballot. One was the liberal republican group, headed by Luís Correa, who had received a small number of votes in the election of 1924 but claimed that he would have received enough, if the votes had been honestly counted, to entitle him to a place on the ballot for 1928 under the Dodds law. César rather naively told Morgan that the conservatives were encouraging Correa, in the hope that he might take enough votes from Moncada to throw the election into Congress.[55] The other was the conservative republican party, which had received a substantial portion of the vote as a part of the victorious coalition in 1924, but which was now hardly a bona fide party. In July, the national board of elections rejected the petitions of both groups, saying that the Dodds law was suspended and that neither group had shown enough evidence of political following to entitle it to consideration. McCoy was very anxious to make sure that one of the parties obtained a majority in the election. If neither did, the new president would be chosen by the Congress, where it was probable that the hold-over members would give the conservatives a majority, and there would be danger that the liberals might not accept the result. If there had been a third party with any substantial following it would have been difficult to exclude it, but it seemed clear that there was not.

During the next two months preparations for the election went forward more smoothly than anyone had anticipated. Both parties were optimistic and both seemed to have confidence in the impartiality of the American electoral mission. Díaz cooperated in measures which the mission considered necessary to assure fair play. All liquor warehouses were put under the control of the guard on September 1 and orders were issued to suspend arrests for non-payment of taxes. The electoral mission, meanwhile, had given three months' training, in special schools in each province, to the marine and navy enlisted men who were to be chairmen of most of the 432 local electoral boards. The chairmen of the 13 departmental electoral boards were for the most part officers from the United States Army.

The insurgents in the North could do little to interfere with the electoral process. After a sensational and destructive raid on the

[55] Morgan's memorandum of April 4, 1928, 817.00/5558.

American-owned mines on the east coast in April, Sandino and his lieutenants were relatively inactive, and by September it was thought that the combined strength of the outlaw bands was not more than 200 poorly armed men. There were two shocking incidents in Jinotega province on September 26 and October 1, when outlaws murdered two liberal officials of a local electoral board and several liberal political workers, but even in Jinotega these murders did not seriously interfere with the registration of voters, which took place from September 27 to October 7. A total of 148,831 registered in all Nicaragua: 28% more than in 1924 and very much more than in any earlier election.

The voters' confidence in the protection offered by the marines and the *guardia* was even more evident on November 4, when the election itself took place. No disorders were reported and nearly 90% of those registered voted. In Nueva Segovia the proportion was only 82%, but this was a remarkable showing in view of the conditions that had existed in the province a few months earlier. Though the American electoral mission considered it unnecessary, both parties insisted that each voter's thumb be dipped in Mercurochrome to prevent repeating. There were practically no complaints of the conduct of the American electoral officials and few complaints of fraud, and the national board of elections unanimously approved the returns except in the case of those from the province of Bluefields, where the conservative member dissented. Moncada was elected president by a vote of 76,676 to 56,987.[56]

The greater part of the newly elected members of Congress were liberals, but the conservatives, with the hold-over members, still had a majority. This caused some apprehension that the Congress might attempt to abuse its constitutional power to pass on the credentials of its new members, but after the legation made very informal representations to the principal conservative leaders the report of the national board of elections was approved in joint session on December 28 with only one dissenting vote. Moncada was inaugurated on January 1, 1929 at an impressive ceremony in which Díaz participated.

The outlook for the future seemed brighter than at any time since the United States first became involved in Nicaragua's internal political problems in 1909. During the campaign, Moncada

[56] These are the figures which Eberhardt gave in his dispatch of Dec. 22, 1928, 817.00/6169.

had told the legation that he would like to enter into an agreement with the conservatives to ask the United States to supervise the presidential election of 1932. The State Department had not permitted us to discuss this proposal with the conservative leaders, but it had expressed sympathy with it and suggested that Moncada himself approach Díaz or Benard. Moncada got in touch with Benard, and just before the election the two candidates called together at the legation. They stressed their satisfaction with the way in which the election was being conducted and their confidence in the American government's impartiality and they asked that the United States agree in advance to supervise the 1932 election. The State Department could not commit a future administration to do this, but it expressed sympathy with the idea. As we pointed out to the department, the disorderly conditions which had caused the United States so much trouble during the past twenty years would continue unless some means could be found to bring about peaceful changes of government, and the United States would be criticized more severely than ever if it permitted one party to perpetuate itself by dishonest elections while it controlled the national guard. The two candidates' agreement, which led to American supervision of Nicaraguan elections during the ensuing four years, was undoubtedly one of the chief reasons why the conservatives made no effort to overthrow the liberal government during that period.

Chapter Eight

THE HOOVER ADMINISTRATION, CENTRAL AMERICA, AND THE DOMINICAN REPUBLIC, 1929-1933

NICARAGUA

With the holding of the presidential election of 1928, the United States had discharged its commitment under the Tipitapa agreement. It was under no further obligation to maintain marines in Nicaragua. The easiest and pleasantest course would have been to withdraw: to turn over to the Nicaraguans the disagreeable task of repressing banditry in the Segovias and to terminate an episode which had exposed the American government to so much criticism at home and abroad. If there had been any evidence that any substantial group in Nicaragua opposed the continued presence of the marines they would probably have been withdrawn after Moncada's inauguration. It seemed clear, however, that most Nicaraguans, though they disliked having the marines there, felt that it was better to have them than to risk another civil war. They insured the government against revolt and their control of the national guard protected the opposition against the sort of mistreatment which the government's enemies would otherwise expect. In January 1929, when I left Managua to go to the State Department as chief of the Latin American division, I thought that there was little anti-American feeling in Nicaragua. Sandino, who had appeared abroad as the leader of patriotic resistance to the American intervention and was regarded as a hero in the other Central American states, had little support in his own country.

The retention of the marines in Nicaragua was distasteful to President Hoover and was opposed by strong groups in Congress, but the State Department felt that an immediate withdrawal might undo what had been accomplished at so much cost since 1927. Colonel Stimson, who became secretary of state on March 28, 1929, took a lively personal interest in Nicaragua's

255

problems. He was justifiably proud of his own part in ending the civil war and he wanted to carry through the program of rehabilitation envisioned in the Tipitapa agreement. He continued to carry on a personal correspondence with President Moncada, who frequently asked his advice. The American government thus continued to be involved in Nicaragua's internal affairs while it was trying to end its intervention in Haiti and exposing itself to criticism for refraining from intervention to end Machado's dictatorship in Cuba.

We felt especially that the marines must remain for the time being to fulfil our commitment to train the national guard. The guard was doing good work, but it had as yet few Nicaraguan officers and it would not be able to function efficiently if the American officers were suddenly withdrawn. So long as marines continued to serve in the guard, the navy felt that it must keep a force in Nicaragua to support them. This force would also be useful if the United States should decide to accept the Nicaraguans' request that it supervise the presidential election of 1932, and its presence would facilitate the impending canal survey. In 1928-1929 there was much interest in government circles in the possibility of building an interoceanic canal in Nicaragua, under the option granted in the Bryan-Chamorro treaty, and on March 2, 1929, the United States Congress authorized a survey of the route. This was carried on by U.S. Army engineers during the next two years. The number of marines in Nicaragua, however, was reduced from more than 5,000 at the end of 1928 to about 1,300, exclusive of men in the national guard, in the latter part of 1929.

The situation in the northern provinces seemed to be better than at any time since 1926. After the outlaws failed to interfere seriously with the presidential election, Sandino went to Mexico, where he was granted asylum. Scattered bands under other leaders continued to commit robberies and murders, and in January 1929, with the approval of the marine command, Moncada created a force of volunteers, under officers who had served with him in the civil war, to work with the marines and the guard in an effort to destroy them. He also obtained from Congress a declaration of martial law in the northern provinces. The State Department, which had earlier opposed the establishment of martial law because it did not want to have Nicaraguans tried by courts set up by the guard, acquiesced on the understanding that Nicaraguan officials would assume all responsibility for enforcing the decree. The volunteers operated under the general control of the guard for some months, but there were unpleasant reports that they were executing prisoners and committing other atrocities, and in July the State Department insisted that they be disbanded.

President Moncada, like many other Nicaraguan leaders, had long thought that Nicaragua should seek help from the United States in her political and economic problems. He had been a prominent member of the government that first asked for American aid in 1910, and he had welcomed American intervention to stop the civil war in 1927. His confidence in Colonel Stimson made him the more disposed to accept American help, but he had traits of character which sometimes made it difficult for American officials to cooperate with him. He was probably one of the ablest and most honest of the Nicaraguan political leaders, but he was contentious and suspicious and jealous of his prerogatives and sometimes vindictive in dealing with opponents. These traits caused friction. It was impossible, for example, to permit the guard to be used to oppress the government's opponents. After the United States undertook to supervise the congressional election of 1930 and the presidential election of 1932, it had a special responsibility for ensuring fair play, and it had to insist that the guard and the electoral supervisers be given a measure of independence which Moncada found it hard to accept. He did not have to accede to the State Department's wishes, but he usually did so because he did not want the United States to withdraw the American officers from the guard or abandon the electoral supervision. He was often angry, however, when foreigners' ideas about propriety interfered with his own freedom of action, and he not infrequently complained to Secretary Stimson about the attitude of American officials in Nicaragua.

In the first months of Moncada's administration, before Stimson became secretary of state, there was a bad situation because the president thought that the American minister and the chief of the guard were personally unfriendly to him. Both of these officials had naturally worked closely with Díaz. Moncada's distrust of Eberhardt and Colonel Beadle was apparently encouraged by General Feland, the brigade commander, who had been regarded as pro-liberal during the presidential campaign and

257

who now aspired to be the principal representative of the United States in Nicaragua.[1]

The *guardia* agreement signed in December 1927 was still awaiting approval by the Nicaraguan Congress, and in January 1929 Eberhardt reported that several objectionable amendments were being proposed. He was instructed to tell Moncada that ratification of the agreement without changes of any sort was of "vital importance." His representations, however, had little effect, and Eberhardt thought that General Feland and Admiral Sellers were encouraging Moncada to disregard them. The State Department finally decided to accept some amendments to obtain ratification, but it still insisted that the guard be the sole military and police force in Nicaragua and that it be under the direct command of the president of the republic. It warned Moncada that it might have to consider withdrawing the American officers and all other marines from Nicaragua if the agreement were amended in a way which affected the guard's autonomy or its non-partisan character. Moncada, Kellogg said, would be responsible for the disorder which would ensue. Moncada replied that he considered one article, exempting *guardia* personnel from the jurisdiction of the Nicaraguan courts, unconstitutional, and that if the State Department insisted on this he would rather have the guard continue to operate under an executive decree without a formal agreement.

A few days later, with his approval, the Congress ratified the agreement with several amendments. Some of these were objectionable, but we felt in the State Department that most of the objections could be met by an interpretative exchange of notes. The chief question at issue was a provision of the original agreement which would have exempted members of the guard from the jurisdiction of the civil courts, and Mr. Stimson, who was now secretary of state, was doubtful about the wisdom of insisting on this. The proposed exchange of notes was discussed for some time, but never carried out, and in the end the guard continued to operate under executive decree until the American officers were withdrawn in 1932. In July 1929 the legation reported that articles for the government of the guard, approved by Moncada, provided that its members should be turned over to the civil courts if the officers, after investigation, found that the offenses

[1] General Feland discussed this aspiration with me before I left Nicaragua.

with which they were charged were not under the jurisdiction of the military courts.

In the meantime Eberhardt and Beadle and Feland had all been transferred to other posts. Matthew Hanna, a career officer with much Latin American experience, took charge of the legation. Under his direction the legation regained its prestige and influence. Moncada's attitude toward the guard became more friendly, for a time, after Colonel Douglas C. McDougal took command of it in March 1929, but problems connected with its administration continued to worry the State Department during the next few years.

Several of these were connected with the operation of the *guardia* courts. The State Department had acquiesced in the declaration of martial law in the North on the understanding that the decree would be enforced by Nicaraguan officials, without perhaps realizing that the chief of the guard would have to take ultimate responsibility for what was done. In November 1929, Hanna reported that seven young Nicaraguans chosen by President Moncada would become second lieutenants in the guard and would be trained in military law so that they could serve on courts-martial. He said, too, that Moncada, shocked by a recent atrocious murder, had issued a decree which would enable extraordinary courts-martial to deal with non-military crimes, even in departments that were not under martial law. The State Department replied that it could not approve of the trial of Nicaraguan civilians by military courts so long as the guard was commanded by American officers. If the ordinary courts were inefficient they could be strengthened. This was the responsibility of the Nicaraguan government, which must "do its part" if the United States were to continue to help it. The legation was authorized to suggest that Moncada discuss the matter with the Supreme Court. This gave no comfort to the American officers in the guard who had the urgent problem of dealing with bandits already in custody and who often hestitated to arrest known bandits because it was almost certain that the courts would release them.

An affair which occurred while these matters were under discussion showed that even the necessary and proper operation of the *guardia* courts could cause embarrassment. In October 1929, a marine corporal named Trogler, who was a first lieutenant in

259

the guard, was killed under suspicious circumstances at Telpaneca, and a few days later the garrison at the post, about forty-one men, deserted, taking with them two other American officers. The latter, and several men who had joined the mutiny unwillingly, soon escaped, while the rest of the party apparently crossed the border into Honduras. Meanwhile Trogler's second-in-command, a Nicaraguan sergeant named Larios, was arrested and charged with Trogler's murder. The State Department raised no objection to his being tried by a court composed of an American president and six Nicaraguan officers, but there were protests in the United States when it was reported, falsely, that Larios had been condemned to death. Willard Beaulac, the American chargé d'affaires at Managua, was instructed to suggest that Moncada commute the sentence as an act of grace, telling the president that the State Department understood that death sentences imposed by the ordinary courts were not customarily carried out in Nicaragua and that the execution of such a sentence by the guard would make it more difficult for the American government to keep marines in Nicaragua. If the president did not commute the sentence, Beaulac was to tell the chief of the guard that no marines should have anything to do with carrying it out or be present in any capacity at the execution. The trial in fact had not yet ended, and when it did Larios was sentenced to three years in prison and a dishonorable discharge.

Nothing came of the State Department's effort to persuade the Nicaraguan government to reform its ordinary courts. Moncada asked the Supreme Court to prepare a plan, but the president of the court thought that an effective reform would require a constitutional amendment and suggested that the matter be dealt with in connection with other constitutional changes which the liberal leaders were considering. Since the Department was opposing the most important of these changes, which would have extended the terms of the president and other high officials, it told the legation to drop the matter in the absence of further instructions.

The State Department was less directly involved in the disagreements that soon arose between Moncada and the New York bankers. When Moncada took office, he showed little disposition to change the financial arrangements which he had inherited from the conservative regime. Irving Lindberg continued to collect the customs duties and to perform the now not very important duties of the resident member of the high commission, without encountering any serious difficulty. Moncada left the management of the national bank and the Pacific railroad in the hands of the Guaranty Trust Company and J. and W. Seligmann and Company, though he was under no obligation to do so, because he appreciated the need for efficient, non-political management of both institutions. Not unnaturally, however, he thought that he should have a voice in the policies of the two companies and was irritated when what he wanted was inconsistent with the bankers' ideas of sound management. He thought that the railroad company should spend less on upkeep and improvements and pay the government larger dividends, and he even accused the railroad management, apparently unjustly, of altering the books to show a smaller net profit. His relations with the national bank became even more strained, in the summer of 1929, when he demanded that the bank make a loan which Rosenthal, the manager, considered unsound. His public criticism of both institutions angered the New York bankers, and they told the State Department in August that they felt that they should withdraw from any connection with Nicaragua's affairs.

Secretary Stimson, in a personal letter, urged Moncada to avoid any precipitate action and offered to arrange a conference to discuss the matter. Moncada promptly agreed, saying that he hoped that the bankers would continue to manage the national bank. The president, in fact, had recently approached the New York bankers with a proposal for a $3,000,000 loan for road and railroad building and had indicated that he would turn over to them the collection of the internal revenues, as well as the customs, to secure it.[2] Unfortunately Moncada named as his representatives at the proposed conference two men whom the bankers particularly disliked, and made matters worse by telling the press that the conference would discuss charges against the bank and railroad managements. In October 1929, without further discussion, the bankers abruptly resigned as bankers under the financial plan and withdrew their representatives from the bank and railroad boards.

The State Department was annoyed by the bankers' action and concerned about its possible consequences. The American government still had a responsibility to the holders of Nicaragua's guaranteed customs bonds, who had accepted the bonds in re-

[2] Hanna to Stimson, June 19, 1929, 817.51/2079.

liance on the continuance of the United States' connection with the customs collectorship and the high commission. The bankers' withdrawal would leave the customs collectorship in an uncertain position, with no one to nominate a new collector general if a vacancy arose. Furthermore, political management of the bank and the railroad could have disastrous consequences for Nicaragua. Secretary Stimson consequently told Hanna to say very informally to Moncada that the State Department would be willing to try to put the Nicaraguan legation in touch with other bankers if Moncada wished it to do so. He said that the department could not ask American bankers to enter into any arrangement with Nicaragua and could not conduct the negotiations, but it would be glad to help with suggestions and advice. Moncada replied that he would leave the matter entirely in Stimson's hands. He thought that the best solution would be to reach an understanding with Seligmann and the Guaranty Trust Company,[3] but the State Department felt that it was too late for this.

As a result of the department's informal efforts, Otis and Company and the Equitable Trust Company and the Whitney National Bank of New Orleans sent a proposal to Nicaragua through the American legation in December 1929. They offered to act as Nicaragua's fiscal agents, with no compensation except for any specific services that they might perform, and to familiarize themselves with the republic's financial problems, in order to be able to give advice. They would nominate a manager for the national bank. Moncada apparently found this generally acceptable but he asked the State Department to suggest a few changes in the plan. When the department said that it could not carry on negotiations for him, he referred the matter to his own representatives, who apparently misinterpreted his instructions and abruptly broke off the negotiations. Moncada was surprised when he learned of this through the American legation, and wished to continue the negotiations, but the bankers declined to do so.

Moncada again appealed personally to Stimson for help and promised to accept any arrangement which the secretary might suggest. After the treatment accorded the Equitable group, which had spent a considerable amount of time and money in preparing a plan, the State Department did not feel that it could

[3] Stimson to Hanna, Oct. 12, and Hanna to Stimson, Oct. 16, 1929, 817.516/194A, 197.

ask other bankers to consider the matter, but it told the Nicaraguan chargé d'affaires, when he asked its advice, that the Bank of the Manhattan Company, with which he had had preliminary discussions, was a strong and reputable institution. In April 1930, the International Manhattan Company told the State Department that its affiliate the International Acceptance Bank had been appointed American depositary and fiscal agent of the National Bank of Nicaragua and the Pacific railway and would be represented on the boards of directors of both companies.

Hanna reported that the new arrangement was well received by the press and the public in Nicaragua. The bank and the railroad became Nicaraguan corporations but their boards of directors, each of them with five Nicaraguan and four American members, continued to sit in New York. The government solemnly promised that both boards would be completely free to manage the companies in the best interests of Nicaragua. Hans Sitars, who had fourteen years of experience as manager of the Banco Alemán Antioqueño in Colombia, became manager of the national bank. The arrangement seems to have worked well. The bankers did not take over any responsibilities under the financial plan, but fortunately no question about the appointment of a collector general of customs arose until after the United States, under the Good Neighbor Policy, ceased to take an interest in such matters. The high commission continued, but one of its functions disappeared after April 1930, when Moncada submitted to Congress a budget which appropriated all expected income without reference to the financial plan's restrictions. Since this did not affect any interests secured by the plan, the State Department raised no objection.[4]

The political situation, during the first years of Moncada's administration, was remarkably tranquil. The conservatives showed little disposition to make trouble. Moncada suspected that some of them were plotting to murder him or to start a revolt and from time to time he arrested a few of the most probable troublemakers, but usually he ordered their release after a few days. In November 1929, Hanna was instructed to tell him that the United States was concerned about the arrest of political opponents or critics of American policy in Nicaragua, because of its obligation to maintain the non-partisan character of the guard.

[4] White to Hanna, May 20, 1930, 817.51/2147.

The State Department also felt that it had to oppose a proposal for constitutional reform which was submitted to the Nicaraguan Congress in March 1930. The sponsors of the plan hoped to make it acceptable to the United States by including provisions which would have removed doubts about the constitutionality of the guard and would have authorized the establishment of commissions to try bandits, but the main purpose was to extend the terms of the president and the members of Congress and the Supreme Court. Moncada asserted that the plan had been presented without his approval. Beaulac, who was in charge at the time, was instructed to say informally that the extension of the terms of officials in office was contrary to the spirit of republican institutions, and that the American government's relationship to the guard and its supervision of the 1928 election would make the project especially unwelcome to the United States. The Congress adjourned a few weeks later without acting on the project.

Moncada meanwhile asked the American government to supervise the congressional election to be held in November 1930, and President Hoover nominated Captain Alfred Wilkinson Johnson of the navy to be chairman of the national board of elections. Fifty-one officers, mostly from the navy and marine corps, and 208 naval and marine enlisted men were sent to Nicaragua to assist in the supervision, and 300 additional marines were sent temporarily to protect the electoral personnel and help maintain order during the electoral period. It was necessary as it had been in 1928 to amend the Dodds law, which was still Nicaragua's basic electoral law. Moncada insisted on doing this by presidential decree, to avoid any discussion of the constitutionality of the amendments, and the State Department reluctantly agreed to this procedure.

The most difficult matter that confronted the electoral mission was the situation in Chontales, a strongly conservative department where Emiliano Chamorro had much of his personal following. Though there was little or no bandit activity there, the government had placed Chontales under martial law in 1929 and had replaced the elected municipal authorities in eight towns with commissions dominated by liberals. The State Department expressed disapproval of this action at the time, and when Johnson arrived he supported Chamorro and his friends in their demand that the elected officials be restored to office. Hanna, however, was unwilling to become involved in what he thought was essentially a personal feud between Chamorro and Moncada, especially as he did not believe that the situation in Chontales would materially affect the outcome of the congressional election. Johnson was bitter about the legation's failure to back him up, but the incident did not impair the success of the electoral supervision. The election took place peacefully on November 2. The liberals, as had been expected, substantially increased their representation in Congress, but the conservatives won in Chontales.

During the last months of 1930 the efficiency of the guard was gravely affected by the Nicaraguan government's inability to provide money for its support. There had never been enough money for it in the government's narrowly restricted regular budget, but while Díaz was president he had given it the greater part of the surplus revenues which were turned over to the government by the national bank at the end of each six months under the financial plan. The annual allotment of $689,000 provided for in the *guardia* agreement of 1927 had proved completely inadequate. Moncada very reluctantly included $1,025,000 for the guard in the budget which he submitted to Congress early in 1930, but he complained to Secretary Stimson about the sacrifice which this entailed. In October, when the government's revenues were falling off because of the depression, he told Colonel McDougal that he must reduce his annual expenditure to $720,000, even though it would mean a sharp reduction in the size of the force. McDougal protested, but both the State and Navy Departments realized that the budget had to be reduced and it was finally agreed that $800,000 per annum should be provided.

The reduction in the guard was untimely because the situation in the North was getting worse. Sandino returned to Nicaragua in the first months of 1930 and assembled several of the outlaw bands for a foray into a more settled part of Nicaragua. *Guardia* patrols, supported by marine aviators, dispersed his forces and Sandino himself was wounded, but the outlaws continued to be more active than they had been. Hanna reported early in January 1931 that a marine patrol of ten men which was repairing a telephone line between Ocotal and San Fernando had been ambushed by a large force and eight of them had been killed and the others wounded. This and other incidents aroused a popular demand for more energetic measures against the bandits and Moncada again urged the creation of a Nicaraguan auxiliary force to work with the guard to control them.

Moncada wanted at the same time to inaugurate a program of road and railroad building to improve communications with the North and better conditions there. Hanna had for some time been insisting that banditry could never be eliminated without doing something about the poverty and chronic unemployment that encouraged it, and had been urging that the United States provide money for a public works program in the Segovias. Stimson and Francis White were interested in the idea, and at their suggestion the Navy Department offered to help with engineers and equipment. They could find no way of getting money from the United States treasury, but the National Bank of Nicaragua, under its new management, agreed in January 1931 to lend the government $1,000,000, to be used at a maximum rate of $75,000 per month. Moncada also obtained the consent of the new fiscal agents to use the net profits of the railroad for road and railroad building, under the direction of an engineer chosen by the railroad's board of directors.

Hanna and McDougal did not oppose the creation of the proposed auxiliary force, but they objected to Moncada's evident intention to have it operate independently of the guard and under his immediate direction. Hanna also objected to the president's plans for the use of the loan, because Moncada wished to divert a considerable part of it to projects outside the bandit area. After some argument, however, Moncada said that he would leave the decision as to the character of the new force to Secretary Stimson. Stimson had already asked Hanna and McDougal to come to Washington for a conference. He had told Hanna to impress on McDougal the imperative necessity to complete the training of the guard so that Nicaraguan officers could take it over "lock, stock, and barrel" on January 1, 1933, if the United States government should decide to turn it over at that time. The guard had by this time taken over most of the patrolling in the North, as well as the policing of the interior, but it had made little progress in training Nicaraguans to replace American officers. Little money had been available for the officers' training school, and only a few Nicaraguans had been graduated from it.

After conferences with Stimson and General McCoy, Hanna returned to Managua early in February 1931, taking with him a

"Statement of Policy in Nicaragua." The American government considered that the new military force should be part of the non-political guard. About $15,000 per month from the new loan would be used to finance it, and another $2,000 per month would be used to enlarge the officers' training school. With the rest of the proceeds the government would continue work on a highway to the east coast and on two railroad lines, one of which would improve communication with the bandit country. All marines must be withdrawn from Nicaragua, at the latest, after the election of Moncada's successor. With the projected increase in the guard, it was expected that all marines could be withdrawn from combat duty by June 1, 1931 and that the brigade would be reduced to a training battalion in Managua plus the aviation force. The statement said that "the feeling here, as represented in Congress and by the public in general, is getting stronger all the time that these steps are necessary and that the United States Government must not be drawn into the position of policing Nicaragua indefinitely."

Moncada, when he was shown the statement, initialled it without raising any serious objection.[5] The plan to reduce the marine brigade to a training battalion of approximately 500 men and to withdraw all marines from Nicaragua immediately after the 1932 election was announced to the press on February 13. It apparently made a good impression in the United States, but Hanna reported that it was received with mixed feelings and some trepidation in Nicaragua.

A few weeks later, on March 31, the city of Managua was destroyed by an earthquake which killed hundreds of people and left thousands homeless. There would have been more suffering had it not been for the relief work carried out by the marines under Hanna's direction, with help from the American Red Cross. While the marine brigade and the guard were concentrating their attention on relief the outlaws in the North took advantage of the situation to stage a foray to the east coast, looting farms and mines and murdering nine American civilians and a number of British subjects. Captain Pefley U.S.M.C., the guard commander on the coast, was killed in an ambush. The guard had only small detachments in the area, but its patrols repulsed the bandits soon after the latter's presence was discovered. The

---

[5] Hanna to Stimson, Feb. 12, 1931, 817.00/6995.

United States sent warships to Puerto Cabezas and Bluefields and landed marines at both places to protect foreigners.

The bandits withdrew westward within a few days, but the wanton murders which they had committed aroused loud demands for better protection of Americans at the mines and fruit farms along the coast. In reply to these, Mr. Stimson on April 16 instructed Hanna and the consul at Bluefields to tell American citizens that the United States could not undertake to protect American citizens throughout Nicaragua, and that those who did not feel safe under the protection of the national guard should leave Nicaragua or at least move to the coast towns where they could be protected or evacuated. They could not expect American forces to be sent inland to protect them. This announcement was represented by the press as a change in policy, but in fact it was not. In times of trouble in Central America the American government had frequently landed marines in seacoast towns to protect foreigners and had occasionally sent them to places inland but it had never undertaken to protect foreigners throughout a Central American country. It had had marine detachments at several places in the interior of Nicaragua since 1927, but by April 1931, these were being withdrawn and the national guard was assuming the responsibility to maintain order. Even if this had not been the case, it would have been impracticable to attempt to protect foreigners at mines and farms scattered throughout the interior.

The State Department attempted to clear up the misunderstanding in a press statement issued April 18. It pointed out that the situation was totally different from that of 1926, when the United States landed marines and set up neutral zones to protect its citizens from the consequences of a war between organized armies. In 1931 outlaws in a "thick jungle country," where it was almost impossible for regular troops to operate effectively, were murdering and pillaging the civilian inhabitants. A Nicaraguan constabulary, specially trained for this purpose, was now available to deal with them. American naval vessels were standing by at all the threatened east coast ports with orders to protect life and property there, and they would remain until the danger was over, but the United States would not send troops into the interior.

Neither the earthquake nor the bandit attack on the east coast seriously delayed the execution of the plan to reduce the American forces. The earthquake, fortunately, had devastated only the area around Managua. The bandits withdrew into the Segovias, where they continued to avoid capture but accomplished little more than that. By June 4, 1931, the marine brigade had been reduced to an instruction battalion of 540 officers and men at Managua, plus the aviation force of 255 which continued to cooperate with the guard. The guard was still almost wholly officered by Americans.

By this time both governments were considering some of the problems that would be involved in American supervision of the presidential election to be held in 1932. After the controversy in Chontales in 1930 the American government felt that it ought at least to make an effort to assure fair play in the municipal elections which would be held throughout Nicaragua in November 1931. It would be more difficult to hold a fair presidential election if all of the municipal councils were controlled by one party. Moncada pointed out that there was no legal authority for an American to act as president of the national board of elections except during presidential and congressional elections, but he agreed that Major Charles F. B. Price of the marine corps, who had been a member of the electoral missions of 1928 and 1930, should come to Nicaragua to observe what took place. Price was in Nicaragua from July until November 1931, but he did not have enough authority to accomplish very much. There was a controversy, especially, over the situation in the departments which were under martial law, where the towns were being governed by boards appointed by the president. Price was unable to persuade Moncada to restore the former elected municipal authorities in these towns, and when his efforts failed the conservatives ordered their followers to abstain from voting throughout the country. Conservative candidates were nevertheless elected in several towns but Price reported that there had been many irregularities and much fraud in the electoral procedure.[6]

In the meantime the State Department had been urging Moncada to have the Congress act on the necessary amendments to the electoral law, so as to avoid the necessity for again carrying on the supervision under a presidential decree of doubtful constitutionality. Moncada insisted, as he had in 1930, that the proposed amendments themselves would be unconstitutional and in September 1931 he revived his proposal for a constitutional reform which would remove doubts about the electoral supervision

[6] For his report see 817.00 Johnson Electoral Mission/268.

269

and the legality of the guard and would at the same time extend the presidential term to six years. He wanted to postpone the presidential election until 1934, and to have a constituent assembly elected in 1932 to act on the amendments. Moncada said that he would himself withdraw from office on December 31, 1932, and that a provisional president chosen by Congress would take over.

The State Department did not take very seriously Moncada's arguments about the unconstitutionality of what it had done in Nicaragua, and it was skeptical about his motives. His plan would enable him and his friends to remain in power for two additional years and probably longer, for the constituent assembly would have power to do whatever the dominant party wanted. Stimson consequently told Moncada, in a personal letter, that he did not like the proposed extension of the presidential term and that it would be difficult to supervise a presidential election in 1934 because public opinion in the United States would not tolerate the maintenance of marines in Nicaragua until that time.[7] Moncada was unwilling to give up his plan but any idea that the State Department might be persuaded to acquiesce in it was dispelled when it announced early in January 1932, that President Hoover had appointed Rear Admiral Clark Howell Woodward as his personal representative to supervise the Nicaraguan presidential and congressional election in November 1932.

Moncada continued to urge his plan for a constituent assembly, but he now took a new position and began to argue that reforms were needed to prevent party strife after the marines were withdrawn. With some difficulty, he persuaded both his own party and the conservatives to send representatives to Washington to discuss measures which would provide for minority representation in the government and promote harmony in other ways. The conservatives, though they were skeptical and unenthusiastic, agreed to go because their party's low morale and bad financial situation made it impossible for them to hope for success in the coming election. The representatives called at the State Department on February 26 and proposed that a constituent assembly, to be chosen at an election supervised by the United States, should reform the constitution and elect Moncada's successor.

[7] Stimson to Moncada, Dec. 9, 1931, 817.00/7271. Attached to this letter is a memorandum from the solicitor's office discussing the constitutionality of the guard and the electoral supervision.

They presented a great number of telegrams from municipal authorities in Nicaragua urging the need for reform.

The State Department was still suspicious of Moncada's motives, and it had reports from the legation at Managua indicating that most Nicaraguans opposed the reform project. Its legality seemed doubtful because the Nicaraguan constitution provided that a constituent assembly should meet if Congress voted for it and the next Congress, after an interval of at least two years, confirmed that decision. The American government did not think that amendments were necessary to make the guard constitutional or to permit the construction of an interoceanic canal, which was one of the problems that the representatives raised. It expressed these views in a memorandum which was handed to the representatives on March 23. It said that the amendment of the constitution was a matter for the Nicaraguans to decide, but that the United States would not continue with plans to supervise the November election if a constituent assembly were to be chosen. The press was told that the secretary of state considered the convocation of a constituent assembly at that time unwise and that the United States was consequently not prepared to supervise any election except one for the presidency. Moncada persisted in his effort to persuade the other party leaders to agree to a constituent assembly, but he was unable to obtain enough support in Congress to go farther with the idea.

The State Department ran into unexpected difficulties when it began to make plans for the supervision of the election. When Admiral Woodward made a preliminary visit to Nicaragua in January 1932, he and the American officials at Managua pointed out that the guard did not have enough men to protect American personnel at hundreds of polling places, especially in the regions where the outlaws were still active. They urged that 1,950 additional marines be sent to Nicaragua during the electoral period. This would cost $750,000, which the Navy Department did not have and which the administration could hardly hope to obtain from the Congress. It would also embarrass the State Department, which had only recently announced that most of the marine brigade had been withdrawn. Consequently after much discussion in Washington, it was decided that the conduct of the election in and near the bandit areas should be left in the hands of Nicaraguans. Admiral Woodward protested that it would be impossible to guarantee a fair election if about 40% of the voters

271

voted at places where no American was present, but he was overruled.

Another problem arose in connection with finances. The American government would pay the salaries of the American personnel, but it expected the Nicaraguan government to provide for
the electoral mission's expenses in Nicaragua, which would
amount to between $100,000 and $200,000. The Nicaraguan government's revenues, however, had decreased from an average of
$546,000 monthly in 1929 to about $155,000 in 1932, and $90,000
of this had to be set aside for the *guardia*. Many government
salaries and bills were going unpaid. The Nicaraguan minister
nevertheless got an unsympathetic reply when Moncada instructed him to ask the State Department to help find funds for
the election,[8] and after the department threatened to abandon the
electoral supervision and withdraw the marines from Nicaragua
immediately, Moncada promised to provide $25,000 each month
for four months. He could not keep up these payments, but in
August the State Department helped him to obtain a loan from
the national bank which provided funds for the election and gave
him $75,000 a month for current expenses. To prevent the mis-
use of the money for political purposes, Moncada was persuaded
to agree, reluctantly, that expenditures from the loan should be
approved by the minister of finance and the resident American
member of the high commission and a third person named by
Moncada in agreement with General Chamorro.[9] The State Department also urged the appointment of an American engineer
to supervise the road and railroad building carried on with
the loan funds, but Moncada refused even to consider this
proposal.[10]

Admiral Woodward had hoped to have the help of a considerable number of officers and enlisted men who had had experience
in earlier Nicaraguan elections, but his plans were disrupted
when the United States Senate approved an amendment to the
naval appropriation bill forbidding the use of funds for sending
marines to Nicaragua for electoral work. This irresponsible gesture could not stop the supervision but made it more difficult for
the American government to carry out effectively the obligation

8 White's memorandum of May 19, 1932, 817.00 Woodward Electoral
Mission/113.
9 Hanna to Stimson, Aug. 12, 1932, 817.51/2348.
10 Hanna to White, personal, Sept. 1, 1932, 817.51/2372.

which it had assumed. It compelled Admiral Woodward to rely on inexperienced men already in Nicaragua and it reduced the number of marines available to protect the electoral personnel.

Moncada could not constitutionally be reelected, and his efforts to control the choice of his successor ran into opposition from the León liberals, who were the strongest single group in the party. Early in 1932 the *Leoneses* got control of the "Grand Convention," which was the party's supreme authority. Moncada and his friends set up a rival convention, which seemed likely to have the advantage in any struggle for control of the party machinery, because the government had the support of local officials throughout the country and could deny its opponents the use of the telegraph and other facilities. Beaulac, who was again temporarily in charge of the legation, suggested that the imposition of a candidate by the administration was hardly compatible with a free election, and recommended that he be authorized to speak to Moncada about it, but the State Department preferred to maintain a policy of non-interference for the time being.[11] When Admiral Woodward went to Nicaragua in June, each faction was claiming the right to nominate the candidates of the liberal party. After considering the claims of both, the Admiral ordered a party plebiscite, to be held before August 7, but before that date arrived he was able to persuade the two factions to settle the dispute. On July 27 the four leading liberal candidates signed a "pact of honor," promising their support to Dr. Juan Bautista Sacasa, who had been the candidate of the León group, and agreeing to divide among themselves the nominations for senators and deputies.[12] On August 22 a convention nominated Sacasa for president and Rodolfo Espinosa, for vice president.

The conservatives nominated Adolfo Díaz for president and Emiliano Chamorro for vice president, but they seemed to have little enthusiasm for the contest. Through most of the campaign Díaz stayed in the United States, ostensibly trying to raise money. In Nicaragua the richer members of the party seemed reluctant to contribute to campaign expenses. During much of the campaign, in fact, Chamorro and his associates were negotiating with Moncada in an unsuccessful effort to reach an agreement for

[11] Beaulac to Stimson, Jan. 30, and Stimson to Beaulac, Feb. 3, 1932, 817.00/7316.

[12] Lt. Stephenson of the electoral mission sent a copy of the agreement to Laurence Duggan on Sept. 17, 1932, 817.00/7567.

a coalition government which would exclude the León liberals. Moncada evidently still hoped to find some way to avoid turning over the presidency to Sacasa. There were few complaints, meanwhile, about electoral abuses, and just before election day Díaz and Chamorro issued a manifesto to conservative voters saying that the election was being conducted with freedom and fairness.

The voting, on November 6, went off quietly, even in the districts where bandit interference had been feared, and Dr. Sacasa received a substantial majority. The number of votes cast compared favorably with the number in 1928. The conservatives elected senators and deputies in the traditionally conservative departments but the liberals had a majority in the new Congress. The conservative member of the national board of elections presented a number of complaints, chiefly it seemed for the record, but no one took them very seriously and General Chamorro made the motion for the acceptance of Admiral Woodward's report when it was submitted to Congress in joint session. Despite this happy outcome, however, Admiral Woodward recommended in his report to the secretary of state that the United States make every effort to avoid again becoming involved in anything like electoral supervision in Nicaragua. Assistant Secretary White recorded his concurrence.[13]

A series of agreements which the leaders of the two parties signed shortly before the election probably made the conservatives more disposed to accept their defeat gracefully. Early in 1932, when they began to realize that the United States actually intended to withdraw the marines at the end of the year, many Nicaraguans began to worry about what would happen. They feared a revival of party strife, and some of them had doubts about the ability of the guard to cope with the northern outlaws after the American officers were withdrawn. Sandino was still at large, and some of the leaders in both parties were worried by increasing evidence that his prestige was increasing among young people in the interior, where he formerly had few sympathizers.[14] Though Moncada's earlier proposals had received little support, because his motives were suspect, many conservatives and liberals thought that a provision for minority participation in the government would offer the best hope for avoiding

---

[13] Note on Duggan's memorandum of Jan. 27, 1933, 817.00 Woodward Electoral Mission/238.

[14] Ex-President Díaz told me this in 1933.

civil war after the marines left. Dr. Carlos Cuadra Pasos, who was one of the principal advocates of the idea, cited the example of Colombia, which had enjoyed a quarter century of peace after a disastrous civil war because the dominant party had regularly given the minority a limited participation in the government. Hanna thought that the legation should encourage the advocates of an interparty agreement, but was told that the State Department, though sympathetic, did not wish to have any connection with the matter.[15]

The party leaders showed little inclination to push the idea of an interparty agreement during the summer of 1932, but a few weeks before the election the idea was revived, partly at least because of Hanna's informal efforts. The State Department did not disapprove of what Hanna did, but it still insisted that it could not assume any responsibility in connection with the proposed agreement. It wanted to make the Nicaraguans realize that they must henceforth solve their own problems, and especially to avoid any situation where either party could claim in the future that the United States had a responsibility for enforcing the agreement.[16] In Nicaragua neither party wanted to take the initiative, but a "patriotic group" of citizens not active in politics brought the party leaders together early in October and a series of agreements were signed.

In the first of these, signed October 14, the two parties declared that the war in the North must be stopped, preferably by agreement with Sandino but by vigorous military action if conciliation failed. The second, signed October 18, called for constitutional reforms which would give the minority party representation in all popularly elected bodies, including the Congress and the municipal councils, and would set up bi-partisan commissions to advise the executive on questions of major policy. It also contemplated steps to assure free elections. Two others, signed October 21 and November 2, provided for minority representation in the administration and in the courts pending the adoption of the proposed constitutional amendments. The governing boards of both parties ratified the agreements immediately after the presidential election.

[15] White to Hanna, personal, May 25, and June 3, 1932, Francis White papers, Box 11.
[16] White to Hanna, personal, Sept. 23, 1932, Francis White papers, Box 11.

The reorganization of the guard had to be carried out hastily after the election. The American officers had done little to train Nicaraguans for the responsibilities of command, partly because there had never been enough money to operate an adequate training school. A number of junior officers had been hastily trained since the reorganization of the military school in 1931, but until very recently there had been only one Nicaraguan officer of a rank higher than second lieutenant. It would clearly be necessary to appoint outsiders who had military experience to take over the higher commands when the Americans left. Hanna and General Matthews, who succeeded McDougal as *guardia* commander, pointed out as early as June 1932, that this would have to be done, and urged that the American officers remain in the guard for about two months after January 1 to help train the men whom the new president might choose. The State Department, however, insisted that all marines must leave Nicaragua immediately after January 1. After the election, Moncada and Sacasa and several other prominent Nicaraguans urged Hanna to recommend that the withdrawal be postponed but the department did not change its position.

The presidential candidates had already agreed that each of them would submit a list of potential officers, and that Moncada would appoint those designated by the winner immediately after the election. This would at least make it possible for the new officers to work for a few days or weeks with the Americans whom they would replace. Each candidate would include in his list an equal number of persons from each party. The idea of non-partisanship, in any Nicaraguan institution, was unrealistic, because almost all Nicaraguans were liberals or conservatives by birth, but the Tipitapa agreement had stipulated that the guard be apolitical, and Sacasa and Díaz, in an agreement signed in Hanna's presence the day before the election, agreed to maintain its apolitical character. What this pact achieved, however, was bi-partisanship rather than non-partisanship, for it stipulated that each party should have an equal number of officers of each rank and that vacancies should be filled by the promotion of a man of the same party. Sacasa, who had been reluctant to sign it, did so on the understanding that the higher staff officers would be selected without regard to party.

Anastasio Somoza, whom Sacasa had chosen as the new chief of the guard, began to work at headquarters with General

Matthews soon after the election. Somoza was a nephew of Sacasa and a close associate of Moncada, under whom he had served for a time as undersecretary for foreign affairs. He had had military experience in the civil war of 1926-1927. Hanna considered him the best man in the country for the position.[17] By the middle of December, American officers were being withdrawn from outlying posts. On January 2, the day after the new president's inauguration, General Matthews turned over his command to Somoza, and all of the American marines left Nicaragua.

Except for one short interval, American marines had been in Nicaragua for more than twenty years, and during that time the United States had exercised a dominant influence in the country's affairs. By 1933 this sort of interference was inconsistent with the policy which the State Department was trying to follow in other Caribbean republics, and it was rather abruptly discontinued when the department felt that the American government's commitments under the 1927 peace agreement had been discharged. When Hanna suggested that Secretary Stimson might encourage Sacasa to go forward with the program embodied in the inter-party agreements of 1932, Francis White replied that he thought that the United States must avoid any appearance of underwriting the agreements and that there must be a clean-cut division between the period before January 1, 1933 and the period after that date, when the United States would have no further responsibility in Nicaragua.[18] The customs collectorship and the high commission continued to function, but they interfered little with the Nicaraguan government's freedom of action.

The withdrawal of the marines did not seem to cause any great rejoicing in Nicaragua. The new government's situation was somewhat precarious. There was much discontent in the guard, where the young graduates of the military academy resented being placed under the command of officers appointed from civilian life. An incipient mutiny was averted by Somoza's tactful handling of the situation, but the affair did not increase public confidence. Meanwhile several people who had been exiled by Moncada for radical or pro-Sandino activities were returning to Nicaragua and contributing to the feeling of unrest. Sacasa was worried, and on January 17 he asked the American government to lend or sell him 2,000 rifles. Hanna supported his request, but the

---

[17] Hanna to White, personal, Oct. 28, 1932, 817.1051.701½.
[18] White to Hanna, personal, Dec. 16, 1932, 817.1051/736.

War Department, which had not been paid for arms bought by Nicaragua in 1921 and 1927, refused to extend further credit and Sacasa had to obtain the rifles from a commercial firm in New York. On January 19 the Congress declared a state of siege in the greater part of the republic.

Sacasa pledged himself in his inaugural address to carry out the interparty agreements. The Congress had already elected new courts of appeal, with a majority of conservative judges in Granada and liberal majorities in Matagalpa, León, and Bluefields, and early in 1933 it passed a bill creating a committee to draft the constitutional amendments which the agreements contemplated. Immediately after the president's inauguration, representatives of both political parties began peace negotiations with Sandino, who was reported to be ready to lay down his arms now that the marines had left Nicaragua. A mission which included his own mother and father was sent to confer with the outlaw leader, and on January 24 Hanna reported that an armistice had been arranged. A week later Sandino flew to Managua on a Mexican plane and on February 3 he signed a peace agreement with the representatives of the liberal and conservative parties. The outlaws were permitted to settle on government lands along the Coco River, and to keep 100 men under arms there to maintain order. Their other arms were to be surrendered. The government would inaugurate public works to give the settlers employment during the first twelve months. After Sandino had executed two of his subordinates who opposed the agreement, the outlaws turned in 354 rifles and 21 machine guns. If these guns were indeed all that they had, they were less well armed than had been supposed.[19]

The peace agreement and the effort to implement the other provisions of the interparty agreements afforded some ground to hope that Nicaragua was entering on a period of orderly constitutional government. This hope was short-lived. Many officers in the *guardia* were disappointed by the peace agreement because they wanted to wind up the long conflict with the outlaws by a military victory, and on February 21, 1934, a *guardia* patrol murdered Sandino in cold blood on the streets of Managua. Sacasa ordered the punishment of the murderers, but Somoza defended them and it soon became clear that he rather than the president

[19] Hanna to Hull, March 8, 1933, 817.00/7782.

was the dominant power in the government. Sacasa remained in office for the next two years, but in 1936, because his relationship to Somoza was a constitutional obstacle to the latter's election as his successor, he was forced out and Somoza took full control. This was the beginning of a family dictatorship which was still in power in 1974.

THE NON-RECOGNITION POLICY IN CENTRAL AMERICA, 1929-1933

The trend toward a policy of non-interference in the internal political affairs of Caribbean states became more pronounced after 1929. There were more frequent expressions of the idea that local leaders should be discouraged from taking their problems to Washington for solution, and fewer occasions when formal public warnings or exhortations emanated from the State Department. Warships were occasionally sent to ports where American lives seemed to be in imminent danger, but on several occasions when American legations suggested that the presence of a ship would have a wholesome influence on the political situation the State Department replied that such a visit would be an unwarranted interference in local political affairs. Nevertheless the American government maintained its policy of withholding recognition from revolutionary governments in Central America after it gave up the use of non-recognition to achieve political ends in other parts of the world. Secretary Stimson had doubts about the wisdom of the policy,[20] but Francis White thought that the American government should not abandon a principle to which it had so definitely committed itself, especially after the State Department had gone through so much trouble and embarrassment to make it credible in Central America.

The advocates of non-recognition argued that it was not inconsistent with a general policy of non-interference. In refusing recognition to governments that did not meet the standards set by the Central American treaty of 1923, the United States did not undertake to say who should be president, but simply applied principles which the Central American states themselves had laid down. In each case it consulted the Central American states and

[20] See the note in Stimson's *Diary*, Dec. 18, 1930, Henry L. Stimson Papers, Yale University Library.

279

tried to act in concert with them. In practice, of course, it was the United States which decided whether the treaty applied in a given case, and its decision could determine the fate of a new administration. In reaching a decision the State Department had to pass judgment on such questions as the fairness of elections, the legality of the procedure followed, and the extent to which a particular individual was involved in revolutionary activity. Inquiry into matters of this sort was hard to reconcile with the idea that the Central Americans should not bring their political problems to Washington for solution.

On the other hand the non-recognition policy had unquestionably done some good. There were no successful revolutions in Central America, except in Nicaragua, between 1924 and 1930. This could not be attributed wholly to the 1923 treaty, but in several cases the knowledge that the leaders of an uprising would not be permitted to profit from it had discouraged potential revolutionists. In Honduras especially, the recollection of what happened after the revolution of 1923 seemed to be a major factor in bringing about a peaceful and democratic change of government in 1929, and in permitting the new government to remain in office during its constitutional term.

In September 1930, the Hoover administration decided to recognize governments that had come into power by revolution in Argentina, Peru, and Bolivia, without waiting, as its immediate predecessors usually did, until the constitutional order had been ostensibly restored by an election. This marked a return to the United States' traditional policy of recognizing a new government if it seemed to have substantial and generally accepted control and seemed able to discharge its international obligations. Francis White feared that it might be interpreted as evidence that the United States was abandoning its opposition to changes of government by force in the Caribbean and urged Secretary Stimson to make clear the difference between the United States' relations with South America and relations with the Caribbean states. The announcement of the recognition of the new South American governments consequently stated specifically that the United States would continue to follow the policy laid down by Secretary Hughes in recognition cases in Central America and that special considerations would also affect its policy in some of the other Caribbean states.

A few months later, the non-recognition policy was tested in Guatemala. General José Manuel Orellana, who became president of Guatemala after the breakup of the Central American Union in 1921, gave the country a stable and fairly efficient government. General Lázaro Chacón, who became president when Orellana died in 1926, met with more opposition. He suppressed a military revolt in January 1929, and executed many of its leaders, but there was still much unrest. When Chacón had a cerebral hemorrhage in December 1930, it seemed likely that the government would break down in a general scramble for power. The cabinet chose Baudilio Palma, the second *designado*, to act as chief executive until Chacón recovered, but on December 16 a part of the army led by General Manuel Orellana seized control, and the Congress, apparently intimidated by the soldiers, accepted Palma's resignation and made Orellana provisional president.

The new government was clearly an unconstitutional, revolutionary regime, which could not qualify for recognition under the Central American treaty. Francis White urged that the United States withhold recognition, Stimson somewhat hesitantly agreed, after White pointed out the good results of the non-recognition policy in Nicaragua and Honduras.[21] No public statement was made, but the American legation in Guatemala was told to explain the American government's policy informally to the new authorities and to leading citizens. The American legations in other Central American countries were given similar instructions. Sheldon Whitehouse, the minister to Guatemala, who was about to return to his post, was told to endeavor to bring about some arrangement for the restoration of constitutional government.

Whitehouse proposed that Chacón resign and that Orellana then return to the Congress the powers that had been conferred on him for the period of Chacón's illness. The Congress would then choose a *designado* to hold office until a new president could be elected. With the State Department's backing, the minister insisted that there be an amnesty, that no one involved in the recent revolt should be a member of the provisional government, and that an election be held as soon as possible, without governmental interference. Orellana was inclined to argue, and Whitehouse protested when the government arrested several

[21] Stimson *Diary*, Dec. 18, and Dec. 20, 1930.

people, evidently in an effort to intimidate the Congress. He was so apprehensive about the general situation that he urged that a warship be sent to the Pacific port of San José. The State Department, however, did not wish to make a show of force to influence the political situation in the absence of immediate danger to American lives and property.

Orellana nevertheless withdrew when Chacón resigned, and the Congress, on December 31, elected José María Reina Andrade as provisional president. Orellana's cabinet remained in office and neither Whitehouse nor the State Department thought it advisable to insist that it be changed. For a time they treated the new administration with some reserve but after trying to assure itself that all constitutional forms had been observed, and that no coercion had been used to obtain the resignations of Chacón and the former *designados*, the State Department suggested to the other Central American states that they join the American government in recognizing Reina Andrade as soon as a call for presidential elections had been issued. Recognition was accorded on January 8, after the provisional government announced that the election would be held on February 6, 7, and 8. In February, General Jorge Ubico, who was the only candidate, was easily elected to the presidency. Some of his opponents complained that they had not had time to organize any opposition to him, but Whitehouse thought that he undoubtedly had the support of a large majority of the voters. Ubico was to rule Guatemala, efficiently but autocratically, until 1944.

The non-recognition policy had been successful, with a minimum of the unpleasantness which had accompanied its earlier applications in Honduras and Nicaragua. The leaders of the revolt had been prevented from profiting by it and constitutional procedures had been maintained. There had, however, been a period of suspense when it appeared that Orellana might not yield and that the State Department might be confronted with an embarrassing situation. Undersecretary Joseph Cotton, who was one of the wisest men who have held the second post in the State Department, was convinced that the American government ought not to risk another test of the policy. He thought it was open to the gravest theoretical and practical objections, and he urged Francis White to find some way to "slide away" from it.[22] If Cotton had not died soon afterward the State Department

[22] Cotton to White, Jan. 5, 1931, 813.00, Washington/375.

might not have again tested the non-recognition policy in El Salvador.

El Salvador, where there had been no revolution for more than thirty years, had up to this time given the State Department less trouble than any other Central American or West Indian republic. Arturo Araujo, who became president on March 1, 1931, was one of the small group of wealthy coffee planters who had long dominated the government and the economy, but he had been supported in his electoral campaign by liberals and radicals and even by some of the communists whose activities had been causing increasing worry during the past three years. After the election, which was one of the freest in the republic's history, there had been doubts whether the oligarchy and the army would permit him to assume office. Warren Robbins, the American minister, had used his personal influence to discourage any attempt to upset the result of the election, and he thought that the State Department's recent action in Guatemala had contributed to the success of his efforts. The conservatives and the army continued to be unfriendly to the new administration, and discontent increased when Araujo seemed unable to cope with the economic problems brought on by the depression.

In the evening of December 2, 1931, units of the army, which had had little pay for several months, seized some of the barracks in San Salvador. Araujo fled to Santa Tecla, seven miles away. Charles C. Curtis, the new American minister, though he was an experienced career diplomat, apparently did not realize that the State Department's first thought in such a situation would be to warn all concerned that a government coming into power by force would not be recognized by the United States. Instead of attempting to discourage the revolt, he went to the barracks to arrange a short armistice between the army units which were supporting and opposing it, and agreed to convey to Araujo the rebels' demand that he resign. The president refused to resign and fled to Guatemala; and the vice president, General Maximiliano Martínez, assumed the presidency.

Martínez had been a candidate for the presidency until just before the election, when he threw his support to Araujo and accepted the vice presidency. He was also minister of war in Araujo's cabinet. His relationship to the revolt was not entirely clear, because his friends asserted that he had been arrested and confined to the barracks on the night of the uprising. Even if this were true, however, he was ineligible for recognition under the 1923 treaty, because he had been minister of war in the ousted government. It was true that the Salvadorean Congress in ratifying the treaty had specifically omitted that portion of Article II which prohibited the recognition of a revolutionary regime if the new president had been a leader of the revolution or a high official of the preceding government; but the State Department considered that this had no bearing on the policy which the United States and the other Central American governments might follow.

The State Department told Curtis and the other Central American governments that its policy would be based on the 1923 treaty, but it tried to get further information before deciding on a definite course. There could be little hope for the restoration of Araujo, who seemed completely discredited. On December 11 Curtis was instructed to ask Martínez for suggestions "as to the manner in which he feels the government of El Salvador can be placed on a basis that will permit its recognition by the United States and the Central American governments." Martínez insisted that his government was constitutional and cited El Salvador's reservations to the 1923 treaty. In reporting the interview Curtis expressed the opinion that Martínez had the support of a great majority of the Salvadorean people and that recognition should not be delayed too long.

The State Department had by this time lost confidence in Curtis because of his failure to warn the revolutionists immediately of the American government's attitude toward revolutionary governments and because his reports since the coup had been unsatisfactory.[23] Stimson consequently decided to send Jefferson Caffery, the minister in Colombia, who had formerly been minister in El Salvador, to look into the situation and make recommendations. Caffery arrived at San Salvador on December 19. On the twentieth, the State Department informed the legations in the other Central American capitals that it had concluded that the Central American treaty precluded the recognition of Martínez because he had come into power by revolution and because he had been minister of war within six months before the revolution. It would not recognize him and hoped that the Central American governments would not. None of them did.

[23] Stimson *Diary*, Dec. 4, and Dec. 9, 1931.

Caffery reported that Martínez had general support among the "better elements" in El Salvador, that he had no intention of resigning, and that any attempt to force him out would arouse much hostility toward the United States. Caffery thought that it might be possible to persuade the other military and civilian leaders to replace Martínez with General Castaneda, the minister of government, but the State Department rejected this idea because Castaneda also seemed to be ineligible under the 1923 treaty. Caffery then recommended that efforts to eliminate Martínez be suspended until a new Congress met in February 1932. This would elect new *designados,* and one of these might assume the presidency if Martínez should resign. When the State Department suggested that he endeavor to obtain assurances from the local leaders that the matter would be settled in this way, Caffery replied that none of the leaders wanted to make definite promises which might turn against them the strong anti-American feeling which his mission had aroused. Furthermore, they were unwilling to agree at that time on the choice of *designados.* He thought that Martínez would leave office only under military pressure, but he thought that the other principal civilian and military leaders realized that the plan would have to be adopted.[24] Caffery left San Salvador in the first days of January 1932.

Curtis was recalled and William J. McCafferty, who had been secretary of the legation in Guatemala, assumed charge at San Salvador. McCafferty was told to make it clear to the *de facto* authorities that Martínez could under no circumstances be recognized. It would be useless for him or his adherents to send a representative to Washington to seek recognition. The department hoped for the earliest possible establishment of a government which could be recognized. It mentioned Caffery's plan and said that any *designado* eligible under the Central American treaty would be acceptable to the American government.

After Caffery left, Martínez was confronted by a communist revolt in several sections of the country. For some years the communists had apparently made El Salvador the chief center of their effort in Central America. Great amounts of printed propaganda had been sent in from abroad and many agitators had

---

[24] Carr to Caffery, Dec. 31, 1931, and Caffery to Stimson, Jan. 1, 1932, 816.01 Caffery Mission/13, 14. See also Stimson's notation in his *Diary* for Jan. 8, 1932.

285

been active in the rural areas, where most of the peasants worked for low wages and under bad conditions. There had been disturbances before Araujo's overthrow, and in January, after thirty persons were killed in an attack on government offices at Ahuachapán, they grew more serious. On January 21 the government declared martial law in much of the republic. Resident foreigners were alarmed, and the American, British and Canadian governments sent warships to provide protection in case of necessity. After a few days of fighting, however, the government got the upper hand. Several thousand communists or suspected communists were reported to have been slaughtered by the government's troops while the movement was being wiped out.

After the suppression of the communist revolt the government's financial situation was even worse than it had been. The American bankers, who had helped in previous emergencies, were unwilling to make a loan to an unrecognized government, and as an emergency measure Martínez took over the customs receipts pledged for the service of the foreign debt under the 1922 contracts. The fiscal agent consequently invoked the contractual provision for the establishment of a customs collectorship in case of default and asked the State Department to transmit to San Salvador the names of two persons, one of whom should be selected by the government to act as collector. This raised a difficult question of policy. Despite Hughes' effort to emphasize the limited character of the obligations which the American government assumed under the contract, the purpose of the provisions linking the secretary of state and the chief justice to the loan had been to make the bonds more attractive to prospective purchasers and thus enable El Salvador to obtain the loan on more reasonable terms. The bondholders would feel that they had been deceived if these provisions proved meaningless. Even if there had been a recognized government at San Salvador, however, the State Department would not have been disposed, in 1932, to take any very vigorous steps to compel it to comply with the provisions of the loan contract. With an unrecognized government, it was doubtful whether the bankers' nominations could even be transmitted without seeming to recognize the *de facto* authorities. There was some difference of opinion on this point in the department,[25] but the final decision was to tell the

[25] See Baker's memorandum of Feb. 26, and Hackworth's of March 10, 1932, 816.51 C 39/131, 132.

bankers and inquiring bondholders that the department could not act because there was no recognized government to which the nominations could be transmitted.[26] No customs collectorship was established. Part of the contractual interest was paid during the next few years, under an agreement between the government and the bondholders, and in 1944 service on the bonds was resumed, at reduced rates, under an agreement negotiated by the Foreign Bondholders Protective Council.

American officials who had misgivings about the Central American non-recognition policy had always feared that the time would come when a government ineligible under the treaty of 1923 would simply remain in office and place the United States in an untenable position. Within a few months it began to seem probable that this had happened in El Salvador. Martínez' position grew stronger rather than weaker and McCafferty reported that his administration was very efficient and honest. The State Department, however, had taken a position from which it was hard to retreat, even though its insistence on a change in the government might well make the government worse rather than better.

Though Martínez faced little formidable opposition and the Congress elected in January 1932 declared him the constitutional president, he apparently did not yet feel strong enough to defy the United States by refusing categorically to cooperate in the establishment of a government that could be recognized. He seemed to acquiesce in McCafferty's suggestion that the Congress choose *designados* who would be eligible for recognition if he should resign. After the election, the State Department told McCafferty that it did not think that Colonel Fidel Garay, who had been chosen as first *designado*, would be ineligible for recognition. Martínez sent word to McCafferty, however, that he feared that his life would be in danger if he withdrew from office at once. He suggested that he might "deposit" his authority temporarily in the first *designado*, retaining his own position as vice president so that he could resume the presidency after six or seven months. The State Department replied that the only solution would be an outright resignation. On March 8 the minister for foreign affairs told McCafferty that Martínez realized that he must resign but he wished to delay action for several weeks be-

---

[26] The correspondence with the bankers and the bondholders is in file 816.51 C 39.

cause there was much opposition in the army to Garay. The minister said that Martínez might wish to be secretary of war. This would of course mean that he remained in control of the government, but the State Department, when McCafferty asked its views, said that the appointment of the cabinet was an internal matter and that the proposed arrangement would not seem to make the new government ineligible for recognition.

McCafferty obtained what he thought was a definite promise that Martínez would withdraw immediately after Easter, and he remonstrated vigorously when the president did not do so. The State Department, however, did not support McCafferty, apparently because it feared that it would be accused of interfering in El Salvador's internal affairs. It mildly rebuked him for speaking of a "solemn pledge" to the United States and reminded him that his talks with the Salvadorean officials had been an "entirely informal and personal" effort to help El Salvador in the difficult situation caused by non-recognition. After this admonition McCafferty made little further effort to bring about a change.

For a time Martínez still pretended that he would resign when he felt it safe to do so, and in April 1932, when Stimson was in Europe, he sent Judge Guerrero of the World Court to tell the secretary that he would turn over his office to Garay on June 1. On June 8, however, he issued a manifesto saying that he would cease his efforts to obtain recognition and would accede to the wishes of the overwhelming majority of the Salvadorean people by remaining in office until the end of his constitutional term. There was little further that the State Department could do. On June 14 it told McCafferty that it was considering closing the legation as an indication of its displeasure at Martínez' failure to comply with his promises but that it did not want to do anything which could be interpreted in El Salvador or elsewhere in Central America as an effort to force Martínez out. McCafferty recommended the proposed step, but Renwick, who was in the United States trying to make arrangements for the protection of the bondholders, opposed it, saying that it would be regarded as a bluff if the department did not follow it up with further action, and might encourage revolutions elsewhere in Central America. After a month of indecision, McCafferty was told that no change would be made for the time being. During the next two years, consequently, the American government maintained informal and not wholly unfriendly relations with Martínez. In September 1932, the British government, which had held off until then only because of earnest representations by the United States, formally recognized the regime. Several other governments soon followed.

The other Central American states continued to withhold recognition, but most of them were unhappy about a situation which cut them off from normal relations with a close neighbor. Nicaragua went along cheerfully with the American policy, but President Mejía Colindres of Honduras, though he welcomed a policy that discouraged any revolt against his own weak government, was worried because he feared that the United States might suddenly recognize Martínez and leave Honduras exposed to retaliation by a more powerful and angry neighbor. The Guatemalan government had from the first been strongly opposed to Martínez and had been impatient with what it considered the weakness of the State Department's policy. It had objected to the department's idea of accepting Garay as Martínez' successor and had urged that efforts be made to bring about the choice of Gómez Zárate, the chief justice, as provisional president. The State Department had discouraged this proposal because it thought that support or opposition to any particular individual, on grounds of fitness or unfitness, would be improper.

The Costa Rican government had been lukewarm about non-recognition because it disliked any North American interference in Central American affairs. After the communist revolt in El Salvador, it had irritated the State Department by suggesting a Central American conference in Guatemala to discuss the communist menace, obviously with the idea of paving the way for Martínez' recognition. There was a suspicion that some members of the González Víquez administration opposed the non-recognition policy because they were themselves contemplating a coup d'état if the opposition should win in the approaching presidential election.[27] Manuel Castro Quesada, the official candidate, did seize one of the barracks in San José when the election went against him in February 1932, but President González, after some hesitation, ordered the rest of the army to suppress the revolt. Minister Eberhardt, who had been transferred to San José from Managua, attempted to restore peace, but instead of urging ac-

[27] Chargé d'Affaires Werlich voiced this suspicion in a telegram of Dec. 7, 1931, 816.01/8.

ceptance of the results of the election and warning the revolutionists of the danger of non-recognition, he agreed to carry the rebels' proposals for a compromise government to President González. The State Department was displeased, but the affair came to a peaceful conclusion when González rejected the rebels' demands and the rebels soon after capitulated. Ricardo Jiménez, who had had a plurality in the election, became president.

By the end of 1932 it was clear that Martínez' successful defiance had destroyed whatever usefulness the non-recognition policy may once have had. In October, Minister Whitehouse in Guatemala wrote Edwin Wilson, the chief of the Latin American division, that the prestige of the United States had been seriously affected. Friends of Manuel Orellana, who had withdrawn from the presidency in 1930, were sorry that they had listened to the State Department's warnings about non-recognition at that time. Whitehouse thought that the United States should still do what it could to force Martínez out.[28] Wilson and White disagreed. Wilson pointed out that the United States had no mandate to enforce the 1923 treaty, and that it would be indefensible to encourage disorder in El Salvador. He thought that it was better to accept a temporary loss of prestige than to embark on a policy of meddling in internal situations in Central America.[29] The United States nevertheless continued through the rest of the Hoover administration to withhold recognition from Martínez. In 1934, the denunciation of the 1923 treaty by Costa Rica and El Salvador gave the other Central American states an excuse to resume relations with El Salvador and the American government cheerfully followed their example.

The one country that clearly benefited from the non-recognition policy was Honduras. Miguel Paz Barahona, who was elected president in 1924 after the United States barred the candidacy of Tiburcio Carías, was not a strong leader, but his conciliatory policy made for peace. He had unobtrusive but effective moral support from George Summerlin, the American minister. The State Department's insistence that the neighboring governments live up to their obligations under the Central' American treaties prevented the sort of interference that had often encouraged revolutions in the past.

[28] Whitehouse to Wilson, personal and confidential, Oct. 19, 1932, 816.01/258.

[29] Memorandum to White, Nov. 4, 1932, 816.01/258.

Paz Barahona's most notable achievement was the holding of a fair election at the end of his term. Early in 1928, the prospect for an orderly election did not seem bright. Carías, though he had from time to time made trouble for Paz, was the candidate of the national or "blue" party which controlled the administration, but Tosta also aspired to the presidency. Summerlin feared that Tosta or the liberal party would revolt rather than take part in an election where Carías would presumably have official support. He thought that the Cuyamel Fruit Company, or its president personally, was financing the opposition groups and might finance a revolution when the time came, and that the United Fruit Company was financing Carías.[30] Many people in Honduras expected a revolution, if only because they could hardly imagine an election without one. On Summerlin's recommendation, the State Department had American warships make frequent visits to the north coast to discourage troublemakers. The danger of a revolt diminished when the liberals and Tosta combined to support the candidacy of Vincente Mejía Colindres and it became evident that the government would give the opposition ticket a fair chance. The election in October 1928 was as free and orderly as a Central American election could be. To the surprise of many observers, Mejía Colindres won, by 62,000 votes to 47,000 for Carías.

There was still some reason to fear that the national party, which commanded the loyalty of most of the government officials and the greater part of the army, would refuse to turn over the government to its opponents. Carías, however, knew that the United States would not recognize him as president if he disregarded the result of the election. He promised Summerlin that he would endeavor to restrain his more militant followers, and both candidates issued manifestos urging their friends to remain calm. When I visited Tegucigalpa soon after the election and talked with the president and both candidates, I was convinced that it was the American government's non-recognition policy which was making a peaceful change of government possible. On January 19, 1929, the Honduran Congress approved the result of the election by a large majority and the danger of revolution seemed to have passed.

With the change in American policy after 1929, Mejía Colin-

[30] Summerlin to White, personal, July 30, 1928, Francis White papers, Box 15.

291

dres received less effective moral support from the United States than Paz had enjoyed. Summerlin left late in 1929 and was succeeded by Julius Lay, another veteran career diplomat. The death of General Tosta, in August 1930, deprived the new administration of its one strong military leader. Nevertheless the country was fairly tranquil until April 1931, when Gregorio Ferrera started a revolution on the north coast. The government's situation was precarious because its forces were dangerously short of arms and ammunition. It had asked the United States in December to sell it 2,000 rifles, but the State Department had refused because too many of the 5,000 rifles which had been furnished to the preceding administration had been handed out to political supporters in times of crisis and thus lost. The State Department also began to enforce more strictly the embargo on private shipments of arms to Honduras, which had been in effect since 1924. It had been issuing export permits only to the Honduran government, but it had learned that the government was selling the permits to German merchants, who then sold the merchandise to the public. When the revolt started, Mejía asked for a loan of arms from the marines' stock in Nicaragua, but the State Department refused, suggesting that anything needed be obtained from private dealers.

The United States sent three cruisers to the north coast to protect Americans and other foreigners; and at his press conference on April 20 Secretary Stimson was asked to compare the situation in Honduras with that in Nicaragua. The correspondent had in mind the secretary's very recent statement about the inability of the United States to protect Americans in the interior of Nicaragua. Mr. Stimson replied that there was apparently a genuine political movement in Honduras, and that the American forces were there to protect American lives and property, and not to participate in military operations. This statement, as reported in Central America, distressed the Honduran government, because it gave the impression that the United States was neutral in the conflict. Lay was consequently authorized to explain that the United States of course continued to give its moral support to the constituted government and maintained its policy with respect to the non-recognition of revolutionary regimes. Furthermore, it was still maintaining the arms embargo and authorizing shipments only to the government. The secretary had intended to indicate that the revolution was an internal matter to be handled solely by the Honduran government.[31]

The revolutionists were also poorly armed, and there was relatively little serious fighting. On May 1 Ferrera took Santa Rosa de Copán, where he massacred the garrison, which had surrendered when its ammunition gave out, and killed several government officials and civilians. Three weeks later a rebel attack on Tela was repulsed and on June 18 Ferrera was decisively defeated near Lake Yojoa. A few days later he was killed and the revolution ended. Other opposition leaders had refrained from joining the revolt because they knew that there would be no hope of recognition from the United States if they won.

Mejía Colindres apparently did what he could to assure a fair presidential election in October 1932. Ángel Zúñiga Huete, the liberal candidate, had the support of most of the government officials and the use of considerable sums of money from the treasury, but he had to contend with the unpopularity of Mejía Colindres' administration and the prestige of General Carías, who was again the national party candidate. There was little disorder during the campaign, but feeling ran high and many feared that there would be violence before the contest ended. Lay suggested that the American government be prepared to send a landing force to Tegucigalpa, where he thought that the danger to foreigners was greater than it had been in 1924. The State Department, however, reminded him of its refusal to attempt to protect Americans in the interior of Nicaragua in 1931 and said that those who felt unsafe should leave Honduras or at least withdraw to coast towns where the United States could protect them. It said that the American government would consider sending an armed force into the interior of a foreign country only with the greatest reluctance and in a most serious emergency when law and order had broken down completely and diplomatic efforts to obtain adequate protection had failed.

After Carías won the election, by a substantial majority, some of the liberals started a revolt. President Mejía, who opposed the movement, suggested through his minister at Washington that liberals who had not yet joined it might be deterred if the United States announced that it would not recognize any regime coming into power by revolution. Francis White told the minister that

[31] Stimson to Lay, May 13, 1931, 815.00 Revolutions/84.

293

American policy had not changed but that the United States wished to keep out of internal political affairs in Central America and the issuance of a statement might be considered as inter-meddling.[32] A few days later the department refused to permit the Honduran government to buy arms from the War Department, in spite of Lay's strong recommendation that the Honduran request be granted. The government's forces might have been in a difficult situation if Carías, who commanded them, had not been able to obtain arms from Martínez in El Salvador. As it was, the revolt was soon suppressed. Carías set up a rather heavy-handed dictatorship, which lasted until he stepped down voluntarily in 1948.

THE DOMINICAN REPUBLIC

Relations between the United States and the Dominican Republic were friendly while Horacio Vásquez was president. The bad feeling caused by the policies of the military government disappeared with surprising rapidity, and the suspicion of American purposes which made the withdrawal of the occupation difficult became far less evident. Evan Young, the new American minister, had friendly personal relations with the president and the other political leaders. Young did not hesitate to give advice and point out mistakes, even when internal political questions were involved, but he avoided anything that looked like dictation.

The country was relatively peaceful and prosperous. The partisan hatreds engendered by the civil wars before 1916 had had a chance to cool. The American-trained constabulary, now called the army, was efficient and its work was facilitated by the new roads and better communications. The government, thanks to the American customs receivership, had ample revenues, and these were augmented by loans, totalling $13,300,000, contracted in the United States between 1926 and 1928. The political situation was less encouraging. The contest between aspirants for the presidency for the next term began almost before Vásquez himself took office. Vice President Velásquez claimed that Vásquez had promised to support him in 1928 in return for the votes which he brought to the *alianza* ticket in 1924, but relations between the two men became strained soon after their inauguration. In 1926

32 White's memorandum of Nov. 16, 1932, 815.00 Revolutions/361.

there was a definite break and Velásquez' followers were removed from official positions. Political tension increased further when it became evident that José Dolores Alfonseca, and not Velásquez, would be the official candidate in 1928.

Alfonseca had many enemies in the president's own *Horacista* party, and in August 1926, Young reported that some of these were arguing that Vásquez had been elected under the constitution of 1908, which would give him a six-year term instead of the four-year term set in the constitution of 1924. The presidential electors had in fact been chosen before the 1924 constitution went into effect but they had voted afterward and it was clearly understood that they were electing the president for a four-year term. Since the proposal was inconsistent with the intent of the plan of evacuation, the State Department approved Young's suggestion that he discuss the matter, as if on his own initiative, and say that action contrary to the 1924 constitution "would be regarded with strong disfavor by the Department." Vásquez professed to be reluctant to agree to the extension, but said that he was under much pressure from his followers, and especially from the senators, whose terms would also be extended. When Young asked for further instructions, he was authorized to intimate that the State Department was surprised that there should be any doubt about the question, and to say that the proposed action "would without doubt have a most unfortunate effect upon the growing confidence in the stability of Dominican institutions." Perhaps as a result of Young's efforts, Vásquez published a statement on September 27 saying that if the Congress decided that he had been elected for a six-year term he would resign at the end of the fourth year.[33]

The Congress took no action, but in February 1927, the plan to continue Vásquez in office was revived. Again Young made informal representations. He was reluctant to urge that the American government take a vigorous stand against the plan, partly because he had a low opinion of Alfonseca and feared that a government headed by him would be weak and possibly corrupt.[34] The State Department now felt that the question was an internal political one, to be decided by the Dominicans, and it told Young to impress on Vásquez the fact that the responsibility

[33] On this matter see 839.00/2996 ff.
[34] Young to Kellogg, March 31, 1927, 839.00/3045.

for what might happen rested solely on him. When the Dominican minister asked the department for an expression of its opinion, he was given no definite answer.[35]

To dispose of any doubts about the legality of the proposed extension, the Dominican Congress in May 1927 authorized the holding of a constituent assembly. Vice President Velásquez and his followers objected, and boycotted the election, but many more votes were cast, or at least counted, than in the hotly contested presidential election of 1924.[36] The assembly, which met in June, adopted a new constitution which extended the terms of the president and vice president to six years. The vice president, however, was to be considered as resigning if he did not take a new oath of office. This eliminated Velásquez, who could hardly take the oath when he denied the validity of the whole procedure. In February 1928, Vásquez announced that he would continue as president until the end of the six-year term in 1930.

Early in 1929 Sumner Welles, who still kept in close touch with Vásquez, persuaded the president to employ a group of American experts to make recommendations for the improvement of the republic's financial administration. The customs collectorship was functioning well, but there was inefficiency and corruption in handling the funds after the government received them. Neither the American minister nor the State Department knew about the project until just before it was publicly announced that General Charles G. Dawes, who was ending his term as vice president of the United States, would head the mission. General Dawes arrived at Santo Domingo on April 2, 1929, accompanied by a large group of eminent business executives and financial experts, and after a stay of three weeks made an impressive report proposing reforms in the government's organization and in its financial administration. The laws which the commission's experts drafted were enacted by the Dominican Congress and Vásquez announced that he would carry out the proposed reforms. Some of them were in fact put into execution, but sharply declining revenues more than offset the economies which were effected.[37]

Meanwhile it had become evident that Vásquez was planning to bring about his own reelection in 1930. Ostensibly he still sup-

[35] See W. M. Wilson's memorandum of May 26, 1927, 839.00/3073.
[36] Young to Kellogg, June 10, 1927, 839.00/3071.
[37] Correspondence about the Dawes mission is in file 839.51A.

ported Alfonseca's candidacy, but not very vigorously, and in August 1928, Alfonseca himself came out in favor of the president's continuing in office. Young tried very informally to dissuade Vásquez from a step which would require another change in the constitution, but he did not think that any official objection should be raised. He thought that the majority of the Dominican people would probably approve the president's reelection. When a constituent assembly was elected in June 1929, few people bothered to vote and in many places the votes were not even counted. The assembly eliminated the constitutional prohibition against the reelection of a president and in October Vásquez publicly announced that he would again be a candidate.[38]

The situation suddenly changed a few days later when Vásquez had to fly to the United States for emergency medical treatment, leaving Alfonseca at the head of the government. The commander of the army, General Rafael Leonidas Trujillo, was one of Alfonseca's chief enemies, and it was soon evident that the bad feeling between the two men would cause trouble. Trujillo had enlisted in the *Guardia Nacional* as a private in 1918, when it was being trained by American marines, and had risen rapidly through the ranks. The marines under whom he worked thought highly of him, and their support, plus perhaps the fact that he was the only *Horacista* in the upper ranks, led Vásquez to make him lieutenant colonel and second chief of the constabulary in December 1924, and then to put him in command of the force in June 1925. He remained as brigadier general in command when the force was renamed the Dominican army. He had thus far seemed loyal to Vásquez, and his friendly feeling toward the American officers who had trained him had made him disposed to cooperate with the American legation. Young had a high opinion of his professional ability.

Young interposed to prevent an open break when Trujillo seemed on the point of revolt, and Trujillo promised to respect the government's authority. The situation was still tense when Young left Santo Domingo to become minister to Bolivia in December 1929, but it seemed to improve when Vásquez returned and resumed control early in 1930. By this time the opposition had chosen Velásquez and Rafael Estrella Ureña as their candidates for president and vice president, and were demanding

[38] Young to Kellogg, Oct. 6, 1928, 839.00/3172; Oct. 26, 738.3915/369; Nov. 2, 839.00/3176; Cabot to Stimson, July 18, 1929, 839.00/3198.

changes in the electoral law to make a fair election more possible. They objected especially to the fact that all of the members of the central electoral board were friends of Vásquez. John Cabot, who was chargé d'affaires after Young's departure, tried to bring about an agreement, and the government was ready to make some concessions, but on February 13, 1930, Velásquez announced that his party would abstain from voting. Velásquez himself perhaps did not know that his associates had made a deal with Trujillo to overturn the government by force.[39]

On February 23 armed partisans of Estrella Ureña, seized the fort at the important northern city of Santiago. It was learned later that Trujillo had ordered the garrison not to resist, and had sent arms from the capital to fall into the rebels' hands. On the twenty-fourth the revolutionists were on their way to Santo Domingo. Vásquez and Alfonseca and a score of other high officials sought refuge in the American legation, but they left when Charles C. Curtis, the new American minister,[40] telephoned to Trujillo and got assurance of the army's loyalty to the president. At Curtis' suggestion, however, they authorized the legation to propose that Alfonseca resign the vice presidency and that Vásquez ask Congress to repeal some recent objectionable changes in the electoral law. Cabot, the secretary of the legation, took these proposals to the rebel leaders, who made counterproposals. The rebels also agreed to a truce, but then pressed forward and entered Santo Domingo on the morning of the twenty-sixth. Meanwhile Consul Bickers, at Puerto Plata, prevented what could have been a bloody fight there. The local garrison, which had no communication with Santo Domingo, was prepared to resist the revolutionists, but its leaders agreed to a suspension of hostilities while Bickers made the long and dangerous journey to Santo Domingo to obtain orders from the leaders of both parties there for a truce. Both Cabot and Bickers were promoted in recognition of the courage and good judgment which they had displayed.

The legation at first acted on the assumption that a real revolution was starting and that the legation's influence should be used to prevent bloodshed. On February 24, Curtis urged that an American warship be sent to Santo Domingo, but the State De-

---

[39] The Dominican historian Luis F. Mejía says that Velásquez was not a party to the plot. *De Lilís a Trujillo, Historia Contemporánea de la República Dominicana* (Caracas, 1944), p. 234.

[40] Curtis was minister at Santo Domingo before he went to San Salvador.

partment thought that there was no imminent danger to American lives or to the operations of the customs service and told the Minister to handle the situation without a show of force if possible. On the twenty-fifth, Curtis learned that the army was conniving with the revolutionists. Trujillo himself stayed in the fort of Santo Domingo, apparently thinking that his inaction would seem to be a partial compliance with his promises of loyalty to Vásquez. There were occasional brawls and skirmishes between the undisciplined rebel troops and people loyal to the government, but on February 27 Vásquez and Rafael Estrella Ureña met at the American legation and signed an agreement which led to a peaceful settlement.

Vásquez resigned, after appointing Estrella Ureña minister of the interior so that he took over as provisional president under the constitution. Curtis, who had told the Dominicans that the legation would under no circumstances recommend the recognition of Trujillo as president, was also inclined to object to giving the position to the leader of the revolution, but he yielded when Vásquez and his advisers insisted that no one else could maintain order. Since legal forms were followed, the State Department told Curtis that it would raise no question of recognition and would give the new administration all proper assistance.

Estrella Ureña had been an *Horacista* and had held important positions under Vásquez, but he had broken with the president because he opposed Alfonseca. He was considered bright but somewhat erratic. He had little real power as acting president because his authority was overshadowed by that of Trujillo. The recent peace agreement had provided that neither Trujillo nor Alfonseca should be a candidate in the approaching presidential election, but Trujillo had not signed the agreement and it soon became clear that he intended to disregard it. In March his friends formally nominated him for the presidency and Estrella Ureña for the vice presidency.

Estrella Ureña declined the nomination and asked Curtis to announce that the United States would not recognize Trujillo as president. Curtis cabled the State Department that a revolution would be inevitable if Trujillo were not eliminated as a candidate, and suggested that either the legation or the department issue a statement insisting that the peace agreement which had been reached through the mediation of the legation should be carried out. Acting Secretary Cotton replied on March 19 that the department could not authorize such a statement. It felt that its scrupulous avoidance of interference in internal affairs had put relations with the Dominican Republic on a very sound basis. It agreed that it was unfortunate that the head of the army should use his position as a means of obtaining the presidency, and it was willing that Curtis should "talk personally, confidentially and in the most friendly manner" with Trujillo, pointing out that he had a unique opportunity, by withdrawing, to help his country to attain stable, constitutional government; but it thought that any effort at "duress" through public statements would defeat its purpose. It warned Curtis against any action that might impair his own relations with Trujillo, because it expected to recognize him and maintain friendly relations with him if he were elected.

The State Department was blamed in later years for permitting Trujillo to take over the presidency. We could hardly foresee at the time that his regime would develop into one of the most atrocious dictatorships in the history of Latin America. If we had had more foresight, we could hardly have prevented his accession without reverting to the sort of interference which had led to unprofitable interventions in the Dominican Republic and other Caribbean countries in the past. If we had been dealing with a Central American state, we should have felt that we could not recognize the new government because of our commitment to apply the principles of the treaty of 1923, but we had no such commitment in the case of the Dominican Republic. We did however make an ineffective effort to dissuade Trujillo from going ahead. Colonel Richard M. Cutts, the brigade commander in Haiti, who had formerly worked with Trujillo in the Dominican guard and was one of his closest friends, went to the border late in March at our request to see Trujillo and try to persuade him to withdraw, but his mission was a complete failure.[41]

Curtis had already made clear his own disapproval of Trujillo's candidacy in an effort to counteract a popular impression that the army chief was acting in accord with an understanding with the legation. The minister continued to urge that the State Department take a stronger stand, but the department felt that it should go no farther than it had gone. As the election ap-

[41] For Col. Cutts' account of this interview, see the Latin American division's memorandum of May 7, 1930, 839.00/3398.

proached, Vásquez' followers joined with the *progresistas* in nominating Velásquez for president and Angel Morales for vice president. The 1924 "coalition" and some smaller groups supported Trujillo and Estrella Ureña, who had apparently been compelled to accept the vice presidential nomination. To comply with the law, Trujillo ostensibly went on leave and Estrella turned over the provisional presidency to Jacinto Peynado. It soon became clear that the army would not permit a free election, and before the voting Velásquez and his followers withdrew from the contest. Immediately after the election Trujillo attempted to conciliate the other leaders and even offered cabinet posts to Velásquez, whom he had just arrested, and to Alfonseca. Neither accepted, but a judicious mixture of terrorism and conciliation caused many lesser politicians to agree to support the new regime.

There were, nevertheless, minor outbreak of disorder, and in July Cabot, who was in charge of the legation, cabled that the provisional government was asking that the United States issue a statement to counteract rumors that it would oppose Trujillo's taking office. The State Department repeated what it had told Curtis: that it expected to recognize Trujillo and to maintain most friendly relations with him. It added that it would designate Curtis as a special representative at the inauguration. It authorized Cabot to make such use of this information as he thought necessary, and Cabot, after consulting Trujillo, told the press of Curtis' designation and pointed out that this showed that the new government would be recognized.

Trujillo was inaugurated on August 16, 1930. Less than three weeks later, on September 3, Santo Domingo was almost totally destroyed by a hurricane. The American Red Cross rushed aid to the city, as did the Haitian government. Trujillo, fearing that his enemies might take advantage of the general confusion, asked through Colonel Cutts at Port au Prince that fifty marines be sent to Santo Domingo to help maintain order and Curtis supported his request, but the State Department felt that another landing of marines would cause misunderstanding elsewhere. The Haitian government also declined to send a detachment of its American-trained constabulary. Fortunately, there were no serious disturbances and on the whole Trujillo's handling of the emergency increased his prestige at home and abroad. Secretary Stimson

301

commented in his diary that we had opposed Trujillo as a "militarist" but that he was turning out to be a very good man.[42]

The economic loss caused by the hurricane aggravated a financial crisis which already confronted the Dominican government. The government's revenues were reduced by the depression and in 1930 there was a sudden increase in the amount required for the service of the foreign debt. In contracting the loans in New York, the Vásquez administration had postponed any repayment of capital until 1930, but had agreed to very large sinking fund payments beginning in that year to assure the repayment of the loans by 1942, when it was thought that the debts contracted by the military government would be paid off and the customs collectorship could be ended. This arrangement imposed an intolerable burden on the treasury. Under the treaty of 1924, the general receiver, who took orders from the United States rather than from the Dominican government, was obligated to remit to New York monthly as much of the customs revenues as was needed to meet the debt service, and the American government was necessarily concerned when it began to appear that the operation of the treaty would leave the Dominican government without funds to carry on essential activities. President Hoover consequently asked Eliot Wadsworth to go to Santo Domingo to look into the problem.

Wadsworth found the situation extremely serious. Many salaries were unpaid and the floating debt was increasing. The budget had been reduced, but there was no prospect that the government could keep up the debt service and at the same time meet its most necessary expenses. In view of his report, the State Department indicated that it would be ready to acquiesce in a suspension of amortization payments, but Trujillo, who probably feared that a default would expose him to demands for increased American financial control, insisted that the full debt service must be maintained. In the last months of 1930 he sent a commission to the United States to endeavor to obtain a loan which would save the government from default and provide funds for rebuilding Santo Domingo city.

The commissioners were received by President Hoover when they came to Washington, but after the State Department expressed doubts about their plan for a loan of $50,000,000, and turned down their request for a gift of $5,000,000 from the

[42] Entry for Oct. 13, 1930.

United States, they made little further attempt to work with the department. Instead they shopped around rather ineptly in New York. Lee Higginson and Company, who had been the republic's bankers, were disposed to make a loan of about $4,000,000 but only if the government agreed to financial reforms which Trujillo would not accept. J. G. White and Company seemed willing to help, but the State Department disapproved their proposal because it would have given them a monopoly of all government construction work in the Dominican Republic. Another engineering firm, Ulen and Company, discussed a plan with the State Department and then presented it to the government at Santo Domingo, without negotiating with the commissioners, but was unable to reach an agreement with Trujillo.

I was not involved in these negotiations, because I had gone to Haiti. Apparently the State Department was increasingly concerned about the situation in the Dominican Republic and disturbed by rumors that the Dominican commissioners were seeking bribes from persons who wished to do business with them. It was also irritated because the commissioners had accused the department of impropriety in discussing a loan with Ulen and Company when they were negotiating with J. G. White. Through their counsel, Ernest Gann, who was Vice President Curtis' brother-in-law, they persuaded Curtis to discuss the matter with Secretary Stimson; but Stimson rejected the commissioners' protests and warned Gann about the rumors of bribery. On February 12 Stimson told the Dominican minister that any bankers who consulted the department about a loan contract would be asked to certify that no improper commissions had been paid. He said that he could not approve the J. G. White proposal as it stood because of its monopolistic character and because its terms were too vague.

At the same time the secretary gave the minister a copy of a statement which was being cabled to the legation at Santo Domingo setting forth the principles which the State Department would follow in considering proposals for Dominican government financing. No proposal would be considered until it was in complete and final form. Financing up to $5,000,000 would be considered reasonable. The department could not approve a loan on conditions so onerous as to constitute improvident borrowing, and this would probably preclude long-term financing under existing market conditions. All disbursements of the proceeds of any loan would be controlled in the same way that expenditures from a small loan had been controlled in 1913: checks drawn on the proceeds by the minister of finance, stating specifically the proposed use of the money, would be countersigned by the secretary of the American legation and by a representative of the general receiver of customs. Only such construction work as was considered eminently desirable by both governments should be undertaken.

The State Department's assumption of the right to approve or disapprove the provisions of contracts between the Dominican government and American businessmen, and its insistence on controlling the expenditure of the loan proceeds, seem inconsistent with the policy which it was following in other matters, but it must be remembered that the treaty of 1924 forbade the Dominican government to contract new loans without the American government's consent. Stimson felt that this consent should not be given, in a situation where the Dominican government's solvency and stability were at stake, without making sure that the transaction was a sound one. The State Department had a responsibility not only to the Dominicans but to the bondholders, who had purchased the bonds in reliance on the American government's commitments under the convention and whose interests could be disastrously affected if unwise measures were adopted.

Francis White had already asked Lee Higginson and Company to work out a financing plan which the State Department itself might submit to the Dominican government. This was an unusual step, but it was clear that the Dominican government urgently needed help and that its own representatives were accomplishing nothing. Lee Higginson had been the republic's bankers for many years, and were apparently the only firm interested in an arrangement which would not also involve a construction program.

There was a slight improvement in the bond market in February 1931 and the bankers thought that a loan of perhaps $4,000,000 might be feasible if this improvement continued. They insisted, however, that there must first be an independent survey of the republic's financial position by an American expert and that the republic must accept financial controls to assure that the budget was balanced and that funds were available for public works and other necessary expenses. They pointed out that such controls could be established under laws which had already been adopted in accord with the recommendations of the Dawes commission. They were ready to consider an advance of $500,000 pending an improvement in the market, but would insist that the Dominican government negotiate only with them and give them an option on any future financing. The department transmitted this proposal through the legation at Santo Domingo, explaining that the bankers had made it because the department asked them to. In a separate cable it suggested that Trujillo might find the bankers' terms onerous and might wish to make a counterproposal.[43]

Trujillo seemed willing to accept the proposal as it stood. He had for some time wished to employ an American expert to advise him on financial matters, and he had asked the State Department to make available the services of Sidney de la Rue, the financial adviser to Haiti. De la Rue could not be spared from Haiti, but the State Department recommended William E. Dunn, a former official of the United States Department of Commerce, who had been director of internal revenue in Haiti from 1924 to 1927. To avoid nationalist criticism, Dunn was appointed as expert adviser to a committee to revise the tax laws. He went to Santo Domingo at the end of March 1931, and completed his economic and financial survey at the end of April. Meanwhile the improvement in the bond market had encouraged J. G. White and Ulen to revive their projects, and on March 25 the two firms told the State Department that they had agreed to work together in Santo Domingo. The State Department seems to have done what it could to discourage them from pushing their projects in a way that would complicate the negotiations with Lee Higginson, and it told Ulen that it would not approve so large a construction program as Ulen was suggesting.[44] The construction firms apparently lost interest after the financial crisis in Europe again made the prospect for financing in New York unpromising.

The crisis also made it impossible for Lee Higginson to consider any actual financing for the time being. When they received Dunn's report, however, the bankers suggested that the republic go ahead with financial reforms which would pave the way for a loan when market conditions should improve. They suggested the appointment of a financial adviser with broad authority to

[43] Stimson to Curtis, March 6, 1931, 839.51/3364A.
[44] Stimson to Curtis, March 6, 1931, 839.51/3365. See also Miller's memorandum of March 10, 839.51/3365½.

control government expenditures and they thought that the State Department should participate in his selection and exercise a considerable measure of control over the country's fiscal policies. They had in mind a loan of about $25,000,000 which would refund the outstanding foreign bonds, with their heavy sinking funds, and thus reduce the annual charge for debt service. The State Department, however, was not prepared to assume any new responsibilities in connection with Dominican finances, or to agree to an arrangement which would prolong the life of the customs receivership for a long period. It suggested that any arrangement for a financial adviser should be one solely between the Dominican government and the bankers and that the new bonds be secured under an arrangement like that in Nicaragua or El Salvador. The department's attitude, and a letter from Dunn saying that Trujillo would not accept the proposed financial controls, discouraged the bankers and in July they politely terminated the negotiations.

The government's financial situation was growing much worse. In August 1931, for the first time since 1908, the customs receipts did not cover the debt service. On August 25 Trujillo wrote to President Hoover, asking his support for a plan which Dunn had drawn up for a new issue of $25,000,000 six percent bonds, a part of which would be exchanged par for par for the outstanding bonds and the remainder would be used to pay the internal debt and to provide cash. Dunn proposed that holders of the old bonds should cease to receive interest if they did not accept the exchange. The State Department could not agree to this feature of the plan, which would have been a gross violation of the bondholders' rights, but it recognized that something had to be done. Assistant Secretary Harvey Bundy, who took charge of the problem, explored the possibility of obtaining the bondholders' consent to Dunn's plan. He found that it would be impossible to reach the bondholders without Lee Higginson's cooperation and that the bankers did not feel that they could properly help. Bundy decided that the only solution was a temporary suspension of sinking fund payments, which would cause less hardship to the bondholders and less injury to the Dominican government's credit than would a failure to pay interest.

The State Department could not formally order or assent to the suspension without in effect changing the provisions of the treaty, which it had no right to do, and without exposing the general receiver to personal liability for failing to apply the customs revenues as the treaty provided. Furthermore, since the 1922 loan had priority over the 1926 loan, it could not properly consent to the payment of interest on the 1926 loan before provision was made for the sinking fund on the 1922 bonds. Bundy thought, however, that the United States, though it could not formally acquiesce in a violation of the treaty, would be justified in not intervening by force to prevent the Dominican government from violating it, and Dunn was asked to come to Washington to work out a plan. Bundy was careful to make it appear on the record that the United States was not a party to the plan and that the department had made every effort to satisfy itself that there was no alternative to default before deciding not to intervene to prevent it from being adopted.

In accord with the plan which Dunn and Bundy worked out, the Dominican minister, in a note delivered October 20, 1931, described his government's financial difficulties and explained how the government proposed to meet them. Each month, all of the money collected by the customs service, after setting aside the amounts required for the expenses of the receivership and for interest on the 1922 loan, would be placed in an "emergency fund." Dunn would administer this fund as "special agent." He would pay from it the interest on the 1926 bonds and not over $125,000 each month to the government, to be used for salaries and other designated purposes. Any excess remaining in the emergency fund after these payments would be delivered to the receiver general to be applied for amortization of the foreign debt. The State Department's reply, on October 23, recognized the seriousness of the situation and the commendable effort which the Dominicans had made to meet it. It stressed the importance of continuing interest payments and of taking steps as soon as possible to return to an observance of the provisions of the treaty, and it pointed out that the arrangement would extend the life of the receivership. The reply did not express any agreement with the plan but said that "it is with an understanding of the special circumstances which you point out that the policy of this government will be guided."

The Dominican Congress immediately passed the proposed emergency law. Since the general receiver could not be asked to violate the treaty by turning the customs revenues into the emergency fund, the three principal customshouses, at Santo Domingo and Puerto Plata and Macorís, were theoretically taken from his control and placed under Dunn's, though there was no actual change in the collecting personnel. Through Dunn the American legation and the State Department kept in touch with the operation of the plan, and Bundy especially watched it carefully to see that there was no improper use of the emergency fund. Trujillo not unnaturally found the restrictions of the plan irksome, and there was some friction between him and Dunn. Arthur Schoenfeld, who succeeded Curtis as minister in October 1931, occasionally had to use his good offices to restore harmony, and in April 1932, the State Department rather gently warned Trujillo that it expected the Dominican government to respect the arrangement. In general, however, the plan worked well. The government had money for essential expenses and the bondholders received their interest. In 1934, by an agreement negotiated with the newly formed Foreign Bondholders Protective Council, the bondholders accepted a reduction in the sinking funds and the general receiver resumed control of the customs service.

In view of its obligations under the 1924 convention the United States could hardly have refused to help the Dominican government to find a way out of its financial difficulties. It could not insist on the full application of the convention without risking a complete breakdown of government in Santo Domingo. This would have been disastrous to the bondholders and might have forced the United States to take action to protect the customs service, as it was obligated to do by the treaty. The obligation to protect the customs service would also have made it difficult to permit Trujillo to try to solve the problem himself, by unilaterally taking over the customs collections and suspending the debt service. The emergency law made it possible for the government to function and at the same time avoided a serious injury to the bondholders.

In cooperating in the operation of the emergency law, the American government of course exposed itself to charges that it was giving moral support to Trujillo's dictatorship. Trujillo had not yet built up the reputation for cruelty and rapacity which he later enjoyed, but he had seized power by treachery and dealt ruthlessly with some of his opponents. The State Department, however, did not want to interfere in the country's internal political affairs, and it had to deal with him if it was to deal with the Dominican government at all.

Chapter Nine

WITHDRAWAL FROM HAITI

President Hoover was more averse than his predecessors to any military intervention in the Caribbean. As he told the Congress, he did not like to be represented abroad by military forces.[1] He permitted the marines to remain in Nicaragua until January 1933, because a democratically elected government had asked that they stay to assure the free election of its successor, but he took steps early in his administration to change the situation in Haiti, where there was more opposition to American intervention. The liquidation of the responsibilities which the United States had assumed in Haiti was a long-drawn-out, complicated business, which was not completed until after Hoover left office.

Opposition to the intervention had grown stronger during President Borno's second term. There had always been resentment of the presence of foreign troops and the authority exercised by foreign officials, and some of the policies of the American treaty officials had made matters worse. The elite had little interest in bettering the lot of the peasants and less in Russell's proposal to build up a middle class which would be a threat to their own position. The mulatto upper class, which had traditionally lived on government salaries and money obtained from the treasury in other ways, had suffered a real hardship from the diversion of government funds to road building and agricultural development, and their situation grew worse with the advent of the depression in 1929. Even among the peasants there was much discontent. Coffee prices were falling and new alcohol and tobacco taxes, for which the financial adviser was responsible, had hurt many small farmers. Efforts to enforce a coffee standardization law, which was intended to make more profitable the exportation of the peasants' chief money crop, had aroused much opposition. The unrest in the countryside was encouraged by upper class nationalists who were glad to have peasant support in their efforts to get rid of the occupation. These efforts centered

[1] Message of December 3, 1929.

309

mainly in the *Union Patriotique,* an organization which seemed to have the support of a large part of the elite, and which was in close touch with the anti-imperialist groups in the United States who had been criticizing American policy in Haiti since the end of the world war.[2]

Neither the American treaty officials nor the State Department seem to have appreciated fully the seriousness of the situation that was developing. When I returned from Nicaragua to take charge of the Latin American division in the spring of 1929, there was apparently no feeling in the State Department that any basic change of policy in Haiti was desirable. There had been no disorder for several years and the treaty services, with Borno's support, were doing useful work. President Hoover, however, decided not long after he took office that the American government's policy in Haiti should at least be reconsidered. He seems to have been influenced not so much by anti-imperialist pressure as by a series of letters criticizing General Russell and his advisers, apparently inspired by the Haitian Corporation of America, which had been having a series of controversies with the treaty officials. In September 1929, the president sent one of these letters to Secretary Stimson and said that he was contemplating the appointment of a commission of "highly important citizens" to reexamine American policy in Haiti. He did not think that he wished to commit himself to the "indefinite policy" of the Coolidge administration and he thought that a study such as he proposed would at least "clarify the atmosphere." Stimson acquiesced in the proposal, but the president took no further action pending the meeting of Congress in December.

In the meantime, a political crisis was developing in Haiti. It will be remembered that the constitution of 1918 provided that an appointed council of state should exercise the legislative power until the president saw fit to hold a popular election for members of Congress. Borno had been elected and reelected by the council of state. The American government acquiesced in this procedure, rather reluctantly. In 1928 General Russell obtained from Borno a promise that there would be a congressional election in 1930, and Secretary Kellogg congratulated Borno on this

---

[2] For a good discussion of the Haitian attitude in 1929 see Professor Rayford W. Logan's article in *The Southern Workman,* LVIII (January, 1929), p. 16.

decision.[3] Russell said later that neither he nor Borno had realized at the time that the first act of the new congress would be to elect a president. When he did realize this, Russell recommended in March 1929 that the American government acquiesce in the postponement of the congressional election until 1932, but on the understanding that Borno would not seek reelection in 1930. It was evident that the president, despite his assertions to the contrary, was seriously considering being a candidate.

The State Department did not reply immediately to Russell's proposal, but it emphatically expressed the opinion that Borno was constitutionally ineligible for reelection. Borno, though he disagreed, said that he would not be a candidate but asked the department's views about the postponement of the congressional election. The department did not reply until August, when it told Borno that the matter was one for him to decide on his own responsibility, and that it would not insist that he act against his better judgment. I shared the responsibility for this decision, because I thought that it would be impossible to hold a meaningful election in Haiti, and that an elected Congress would be no more representative of the wishes of the Haitian people than an appointed council of state. A Congress would inevitably provoke controversies with the treaty officials and obstruct or destroy the constructive programs which we were trying to carry out. It was important to have concrete results from these programs before the treaty of 1915 expired in 1936, and the logical time to have an elected congress would be when the treaty expired.[4] In the light of hindsight, the wisdom of the decision seems doubtful. The consequences of holding an election might have been less embarrassing to the United States than what did happen.

Borno let it be known in November that there would be no congressional election. This meant that he and his friends would select his successor, even if he did not decide at the last minute to seek a third term for himself. His announcement infuriated his enemies and increased their hostility toward the American occupation. In the last weeks of 1929 the first serious disturbances which the country had seen in nearly ten years erupted in Port au Prince.

[3] Russell to Kellogg, April 13, and Kellogg to Russell, April 17, 1928, 838.00/2457.

[4] Memorandum of April 23, 1929, 838.00/2519½.

The trouble started at the Central School of Agriculture, where the *Service Technique* was training agricultural technicians and teachers for the farm schools which it was setting up throughout the country. The Americans in charge had been worried because most of the scholarships which the school offered had gone to boys from the elite of Port au Prince, who rarely had any interest in agriculture or in teaching peasant children; and to encourage peasant boys to come they had set aside $10,000 from the scholarship funds to pay wages at the rate of ten cents an hour for manual work around the school. This precipitated a student strike, which started on October 31 and soon spread to the *Service Technique's* other schools. Borno, with Russell's approval, tried to placate the strikers with rather generous concessions, but it soon became clear that the students were being encouraged by Borno's enemies to continue the strike as a demonstration against the president and the American occupation. By the end of November students were striking in other towns and many of the *Service Technique's* Haitian employees were stopping work. The *garde* did not interfere with parades by the strikers and their sympathizers, and Russell dissuaded Borno from arresting a number of politicians who were fomenting anti-American demonstrations, but when Haitian employees in the other treaty services began to go out, and there were even doubts about the loyalty of the enlisted men in the *garde*, Russell felt that he had to take drastic action to avert bloodshed. He asked that 500 additional marines be sent to Haiti and on December 4 he ordered the bridgade commander to issue a proclamation making effective the state of martial law which had been established in 1915 and never formally abolished.

In the State Department we were extremely reluctant to have more marines go to Haiti. We tried to stop Russell from invoking martial law, but the proclamation had already been issued when our message reached Port au Prince. When we received more information, we felt that Russell had acted wisely. His prompt action had brought about the immediate restoration of order, and it was not necessary to send additional marines. During the short period that martial law was in force, there was little effect on the normal activities of the population. Just after the proclamation of martial law, however, there was a painful incident at Aux Cayes, where a small marine patrol fired on an advancing mob and killed several people.

These events confirmed President Hoover's belief that a change in policy was needed, and on December 7 he asked Congress to authorize the appointment of a commission to look into the situation. After the Congress acted, he chose W. Cameron Forbes, the former governor general of the Philippines, to be chairman of the commission, with four other members: Henry P. Fletcher, the career diplomat who had been Undersecretary of State in 1921-1922, Elie Vezina, a prominent Catholic layman, and James Kerney and William Allen White, who were newspaper editors. The group represented both political parties and several different points of view. The president told the commission that its task was to consider "when and how we are to withdraw from Haiti" and "what we shall do in the meantime." He did not contemplate an immediate withdrawal, because "every group in Haiti considers that such action would result in disaster to the Haitian people," but he pointed out that the treaty of 1915 would expire in 1936 and it was necessary to "build up a certainty of efficient and stable government" after the United States withdrew. He praised General Russell for what had already been accomplished.[5]

The situation at Port au Prince was still potentially explosive when the commission arrived on February 28, 1930. On the twenty-seventh, a false rumor that the council of state was about to choose a new president had touched off a disorderly demonstration which was quieted with some difficulty by the police. The tension increased when the commission began to hold public hearings. Nearly all of those who appeared were presented by a committee representing the various anti-Borno groups, and their denunciations of Borno and the occupation, and the publicity which their charges received in the North American press, aroused much public excitement. It was soon clear that there might be serious disorder unless the opposition was assured of an opportunity to participate in the choice of the next president.

Fortunately, General Russell was able to work out with Borno a compromise which the commissioners persuaded the opposition to accept. Eugene Roy, a businessman who had not been active in politics, would be elected by the council of state to succeed Borno at the end of the latter's term in April, with the understanding that he would summon the people to elect a congress

[5] *Report of the President's Commission for the Study and Review of Conditions in the Republic of Haiti* (Washington, 1930), pp. 1, 2.

and then resign in favor of a new president whom the congress would choose. This agreement relieved tension, for the time being, and the commission was able to proceed with its hearings, in the capital and elsewhere. It left Port au Prince on March 16 and submitted its report to the president on March 26.

The report did not call for any very radical change of policy. The commission thought that the occupation should continue until the expiration of the treaty in 1936, and that it was "too early to suggest in what form the American Occupation should be liquidated upon the expiration of the treaty or in what form such further aid and assistance as the Haitian Government might desire from the United States should be provided."[6] It did not recommend any immediate reduction in the marine brigade, and its proposal that naval and marine officers be detailed to the treaty services for a minimum of four years, in the hope of building up a force of doctors, engineers, and police officers who might be available after 1936 for continued assistance to the Haitian government,[7] suggested that the commissioners did not think that the United States should withdraw completely when the treaty expired. They were "under no delusions as to what may happen in Haiti after the convocation of the elected legislative assembly and, to a greater extent, after the complete withdrawal of the United States forces. . . . Until the basis of political structure is broadened by education—a matter of years—the Government must necessarily be more or less unstable and in constant danger of political upheavals."[8]

The commission praised the "fine record of accomplishment" under the leadership of President Borno and General Russell, but it criticized some aspects of the treaty services' work. It pointed out that the occupation's public health and public works and educational programs, which were designed to pave the way for a more democratic government in Haiti, had alienated the Haitian elite, who saw the programs as a threat to their own leadership. It said that

The failure of the Occupation to understand the social problems of Haiti, its brusque attempt to plant Democracy there by drill and harrow, its determination to set up a middle class—however wise and necessary it may seem to Americans—all

[6] *Ibid.*, p. 9. 　　　　　　　　　[7] *Ibid.*, p. 19.
[8] *Ibid.*, p. 9.

314

these explain why, in part, the high hopes of our good works in this land have not been realized.[9]

More specifically, it criticized General Russell and the treaty officials for not making a greater effort to train Haitians for the responsibilities which they would have to assume when the treaty of 1915 expired. The commission recommended an increasingly rapid "Haitianization" of the treaty services. It also recommended that General Russell be replaced, at the end of his tour of duty, by a civilian minister, who would carry out a program of Haitianization and would negotiate agreements "providing for less intervention in Haitian domestic affairs and defining the conditions under which the United States would lend its assistance in the restoration of order or maintenance of credit."[10]

The commission's report evidently represented a compromise between the rather conservative views of Cameron Forbes and Henry Fletcher and the views of the more liberal members, of whom William Allen White was the most outspoken. Each member apparently wrote a section of the report, and the recommendations in one section were sometimes incompatible with those in another. The commission's basic purpose, however, was clear: the United States was to reduce its interference in Haiti's internal affairs as rapidly as practicable. Immediately after he received the report, Hoover told the State Department that he was accepting it as the basis of his administration's policy in Haiti.[11]

Neither the American officials in Haiti nor those who were dealing with Haiti in the State Department were happy about the commission's work. General Russell and his coworkers complained that the commission had spent nearly all of its time listening to opponents of the occupation and had made little effort to learn the views of the treaty officials. They thought that some of the commission's statements about their work were based on misrepresentations and were unfair. They believed that the task which the United States had assumed in Haiti could not possibly be completed by 1936 and that a substantial amount of American control would have to continue after that date. At Washington, though the question had never so far as I know been seriously considered by the secretary of state, the Latin American division had been acting on the tacit assumption that American help

[9] *Ibid.*, pp. 18-19. [10] *Ibid.*, p. 21.
[11] Cotton to Russell, March 29, 1930, 838.00/2773A.

to Haiti would have to continue after the treaty expired in 1936. We thought that a great deal had been accomplished but that more would have to be done before we could withdraw without risking a return to the conditions that prevailed before 1915. Continued control was inconsistent with the State Department's general Caribbean policy but the obligations which we had assumed in the treaty of 1915 made Haiti a special case. The commission had not urged a complete withdrawal in 1936, but the early Haitianization of the treaty services which it had recommended seemed certain to put an end to any constructive work. Secretary Stimson, who was in London at the head of the American delegation to the naval conference and who apparently had had no chance to see the commission's report before the president adopted it as the basis of administration policy, was never happy about what the commission had done.[12]

The commission had hardly mentioned one matter that seemed very important to us. It will be recalled that the protocol of 1919 had provided that the bonds to be issued under it would be secured by liens on all of Haiti's revenues and that the control of the collection and allocation of these revenues by officers nominated by the president of the United States should continue so long as the bonds were outstanding. When the loan of 1922 was issued, Secretary Hughes, with President Harding's approval, had assured the bankers and the prospective purchasers of the bonds that the United States intended to exercise the authority which this provision gave it. This meant, we thought, that any plan for withdrawal from Haiti would have to provide for a considerable measure of financial control for some years after 1936.

It was clear that the new policy would make the situation in Haiti very different from that in which the high commissioner and the treaty officials had been working since 1922. The government which emerged from the popular election would almost certainly be less friendly and less cooperative. The nationalists thought that they had already won a notable victory over Borno and the occupation, and it seemed likely that they would foment new disorders in an effort to get further concessions. The American treaty officials were resentful and uncertain about the future. The State Department, however, told them that they should carry on as usual until the election of a new permanent presi-

---

[12] This was my impression based on several conferences in which he gave me oral instructions, and it is borne out by entries in his diary.

dent. It said that the marines and the *garde* must maintain order and that there should be no change in the financial administration.

The immediate problem was to see that the plan for the election of a temporary president was carried out. Borno, though he had agreed to the election of Roy, began to argue that the plan was unconstitutional and that he should not be asked to go ahead with it. The council of state opposed the plan, especially after the opposition groups held a convention on March 20 and "elected" Roy as president. Russell firmly insisted that the plan be carried out, and on April 11 the State Department strengthened his hand by telling him, for his "discreet use," that the United States would if necessary install Roy in the presidency when Borno's term expired. The council elected Roy on April 21, after Borno had replaced twelve of its members.

There was still much anti-American feeling. In April and May the brigade commander's house was burned to the ground in a fire of suspicious origin and there were unsuccessful attempts to burn the houses of two other marine officers and of Dr. Colvin, the acting head of the *Service Technique*. There were minor disturbances at Jacmel and several members of the *garde* were injured in an encounter with a mob at Aux Cayes. The situation improved, however, after Roy was inaugurated on May 15. The new president appointed some of the extreme nationalist leaders to his cabinet but he himself seemed disposed to work harmoniously with the treaty officials and with Stuart Grummon, who was in charge while Russell took leave during the summer. Roy's moderate attitude and Grummon's diplomacy made it possible to avoid serious conflicts when the nationalists in the cabinet showed a disposition to make trouble for the treaty officials. Roy acquiesced when the State Department insisted that there be no changes in the organization or operations of the treaty services during the life of the temporary government and urged that the government confine its activity to preparation for the congressional election.

The United States left the conduct of the election entirely in the hands of the temporary government and enjoined a strict neutrality on all of its officials in Haiti. The *garde* maintained order and prevented violence and overt intimidation of the voters. The *garde's* reports indicated that the people at large seemed to take little interest in the contest, though the candidates tried to arouse enthusiasm with speeches, dances, and cockfights.[13] Most of the candidates represented one or another of the two groups which had sought control of the government throughout Haiti's history: the mulatto elite and the more radical and nationalistic black politicians. The result of the voting, on October 14, was an overwhelming victory for the black nationalists.

The mulatto leaders at Port au Prince were distressed and apprehensive. Most positions in the Haitian government had been held by members of the elite since the American occupation and they looked back with dismay on the chaotic period before 1915 when a series of black generals had been in power. When the Congress met in November, some of them made a desperate effort to bring about the election of one of their own number as president, and they were able by inducements of one sort or another to obtain the election of Stenio Vincent. Vincent had been an active leader in the campaign against the occupation, but he had closer ties with the aristocracy than did Seymour Pradel, a prominent lawyer who was his chief rival. Jolibois *fils*, the newspaper man who had spent so much time in jail because of his attacks on Borno and the occupation, was probably the most popular nationalist leader, but he was constitutionally ineligible for the presidency because he was only thirty-nine. He became president of the new Chamber of Deputies.

Soon after the Forbes commission recommended that the high commissioner be replaced by a civilian minister, I was told that I would be appointed to the post. The commission had proposed that the change be made after the inauguration of the permanent president, but Russell decided to leave Port au Prince on November 12 and I arrived there on November 16, just before Vincent's election. I was instructed to take over the direction of the American treaty services and of those activities of the marine brigade which affected its relations with the Haitian government and the Haitian people. The department said that the president wished to withdraw the brigade when this was possible, and in the meantime the marines were to take no action under martial law without consulting the legation. The legation was to bend every effort to create a situation where the United States could withdraw completely from participation in Haiti's affairs and one of its first duties would be to work out a plan for the Haitianization of the treaty services. The American government was prepared to give up part of its authority under the treaty before

[13] Russell to Stimson, Sept. 23, 1930, 838.00/2887.

1936 if the Haitian government wished it to do so and if the purposes for which the authority was granted seemed to be fulfilled. It would, however, insist on the full recognition of the rights and authority that it retained because it could not otherwise discharge its responsibilities under the treaty. It would expect the president of Haiti to appoint promptly any persons nominated as treaty officials and to continue submitting to the American legation for prior approval any legislation bearing on the objects of the treaty. The legation was not to interfere with legislation or government contracts or decisions by the Haitian courts unless it was absolutely necessary.

These instructions contemplated a gradual relaxation of American control rather than an early and complete withdrawal. Because of the assurances that Secretary Hughes had given to purchasers of Haiti's bonds, the State Department felt that it could not agree to any important changes in the treaty provisions governing the *garde* or the financial services before 1936 and that the United States would have to maintain some form of financial control after that year. About $16,000,000 of bonds issued under the protocol of 1919 were still outstanding in 1930 and it was unlikely that they could all be retired before 1942 at the earliest. The American government's control of the *garde*, the public works and public health services and the *Service Technique* would presumably end in 1936, and we had an obligation to endeavor to train Haitian personnel so that these services would be efficient organizations when the Haitian government took them over.

Some of the treaty services had already made substantial progress in training and promoting Haitian employees. In the public works administration, six of the eight district offices were headed by Haitian engineers at the end of 1930, and Haitians were being trained for the principal administrative positions in Port au Prince. Haitian doctors played an important role in the health service. There had been less progress in the *Service Technique*, which was newer and had been forced to start from scratch in developing agricultural experts and teachers for its vocational schools. In the *garde*, efforts to develop officer material had begun in the first years of the occupation, but progress was slow because few members of the literate upper class were interested in a career in the police. At the time of the Forbes commission's visit, only 35% to 40% of the officers were Haitians, and none of these had reached a rank higher than captain. The commission,

319

however, approved a plan presented by the *garde* commander which contemplated the replacement of all American officers by Haitians not later than 1936.

Immediately after President Vincent took office we began to discuss a program for the further Haitianization of the treaty services. At first, the prospect for an agreement seemed good. The president and the new foreign minister, H. Pauleeus Sannon, were reasonable and pleasant to work with, and they seemed interested in assuring the proper training of the Haitian employees who would eventually take over the treaty services. If they proposed a more rapid transfer of responsibility than we thought practicable, they seemed willing to discuss the subject in a friendly way. They were pleased when the *garde*, as a step toward Haitianization, placed one of the five military departments under the command of Major Demosthenes Calixte, who had enlisted as a private in 1915.

The Haitianization negotiations, however, were soon interrupted by a series of controversies about the current operations of the treaty services. Whatever our plans for the future, for the time being the financial adviser was responsible for the financial administration and the *garde* had to maintain order. Roads and irrigation systems must be maintained and the health service had to continue its work. The efficient conduct of all of these activities required cooperation between the treaty officials and the ministers to whose departments they were attached. The American government had always insisted that the treaty officials have complete control of the personnel of their services and a free hand in carrying out the work entrusted to them, but they were supposed to keep their ministers fully informed about what they were doing and to obtain the Haitian government's approval for new projects which they undertook. The treaty of 1915, however, did not precisely define the extent of their authority, and disputes about this had caused much trouble between 1916 and 1922. While Borno was president the treaty officials had worked fairly harmoniously with the Haitian department heads, and disagreements had been settled by the president and the high commissioner in a spirit of give and take. Frequently Borno's views prevailed, for he was by no means a puppet.[14] An intricate system of

[14] This statement is based on my recollection of conversations with General Russell and the treaty officials before 1930 and on what I learned

320

relationships and practices, which sometimes had little basis in the treaty, had grown up to facilitate the conduct of business.

This system tended to break down under the new administration. After the events of the past twelve months, the Haitians expected American control to be relaxed much more quickly than the American government intended that it should be. While the Forbes commission was in Haiti some of its members had apparently made unguarded statements which encouraged this idea, and many of the candidates in the congressional election had promised that the new government would put an end to the American intervention. The new president and his advisers were disappointed when they took office to find that they had little control over the expenditure of the government's money and that they had few jobs to which they could appoint political friends. Some members of the cabinet were ardent nationalists who opposed continued cooperation with the Americans in any form. One or two of them, especially, seemed determined to do what they could to make trouble, by unreasonable demands on the treaty services and unjustified accusations against individual officials. This further upset some of the treaty officials, whose morale was already low.

We had to maintain the independence and the integrity of the treaty services so long as we were responsible for their work. We had to object, for example, when the government wished the public works service to build a road which would benefit only a few politicians. We could not consent to patently corrupt expenditure of government funds. We had to maintain the right of the treaty officials to appoint and remove their Haitian employees, because political appointments and promotions would have destroyed morale and efficiency. We tried to meet the Haitian government's wishes when we could do so without too great a sacrifice of principle, but a desire to make a show of anti-Americanism on the Haitian side and an increasing feeling of resentment and suspicion on the part of the treaty officials often made it hard to settle disputes even about minor questions.

Vincent and Sannon repeatedly helped to patch up quarrels between their colleagues and the treaty officials, but it was evident that they were under increasing pressure to provoke a

---

later in Haiti about specific cases, rather than on anything that appears in the record.

showdown over the question of American control. Apparently many of the nationalists who thought that the Forbes commission and President Hoover had promised an early withdrawal of the occupation were beginning to suspect that the State Department did not want to withdraw, and some of them had the idea that a new demonstration of discontent in Haiti might bring about a further change in policy. There were many attacks on American officials in the press. Vincent and I had agreed informally not to enforce the press law, under which Borno had frequently jailed unfriendly editors, and the newspapers were enjoying and sometimes abusing their new freedom. Their principal target was Commander Duncan, the engineer-in-chief, whose public works administration was especially interesting to politicians because its payroll was large and because the location of roads and irrigation works was important to local landowners.

The showdown came early in January 1931, when the minister of public works sent Duncan commissions to be delivered to three Haitians who were already working in the service. We suspected that this totally unnecessary action was intended to assert the Haitian government's right to make appointments to subordinate positions in the public works service, and this suspicion was confirmed when I mentioned the matter to Sannon and was told indignantly that the government had a right to make appointments in all of the treaty services. I consequently instructed Duncan to return the commissions with a courteous note. At the same time I set forth the American government's position about appointments in the treaty services in a formal communication to Sannon.

The Haitian press immediately urged the populace to stage tumultuous demonstrations against what was represented as an affront to the president. Vincent assured me that he did not feel affronted, but it was clear that he and his associates were encouraging the agitation. The situation grew more serious when most of the Haitian employees of the public works administration went on strike, apparently in response to pressure from the nationalist leaders. It seemed clear that the nationalists were trying to create a situation like that which had attracted attention to Haiti in the American press a year earlier. The American press, however, hardly knew about the crisis before it was over. The Haitian government realized that public demonstrations might be directed against it as well as against the occupation, and when excited crowds began to gather in the streets, the president sent Sannon to the legation to say that the situation was getting out of hand and to ask for help in dealing with it. Sannon said that the government would be forced out of office if the president withdrew the commissions, and he eagerly accepted a proposal that we permit the delivery of the commissions to the three employees in return for a written promise that the government would make no further attempt to change the status of employees in the treaty services pending their Haitianization.

This agreement was kept secret, and Vincent was able to claim a diplomatic victory which strengthened his rather shaky political position. This was desirable from our point of view, because it would be much more difficult to work out a satisfactory Haitianization agreement with a weak and unstable government. Some of the treaty officials were unhappy about what they regarded as a blow to American prestige, but on the whole the settlement strengthened our position because it discouraged, though it did not entirely stop, further attempts to control appointments in the treaty services. It also averted a very real danger of a serious outbreak of disorders. We were confident that the *garde* could control any situation that developed, probably without help from the marines, but reports of rioting and bloodshed in Haiti would have made an unfortunate impression in the United States.

It was by this time becoming clear, however, that neither Haiti nor the United States would benefit from our maintaining full control of all of the treaty services until 1936. The Haitian government's attitude toward the services made it improbable that they could accomplish very much useful work during the next five years, or even make substantial further progress in training their Haitian staffs. Even if the Haitians should become more cooperative, the sharp decline in the government revenues, caused by the depression, would make it hard to inaugurate new constructive programs or even to carry on existing programs effectively. Furthermore Commander Duncan and Captain Stuart, the head of the health service, thought that their principal assistants had reached a point where they would profit little from further training under foreign control. We could not give up the financial services, and we could hardly withdraw American officers from the *garde* until Haitian officers were ready to take their places, but there was less reason for continued participation in other activities of the Haitian government. I consequently recommended that we agree to an early and almost complete Haitianization of the public works administration as a part of the general Haitianization agreement which we were still discussing. The State Department approved. This decision made the conduct of the negotiations easier, and early in March we seemed close to a tentative agreement which would cover all of the treaty services but would leave for later consideration the particularly difficult question of financial control after 1936.

There was one matter that had to be settled before an agreement could be concluded. In June 1930, President Hoover had nominated Dr. Carl Colvin to be director of the *Service Technique,* but the Haitian government had not yet accepted the appointment. Colvin had been assistant director of the service and had become acting director when Dr. Freeman left Haiti in April 1930. He was a man of unquestioned ability and he was liked by the Haitians who knew him. In the State Department we thought that the service must have a new head if it were to continue to operate and we hoped that Colvin might be able to repair some of the damage which the service had suffered from the student strike. The nomination, however, was ill-timed. It met with violent opposition from the nationalists in the temporary government, simply because of their hostility to the *Service Technique.* Furthermore, President Hoover, when he appointed the Forbes commission, had asked Dr. R. R. Moton of Tuskegee Institute to head a separate group to study educational problems in Haiti, and this commission was in Haiti in June. Its members were naturally offended when Colvin's nomination as director of the American eduational effort in Haiti was presented without consulting them.[15] Partly because of the commission's reaction, the State Department had not insisted that President Roy act on the appointment.

The delay made it more difficult for Vincent to accept the appointment when the matter was taken up with him. The report of the Moton commission[16] did not make the situation easier. The commission approved the general program and objectives of the *Service Technique* but criticized some aspects of its perform-

[15] Moton to Hoover, July 23, 1930, 838.61/188. Also Russell to Stimson, Oct. 2, 1930, 838.61/173.

[16] *Report of the United States Commission on Education in Haiti* (Washington, 1931).

ance. It also deplored the fact that the service's schools received much more financial support than the ill-equipped and inadequately staffed schools administered by the Haitian government. These statements, made by persons whom the Haitians regarded as spokesmen for the American government, encouraged the nationalists in their opposition to Colvin's appointment.

Under instructions from the State Department, the legation had repeatedly told the Haitian government that Colvin's appointment would have to be accepted before a Haitianization agreement could be signed. We knew that we would probably want to turn the *Service Technique* over to Haitian control in the near future, but it would be very much harder to discharge our continuing obligations with respect to the financial services and the *garde* if Haitians in the treaty services thought that their appointments and promotions might depend on the good will of Haitian politicians. We had refrained from forcing the issue while other matters involved in the Haitianization agreement were being discussed, and we had been exploring, unsuccessfully, the possibility of a face-saving compromise. I still felt that a firm insistence on our treaty rights would cause less trouble in the long run, but I felt that I had to warn the department that if Vincent were compelled to make the appointment the immediate results might be a political storm which at the very least would destroy such usefulness as the *Service Technique* still had.

I did not know that President Hoover had been urging Secretary Stimson to make a change in our policy in Haiti. The president had probably not seen my dispatches, but he had read some pessimistic personal letters which one of the treaty officials had written to a friend in the Department of Commerce, and his reaction had been that we ought to withdraw at once and completely. When Stimson convinced him that we were obligated to retain control of Haiti's finances, he thought that we should proceed more rapidly in relinquishing control of other governmental activities.[17] The State Department had consequently been considering a new course of action which it thought would avoid further disputes with the Haitian government and lessen the possibility of new disorders in Haiti. My warning about the Colvin matter, and probably a dispatch forwarded in March saying that the Haitian government might attempt to disregard the financial

[17] Stimson, *Diary*, Feb. 21, and March 11, 1931. See also Francis White's personal letter to me, March 5, 1931, Francis White papers, Box 5.

adviser's authority in formulating the budget for the coming year,[18] apparently made the need for a change in policy seem more urgent.

On March 18, the State Department told us that it contemplated a new approach. It proposed to offer the early, complete Haitianization of the public works and public health services and the *Service Technique*, but only on condition that the Haitian government accept a new treaty which would ensure the continuance of American financial control and the continued efficiency of the *garde* while the bonds of the 1922 loan were outstanding. This proposal was obviously unworkable. The new treaty, as the department had drafted it, would have repeated word for word almost all of the articles of the hated treaty of 1915. This fact alone would have made it offensive to Haitian pride. After the commitments which we had already made with respect to Haitianization, the requirement that the treaty be signed before any further steps toward Haitianization were taken would have been regarded as a breach of faith. We were already close to an agreement that would have turned over public works and public health and the *Service Technique* to Haitian administration. From the standpoint of relaxing our control, the proposal was a step backward rather than forward, for it would have prolonged American control of the *garde* after 1936 and would have provided for a more complete control of the finances than was really needed to protect the interests of the bondholders.

The State Department was very reluctant to give up a plan which seemed to it a neat and simple solution of the Haitian problem, but after a long debate, first by cable and then at conferences in Washington, it authorized me to continue negotiations for the early Haitianization of any parts of the treaty services which could be turned over immediately and to leave until later the question of financial control after 1936. The Secretary obtained President Hoover's approval for this procedure. The State Department said, however, that the question of financial control must be dealt with in a new treaty rather than by executive agreement. I had urged an executive agreement because I knew that it would be hard to obtain the Haitian Congress' approval for any treaty that we might sign.

Sannon seemed pleased with our new proposals and it looked for a time as though we might reach an early agreement, not only

[18] 838.51/2241.

on Haitianization but also on the text of a treaty covering the financial administration after 1936. Sannon gave me the impression that Vincent would be willing to confirm Colvin's appointment as part of a general settlement. The situation suddenly changed when the Haitian Congress, which met for its regular session in April, insulted two of the president's ministers and caused the entire cabinet to resign. Sannon's successor was Abel Léger, a prominent lawyer and a diplomatic historian, who proved to be more aggressive and less cooperative.

When the new foreign minister proposed to resume the Haitianization negotiations, I pointed out that the Colvin case would have to be settled before a final agreement could be signed. Léger expressed surprise, and a few days later he said that the president and the cabinet had unanimously decided that the events of the past eighteen months made the appointment impossible. If Colvin would resign, however, the government would agree that he be paid the full salary of the director for the entire period that he had served as acting director. I submitted this proposal to the State Department, suggesting that it avoided a surrender of principal by either government and protected Colvin's interests. I pointed out that the department and its representatives were partly responsible for the long delay which made it extremely difficult for president Vincent to make the appointment. The department very reluctantly authorized me to accept the proposal, but before the matter was settled the Haitianization negotiations were again held up, this time by a dispute about appointments in the *garde*.

There had been relatively little friction in connection with the *garde*, where the appointment and promotion of Haitian officers was ahead of the schedule which the Forbes commission had recommended, but there had been a difference of opinion about the rural police, who were local people chosen by the *garde's* subdistrict commanders. The Haitian government thought that it should control these appointments, but we had insisted that the *garde* must have full authority over its personnel so long as American officers were responsible for it. There had been an especially unpleasant dispute about one rural policeman in the district of Las Caobas, who was disliked by the president's political friends there. Vincent had been told that Lieutenant Aarons, the Haitian officer who appointed the man, had made disrespectful remarks in discussing the matter, and when the chief of the

327

garde promoted Aarons to a captaincy the president refused to sign his commission. At the same time he refused to sign the commissions of two American officers who were being nominated to fill vacancies for which no Haitian officers were available. Léger wrote me that the Haitian government would object to further appointments of American officers in the *garde*. This provoked the most serious conflict that we had had with the Haitian government. The State Department refused to go ahead with the proposed settlement of the Colvin case or with the Haitianization negotiations until it received specific assurances that the treaty provisions about the *garde* would be respected.

Léger refused to give assurances, but in June he made new proposals. He asked that the public works and health services and the *Service Technique* be turned over to Haitian control on October 31, 1931, which was three months earlier than the date which we had proposed, and that the Colvin case be settled in accord with his earlier suggestion. The government offered to pay generous indemnities to Colvin and the other American experts in the *Service Technique*, many of whom, being teachers, might not be able to find new positions for several months. It would promise also to respect the treaty provisions covering the *garde*, and the president would sign commissions for American and Haitian officers already nominated or nominated in the future, except in the case of Lieutenant Aarons, where the president's dignity and prestige were involved.

I felt that we could not accept this proposal, because we could not permit the Haitian officers in the *garde* to feel that they would not be promoted if they offended politicians. When I was in Washington in April, Secretary Stimson had said emphatically that we must retain full control of the *garde* so long as we were responsible for it. The government's promises of future good conduct would mean little if one Haitian officer was sacrificed in what his fellow officers were watching as a test case. A board convened by the *garde* commander had explicitly exonerated Aarons of the charge that he had made disrespectful remarks about the president. After Vincent reiterated his refusal to sign Aarons' commission I recommended to the State Department that we make public the program of Haitianization which we had worked out and announce that we would carry it out unilaterally. We would still be prepared to discuss details if the Haitian government wished, but we should not permit the government's obstructive attitude to prevent us from carrying out our plans for withdrawal.

The department had earlier approved the idea of proceeding unilaterally if we could not reach an agreement with the Haitian government, but it was alarmed when it considered the possible consequences. It foresaw a situation in which American officers might have to work in the *garde* without Haitian commissions and the financial adviser might have to make payments to the treaty services without authorization from the minister of finance. This it thought would be tantamount to a "military occupation" and would lead to severe criticism in the United States. At Port au Prince the prospect seemed less alarming. We already had a military occupation. Since Vincent's inauguration, we had tried to avoid interfering in the Haitian government's actions, even when we thought that these actions were unwise or improper, but we had often had to do so, and we had occasionally had to disregard orders of the Haitian courts, when they affected the work of the treaty services. Once or twice we had acted or threatened to act under authority of martial law. I was confident that we could handle the situation in a way that would lead to an early resumption of the Haitianization negotiations, and that we would face more trouble in the future if we did not take a firm stand in the Aarons case.

I argued vigorously for this point of view, but on July 3 Undersecretary Castle, who was in charge in Stimson's absence, cabled that "we absolutely cannot get support in this country in this individual case," and instructed me not to insist that Aarons be commissioned. Fortunately, we had already learned indirectly that Vincent was reconsidering his own position. He too was under political pressure to show progress in Haitianization. Before we had to act on the department's instruction, we received his assurance that he would sign Aarons' commission when a Haitianization agreement was concluded. This opened the way for a resumption of the negotiations without further discussion of the Aarons case.

In its instruction of July 3, and on previous occasions, the State Department criticized the legation for permitting the negotiations to be interrupted constantly by controversies about other matters. Francis White thought that we would make more progress if we simply told the Haitian government what the United

States was prepared to do about Haitianization and insisted on a reply. I felt that this procedure would be unreasonable and unproductive. The Haitian government had a right to discuss each aspect of the Haitianization problem in detail if it wished to do so. Most of the difficulties that we had arose not from differences of opinion about Haitianization but in connection with the multifarious questions that arose in the day-to-day operations of the treaty services. These also required discussion, and usually were amicably settled after some argument. Since we were trying to reduce our control, we made any concessions that we could. In some cases, especially where the Haitian government was trying to assume control in fields of action where we were not prepared to relinquish authority, unpleasant disputes were inevitable. I could not see how the course of action which the department envisaged would avoid controversies of this sort.

One such controversy again interrupted the Haitianization negotiations just when we seemed to be about to bring them to a successful conclusion. On July 17, without obtaining the accord of the financial adviser, the government sent Congress a budget which contained several objectionable features and authorized expenditures greater than the anticipated revenues. This violation of the treaty was especially serious, because the government's revenues had fallen to a point where only the most careful financial management would enable it to meet essential expenses. The State Department at once instructed the legation to make a formal protest and to demand that the budget be withdrawn. Léger offered instead to obtain congressional authorization for any changes in the budget which might be required by the prospective Haitianization agreement, and explained that this would enable the government to adjust the budget in consultation with the financial adviser. In order not to delay the conclusion of the Haitianization agreement, we reluctantly acquiesced in this plan.

Léger and I signed the Haitianization agreement on August 5, 1931. It provided that the Haitian government should take over the administration and control of the public works and health services and the *Service Technique* on October 1, but that an American scientific mission should have charge of sanitation and chlorination of water in Port au Prince and Cape Haitian as long as American troops were stationed in those cities. The 1918 agreement, providing for the submission of legislation to the legation before enactment, was abrogated, as was the requirement for the financial adviser's visa on all orders of payment. The Haitian government, however, specifically recognized its continuing obligation to obtain the financial adviser's approval for all expenditures and for measures affecting sources of revenue. One article, which was especially important to Vincent in his relations with the Congress, stipulated that the Haitian senators and deputies would be paid representation allowances which they had voted themselves but which the financial adviser had not yet approved. Americans who were leaving the treaty services would be given suitable indemnities. While awaiting a final settlement of the status of the *garde*, the two governments agreed to maintain the status quo established by existing laws and agreements.[19] The Haitianization agreement was not a treaty and required no further approval or ratification by either government. Léger got an enthusiastic ovation when he announced it to Congress, and the Haitian legation in Washington was instructed to express the government's "sincere joy" and to thank President Hoover. Captain Aarons received his commission a few days after the agreement was signed, and Colvin received a letter of appreciation from Vincent, as well as the balance of the salary which he would have had as director.

During the negotiations the Haitian government asked for a "protocol of evacuation" and the abolition of martial law, which had been in effect since the first days of the intervention. The State Department was unwilling to set a date for the withdrawal of the marine brigade, because it intended to keep a force in Haiti as long as American officers were serving in the *garde*. It did agree, however, that the brigade commander should issue a proclamation suspending martial law on the day when the Haitianization agreement was signed. Martial law had been little more than a technicality for some years, except for a brief period during the strike in December 1929, but it had given the American officials great potential authority and responsibility.

The Haitian Congress adjourned its regular session on August 6. It had made less trouble than anyone expected, chiefly because its members were too inexperienced and undisciplined to agree on any definite course of action. After it forced the resignation of the cabinet in May, Vincent tried to placate it by agreeing, with the financial adviser's consent, that its members should have representation allowances like those which the council of

[19] For the text, see *Foreign Relations, 1931*, Vol. II, pp. 505-508.

state had had. The congressmen promptly voted themselves larger allowances than de la Rue thought reasonable, but the Haitianization agreement provided that they should receive them. No one paid much attention to resolutions which the Congress passed declaring the treaty of 1915 invalid and calling on the executive to terminate the customs receivership, and the provisions of several other laws which it enacted were arbitrarily amended by the president before publication.[20] In the last days of the session the budget for 1931-1932 was approved with a provision authorizing the president to make any necessary changes. This seemed to open the way to settling the controversy which had been pushed aside in the last days of the Haitianization negotiations, especially as the Haitianization agreement specifically recognized the financial adviser's authority over expenditures.

In September, however, when both de la Rue and I were on leave, the government flagrantly violated the Haitianization agreement by promulgating two of the budgetary laws with provisions to which the financial adviser had objected. It also refused to submit proposals for detailed appropriations until a few days before the fiscal year ended on September 30. Léger evidently thought that the legation and the financial adviser would have to acquiesce in the government's action because otherwise there would be no legal authorization to spend government funds or to pay salaries and indemnities to treaty officials who would leave Haiti after October 1.

This action provoked another crisis, but Joseph McGurk, the chargé d'affaires, and Rex Pixley, the acting financial adviser, handled the situation with courage and tact. Léger was defiant and aggressive, but he changed his attitude when the State Department said that if necessary it would itself order the financial adviser to pay the expenses of the remaining treaty services and the essential expenses of other government departments. The Haitian government agreed to discuss the budget in the usual way with the financial adviser and to work under a reduced provisional monthly budget in the meantime. Nevertheless, a long and unpleasant controversy took place before a final agreement was reached. At one point the government tried to enlist anti-imperialist support in the United States by spreading a totally

[20] McGurk to Stimson, Oct. 10, 1931, 838.00 General Conditions/59.

332

untrue story that the legation was threatening to cut off the salaries of all Haitian officials because it disapproved of some governmental appointments. Finally, most of the questions involved were settled in principle by an exchange of notes, and on November 27 the financial adviser was able to approve the completed budget. Both sides made concessions. The Haitian government recognized the financial adviser's authority to see that the budget was balanced and that provision was made for essential government services, while we agreed that the government should have more freedom in determining the distribution of funds between its various activities. We could do this because we were no longer responsible for the work of the services which had been turned over to Haitian control.

President Hoover, in describing the Haitianization agreement in his message to Congress on December 10, 1931, referred to the fact that both the American and the Haitian governments were obligated to continue American financial control in Haiti because investors had bought the 1922 bonds in reliance on the promise that the control would continue during the life of the bonds. This caused a brief flareup of resentment in Haiti, where there had been a belief that Hoover was more sympathetic to Haitian aspirations for complete independence than the State Department was. Léger angrily responded in a formal note which for the first time officially questioned the continued validity of the treaty of 1915 and the protocol of 1919. I thought that it was unnecessary to reply to this, because our views had already been made clear, but the State Department, after some weeks of consideration, decided to take the occasion to assert again in some detail its position with regard to the rights and duties of the United States under the treaty and the protocol. I delivered the reply on April 6, 1932.[21]

During the last few weeks of 1931 there were relatively few disputes with the Haitian government, partly because the energies of the administration were absorbed in politics. A new Chamber of Deputies and half of the Senate were to be chosen in January 1932. Vincent's opponents, led by Seymour Pradel, were

[21] The president's message was published in State Department *Press Releases*, December 26, 1931, p. 601. For Léger's note of December 22, 1931, and the legation's comments see my dispatch of January 6, 1932, decimal file 838.51A/220. The State Department's reply was printed in *Press Releases*, April 23, 1932, p. 365.

aggressive and some of their candidates had much popular support. We did not feel that we should attempt to supervise the election, and no political group asked us to do so, but the campaign raised problems for the *garde*. We told the *garde* commanders not to execute the local authorities' orders to make arrests which were clearly political. When one of the government's candidates was murdered at Las Caobas on November 14, the government thought that this was the first step in a campaign of terrorism and ordered many arrests including that of Jolibois, who was running for senator against the president's brother. I did not feel that I should countermand an order which the government considered necessary to prevent further murders, especially in view of Jolibois' reputation for erratic and unorthodox conduct. Toward the end of the campaign, however, I insisted that the government issue orders that no arrests be made on election day except in cases of *flagrante delicto*. The masses of the people did not seem greatly interested in the campaign, and there was no serious disorder on election day. Since the registration and voting were controlled by local boards in which the representative of the communal government had the deciding vote, and since the communal authorities were in practice appointed and removed by the president, it was not surprising that the government's candidates won in every district.

During the first months of 1932 there was a welcome change in our personal relations with the Haitian leaders at Port au Prince. Until that time the president and his ministers for foreign affairs had been courteous and the legation staff had been invited to official functions, but we had little informal social contact with Haitians. Few Haitians, however friendly, dared to expose themselves to nationalist criticism by accepting an invitation from an American. The government too often seemed to think that an antagonistic attitude, with recurrent threats of strikes and disorders, would get support from anti-imperialists in the United States and cause the American government to make concessions. This obstructive policy had indeed produced some results, but by the end of 1931 it was probably fairly clear that it was not likely to affect our attitude with respect to the status of the *garde* and the financial services, which was the principal question still pending. The abandonment of the policy became easier, politically, after the Haitianization agreement showed that the United

States was sincere in its desire to reduce its interference in Haiti's internal affairs.

In February 1932 it began to appear that the leaders of the elite had decided to abandon their social boycott of the American official community. We received intimations that there might be a friendly response if we took the initiative in seeking better relations. Rather diffidently, we arranged a large party on Washington's birthday. This was successful, and from then on many Americans had pleasant social contacts even with some of the leaders who had been most hostile. One of those who did most to promote these contacts was Colonel Louis McCarty Little, the brigade commander, whose horse races were enthusiastically attended by crowds of people of both nationalities. The changed atmosphere made the work of the remaining treaty officials much easier. Disagreements about financial questions could usually be settled amicably and there was no further serious effort to interfere with appointments in the *garde*. The president in fact went out of his way to express appreciation of the *garde*'s work and in March he pinned a decoration on General Williams, its commander, at a public ceremony.

The Haitianization of the *garde* was still ahead of the Forbes commission's schedule, but at the end of March Léger proposed that it be speeded up to assure a complete turnover to Haitian officers by the end of 1934. He also asked that the United States promise to withdraw the marine brigade by the end of 1932 and the scientific mission by August 5, 1933, and added that the Haitian government would reserve the right to employ a military mission to complete the training and discipline of the *garde* if this seemed necessary.

The American officials in Haiti thought that this proposal should be seriously considered, insofar as it related to the *garde*, because a military mission with adequate authority would offer some hope for the maintenance of the *garde*'s efficiency. Some members of the government and many other responsible Haitians were worried, as we ourselves were, about what would happen after the American officers left. The effort to keep the *garde* free from political influence had encouraged a rather dangerous spirit of independence among the Haitian officers, and the seizure of power across the border by General Rafael Trujillo at the head of an American-trained military force had set them a bad example. Léger's proposal seemed to be a serious effort to deal with this problem. The State Department was reluctant to make any further commitments about the *garde* or the withdrawal of the marines until the question of financial control after 1936 was settled, but the legation urged that these matters be considered together, because no Haitian government was likely to agree to the financial control that we had to demand unless it could point to concessions obtained in return. Acceleration of the Haitianization of the *garde* and of the withdrawal of the marine brigade would provide such concessions and might save us from having to impose a solution by arbitrary action.

De la Rue had been working for some time on a plan for control of Haiti's finances after 1936. The problem was to give the bondholders the protection which both governments had promised them, and at the same time to make all practicable concessions to the Haitians' desire for greater fiscal independence. After 1936, when nine or ten million dollars of the bonds would still be outstanding, the debt service would consume nearly one-fifth of the government's normal revenue. It seemed essential to retain effective control over the collection of the customs, which were by far the largest source of revenue, and enough control over budget policies and expenditure to assure that funds would be available for the debt service after meeting indispensable government requirements. This control, however, could be given a form less offensive to Haitian pride than the existing arrangements. Some of the powers which the financial adviser exercised under the treaty of 1915 could be given up. The principal substantive change which we recommended was to relinquish control of the collection of the internal revenues. Like the customs receipts, these were pledged for the service of the bonds, but the refusal of the Haitian courts to support the collectors and the unpopularity of the alcohol and tobacco taxes made their collection troublesome. We thought that it would be wise to give up a responsibility that was certain to involve American officials in conflicts with native taxpayers.

The State Department was still inclined to inisist qn maintaining the financial control without essential change, but Secretary Stimson authorized me to submit our plan, with the stipulation that the proposed concessions should be made only if an accord were reached in the immediate future. He also approved a draft agreement for completing the Haitianization of the *garde* and establishing a military mission, to be signed with or after the financial agreement.

Meanwhile, the Haitian Congress was drafting a new constitution to replace that of 1918. The congressmen's first thought was to increase their own powers at the expense of the executive and to extend their own terms. There was an acute political crisis when the president blocked these efforts by suspending the session, but after a few days a compromise allowed the session to be resumed. Contrary to expectations, the new constitution, adopted in July, contained no provisions which seriously affected American interests. It asserted Haiti's sovereignty over Navassa Island, which the United States claimed under the Guano Act and where we had a lighthouse, but the American government avoided what would have been a futile argument by making merely a formal reservation of its rights. The much criticized article permitting resident foreigners to own land in Haiti was retained in a slightly less liberal form, although we made no effort to discourage its elimination. As a matter of fact, the hoped-for influx of foreign capital to develop Haiti's agricultural resources had never materialized, and foreigners had acquired little land since 1918.

At least partly in an effort to improve relations with the Congress, Vincent accepted Léger's resignation in July. Albert Blanchet, the new foreign minister, accepted our proposals about the *garde* and the financial administration as a basis for negotiations and we moved rapidly toward an agreement. The Haitians became more anxious to reach a settlement when they began to realize that Franklin D. Roosevelt, Assistant Secretary of the Navy in 1915, who had once said publicly that he had written the 1918 constitution, would probably be the next president of the United States. Even the nationalists, who could not foresee the Good Neighbor Policy, began to urge the government to reach a settlement while Hoover was still in office.

Blanchet pointed out, however, that the Haitian Congress would be unlikely to approve a treaty which extended American financial control beyond 1936 without bringing any immediate benefit to Haiti. He asked that the new treaty abrogate some of the objectionable features of the treaty of 1915 and put into effect immediately the modified plan of financial control. The State Department somewhat reluctantly agreed to this, and we signed a new treaty at Port au Prince on September 3, 1932. The articles of the 1915 treaty under which the recently Haitianized treaty

337

services and the claims commission had been established would be abrogated at once. Those dealing with the financial administration and the *garde* would be abrogated on December 31, 1934 and replaced by two protocols designated A and B. The only substantive provisions of the original treaty which would remain in effect until 1936 were Article I, in which the United States promised to aid Haiti in the development of its resources and the improvement of its financial administration; Article XI, in which Haiti agreed not to alienate any of her territory or to enter into any treaty that might impair her independence; and Article XIV, which authorized the contracting parties to take any steps necessary for the full attainment of the objects of the treaty and provided that the United States would aid in the preservation of Haitian independence and the maintenance of a government adequate for the protection of life, property, and individual liberty.

The two protocols would continue to govern relations between the two countries after 1936. Under Protocol A the *garde* was to be completely Haitianized by December 31, 1934. The United States was to withdraw the marine brigade and the scientific mission at that time, or earlier if practicable. To complete the training of the *garde*, the president of the United States would designate a military mission, with powers to be defined in a separate agreement. The Haitian government promised to maintain strict discipline in the *garde* under its existing regulations so long as any bonds issued under the protocol of 1919 were outstanding.

Protocol B provided that a "fiscal representative" and a "deputy fiscal representative" appointed by the president of Haiti on nomination by the president of the United States should collect Haiti's customs duties and see to the debt service from December 31, 1934 until the bonds issued under the protocol of 1919 were retired. The employees of the customs service were to be commissioned by the president of Haiti but they were to be appointed and removed on the fiscal representative's recommendation. The internal revenue service would be completely Haitianized, but the fiscal representative would have authority to supervise its operations. He would also assist in preparing the budget, which the government promised to keep in balance. Except for the amounts required for the debt service and the expense of collecting the customs, all government funds would be deposited in the national bank to the credit of the Haitian government, instead of remaining as hitherto in the custody of the financial adviser. All disbursements, however, would continue to be made by checks prepared by the service of payments in the fiscal representative's office.

The treaty would have reduced considerably the control still exercised by the United States under the treaty of 1915. The *garde* would have been turned over to Haitian officers and the marine brigade and the scientific mission would have been withdrawn at least sixteen months before the treaty of 1915 expired. The Haitian government would have more freedom in deciding what taxes it would impose and where it would spend the funds remaining after the debt service had been met, and would control the politically important internal revenue service. The fiscal agent's power to prevent illegal expenditures through the service of payments should have been less objectionable than the existing arrangement by which he passed on the expediency as well as the legality of each order of payment.[22]

When I resigned as minister immediately after signing the treaty, it was generally expected that the Haitian Congress would ratify it. The president had some enemies in the Senate, but all of the deputies had been elected in January 1932 as supporters of the administration. Though they had quarreled with the president about the new constitution, better relations had since been restored. There was little criticism when the terms of the treaty were made public. President Vincent, however, made no effort to line up support for it, and when it was submitted to the Congress some of the leaders decided to humiliate him by opposing it with a show of patriotic indignation. No one dared to seem unpatriotic, and on September 15 the Congress, sitting in joint session, rejected the treaty by a unanimous vote.

The treaty of 1915 thus remained in force. The State Department rejected the Haitian government's proposal for a new agreement dealing only with the *garde* and the withdrawal of the marines and insisted that it could make no further concessions with regard to the financial administration. It even intimated that the Haitianization of the *garde* might be delayed, but soon realized that this was unwise. There was no immediate change in policy after the Roosevelt administration took office.[23] The Haitian

[22] For the text see *Foreign Relations, 1932*, Vol. V, pp. 671-680.

[23] See Latin American division's memoranda of March 31, and April 3, and Secretary Hull's telegraphic instruction of April 13, 1933, *Foreign Relations, 1933*, Vol. V, pp. 735-738.

government for some time professed to hope that the treaty signed in September would eventually be ratified, but by June 1933 there was clearly little hope for congressional approval, so that the questions still pending would have to be dealt with in some other way.

Fortunately, relations between Haitians and Americans continued to improve. Norman Armour, the new American minister, soon won the Haitians' confidence. Questions arising in the treaty services seemed to cause little friction, and even the question of the budget, which had made so much trouble in 1931, was settled amicably in the fall of 1932. When the State Department finally decided that the major problems still outstanding might be dealt with by an executive agreement—a procedure which it had refused to consider a year earlier—it was possible to negotiate a final settlement.

On August 7, 1933, Armour and Blanchet signed an executive agreement which provided for the termination of the American occupation. Progress achieved during the past eleven months made it possible to advance the date for the complete Haitianization of the *garde* to October 1, 1934, and the marine brigade and the scientific mission were to be withdrawn within thirty days thereafter. A military mission would be established if the president of Haiti thought it desirable. The treaty of 1915 would remain in force until 1936, because it could not be abrogated by executive action, but the United States in effect agreed not to exercise all of the powers which it had claimed under the treaty. A fiscal representative, with not more than eighteen American assistants, would take over the services of the financial adviser-general receiver in January 1, 1934, a year earlier than the unratified treaty had contemplated. With a few verbal changes to make it more palatable to the Haitians, the agreement provided for the same financial control which Protocol B would have established.[24]

The Haitian political leaders and even the nationalist press greeted the agreement with approval.[25] Sidney de la Rue, whom the Roosevelt administration left in office at the request of the Haitian government,[26] became fiscal representative. The Haitian-

[24] The text is printed *ibid.*, pp. 755-761.

[25] See Armour's telegram of August 9, 1933, reporting conversations with several of the leaders, and Heath's dispatch of August 14, transmitting comments of the Haitian press, 838.51/2689, 2695.

[26] State Department *Press Releases*, June 10, 1933, p. 427.

ization of the *garde* was completed ahead of schedule, in August 1934, and the marines and the scientific mission were withdrawn immediately afterward. The government did not ask for a military mission.

The Haitians' attitude changed when anti-imperialist critics in the United States accused the Roosevelt administration of prolonging the occupation of Haiti in order to collect debts. Within a few months President Vincent was urging further changes in the system of financial control. The American government politely turned him down at that time, but a new agreement signed in 1941 abolished the office of fiscal representative and entrusted most of its functions to the National Bank of Haiti, which was reorganized with three American and three Haitian directors and an American as manager. Nearly $8,000,000 of the 1922 bonds were still outstanding at that time because low coffee prices and later the war in Europe caused the government to suspend all but token payments into the sinking fund. In 1947 the government redeemed its bonds with the proceeds of an internal loan and the United States ceased to have any responsibility for Haiti's foreign debt.

Chapter Ten

NON-INTERVENTION IN CUBA,
1925-1933

General Crowder's mission to Cuba in 1921-1923 had been criticized as an improper interference in Cuba's affairs. Ten years later the American government's failure to interfere to put an end to Machado's dictatorship met with even more criticism. The State Department's refusal to act was partly a response to anti-intervention sentiment in the United States, but the history of our relations with Cuba during the last years of the Hoover administration showed that many of those who opposed intervention in principle would not support a hands-off policy when their indignation was aroused by reports of oppression and cruelty in a nearby country.

During his first years in office, Gerardo Machado seemed one of the best presidents that Cuba had had. He was a good administrator and he corrected some of the bad practices that characterized Zayas' regime. Before his election he announced that he would try to make the Platt amendment inoperative, not by defying the American government but by conducting such a good government in Cuba that there would be no occasion for threatening notes from Washington.[1] Francis White thought in 1926 that Machado had "done wonders" in putting the government's finances on a sounder basis and in trying to eradicate graft, and that "he deserves all the support and encouragement we can give him." White was especially pleased because he thought that the State Department's refusal to intervene in Cuba during the Zayas administration had made the Cubans realize their own responsibility for improving their government. If the trend continued, he thought that the country should be on the way to "decent independent government" within the next ten or fifteen years.[2]

As White implied, political conditions in Cuba still left much to be desired. General Crowder, in commenting on Machado's

---

[1] Crowder to Hughes, August 14, 1924, 837.00/2539.

[2] White to Herbert Stabler, May 15, 1926, Francis White papers, Box 35.

idea of making the Platt amendment inoperative by giving the American government no occasion to invoke it, pointed out in 1926 that "liberty and property" would not really be secure in Cuba until there had been basic reforms in the courts and in the provincial and municipal governments.[3] As a matter of fact, many of the evils against which Crowder had inveighed in his famous memoranda persisted. Graft was perhaps less blatant and omnipresent, but even the highest officials continued to profit in various ways from their control of the government and especially from the national lottery, where the old abuses continued unchecked. It was chiefly through the distribution of *colecturías* that Machado was able to hold the support of his followers and to win over many of the conservatives so that he had no real opposition during his first term.[4] This gave the political situation an apparent stability which made it seem less necessary to press for reform.

The worst problem that confronted Machado during his first term was the bad situation in the sugar industry. Cuba's livelihood still depended on the sale of the greater part of her sugar in the United States, where the reciprocity treaty of 1902 gave her a decisive advantage over all other foreign producers. Sugar prices rose in the early 1920's, after the post-war depression, but beet growing in Europe was reviving and tariff increases in the United States in 1921 and 1922 encouraged production in the Philippines and Hawaii and Puerto Rico. By 1925 the price of Cuban sugar was falling below the cost of production. The Cuban government's efforts to cope with the situation by restricting production and by crop limitation agreements with other countries did little good.

In March 1926 Machado asked Crowder to find out whether the American government would be willing to consider a revision of the reciprocity treaty to encourage the importation of Cuban sugar into the United States. The State Department replied that it would take up the matter with the Department of Commerce and the tariff commission. It warned Crowder to express no opinion about a revision until he received further instructions, but the Cuban government pressed for a reply and Crowder reported that there was so much public interest in the matter that a refusal

[3] Crowder to Kellogg, Sept. 2, 1926, 711.37/85.
[4] Guggenheim's dispatch of March 16, 1933, 837.513/125, describes the operation of the lottery under Machado.

by the United States to negotiate would hurt the Cuban government's prestige. The State Department said that it was still awaiting the views of other departments. When Orestes Ferrara, the Cuban ambassador, attempted to push the matter, Secretary Kellogg told him that it was doubtful whether any revision of the reciprocity treaty would be approved by the United States Senate.

Ferrara nevertheless made concrete proposals for changes in the reciprocity treaty, but he got no reply for several months. In June 1928 he was informed, rather curtly, that his proposals seemed to be based on the assumption that the reciprocity treaty benefited the United States more than it did Cuba, an assumption which a report from the tariff commission showed to be wrong. Kellogg evidently did not want to become involved in the political conflict which any effort to change the reciprocity treaty would have aroused. In 1921 and 1922 there had been fierce battles over the sugar tariff between the beet growers in the United States on the one hand and the New York banks which controlled much of Cuba's sugar production and exporters who wished to sell goods to Cuba on the other. The beet growers, with the support of Senator Smoot, the chairman of the Senate Finance Committee, had had the best of the contest.

Machado received kinder treatment in connection with his ambitious public works program, which included the construction of a central highway from Habana to Santiago and a new capitol in Habana. A law enacted in July 1925 created a number of special taxes for this and provided that the work be carried on from the product of the taxes, without resort to loans.[5] This last provision was troublesome, because the $15,000,000 each year which the taxes were expected to produce would not be enough to carry out the program as rapidly as the government wished. Machado got around it in January 1927 by obtaining an advance of $10,000,000 from the Chase National Bank, to be repaid out of the public works taxes as they were collected. He maintained that this was not a loan. The State Department thought that it was an increase in the public debt, about which the United States should be consulted under the Platt amendment, but since it did not want to seem to interfere it told Crowder to say that it saw no reason to object and would not ask that it be formally consulted.

[5] For the text, see Crowder's dispatch of July 31, 1925, 837.15/19.

The ambassador reported that Machado was much gratified by the department's attitude.[6]

Machado could have gone down in history as one of Cuba's best presidents if he had been content to retire at the end of his first term in 1929. During the electoral campaign in 1924 and again after his inauguration, he had declared that he would not seek a second term. In March 1927, however, he let it be known that he had changed his mind. He thought, and General Crowder was inclined to agree with him, that a majority of the Cuban people would wish him to continue in office and that he should do so to assure the success of his public works program.[7] There was no legal obstacle to his reelection. Crowder was disturbed, however, when he learned that the president and his supporters were secretly planning not to have an election but to extend the terms of the president and of members of congress then in office by a constitutional amendment. He thought that this would meet with opposition in Cuba, and he suggested that the State Department discuss the project "emphatically" with Machado during the president's impending visit to Washington.[8]

The State Department did not seem greatly concerned. Stokely Morgan, the new chief of the Latin American division, thought that the extension of the presidential term would be "somewhat objectionable" but that the United States should not object unless the matter was handled in a way that seemed likely to cause trouble.[9] When he escorted Machado from Key West to Washington on April 20-22, he discussed the proposed constitutional amendments and expressed some misgivings about them. He suggested that a normal election would be better but Machado replied that he had always opposed the reelection of a president and that an election would cause expense and disturbances. He said however that he had not yet fully made up his mind.[10] On April 23 Machado explained the proposed amendments to President Coolidge, saying that he wished to have his term extended only for two years. Coolidge replied that the American govern-

[6] Kellogg to Crowder, Dec. 11, 1926, 837.154/59, and Crowder to Kellogg, Dec. 13, 837.154/64.

[7] For Crowder's views see his personal letter to Kellogg, Feb. 14, 1927, 837.00/3637.

[8] Crowder to Kellogg, April 16, 1927, 837.00/2646.

[9] Morgan's memorandum to Kellogg, April 11, 1927, 837.00/2681.

[10] Morgan's memorandum of April 25, 1927, 837.00/2655.

ment's views would be expressed through Ambassador Crowder, but that the amendments were a matter for the Cuban people and their government to decide.

The State Department could not approve a project so clearly inconsistent with the principles of republican government, but it wanted to avoid interference in Cuba's internal affairs. It wrote Crowder in May that "for reasons of policy the department does not consider that in the circumstances it would be justified in raising any objections to these amendments," but it authorized the ambassador, if Machado consulted him, to explain his own views orally and informally. It said that it understood that Crowder's views were in accord with those of the department. Crowder discussed the amendments with Machado and other officials just before his final departure from Habana. On June 16 the Cuban ambassador was called to the State Department to discuss the matter further with the secretary and Crowder and Francis White, who had just returned to Washington as assistant secretary of state in charge of Latin American affairs. Some changes were made in the proposed amendments as a result of these discussions. Machado's term was to be extended only until 1930, with a proviso prohibiting his immediate reelection. The senators' term was to be nine years, instead of twelve, and the deputies' six years. On June 21, 1927 Machado signed a bill authorizing the submission of the amendments to a constitutent assembly.

As Crowder had anticipated, Machado's scheme for remaining in office aroused opposition. The administration had already had some trouble with the students at the University of Habana and with the labor unions. Several labor leaders had been imprisoned or exiled and some of them, it was said, had been murdered by the police. Machado still had the support of the regular party organizations, but when it became clear that he planned to remain in office, several liberals and conservatives whose support he had not been able to buy formed a new party, called the *unión nacionalista*, under the leadership of Carlos Mendieta.

Machado, confronted for the first time by a serious threat to his power, made it clear that he would not permit any effective opposition. A meeting called by the students in April to discuss the proposed constitutional amendments was roughly broken up by the police. The police also interfered with meetings of the *unión nacionalista* and suppressed the newspaper which it tried to publish. The opposition leaders were kept under surveillance and some of them were arrested or forced to leave the country. Nevertheless Machado's position seemed to grow stronger during the latter part of 1927. He still had the support of most of the other political leaders and he dominated the Congress.

The United States was represented by chargés d'affaires for several months after General Crowder left Habana in May 1927. Crowder's successor, appointed in November, was Noble Brandon Judah, a lawyer from Chicago who had had no previous diplomatic experience. The choice of a political appointee suggested that the American government did not intend to continue the close surveillance of Cuba's affairs which Crowder had thought necessary. In December, in fact, when the Cuban Congress passed an amnesty bill, an officer in the Latin American division commented that the effect would be bad and that Crowder would probably remonstrate with Machado if he were there; but suggested that it would be better to avoid antagonizing the Cuban Congress and arousing criticism of foreign interference at a time when a new ambassador was going to Habana and a Pan American conference was about to take place there. Assistant Secretary White concurred.[11]

The constituent assembly was chosen on March 5, 1928, in an apathetic election in which the *unión nacionalista* did not participate. Under the constitution, the assembly apparently could only approve or reject the amendments proposed by Congress, but when it met Machado had changed the text to provide for a presidential election in 1928 and to exempt the president then elected from the prohibition against reelection for a third term. The terms of the president and members of Congress were lengthened. A committee of the assembly proposed that the new president serve for eight years, but there was so much newspaper criticism that the term was reduced to six years. Ambassador Judah and the State Department's solicitor thought as many Cuban lawyers did that the modification of the text voted by Congress was unconstitutional.

There seems to have been some difference of opinion about the position which the United States should take. Francis White evidently did not think that it should acquiesce unquestioningly in Machado's plan to perpetuate his tenure of the presidency. In

[11] MacVeagh's memorandum of Dec. 28, 1927, attached to Curtis' dispatch of Dec. 16, 837.00/2689.

answer to a question asked by Ambassador Ferrara, he made it clear that he thought that the convention had no right to modify the amendments voted by Congress. He said however that the American government had as yet taken no official position. Judah, on the other hand, thought that the American government should not object. ". . . in my judgement," he wrote, "the United States ought not, at this time, to take the responsibility of maintaining that it, and not the Supreme Court of Cuba, is the proper interpreter of the acts of the Cuban Congress, or of the Cuban Constitutional Convention, or of the candidacy by the authority of the exact wording of the amended constitution of any presidential candidate." In a personal letter to White, he argued that Machado's administration seemed to be by far the best that Cuba had had and that no one equally good was in sight to succeed him. Secretary Kellogg did not wish to interfere, and White wrote Judah that the United States would not raise any question about the amendments on its own initiative unless a serious political situation developed.[12]

The State Department showed an equal unwillingness to interfere when Machado proposed in May 1928 to borrow $40-50,000,000 to continue work on the central highway. The loan was to be repaid from the proceeds of the public works taxes after 1931. This raised a more serious question than the earlier short-term advance had raised. Article II of the Platt amendment provided that Cuba should not contract any debt which could not be served from the ordinary revenues after meeting the current expenses of the government, and the United States had insisted in the past that it should be consulted in each case where the government contracted a loan to make sure that the transaction met this requirement. It was not clear that Machado's project did meet it, because the government's ordinary revenues were falling off and there was talk of diverting the proceeds of the public works taxes to cover the deficit. It was clear however that any demand for prior consultation would be resented. To avoid seeming to raise the question the State Department told the chargé d'affaires at Habana that it would like to have information about the project to be used in answering inquiries from Ameri-

[12] See White's letters to Judah, May 17, June 4, and June 9, 1928, in his papers, Box 5. For the solicitor's opinion, see 837.011/35, 36, 41. Judah's views were expressed in his dispatch of May 31, 1928, 837.011/29, and in his letter to White of May 31, which is in White's papers, Box 9.

can banks which would consult it before undertaking the loan. When the Chase Bank did consult it, the department told the bank and also the Cuban government that it did not wish to raise any objection to the transaction. Ambassador Judah was authorized to say orally that any use of public works funds for ordinary expenses would create a bad impression, but Judah thought it better not to make this statement because the diversion of the public works funds had already been approved by the Cuban Congress. In June 1928, the Cuban Congress approved a contract by which the Chase Bank agreed to lend the government $60,000,000 at 5½%. At the same time it amended the public works law to abrogate the prohibition against loans.

Machado had no difficulty in bringing about his reelection. He was nominated by all three officially recognized political parties. This would have been impossible under Crowder's 1919 electoral law, but the law had been changed in 1920 to permit Zayas to run on the conservative as well as the popular ticket. The provision of the Crowder law which required that the governing bodies of the political parties be renewed every two years had been ignored in practice, and was changed in 1925, so that the party machinery remained in the hands of persons whose support Machado had purchased in one way or another. Menocal and Zayas, the heads of the conservative and popular parties, were said to have received great sums from the national treasury.[13] Another amendment to the electoral law, adopted in 1925, made it almost impossible for a new party to obtain a place on the ballot and prevented the *unión nacionalista* from nominating a candidate. The embassy reported that the public seemed to take little interest in the election, which was held in November 1928.

Charles Curtis, who was in charge while Judah was on leave, thought that the embassy should not congratulate Machado on his victory. A year earlier Curtis had thought that Machado was giving Cuba "one of the most beneficial administrations of Cuban history,"[14] but he now felt that the president had "developed into a Latin American dictator of a type not far removed from the worst." Curtis said that Machado had ordered the murder of at least one political opponent, that he was using the power of the government for his own enrichment, and that he controlled the press, partly by bribery and partly by intimidation. His reelec-

---

[13] Curtis to Kellogg, Oct. 29, 1928, 837.00/2714.
[14] See his dispatch of Nov. 23, 1927, 71OF/149.

tion under the recent constitutional amendments was generally considered illegal, and Curtis thought that the American government should not seem to approve what was being done. The State Department, however, instructed him to deliver the usual formal message of congratulation.[15] A departure from the customary practice would have implied disapproval of what Machado was doing, and a public expression of disapproval could only have been regarded as an interference in Cuba's internal politics. The department probably thought that Curtis exaggerated the evil aspects of Machado's regime, because it had been getting a very different picture from Ambassador Judah and from American businessmen in Cuba.

Machado's conduct had as yet attracted little unfavorable attention in the American press. The *New York Times* said editorially on November 3, 1928, that the president's reelection promised continued stability in Cuba and good relations with the United States. By the end of 1928, however, many people in the United States were beginning to think that the American government should do something about the situation in Cuba. The American Federation of Labor had been concerned for some time about the imprisonment and alleged killing of Cuban labor leaders and many liberal-minded observers were shocked by reports about the government's treatment of its opponents. The situation grew worse in January 1929 when there were many political arrests and when the radical Cuban student leader Juan Antonio Mella was murdered in Mexico under circumstances that cast suspicion on the Cuban government.

The State Department's own misgivings about the situation increased in March 1929 when a bill providing for the severe punishment of anyone who attempted to bring about foreign intervention was presented to the Cuban Congress. Judah was instructed to tell Machado that this was an affront to the United States and a challenge to its treaty rights. He was to point out that the United States could not fulfill its duties under the permanent treaty unless it had free access to information about conditions in Cuba and that citizens of Cuba would be the most important source of such information. The ambassador was also authorized, unless he saw some serious objection, to say that the

[15] Curtis to Kellogg, Sept. 27, Oct. 29, and Nov. 2, and Kellogg to Curtis, Nov. 3, 1928, 837.00/2710, 2714, 2713.

United States' rights of intervention in Cuba were not created by the Platt amendment but dated back to the general obligations which the United States assumed before the world by expelling Spain from Cuba and turning the government over to the Cuban people. Judah, perhaps wisely, refrained from making this last statement, which the Cuban government could hardly have accepted without an argument. When he read the rest of the department's instruction to Machado, the president promised to see that the bill did not become law.[16]

The increasingly alarming newspaper reports about conditions in Cuba forced the State Department to consider whether it should follow its usual practice and designate a special representative to attend Machado's inauguration in May. When Francis White wrote informally to ask Judah's opinion about this, the ambassador replied that there was no reign of terror; that Machado was a dictator but there had been no political executions or exilings, and the government seemed pretty generally popular.[17] In a subsequent telegram, Judah referred to the appointment of the American Minister to Ecuador as special ambassador to attend the inauguration in that country and argued that a failure to take similar action in Cuba could only be regarded as an expression of disapproval of Machado's regime.[18] White recommended to the secretary that Judah be designated as special ambassador for the occasion. Machado's reelection, he said, was "probably unconstitutional" but it would probably be unwise to raise any question about it unless the United States were prepared to intervene. If we did not intervene, we would have to work with Machado for six years and it would be better to have him as friendly as possible.[19]

Rueben Clark, the undersecretary, agreed with White that any interference in Cuba's affairs would cause a bad reaction in other Latin American countries, but he argued that the peculiar nature of our relations with Cuba made it unwise to ignore the really serious situation which was said to be developing there. The

[16] Judah to Stimson, March 21, 1929, 837.00/2730; Stimson to Judah, April 23, 1929, and Judah to Stimson May 2, 1929, *Foreign Relations, 1929,* Vol. II, pp. 894, 896.

[17] White to Judah, April 1, 1929, Francis White papers Box 5, and Judah to White, April 12, *ibid.,* Box 9.

[18] Judah to Stimson, April 22, 1929, 837.001 M 18/24.

[19] Memorandum of April 25, 1929, 837.001 M 18/34.

United States had a responsibility to see that its power was not used to support corrupt and despotic rule and if the accusations against Machado were true it was questionable whether the United States should continue to support him. Clark thought that the appointment of a special representative to the inauguration would be regarded as an expression of approval. He thought the United States should make a full investigation, but not through Judah, in whom he had no confidence.[20]

The secretary decided that Judah should be designated as special ambassador. At the same time, however, Judah was asked to make a comprehensive report on the situation in Cuba and especially on accusations recently made in American newspapers by a Cuban exile named Seigle and on those made in a resolution which Senator Shipstead had presented to the United States Senate in April 1928.[21] This resolution, which called for an investigation of allegations that American citizens were being unlawfully deprived of their property in Cuba, was based on information supplied by Joseph Barlow, who had been trying for several years to establish his claim to the ownership of a valuable tract of land in Habana. The embassy at Habana had not supported the claim because Barlow had not exhausted his legal remedies in Cuba and because his case was not very strong. He had bought into the property when he knew that the title was under litigation. Failing to obtain diplomatic support, and convinced that he could not obtain justice in the Cuban courts, Barlow had asked help from Senator Shipstead. The senator's resolution had attracted little attention when it was introduced, but some months later, when hearings were held on it, Barlow's charges were given much publicity.

Judah, in reply to the department's instruction, said that practically all of the charges in the Seigle articles and the Shipstead resolution were either untrue or unproved. He thought that Cuban public opinion was not greatly concerned about the illegality of the recent constitutional amendments. It was even less concerned about the alleged terrorism, which, if it existed at all, was directed against persons who were preparing acts of violence. The government was permitting far greater freedom of the press than it had previously. There was discontent because of

[20] Memorandum of April 26, 1929, 837.00/2749.
[21] Stimson to Judah, April 27, 1929, 837.00/2731.

the bad economic situation, but he saw no sign of any immediate outbreak of disorder.[22]

The ambassador's estimate of the situation probably reflected the views of the Cubans and Americans with whom he came into contact. Machado still had the support of most of the political leaders and the only overt opposition seemed to come from the university students and the *unión nacionalista*. The latter, according to Curtis, who was by no means partial to Machado, had relatively few adherents.[23] The administration's efficiency and the relative decrease in petty graft had made the president popular in the Cuban and American business communities. In September 1929, when the Senate Committee on Foreign Relations at Washington was considering the subcommittee's report on the Shipstead resolution, the American Chamber of Commerce and the American Club at Habana and the Cuban Chamber of Commerce in the United States all sent communications to the State Department denying the charges which were being made against Machado.[24] These testimonials were perhaps not wholly spontaneous, but they probably represented the views of most of the signatories.

Stimson told the foreign relations committee, and told the press, that the State Department had no information which would substantiate the charges of misgovernment contained in the Shipstead resolution. This statement, like many which secretaries of state have to make, was not wholly candid, but the secretary probably felt that it was justified by the embassy's reports. As a result of the hearings, the foreign relations committee seems to have been convinced that there was at least no occasion for American intervention in Cuba. Senator Borah, however, asked the secretary to do something to help Barlow, who had convinced the committee that he had been badly treated. By this time Barlow's much publicized complaints were arousing unfriendly feeling toward Cuba in the United States and anti-American feeling in Cuba, where his criticism of the Cuban courts was resented. Ambassador Harry F. Guggenheim, who was appointed to succeed Judah in October 1929, was consequently

[22] Judah to Stimson, May 10, 1929, 837.00/2747. See also Judah's letter to White, April 30, 1929, Francis White papers, Box 9.

[23] Curtis to Stimson, Nov. 20, 1929, 837.00/2776.

[24] 837.00/2759, 2760, 2762.

asked to make a new study of the case, and turned the matter over to his legal adviser, Philip Jessup, whose investigation confirmed the opinion that there was no ground for diplomatic intervention. In the hope of disposing of the matter, however, the embassy proposed an impartial arbitration. The other claimants accepted this proposal but Barlow rejected it.

The new ambassador had had Latin American experience as executive director of the Chile Copper Company and had taken a prominent part in diplomatic activities connected with international aviation. He seemed to be energetic and ambitious to make a success of his mission. Besides Jessup, he had on his staff Grosvenor Jones, a former chief of the finance and investment division of the Bureau of Foreign and Domestic Commerce, to act as economic adviser. He was not expected to make any radical changes in the embassy's relations with the Cuban government. The State Department was worried about what was going on in Cuba, but it saw nothing in the situation to justify active interference or even a refusal to cooperate with Machado in matters in which both governments were interested.

This was evident in the department's attitude when the Cuban government decided to resort to long-term borrowing to complete the public works program. Without new financing it would be necessary to suspend work on the central highway, which would have meant the loss of much of the money already spent on the road and would have left thousands of men without employment. The Chase Bank proposed in January 1930 to issue $80,000,000 in 5½%, fifteen-year bonds, of which $40,000,000 would be sold to refund advances already made by the bank and $40,000,000 would be held as security for a new short-term credit of $20,000,000. After Jones investigated the government's financial condition, and reported that there was no reason to object to the loan under the terms of the Platt amendment, the State Department told the Chase Bank that it saw no occasion to object and had Guggenheim inform Machado that it had done so. Again, the American government had sought to preserve its treaty rights without compelling the Cuban government to recognize them explicitly.

This arrangement made it possible to complete the central highway early in 1931, but it proved costly to all concerned. When the new short-term credit was exhausted, it was impracticable to market the second $40,000,000 of bonds, and Warren

Brothers, who were building the road, were compelled to take treasury notes in payment for the rest of their work. After Machado fell in 1933 the new government stopped payment not only on the Chase credit and the contractors' treasury notes but also on the bonds which had been sold to the public. Several years passed before the indebtedness was adjusted.

The continuation of work on the central highway only partially offset the effects of the steadily deteriorating situation in the sugar industry, and both economic and political conditions continued to grow worse. In November 1929, the American military attaché at Habana reported that some of the leading American businessmen and some anti-governemnt Cubans thought that Machado had passed the peak of his power and that the pendulum of public opinion was swinging slowly against him. Until a short time before, everyone had spoken of the president "with reverence," but now there was much criticism of him and his supporters and of their private business ventures, which included two newspapers and a bank and several importing and contracting firms.[25] Ambassador Guggenheim also thought that the situation was becoming worse. Like Judah, he was convinced that the increasing discontent arose more from economic hardship than from resentment at the president's dictatorial conduct. In April 1930, in an effort to help, he sent the president a study which Jones had made discussing the precarious state of the government's finances and urging the need for economies. Machado thanked him courteously but paid little attention to his recommendations.

Early in 1930 Machado seemed disposed to allow somewhat more freedom of political discussion. The *unión nacionalista*, which had been carrying on its propaganda through clandestinely circulated fly-sheets and newspapers which were suppressed as soon as they appeared, began to receive some notice in the more established newspapers. In January the opposition leaders asked permission to hold a meeting in one of the Habana parks. Machado replied by prohibiting all political meetings during the cane grinding period, but the Supreme Court declared this decree unconstitutional and permission was granted. When 5-10,000 people attended the meeting on April 19, it was clear that the administration could no longer claim that it had the support of all organized political groups. The meeting passed off without dis-

[25] Report of Major J. J. O'Hara, Nov. 26, 1929, 837.00/2780.

order, but in May the rural police broke up another opposition meeting at Artemisa and four persons were killed.

A few days after this affair, Carlos Mendieta asked Guggenheim to try to bring about an agreement between Machado and the opposition. He said that the *unión nacionalista* wanted a new census, a revision of the electoral law to restore the safeguards which the Crowder law had contained, and a reorganization of the political parties, all of which were still controlled by small groups subservient to Machado. He also demanded that a presidential election be held within the next twelve months. Guggenheim refused to discuss the last point, which would have meant a curtailment of Machado's term, but he offered his mediation to bring about an agreement on the nationalists' other demands. During the next few weeks he negotiated with both sides. Machado seemed willing to agree to the proposed changes in the electoral law but the leaders of the *unión nacionalista* refused to consider any arrangement that did not assure a new presidential election within the next three years. They had always insisted that the extension of Machado's term to 1935 was unconstitutional.

Guggenheim blamed Mendieta's stubbornness for the failure of his efforts, and he suggested that Machado go ahead with electoral reforms on his own initiative. In July 1930 the president asked the Congress to make the proposed changes in the electoral law, in order to permit the *unión nacionalista* to take part in the congressional election scheduled for November. The opposition leaders, however, publicly rejected this proposal and the president permitted its defeat when it came to a vote. Mendieta's friend Antonio González Mendoza, a businessman who had worked closely with Guggenheim in the negotiations, then proposed that the congressional election be postponed until March 1, 1931 and that Machado should promise to resign on May 20 of that year if the nationalists elected a majority of their candidates. Mendoza insistently asked the embassy's support in this effort, but Edward Reed, who was in charge while the ambassador was on leave, refused to go farther than to express a purely personal opinion that the ambassador might use his good offices to encourage both sides to abide by an agreement if one were reached. Nothing came of Mendoza's proposal or of subsequent nationalist demands that the election be postponed.

Public opinion in the United States was becoming more concerned about the situation in Cuba, and the State Department was under increasing pressure to do something about it. Some of the anti-imperialists who had condemned the interventions in Haiti and Nicaragua were demanding that the United States intervene to oust Machado.[26] They denounced the State Department for seeming to approve what was evidently becoming an increasingly repressive dictatorship. Guggenheim, because he refused to support the opposition's demand that Machado withdraw and also perhaps because he failed to hide his belief that this demand was unreasonable, was accused of supporting the dictatorship. In the State Department, where I had to deal with the problem as chief of the Latin American division from the spring of 1929 until the summer of 1930, we were worried about the situation but we could not see that there was much that the United States could do. An expression of disapproval of Machado's conduct, if it were vigorous enough to have any effect, could only have encouraged disorder and would probably have made the situation worse. After years of trying to cut down interference in the Caribbean states, we were not prepared to recommend that the United States intervene either by diplomatic pressure or by force to oust an established government.

It could be argued that the Platt amendment, which provided that the United States might exercise a right to intervene for the preservation of Cuban independence and the maintenance of a government adequate for the protection of life, property, and individual liberty, imposed a special obligation on the American government with respect to Cuba. Guggenheim discussed this aspect of the situation when he came to Washington for conference in September 1930. He suggested that the embassy make a thorough study of economic and political conditions so as to be able when asked to give expert unofficial advice, but he thought that the American representatives had no right or duty to go farther than this unless there was a complete breakdown of government in Cuba or an attack from abroad. He mentioned the Cubans' sensitiveness about the Platt amendment, and pointed out that Secreatry of War Root, when the amendment was under

[26] Senator King of Utah, for example, in a telephone conversation with me in the summer of 1930, angrily insisted that we force Machado out. I was then still in the Latin American division.

consideration, had assured the Cuban constitutional convention that the intervention which the amendment authorized was

> not synonymous with intermeddling or interference with the affairs of the Cuban Government but the formal action of the Government of the United States, based upon just and substantial grounds, for the preservation of Cuban independence and the maintenance of a government adequate for the protection of life, property, and individual liberty and adequate for discharging the obligations with respect to Cuba imposed by the Treaty of Paris on the United States.[27]

Guggenheim thought that the American government should be guided by this interpretation. He told Stimson that Machado was in control in Cuba, with the help of the army, but that economic conditions were bad. The secretary was unwilling to approve any detailed statement of policy, in advance of contingencies that might arise, but he said that he would be guided by Root's interpretation of the Platt amendment.[28]

The secretary had not known previously about Root's assurances to the Cuban constitutional convention.[29] During the past twenty years the State Department had frequently taken the position that the Platt amendment authorized and in fact obligated the United States to attempt by advice and diplomatic pressure to discourage policies which might create a situation where intervention would be necessary. During the Taft administration, and between 1919 and 1923, there had been much "intermeddling or interference" in Cuba's internal affairs. The State Department's policy since 1923, however, had been close in practice to that envisioned by Root, and it was perhaps for this reason that there had been no occasion for the secretary's advisers to tell him about Root's telegram. After 1930 the telegram was frequently cited in replies to critics who urged intervention. Stimson read it to the correspondents at his press conference on October 2 and said that the United States had never intervened in Cuba, except in 1906 when there was no government in the island.

[27] This telegram was printed in the *Report of the Secretary of War, 1901,* p. 48.

[28] See Guggenheim's memorandum to the secretary, Sept. 17, 1930, 711.37/148, and Stimson's *Diary*, Sept. 18, 1930.

[29] On Nov. 25, 1930, Mr. Stimson wrote in his diary that he "had recently discovered" Root's message to the constitutional convention.

A few days later, when President Hoover expressed concern about reports from Cuba, the secretary told him that there seemed to be no occasion for American intervention. Machado's administration, after a good beginning, had been disappointing, but the president had the support of the army and there was no question of anarchy or of failure to protect American life and property. Hoover seemed to approve of the policy which the State Department was following.[30]

In Cuba, the leaders of the *unión nacionalista* continued to insist that the congressional elections be postponed, but the embassy did not support their demands and Machado paid little attention to them. The elections were held on November 1, 1930, with no more violence than was customary. They were of more than usual importance, for under the recent constitutional amendments two-thirds of the senators and half of the representatives were elected, for terms of ten years in the case of most of the senators and of seven years in the case of the representatives. Guggenheim reported that the opposition got a limited response to its efforts to persuade the voters to abstain. Unfortunately the State Department gave this telegram to the press, and it was seized on in Cuba as evidence of the ambassador's partiality to Machado.

The students at the University of Habana, who had opposed Machado's reelection when all but a few of the politicians had acquiesced, were still among the government's most active adversaries. In the hope of discouraging their activities, the government had postponed the opening of the university in September 1930, and on September 30 there had been a clash between the police and about 200 students and sympathizers. It was not clear who fired first, but several students were shot and one of them died the next day. The affair made an exceedingly painful impression in Cuba and abroad. The students continued their agitation in Habana, though the university was kept closed, and students in other cities went on strike in sympathy. In November even the secondary schools had to be closed. Disorderly demonstrations, in which many older people took part, began to occur daily in Habana and the government suspended constitutional guaranatees in the city on November 13. It imposed a press censorship which caused nearly all of the newspapers to suspend publication.

[30] Stimson *Diary*, Oct. 10, 1930.

The disorders decreased as these measures took effect, and in December the government restored constitutional guarantees and reopened the university. It even indicated that it was willing to grant the university the autonomy which the students had been demanding. The students, however, refused to attend classes and forced the rector to resign. They were supported by students in other centers, and there were more demonstrations and riots. The government again suspended constitutional guarantees and closed the university and imprisoned many students. On January 8 there was rioting in the central part of Habana when a group of women assembled near the presidential palace with banners demanding Machado's resignation. Many men joined them and when the police dispersed the crowd five persons were wounded and 70, including 46 women, were arrested. The embassy reported that there were small bomb explosions every day and that social gatherings were often disrupted by tear gas or stink bombs.

Guggenheim still thought that much of the unrest was caused by economic hardship. The situation in the sugar industry was even worse than it had been. The Smoot-Hawley tariff of 1930 had raised the American duty on Cuban sugar to 2 cents per pound. This was less than the domestic growers had demanded, but it increased Cuba's disadvantage in competing with sugar grown under the American flag, and had a psychological effect in Cuba out of all proportion to its real importance. The State Department had been concerned about the proposed increase and also about provisions affecting meat imported from the River Plate countries, and in June 1929, Stimson had sent the president a memorandum warning of the damage which the tariff might do to our relations with Latin America. This apparently had little result. After the tariff passed, the American producers in Cuba tried to bring about an international agreement for the stabilization of the sugar trade, but the growers in the United States and the insular possessions would not participate. The situation in the sugar industry was not improved materially by the Chadbourne plan, under which Cuba entered into a crop restriction agreement with several other sugar-producing countries in February 1931. The political disturbances made economic conditions worse.

Guggenheim was still anxious to help to restore peace. On November 14, 1930, he reported that he was using his "unofficial good offices" for a "modus vivendi" between Machado and Mendieta and ex-President Menocal, who had emerged from political retirement in September and seemed to be seeking to build up an opposition to Machado in the conservative party. The State Department was disturbed at the idea of doing anything to encourage the opposition in Cuba "at this critical time" and urged him to avoid any move that might be interpreted as interference by the United States or by himself personally. The ambassador had in fact already ceased his efforts when this instruction was received, but he was increasingly convinced that something would have to be done. In December he wrote that "the Cuban people are undeniably overwhelmingly opposed to the President, attributing to him the responsibility for the present economic situation,"[31] and on January 20, 1931, he reported that he had told Machado that he would soon face a situation like that which had recently caused the overflow of Leguía in Peru and suggested that the president resume negotiations with his political opponents. Ten days later he wrote personally to Stimson to ask permission to send Machado a letter pointing out that continued repression could only make matters worse and urging the imperative need for a political settlement. Guggenheim thought that both parties were in a mood to compromise. The secretary, however, felt that the proposed action would be inconsistent with the American government's policy of non-interference.[32]

Nevertheless, the secretary could not ignore the evidence that Machado's administration was no longer a government "adequate for the protection of life, property, and individual liberty." Stimson was especially concerned at reports that great numbers of people were being held in prison illegally. He asked the embassy to investigate these, and when Guggenheim reported that he did not think that the government had acted illegally but that it was difficult to obtain full information, the secretary took the matter up on April 10 with the Cuban ambassador. He emphasized the American government's disapproval of illegal arrests and the imprisonment without trial of political opponents, and said that he himself was interested because he would be accused of dereliction in not seeing that Cuba had the sort of government which the Platt amendment contemplated. He especially wanted to

[31] Guggenheim to Stimson, Dec. 11, 1930, 837.00/2927
[32] Copies of the proposed letter and the secretary's reply are attached to Guggenheim's dispatch of March 29, 1931, 837.00/3481.

avoid revolution with its concomitant of possible intervention.[33] The ambassador argued that the hostility to Machado arose chiefly from the economic situation and said that Machado had in fact weakened his position by being too lenient with subversive elements.

During the disturbances in January 1931 Machado had broken off talks with the Cuban leaders who were still trying to find a basis for a political settlement. A few weeks later the talks were resumed and for a time it seemed possible that an agreement might be reached on the basis of a plan put forward by Senator José Manuel Cortina. This contemplated constitutional amendments which would establish a sort of parliamentary system and would reduce the terms of the officials elected in 1928 and 1930. A general election would be held in 1932, and Machado would turn over his office to a successor in May 1933, rather than in May 1935. Machado was apparently willing to agree to the curtailment of his own term and to a two-year reduction in the terms of the recently elected congressmen, but Menocal and Mendieta wanted an election in 1931 and a greater reduction in the terms of the congressmen. Guggenheim told them that it was not practicable to hold an election so soon and urged them to negotiate on the basis of Cortina's plan, but the rivalry between Mendieta and Menocal made it difficult for the opposition leaders to agree among themselves and made progress slow. Guggenheim, though he was instructed not to participate in any way in the negotiations, continued to urge both sides to adopt a conciliatory attitude. The prospect for an agreement did not seem bright when the ambassador went to Washington for consultation in May but there had been some improvement in the general situation. The state of siege had been lifted in all of the provinces except Habana and political prisoners who were being held without formal charges had been released. There had also been a marked decrease in terrorist activities. For the first time in the republic's history, however, there were no ceremonies or public demonstrations on Independence Day, May 20.

At Washington, Guggenheim seems to have persuaded the State Department to approve his taking part in the negotiations between the Cuban factions. A memorandum dated May 19, 1931, prepared by Guggenheim and White and approved by

[33] White's memorandum of April 10, 1931, 837.00/3044. Part of this memorandum is printed in *Foreign Relations, 1931*, Vol. II, p. 51.

Stimson, authorized the ambassador to discuss the political situation with the opposition leaders, but only if they came to him and gave him a written statement indicating their attitude toward a settlement based on the Cortina plan. He was to tell Machado that the State Department had been following the situation with much interest and great concern. It had felt that the constitutional amendments were unwise and unconstitutional, but in accord with its traditional policy it had not wished to go beyond an informal statement, which it had made when its opinion was asked. It would favor the Cortina plan if the terms of the senators and representatives were reduced in a way that satisfied public opinion, and it hoped that a satisfactory solution could be reached on this basis. The ambassador was to have nothing to do with the opposition leaders if they did not put their views in writing; but if they did so and the only point at issue was the date when the congressmen would retire, he might try to reconcile the views of the two parties.

The memorandum also set forth what the United States would do if a revolution occurred. It would send warships to Cuba's ports to protect American and foreign lives, and it would expect any government that existed in Cuba to protect American lives and property rights. The United States would not interfere except for the protection of lives and property but would let the rival factions fight it out so long as there was a government in the island. If the government disappeared, as it did in 1906, a military occupation would have to be considered. This was probably the most explicit statement of policy in the event of a revolution in Cuba that any secretary of state had ever made, and it represented an important departure from the State Department's usual policy of opposing revolution and giving moral support to constituted governments.[34]

When Guggenheim returned to Habana the opposition leaders showed no disposition to go ahead with the Cortina plan. Guggenheim attributed their intransigence largely to the rivalry between Menocal, with his conservative followers, and the liberals who controlled the *unión nacionalista*, but there were undoubtedly other reasons. It was hard for the opposition to accept Machado's continuance in office until 1933, because their whole case against the regime was based on the alleged illegality of his

[34] This memorandum is in the National Archives in the post records of the embassy at Habana (R.G. 84), Vol. 10, Class 800.

election. Furthermore, though the Cortina plan contemplated amendment of the electoral laws and the appointment of a coalition cabinet, there would be no assurance of a really fair election in 1932 so long as Machado remained in the presidency and controlled the army.

Since an agreement seemed impossible, Guggenheim urged Machado to put the Cortina plan into effect by congressional action. He thought that this might satisfy public opinion and deprive the opposition of their chief issue. The president was reluctant to agree to a substantial reduction in the terms of the senators and congressmen and threatened to resign when Guggenheim pressed him. In reporting this conversation, the Ambassador remarked parenthetically that he thought that the threat to resign was a bluff but that anyway the United States could not urge Machado to remain in power to "carry on under the repressive measures and the ill-advised fiscal policies that he will have to pursue unless he solves the political problems of Cuba." He thought that the chief reason for Machado's determination to remain in office was a desire to recoup the large sum which he had allegedly paid Zayas for the presidency.[35]

During the summer of 1931 unemployment was increasing and the unemployed frequently joined with the students in demonstrations which led to clashes with the police and then to more violent demonstrations against police brutality. The opposition leaders were still adamant in their refusal to negotiate on any terms which Guggenheim considered reasonable. They had been hoping that the Supreme Court, which was not wholly subservient to Machado, would declare that the president and Congress had been illegally elected. The court, however, dismissed three suits in which the question was raised. This disappointment made the opposition leaders more desperate, and in the expectation that they would now resort to violence, the government reestablished the press censorship and made many arrests. It nevertheless made a conciliatory gesture when the house of representatives on July 20 approved in principle a series of constitutional reforms based on the Cortina plan, reducing by two years the terms of most of the officials elected in 1928, calling for a general election in November 1932, and establishing a modified

[35] Enclosure to dispatch of May 29, 1931, 837.00/3075. The dispatch but not the enclosure is printed in *Foreign Relations, 1931*, Vol. II, p. 60.

form of parliamentary government.[36] This program, if honestly carried out, might have given the opposition as much as they could reasonably ask.

The opposition leaders, however, still had no confidence in Machado, and on August 9 they started an armed revolt, with small uprisings in several sections of the country. The movement was poorly planned and it met with little popular support. The army, which was loyal to Machado, easily controlled the situation, and within a week both Menocal and Mendieta had been captured with their staffs. A few days later the revolt was over. Machado held many of the rebels in prison for a few months but there were no executions. While the fighting was going on, the United States attempted to enforce its neutrality laws, but it refrained from making any statement in support of the constituted government.

After the revolt, Guggenheim strongly urged Machado to go ahead with the reform program which the house of representatives had been considering. Machado was willing to do so but he would not agree to Guggenheim's suggestion that he announce that he would retire in September 1932 and leave the conduct of new elections in the hands of a vice president chosen by the Supreme Court. He said that he would lose the support of his friends and of the army if he did this. When he did urge the reform program on Congress, he added a proposal that the scope of parliamentary immunity be more clearly defined. This looked like an effort to correct one of the glaring evils in Cuba's political life, but it was calculated to arouse opposition to the whole program in Congress, where the freedom to commit murders and other crimes with impunity was a cherished privilege. The suspicion that the president was not acting in good faith increased when the house of representatives, with his approval, eliminated from the reform program a provision for electing a vice president, so that Machado's successor, if he withdrew, would be the secretary of state. The house approved the program on September 16, but the Senate delayed action on it for another two months. Neither the opposition leaders nor the public in general seemed to take much interest in it, and Machado himself put an end to any hope for a settlement when he announced on Decem-

[36] The proposed reforms are described in a report of the military attaché at Habana dated July 24, 1931, 837.00/3122.

ber 22 that he would remain in office until May 20, 1935. Guggenheim thought that the president had been encouraged to disregard the embassy's pressure to make concessions because the Cuban ambassador in Washington had assured him that the United States would not interfere in Cuba's internal affairs.

The embassy at Habana thought that one reason for the opposition's lack of interest in a settlement was the hope that the government would soon find itself unable to continue the service of its foreign debt, and that a default would compel the United States to intervene.[37] Several million dollars of serial certificates issued to finance work on the central highway would come due on June 30, 1932 and several million more on December 31, 1932. There was also a short-term credit of $20,000,000 due the Chase Bank and its associates. The bank would obviously have to renew this, but it seemed unlikely that the government could pay the serial certificates, which were in the hands of the public, or the service on the bonded debt. A default was averted for the time being, however, when the banks agreed to help the government to meet the payment due in June.

In 1932 the situation in Cuba grew very much worse. When Machado's enemies found that they could not oust the President by political pressure or by armed revolt, they resorted to terrorism. Several secret societies, of which the A.B.C. was the most important, joined with the students in a campaign of sabotage and destruction and in attempts to kill government officials. On January 12 there were twelve bomb explosions in Habana, and on the twenty-fifth the police discovered an automobile loaded with dynamite and nails and glass and arrested three students who admitted that they planned to "blow up Habana." Most of the persons imprisoned after the August revolt were released in January, but in May, when infernal machines were sent to a number of army officers and one was killed, hundreds were again arrested, including the chief leaders of the *unión nacionalista*. Menocal, who took refuge in the Brazilian legation, was permitted to go into exile. Between July and September the chief of the secret police and the president of the Senate and four other prominent politicians were murdered. The army and the police responded with harsh measures of repression. Persons accused of acts of terrorism were tried by military courts, or in many cases, appar-

[37] Reed to Stimson, Sept. 14, 1931, 837.00/3161.

ently, were shot without trial. The American military attaché reported that the authorities seemed to think that it was better to do away with known enemies whether or not there was any immediate justification for killing them.[38]

The State Department still felt that the Cubans should solve their own political problems without American intervention. In January 1932, when terrorism was beginning to increase, Guggenheim urged that the United States make clear its disapproval of Machado's policies. He thought that a peaceful settlement might still be possible if it were not for Machado's belief that the United States had no interest in the maintenance of political freedom in Cuba. Stimson replied, two months later, that it was still his considered opinion that the United States should continue to refrain from any semblance of interference and that he could not acquiesce in the view that non-interference involved the United States in any responsibility for what happened. In July 1932, Stimson explained his position in a personal letter to Assistant Postmaster General Glover, who had sent him an alarming letter from the United States postal agent in Habana. Dissatisfied elements in Latin American countries, the secretary wrote, were constantly asking the United States to intervene, and if the United States complied it would have its hands full and would become extremely unpopular in Latin America. The United States had never intervened in Cuba except when there was anarchy and no government there and it had always interpreted the Platt amendment as not giving it the right to meddle promiscuously. To advise Machado to resign would be a very serious intervention, which would tend to break down the Cuban people's feeling of responsibility for their own government. To supervise an election would be even more of an intervention. We had done this in Nicaragua, but only at the request of all factions. Even in that small country the supervision had involved us in much expense and difficulty, and under present conditions in Cuba a supervision would be out of the question.[39]

As the end of 1932 approached, the government again faced the possibility of a default on its foreign debt. The Chase Bank was disposed to help, but it was alarmed when it received a letter from the A.B.C. threatening reprisals and it suggested that the

[38] Report of July 29, 1932, 837.00/3319.
[39] Stimson to Glover, July 5, 1932, 837.00/3454.

State Department do something about the financial situation. The department, however, refused to interfere. The arrangement that was finally worked out involved an advance of about $1,500,000 from the American oil companies in Cuba, against the import taxes which they would pay during the next six months. Guggenheim thought that this raised questions under the Platt amendment and might expose the United States to criticism for "bolstering" the dictatorship, but the State Department replied, rather tartly, that to disapprove of a plan voluntarily worked out by the interested parties would be an unwarranted interference in Cuban affairs. It told the ambassador to make it clear that the United States was taking no position in the matter.[40]

Reports of what was going on in Cuba shocked public opinion in other countries but there was little evidence that the terrorism would soon cause the collapse of the government. Machado still had substantial support from most of the liberal leaders and from many conservatives who had not followed Menocal when he joined the opposition. Guggenheim thought that some of the liberal leaders were beginning to turn against Machado, but that the attitude of the civilian politicians was relatively unimportant so long as the administration had the support of the army and the police. These seemed likely to stay loyal because they were themselves the victims of terrorist attacks and were eager for vengeance. Machado in fact felt strong enough in November 1932 to release a large number of political prisoners, and on December 1 he restored constitutional guarantees, except in the province of Habana. There was no let up, however, in the terrorism, and both the government's forces and its enemies became increasingly reckless and brutal.

In November 1932 Guggenheim wrote Francis White that he was making a final effort, by friendly advice, to make Machado see the inevitable result of the course which he was pursuing. He suggested that White might say something helpful to the Cuban ambassador. Neither White nor Stimson, however, thought that the United States should interfere.[41] Stimson, in fact, told President-elect Roosevelt in January 1933 that Cuba had caused him less anxiety than most Latin American countries because the

[40] Guggenheim to Stimson, Nov. 29, and Stimson to Guggenheim, Dec. 3, 1932, 837.51/1533.

[41] Guggenheim to White, Nov. 23, and White to Guggenheim, Nov. 28, 1932, Francis White papers, Box 11.

army, trained by American officers and keeping out of politics, had enabled Machado to retain firm control. He explained on another occasion that he did not approve of Machado or of what he was doing, but he was strongly opposed to intervention or interference by the United States.[42]

The policy of non-interference was abandoned, temporarily, after President Roosevelt took office in March 1933. In May of that year, Sumner Welles, who had returned to the State Department as assistant secretary, was sent to Cuba as ambassador, with instructions to offer his friendly mediation for a truce which would permit a new constitutional government to be elected. Machado and some of the revolutionary groups were willing to accept mediation, but other groups, including the university students, were not. No agreement had been reached when a general strike paralysed Habana and led to new disorder, and on August 11 the army turned against Machado and compelled him to resign. Before he left, Machado named Carlos Manuel de Céspedes, whom Welles had suggested for the presidency of Cuba in 1921, as secretary of state and thus as his constitutional successor. De Céspedes, however, was overthrown after a very short time and a period of turmoil ensued. It was not until 1936 that constitutional government was reestablished.

There were many critics who thought that the United States should have stepped in before it did to stop the cruelty and bloodshed which assumed such shocking proportions during the last two years of Machado's rule. They blamed the American government for what was happening because they thought that the dictator could not have remained in office if he had not had the moral support of the State Department and the embassy. In Cuba, much of the criticism was directed against Guggenheim, who displeased the opposition leaders by his unwillingness to support some of their demands and by his refusal to insist on Machado's withdrawal from office. Guggenheim considered the opposition leaders stubborn and unreasonable, and was indignant about their circulation of rumors and untrue reports in an effort to show that he was partial to the dictatorship, but it is clear that it was not he but the State Department that was responsible for the policies that the opposition criticized. Guggenheim tried earnestly and persistently to bring about a settlement which would have given the opposition an opportunity to partici-

[42] Stimson *Diary*, Jan. 9, and Jan. 10, 1933.

pate in the restoration of constitutional government. He would have put more pressure on Machado to agree to a settlement if he had not been restrained from Washington when he proposed to do so.

In the State Department there was some difference of opinion about the attitude which the American government should take. The officials who dealt with Cuba had been favorably impressed by Machado's performance during his first years in office, but they did not approve or encourage the unconstitutional procedure by which he was reelected or his increasingly rough treatment of opponents. During the 1931 revolt they avoided any expression of support for the constituted government. If they refrained from any public expression of disapproval of Machado's conduct, it was because they wished to avoid any appearance of interference in Cuba's internal political affairs. In naming Judah as special ambassador to Machado's inauguration and in at least not hampering Machado's efforts to deal with the public works debt, they tried to treat the government as they would any government with which the United States had normal relations, because a refusal to do so would have been regarded as a public expression of disapproval.

This policy seemed more defensible before 1932 than it did when the opposition's campaign of terrorism and the government's repression created one of the most appalling situations that ever confronted American policy makers in the Caribbean. Even in this situation, however, it was hard to see what the American government could usefully do so long as it was determined not to intervene by force of arms. Interference not backed by a credible threat of intervention might have done more harm than good. If we had tried by diplomatic pressure to make Machado retire before the end of his illegally extended term we might have encouraged his opponents to stage a new revolution, but Machado was probably too firmly entrenched in power to be ousted by a revolt so long as the army supported him. He was not likely to be ousted by diplomatic pressure so long as he knew that the United States would not intervene. When he fell in 1933, after the change in administration at Washington, it was apparently a threat of intervention, explicit or implied, that caused the Cuban army to turn against him.

Chapter Eleven

THE TRANSITION FROM
INTERVENTION TO THE GOOD
NEIGHBOR POLICY

The years between 1921 and 1933 were a period of transition from Taft's and Wilson's policies in the Caribbean to the Good Neighbor Policy of Franklin Roosevelt. Before 1921, the American government had insisted that the Caribbean states accept its help in trying to stop the disorder and financial mismanagement which had kept them backward and at times had involved them in trouble with foreign powers. It discouraged revolutions, sometimes by force or threats of force, and in several countries it demanded that Americans be given a measure of control over the financial administration. In extreme cases it resorted to armed intervention. In 1921 the Dominican Republic and Haiti were under American military occupation and in Haiti American officials controlled the government's most important activities. A legation guard of American marines was keeping a minority government in power in Nicaragua and in Cuba a personal representative of the president of the United States was directing efforts to settle a disputed election and to deal with an economic crisis.

Twelve years later the situation was different. Americans were still collecting the customs revenues in the Dominican Republic and Nicaragua, but in other respects these countries were freely managing their own affairs. In Haiti a greater measure of financial control continued but the rest of the American treaty services were being dismantled and plans had been worked out for the withdrawal of the marines. The Platt amendment still governed relations with Cuba, but the American government had adopted an interpretation of the amendment which would permit intervention only in the gravest emergency. The United States was in fact being criticized for its failure to intervene in Cuba to terminate Machado's dictatorship.

371

Earlier policies had not been completely abandoned. The State Department still thought that disorder in the Caribbean could endanger the security of the United States. It had been slow to abandon some activities, like the effort to train efficient police forces, which seemed likely to promote stability. It maintained its connection with the customs receiverships in Haiti and the Dominican Republic and Nicaragua because it felt that it had a moral obligation to the people who had bought the bonds of these countries in reliance on the American government's assurances that the receiverships would continue. It had not made up its mind to abrogate the Platt amendment, and it was reluctant to give up the non-recognition policy in Central America, after going through so much agony to convince the Central Americans that it would adhere to it. It still insisted on its right and duty to ask the navy to protect American lives and property by force when local authorities were unable to do so. Nevertheless, the department's attitude toward Caribbean problems was quite different in 1933 from what it had been in 1921.

The transition was a gradual one. When Secretary Hughes first took office he did not make any immediate changes in the policies of his predecessors. In withdrawing the military government from the Dominican Republic and in trying to create conditions that would make possible the safe withdrawal of the legation guard at Managua he was continuing the previous administration's efforts to correct situations that were obviously unacceptable. He showed no inclination to relinquish the American government's treaty rights in the Dominican Republic or in Haiti, and in fact made the American control in Haiti more effective. In Cuba he supported General Crowder in his insistence on reforms. The first indication of a change in policy, perhaps, came when President Zayas rebelled against Crowder's dictation and it became clear that the "moralization" program would fail unless the State Department backed up the general with at least a threat of intervention. Hughes thought that intervention would not be tolerated by American public opinion, and refused to make a threat which he was not prepared to carry out. The State Department consequently made no effective effort to bring Zayas into line. The elimination of intervention as a possible last resort also affected relations with other states. Throughout the Caribbean, the belief that the American government might use force if persuasion failed had given credibility to its diplomatic representations and to the comminatory public statements by which it had sometimes tried to prevent revolutions or bring about reforms. We could not make threats or peremptory demands when we knew that we could not back them up.

At the same time some officers in the State Department were beginning to doubt whether insisting that political conflicts be settled in the way that seemed most proper to us and officiously opposing measures that we considered unwise was the best way to improve political conditions in the Caribbean. In its efforts to discourage the use of force and to encourage constitutional procedures, the State Department had frequently put itself in a position where it was telling the political leaders what they could and could not do, so that the leaders tended more and more to expect their disagreements to be decided in Washington rather than by themselves. This diminished their sense of responsibility for their own actions and imposed on the State Department a responsibility which it ought not to assume. It made more credible the charges of imperialistic designs which hurt our relations with the other American countries. During the last two years of Hughes' tenure as secretary of state, and during the two administrations which followed, there was a definite trend toward a policy of less interference in the internal political affairs of the Caribbean states.

The intervention of 1926-1927 in Nicaragua tended to obscure the fact that this change was taking place, but it did not really signify a return to earlier policies. The marines were sent to Nicaragua in 1926 primarily to protect Americans and other foreigners, just as they had repeatedly been sent to other places in the Caribbean where Americans were in danger. The fact that the United States had been so involved in Nicaragua's political affairs during the past fourteen years and that it still had a responsibility for the customs service and the high commission made the landing of the marines seem more necessary. The American forces were instructed to maintain complete neutrality between the contending factions, and these instructions remained in force even after Secretary Kellogg became convinced that Mexico's intervention in the struggle posed a grave danger to American interests. Kellogg gave Díaz a considerable amount of moral support, though not so much as Díaz wanted, but he tried to avoid any military support. Nevertheless, the landing of marines to protect foreigners, and the landing of more marines to back up the first ones and to keep their communication lines open, created a situation where much of the country was under American control and where the involvement of American forces in the civil war would sooner or later be unavoidable. Colonel Stimson was able to bring about a settlement by negotiation, but only by promising that the United States would supervise the presidential election and that it would maintain order while the armies of both parties were being disbanded and until a non-partisan police force could be trained. It was this promise that involved the American marines in the long and frustrating effort to stop Sandino's depredations.

In explaining their actions to the American public, Kellogg and Coolidge talked about the right to protect Americans and the special interest of the United States in Nicaragua in language that sounded more imperialistic than anything that had been heard in Washington for years, but this was apparently an attempt to rationalize a course of action which had been undertaken under the pressure of circumstances and without any clear idea where it would lead. In dealing with other countries, Kellogg seemed even more reluctant than Hughes had been to interfere in the Caribbean states' internal political affairs or to assume new responsibilities in connection with their finances. One conspicuous example was his failure to oppose the illegal procedure by which Machado had himself reelected and extended his term in 1928.

The worst consequence of the Nicaraguan intervention was a resurgence of hostile feeling in Latin America. The State Department had hoped that the withdrawal from the Dominican Republic and the withdrawal of the legation guard from Nicaragua would have a good effect on public opinion in other American countries. In 1926 Francis White told Herbert Stabler, who was succeeding him as chief of the Latin American division, that one of the division's chief accomplishments during the past five years had been to make progress toward convincing the Latin Americans that the United States had no imperialistic designs.[1] When the Sixth Pan American Conference met at Habana in January 1928, it was evident that the situation was worse than ever. There was an unpleasant conflict when several governments urged the adoption of a resolution stating that "no state has the right to intervene in the internal affairs of another." Ex-Secretary

[1] White to Stabler, May 15, 1926, Francis White papers, Box 35.

Hughes, who was the chairman of the United States delegation, made a vigorous statement opposing it. The American government, he said, did not wish to intervene in the affairs of any American republic, but it could not give up its right under international law to protect the lives and property of its citizens if local governments could not do so. It was finally agreed that the resolution should be considered at the next Pan American conference, but the incident did nothing to improve inter-American relations. President Hoover, when he visited the other American countries before his inauguration, was painfully impressed by what he heard there, and the experience undoubtedly made him more anxious to withdraw as rapidly as possible from Haiti and Nicaragua.

Some of the hostile feeling in Latin America was directed at the Monroe Doctrine, and especially at Theodore Roosevelt's "corollary" to the doctrine—the idea that the United States, if it wished to prevent European intervention in the Caribbean, must try to do away with the disorder and financial mismanagement which invited intervention. It was this idea that inspired the policies which in some cases had led to intervention by the United States itself. Secretary Hughes, in 1923, had emphatically denied that the Monroe Doctrine gave the United States any right to exercise a sort of hegemony in the Americas,[2] and in the fall of 1928 Secretary Kellogg decided to explore the possibility of making an official statement along the same line. As he said later, he "believed that statements had from time to time been made as to this doctrine which were not justified, and that it furnished no ground whatever for intervention or interference with the internal affairs of any Central or South American country, and that there was much misunderstanding on this subject."[3] The secretary probably realized that questions about the doctrine would be raised when his newly signed treaty for the renunciation of war came before the Senate for approval. As a first step, he asked Reuben Clark, the undersecretary of state, to look into the matter.

Clark's *Memorandum on the Monroe Doctrine*, completed a few months later, was a collection of documents and authoritative statements showing how the doctrine had been interpreted

[2] See for example his speech on "The Centenary of the Monroe Doctrine," delivered at Philadelphia, Nov. 30, 1923.

[3] Kellogg to Stimson, June 25, 1930, 710.11/1449.

by the American government since 1923. In a covering letter to the secretary of state, Clark expressed his personal views about the doctrine's scope and significance. He discussed at some length the right of self-preservation, on which the doctrine was based, but he pointed out that the security of the United States might also be endangered by acts to which the doctrine did not apply. He emphasized the view that the doctrine applied to relations between European states and the countries of the western hemisphere, and not to relations between the United States and Latin America. The Roosevelt corollary was thus not justified by the terms of the doctrine, "however much it may be justified by the application of the doctrine of self-preservation." He thought that the effect of his study would be to "relieve that Doctrine of many of the criticisms which have been aimed against it."

Shortly before he left the department, Kellogg, with Clark's help, drafted a statement about the Monroe Doctrine which he proposed to communicate to the other American governments. This was sent to the diplomatic missions in Latin America, with instructions not to deliver it to the governments to which they were accredited until the department should tell them to do so. Kellogg evidently felt that the incoming president and secretary of state should have an opportunity to consider the matter before final action was taken. The statement declared that the Monroe Doctrine "has nothing whatever to do with the domestic concerns or policies or the form of government or the international conduct of the peoples of this hemisphere as among themselves," or with the treaties which the United States had made with certain Caribbean states or the occasional landing by any power of forces to protect foreign nationals in time of disorder. "It is high time," it said, "that misunderstanding as to the meaning of the Monroe Doctrine shall cease, that international troublemakers shall find so clear a conception of the Doctrine in the minds of the people of this hemisphere that false representations concerning it shall no longer find lodgment in the prejudices upon which such misrepresentations have heretofore lived, that irresponsible exploiters of great economic resources shall not be able hereafter to invoke an untrue concept of the Doctrine to justify and induce unwarranted international attitudes and actions; that poorly visioned, grandiose schemes of the dreamers of unrighteous dominion shall no longer be built upon erroneous principles unknown to the Doctrine. . . .

"The Monroe Doctrine is not now and never was an instrument of aggression; it is and always has been a cloak of protection. The Doctrine is not a lance; it is a shield."

Kellogg's project seems to have been forgotten after he and Clark both left the department in 1929. I do not remember that I was told about it when I took charge of the Latin American division in the spring of that year, or that there was any discussion about the implementation of the instruction. Stimson apparently did not hear about it until June 1930, when Kellogg inadvertently mentioned it to a newspaper correspondent and the press made inquiries at the State Department. Stimson at once read Kellogg's statement and suggested to Hoover that the diplomatic missions be instructed to communicate it to the Latin American governments. The president, however, felt that "it would be undesirable to put this out at the present time as it will provoke a great deal of debate and may cause embarrassment in other matters."[4] Seven months later, when Stimson took the matter up again, he found the president "still opposed to the distribution of Reuben Clark's memorandum."[5] The secretary was evidently referring to the instruction of February 1929 rather than to the *Memorandum on the Monroe Doctrine*.

The *Memorandum* had already been distributed as a publication of the State Department[6] and also as a congressional document. The printing had apparently been authorized before Kellogg left the department, but the book was not published until March 1930. Some scholars have speculated on the possible significance of the delay. Clark, sixteen years later, remembered only that there had been long discussions about the number and character of footnotes and delays in printing and proofreading.[7]

Several diplomatic historians have thought that the State Department, in publishing the *Memorandum*, officially repudiated the Roosevelt corollary. I do not believe that anyone in the department thought at the time that the appearance of the book signified a change in policy. Clark himself later told me emphat-

---

[4] Hoover to Stimson, June 26, 1930, 710.11/1450.

[5] Memorandum of conversation with the president, Feb. 9, 1931, 890 F01/29½.

[6] *Memorandum on the Monroe Doctrine*, prepared by J. Reuben Clark (Washington, 1930).

[7] I discussed the history of the memorandum with Clark on October 15, 1946.

ically that he had had no such idea and no such idea occurred to me when I read the *Memorandum*. I had previously known nothing about it, though I had been chief of the Latin American division for nearly a year. I was disturbed about the book, because I thought that any public discussion of the Monroe Doctrine was likely to arouse unfriendly feeling in Latin America. I did not see that it made any great practical difference whether interventions to prevent violations of the Monroe Doctrine were based on the doctrine or on the right of self-preservation. Francis White seemed equally unaware that the *Memorandum* announced a change in policy. He told me that he had known vaguely about its existence but had not read it and had not been consulted about its publication. There seems to be no evidence that Stimson had been consulted. There was no indication that he knew that the Roosevelt corollary had been repudiated when he told the Council on Foreign Relations a few months later that the Caribbean was "the one spot external to our shores which nature has decreed to be most vital to our national safety, not to mention our prosperity."[8]

It has been suggested that Kellogg and Stimson did in fact intend to repudiate the Roosevelt corollary but that other officials of the department disagreed and were able to bring about a "repudiation of a repudiation."[9] The basis for this seems to be the fact that officers of the department, in answering inquiries, emphasized the unofficial nature of the comments in Clark's covering letter. It is difficult to see how they could have answered inquiries in any other way. The fact was that the American government had not taken any new official position about the Monroe Doctrine or about the Roosevelt corollary. Clark himself had not questioned the validity of the idea that disorder in the Caribbean would affect the security of the United States. His point was that it was not the Monroe Doctrine but the right of self-preservation that might justify efforts by the American government to improve conditions there.

The effort to dissociate the Monroe Doctrine from policies which had been unpopular in the rest of the continent was a

[8] *The United States and the Other American Republics*, address before the Council on Foreign Relations, New York, February 6, 1931, published by the Government Printing Office, Washington.

[9] Robert H. Ferrell, "Repudiation of a Repudiation," *Journal of American History*, Vol. LI (March, 1965), pp. 669ff.

laudable one. The *Memorandum* brought forth many expressions of approval in the South American press.[10] It can hardly be said, however, that the *Memorandum* marked a turning point in American policy. There must have been some confusion in ex-President Hoover's mind when he told a biographer in 1947 that he had resurrected it from the State Department's files and made it the basis of his Latin American policy.[11] As a matter of fact, he had twice refused to approve the publication of an official statement based on it. It is hard to see that the ideas in the *Memorandum* had any great effect on what the United States did. Most of the people dealing with Latin American affairs in the State Department continued to believe that disorderly conditions in the Caribbean were a potential danger to the security of the United States. If the need to interpose to correct bad conditions seemed less urgent in 1930 it was because there seemed to be little immediate probability that some unfriendly power would attempt to get a foothold there. In 1930 neither fascism nor communism seemed to pose any serious threat to the development of free institutions in the Americas.

Other misconceptions about the policy of the United States in the Caribbean before 1933 still appear from time to time in discussions of our Latin American relations. One is the idea that this policy was inspired in part by a desire to help American bankers and businessmen to make money. Several scholars have shown that there is little evidence to support this idea, but it still persists. During the 1920's the State Department took an active part in the negotiation of loans to several Caribbean governments because it thought that the loans would forward its own policy objectives. The Morgan loan was an essential part of Crowder's plan for the rehabilitation of Cuba, and the National City Bank's loan to Haiti was essential to the American government's program there. Keith's loan to El Salvador relieved an acute financial crisis in that country. In all of these cases, and in the case of the loans obtained by the Dominican government after the withdrawal of the occupation, the American government's cooperation secured better terms for the borrowing government than it could otherwise have obtained. The bankers expected to make

[10] Donald Marquand Dozer, *Are We Good Neighbors?* (Gainesville, 1959), pp. 12-13.

[11] Alexander de Conde, *Herbert Hoover's Latin American Policy* (Stanford, 1951), p. 49.

a profit out of each transaction, but the State Department tried to make sure that the profit was reasonable and that the arrangement as a whole was beneficial to the borrowing country. I participated in the discussions about many of these loans and I can testify that the people in the State Department showed no interest at all in the idea that the loans would be profitable to American bankers.

In some cases, as we have seen, the department went out of its way to block projects that it considered unsound or unfair. In dealing with loans to Caribbean states, Francis White wrote, the department considered itself in the position of a trustee. It had to scrutinize loan projects to protect the inexperienced governments from harsh terms and to protect the people of the country from efforts to obtain unfair contracts by corrupting government officials. Our relations with the Caribbean states were so close that we should be held responsible for what happened, whether we assumed responsibility or not.[12] The department had a somewhat similar attitude toward other investments in the Caribbean countries. In general, it was interested in promoting trade and finding profitable opportunities for the investment of American capital abroad. Helping Americans who found themselves in difficulties in foreign countries was an important part of its work. But in dealing with some of the Caribbean countries it felt that the political influence which it exercised imposed an obligation to give prior consideration to the interests of the local community where these conflicted with the interests of Americans. This was especially true in Haiti.

In practice, many of the larger American companies doing business in the Caribbean seemed to take care of themselves. The State Department had little to do with the great increase of American investments in Cuba after 1921 or with the growth of the sugar industry in the Dominican Republic. In both countries, in fact, the development of American policy during the 1920's if anything made the climate for foreign investment less attractive. The fruit companies in Central America often took care of their own interests in ways that the department strongly disapproved of.

We were perhaps more concerned than some of our successors were about living up to the explicit or implied commitments

[12] Unsigned memorandum dated Feb. 6, 1931, Francis White papers, Box 32.

which the American government made in its efforts to help borrowing states to obtain loans. The State Department felt that it had to maintain the customs collectorships in Haiti and the Dominican Republic and Nicaragua, and its effort to withdraw from Haiti was seriously complicated by the fact that it felt that it had to maintain a measure of financial control there. Its attitude, of course, benefited not the bankers but the private investors who had bought the bonds in reliance on the American government's connection with the transaction. How far respect for the sanctity of contracts should outweigh other considerations of policy is perhaps a matter of opinion.

Another misconception, still prevalent, is the idea that the United States, before 1933 and since then, has often supported dictatorships in the Caribbean because it wanted political stability and because dictatorships were often more friendly to American interests. Any adequate discussion of this question would require a lengthy essay on Latin American political institutions and a detailed study of our relations with the numerous dictatorships that have flourished in Latin America during the past sixty years. So far as the period 1921-1933 is concerned, I do not think that the American government could fairly be charged with an undue partiality to dictatorial government. The people who dealt with Latin American problems thought that the only way to attain lasting political stability in the Caribbean was to create a situation where there could be free elections. In the light of what has happened during the past half century, I think that we oversimplified the problem, but we could hardly be accused of not being interested in the development of democratic institutions.

We certainly tried to encourage the holding of free elections wherever it seemed practicable to do so. In 1933, as a result of the State Department's efforts, there were democratically elected governments in Nicaragua and Honduras, and a president in Guatemala who apparently had popular support and who had come into office after the United States refused to permit a military clique to seize power by force. Costa Rica had had real republican government for many years. The only Central American government which owed its position to the use of force was that of El Salvador, which the United States still refused to recognize. There were dictatorships in Cuba and the Dominican Republic, with which the United States maintained normal diplomatic relations. The State Department might have been able to discourage their establishment and continuance, but it was deterred by its reluctance to interfere in the two countries' internal affairs from making any but very feeble and ineffective efforts to do so. The one case where the American government might have been accused of a cynical disregard of democratic principles was in Haiti, where the State Department until 1930 could not make up its mind to face the troublesome consequences that would have ensued if it had compelled Borno to hold a popular election.

There were some Caribbean republics, like Guatemala and El Salvador, where free elections had rarely if ever been held and presidents supported by the army and by powerful social or economic groups remained in power or passed on the presidency to political associates so long as the opposition did not become strong enough to overthrow them. Regimes of this type were not necessarily unpopular. They usually had enemies who complained with justification about the treatment which they received, but undemocratic procedures did not prevent them from being accepted, more or less willingly, by the majority of the people. The State Department usually maintained normal diplomatic relations with governments of this sort and discouraged attempts to overthrow them by force. The hope that the relative stability which they provided would encourage progress toward more democratic government seems to have been justified, for Guatemala and El Salvador have elections today in which most of the citizens seem to participate.

The situation became more difficult when a regime developed into a notorious dictatorship, as Machado's government in Cuba did after 1929. The reign of terror started by Machado's enemies and the cruel repression with which the government responded shocked public opinion abroad and the State Department was criticized for its apparent indifference to the situation. The department had not approved of Machado's illegal continuation in power, and when a revolution began it conspicuously failed to give him the moral support which it had given other Cuban presidents under similar circumstances, but it resolutely avoided any effective interference. The American ambassador tried to bring about an agreement between Machado and his opponents, but the department, in its reluctance to interfere, gave him little support.

The policy of non-interference, continued and carried farther in Franklin Roosevelt's Good Neighbor Policy did much to bring about the improvement in inter-American relations which made possible the close cooperation of nearly all of the American republics during the second world war. The Good Neighbor Policy, however, was not the answer to all of the problems which confronted the United States in the Caribbean, because a political breakdown in a Caribbean country could still endanger the security of the United States. If the danger seemed less in 1933, it again became evident when nazi activity appeared throughout Latin America a few years later, and still more evident as the cold war developed. In the meantime, some of the Caribbean states have made progress toward more stable government. Others have not. The problems which still confront the American government in the area are often much like those with which the State Department had to deal in the first three decades of the century.

INDEX

385

Library of Congress Cataloging in Publication Data

Munro, Dana Gardner, 1892-
   The United States and the Caribbean republics, 1921-1933.

   1. Caribbean area—Foreign relations—United States.
2. United States—Foreign relations—Caribbean area.
I. Title.
F2178.U6M86   327.73'0729   73-16767
ISBN 0-691-04623-9